HANDBOOK FOR Teaching the Bible

IN LITERATURE CLASSES

HANDBOOK FOR
Teaching the Bible
IN LITERATURE CLASSES

Thayer S. Warshaw

Abingdon
Nashville

HANDBOOK FOR TEACHING THE BIBLE IN LITERATURE CLASSES

Copyright © 1978 by Thayer S. Warshaw

Library of Congress Cataloging in Publication Data

WARSHAW, THAYER S 1915-
  Handbook for teaching the Bible in literature classes.
    1. Bible as literature—Study and teaching.
  2. Bible in literature—Study and teaching. I. Title.
BS535.W34   220'.07   78-668

ISBN 0-687-16623-3

MANUFACTURED BY THE PARTHENON PRESS AT
NASHVILLE, TENNESSEE, UNITED STATES OF AMERICA

The Indiana University Institute on Teaching the Bible in Literature Courses offers three kinds of experiences for teachers: (a) introduction to biblical scholarship, (b) literary analysis of the Bible *as* literature and the Bible *in* literature, and (c) practicalities of the classroom and community. Our books, most of them published by Abingdon in a series called The Bible in Literature Courses, have grown out of the institute and address themselves to the same three concerns.

Two of our books present a scholarly approach to the historical and cultural backgrounds of the Bible: *An Introduction to New Testament Literature* (Abingdon, 1978), and *Teaching the Old Testament in English Classes* (Indiana University, 1973).

Two more are collections of critical essays by literary scholars. *Literary Interpretations of Biblical Narratives* (Abingdon, 1974) focuses on the Bible *as* literature. *Biblical Images in Literature* (Abingdon, 1975) deals with the Bible *in* literature.

While these four books are useful to teachers who wish to use the Bible in secondary school or college literature courses, they do not confront the more practical questions of *what* to teach in such courses and *how* to teach. The present book is the keystone of our work in this area. It accompanies and underlies our *Bible-Related Curriculum Materials: A Bibliography* (Abingdon, 1976) and the forthcoming *Religion, Education, and the Supreme Court*.

Considerations of classroom and community practicalities stand between the teacher's command of both biblical scholarship and literary criticism on the one hand and the actual teaching/learning situation on the other. We feel, therefore, that this handbook links all our other books with what goes on between teacher and student. It also provides necessary background for using our classroom textbook, *The Bible as/in Literature* (Scott, Foresman, 1976).

All our books have drawn substance and strength from our Indiana University institute, now in its ninth year. Our alumni/ae include over five hundred school and college teachers, from all fifty states and several foreign countries. They have expressed the concerns and needs that this book seeks to answer; indeed, they have furnished many of the answers from their own vast and varied experience.

We have come to look on this handbook as the "Bible-teacher's bible"—not that it is inspired, but it seems to be the most comprehensive and essential book yet offered in its field, containing information and suggestions for a wide range of classroom situations. We suggest that it may also prove as useful to people interested in teaching about religion in public schools as to those who teach the Bible in literature courses.

James S. Ackerman, Director
Thayer S. Warshaw, Associate Director

Preface

This book speaks to people involved with or concerned about the use of the Bible in literature courses—to secondary school and college teachers, teacher educators, administrators, special-interest groups, and other individuals to whom the subject is important.

Much of the book focuses on matters related to teaching in public secondary schools, for several reasons. First, a teacher's handbook draws its vitality and validity from experience, and most of my own experience as a teacher and teacher educator has been in public secondary schools. Second, the Bible in secondary school literature courses presents an enormous need and challenge. Thousands of teachers would like to use the Bible but worry about questions of sectarianism and secularism and feel hesitant about methods and materials. Hundreds of others do use Bible passages in their classrooms but are inadequately equipped to cope with the many sensitive and often subtle problems involved in such an activity. Third, the arena of public secondary school teaching most clearly exposes for teachers elsewhere—at independent schools and at colleges—questions about teaching the Bible that all teachers face (or should face), not necessarily as a matter of law but as a moral obligation in an open society.

The contents of this handbook apply to many different aspects of teaching the Bible in literature courses. Some of its curricular materials are directly useful for daily classroom activities: e.g., "Student Materials," chapter 9, Part III; "Study Questions and Quizzes," Part IV; and "Fun and Games," chapter 10, Part III. Some sections are handy references for teachers: e.g., "Teacher Materials," chapter 8, Part III; the Glossary in Part V, and the list of "Biblical Sources of Some Religious Beliefs and Practices," chapter 7, Part II. The rest, Part I and chapter 6, Part II, deal with some of the larger issues: overall approaches and emphases for a course or unit and some possible classroom problems arising out of religious sensibilities.

In discussing these issues, I have concentrated on presenting possibilities—both the opportunities and the pitfalls—and have used examples from teaching experience, my own and that of others. Among the opportunities, my principal interest is to expose alternatives. I have not hesitated to express preferences among them and to offer suggestions here and there. Some of my opinions seem, at least to my not unbiased eye, unexceptionable; others are obviously controversial. All, however, are primarily intended to stimulate the reader into thinking about the alternatives and making his or her own judgments.

Our institute has always assumed that its primary tasks are to provide information, to raise issues, and to make its participants aware of possibilities. We are convinced that with such a background an intelligent and sensitive teacher will then be the best judge of what and how to teach most effectively in his or her own classroom or lecture hall.

The 1963 Supreme Court decision ending devotional use of the Bible in the public schools made many people realize that students weren't being taught much about the Bible as part of our literary heritage. Students are generally ignorant of its contents, its literary excellences, and its relation to other literature. Since that decision, teachers have increasingly accepted the freedom and responsibility for filling this lamentable educational gap. We find that teachers need only encouragement, guidance, examples, and information of the kind that this handbook attempts to provide.

This book represents fifteen years of teaching the Bible at Newton (Massachusetts) North High School, eight summer institutes at Indiana University, and countless contacts with other teachers in conferences throughout the country. I acknowledge my great debt to my high school students and to the teachers who have been participants at our institute. They have all contributed, directly or indirectly, to this book—for whose deficiencies, however, I take the full measure of responsibility.

Particular thanks are due to those who have invested the greatest amount of time and effort in helping me develop the insights embodied in this book. Henry Bissex encouraged and guided me at the outset at Newton High and for many years was a source of strength. Jim Ackerman at Indiana University has expanded my horizons, kept me on the right track, and made many contributions to this handbook. And Bernice has supported me throughout, even when it has meant giving up many opportunities to fulfill her own interests.

Thayer S. Warshaw
Andover, Massachusetts

Contents

PART I
CLASSROOM
APPROACHES AND EMPHASES

CHAPTER	Introduction

1

A Question of Goals—Human and Literary

What are a teacher's primary goals for students when teaching literature in a secondary school English or language arts class? Consider two kinds of objectives, represented by two groups of questions: Does the teacher normally teach literature to help students—

expand their understanding of humankind and of themselves;

find meaning in their lives and in the universe;

fulfill themselves as individuals and as members of society;

become more valuable people;

enlarge their minds and spirits?

Or is the first priority to help students—

improve their reading skills;

be more sensitive to language and to literary craftsmanship;

become acquainted with our literary heritage;

enjoy reading;

appreciate good literature?

More than likely a teacher's goals will include at least some from both lists, perhaps adding other formulations that will fall within one group or the other. There will probably not be an even balance: Some teachers of literature, for theoretical and for practical reasons, tend to favor the first, or "human," type of goal; and some emphasize the second, or "literary," goal.

Which kind of preoccupation will dominate may even vary from one piece of literature to the next. The initial approach to the play, poem, story, or essay, as well as the main emphasis of the exercise of reading and analysis, will serve either one kind of goal or another. The choice of main focal, organizing, and controlling principle will depend on the teacher's own educational philosophy, the nature of the piece being studied, the abilities and maturity of the students, the overall plan of the course or unit, and even the shifts in the immediate classroom situation.

Granted, the dichotomy implied by presenting separate lists is artificial for most actual teaching/learning activity. In language arts courses, no matter how dedicated a teacher is to human goals as a first priority, it is fair to assume that he or she will want to expose even the most reluctant or least able students to good writing. Conversely, it would be difficult to ignore human goals and to concentrate exclusively on technique.

Suppose, for example, that the class is pursuing mainly literary goals. The teacher may legitimately decide to help students understand the relationships among the content, craftsmanship, and issues in a work of literature by having them become personally engaged in the world of the text. The students may be asked to relate the situation or the issue presented in the text to their own experience or to respond to it with a value judgment or with an imaginative treatment.

When students are thus invited to become creatively involved with the literature, they are exercising and developing their minds, imaginations, and spirits—fulfilling the human goals. And even if the teacher did not assign such an activity or stimulate such a discussion, the students would probably be growing in mind and spirit merely by having been exposed to, and having confronted, the new kinds of experience and the new ways of looking at life that the literature offers. They nibble at the apple.

However intertwined the human and literary aspects of the study of literature may be, the teacher does have options with any piece of literature the class is to study—both for initial approach and for overall emphasis. Which of the two kinds of goals will be primary?

Consider three novels, related by their common interest in racial questions, that are often taught in secondary schools: *Huckleberry Finn; Cry, the Beloved Country;* and *Uncle Tom's Cabin.* Few teachers read them with their classes only for their literary attributes, their place in the history of literature, or even for their interesting stories. The books are at least as important for the issues they raise and the values they espouse or oppose.

Huckleberry Finn has been condemned, even banned in some schools, because of the close interracial friendship of Huck and Jim and because of the book's seemingly one-sided sympathy for Jim and its ridicule of white people's values. Others object that it denigrates blacks, and they point to Huck's use of the word *nigger.*

Won't the teacher raise these issues? Might the teacher not ask students to comment on questions of values that are implied by the way Twain treats Pap's encounter with the black "p'fessor"? by the cowardice of the lynching mob when confronted by one man of character with a gun? by the idea of feuding families taking their guns to church, where the sermon is "all about brotherly love, and such-like tiresomeness"? The teacher will probably not be content with merely pointing out that in these instances Twain is using the literary device of irony.

Cry, the Beloved Country (to be discussed at greater length below) presents some characters, both black and white, who feel that their country's problems can be settled only through power: for the whites, to keep the blacks in line; for the blacks, to gain their freedom. Other people, both black and white, say that the answer is not power but love.

Won't the teacher ask students to think about Africa today and Msimangu's now prophetic words, "I have one great fear in my heart, that one day when they [white people] are turned to loving, they will find that we are turned to hating"? Might the teacher not mention the slaughter of white people in some African countries when black people finally achieved independence? the awful tribal wars that have resulted?

The teacher may not confine discussion to the world of the novel. The students may be invited to compare or contrast the horrors of apartheid and baaskap with the inequities of our own democracy, to contrast the repressive but forthright official South African position that "there shall be no equality among the races" with the idealistically humane but ironically unfulfilled statement of our own Declaration that "all men are created equal." Or the teacher may stop with the literary observation that Paton's novel, though otherwise carefully wrought, uses two-dimensional figures who embody the two opposing camps—proponents of power and proponents of love.

Uncle Tom's Cabin, our third example, has been praised and condemned since it first appeared. The teacher might ask students to speculate why this book, with all its literary ineptitudes, was so much more successful as a social protest than the far more artistically crafted *Cry;* why Uncle Tom has become a pejorative epithet; what message the novel has had for its readers down through the years, and what its relevance is today. Or will the teacher avoid these ethical issues and focus only on such aspects of the book as the author's use of coincidence and thread-weaving, the sentimentality, the obtrusive narrator, and the shadings of character and conflict?

These are novels. Other kinds of literature present much the same options. Poetry, drama, nonfiction—all may be treated as lessons in the art of either literature or life.

Teachers often select a piece of literature for their students to read primarily because it will hold their interest and will raise moral issues that will stimulate discussion or writing. They often feel that to insist too much on the subtleties of literary craftsmanship with younger or less able students might endanger or even destroy their pleasure of reading and alienate them from books. In such cases, teachers ask students only to weigh the issues against their own experiences and values.

With the older, more able students, such human questions may not be the only focus for the class; but very often these questions are by far the teacher's major reasons for having students read literature. More important, the students themselves see those ethical issues as primary. Their "book reports" usually consist largely of evidence that they have read the novel or play (listing characters, retelling the story), plus their reactions to its issues. Rarely do they discuss its craftsmanship and artistry.

This emphasis does not arise merely from the teacher's personal interest in human goals, nor is it to be condemned. The U. S. Supreme Court has recognized the obligation of public school teachers to foster moral values among their students. Nearly every state in the union has a similar requirement. The California Board of Education spells out the schools' "duty concerning instruction of pupils concerning morals, manners, and citizenship." New York State's Board of Regents has published a "statement on moral and spiritual training in schools" which lays down guidelines.

When the teacher asks students to react to a piece of literature, to the issues it raises, and to the values it seems to commend or condemn, the teacher is, it seems, challenging students. The student is invited to examine the validity of his or her own preconceptions and dispositions; to judge the worth of the literature as a human document; and to comment on the author's values as expressed or implied by the characters, the narrator, or even the author's own manipulations of both character and narrator.

The purpose of such a challenge, if not the result, is to help students grow. Some teachers see their role in this activity as that of a midwife, helping students to give birth to their own ideas. Other teachers are sculptors, forming students' minds in someone's, or Someone's, image. The difference between these two ways in which teachers see their role is similar to the difference between the relatively new, analytic pursuit of "value clarification" and the more traditional, but recently revived, prescriptive "moral education." The difference in each pair is that in the former kind of activity one at least tries to be Socratic.

This brings us back to our original two lists of goals, human and literary, for the teaching of literature. It seems that *the teaching goals represented by the first group, tending toward enlarging students' minds and spirits, are those of education in general.* They are shared by all teachers, whether of English, biology, or physical education.

Both value clarification and moral education, as separate disciplines, are simply the extreme, the purest form, in which such education takes place. Not only are their goals focused on human values, but so is their subject matter. In other disciplines, subject matter and human values are distinguishable, if not entirely separable. Human values are related to the specific subject matter of nearly any discipline. A biology teacher's subject matter leads to questions about the value of life, and an athletic coach deals with fair play.

The second, or literary, group of goals listed for the English teacher tend toward the appreciation of good literature, and they are specific to the discipline of English or language arts. These goals ask students to learn *facts* about our literary heritage and the tools of literary criticism, *skills* in recognizing literary craftsmanship, and a *disposition* to pick up and enjoy a book when they don't really have to for an assignment.

The teacher of literature shares the first set of goals, human development, with colleagues from other departments, along with parents and others interested in the mental and spiritual growth of the students. The second set of goals are the teacher's special responsibility.

With all this in mind, what shall one say when the literature being studied in the public school class is taken from the Bible? Should a teacher ask students to judge the worth of the literature as a human document and to comment on the values expressed or implied by the characters, the narrator, and the author? Should teachers themselves do so? Both intervention and abstinence have their pitfalls.

One teacher intervened. She reported that her obligation to the Bible and to the moral health of her students simply would not let her remain silent when her students expressed horror at the "eye for an eye" in the Pentateuch. It was destroying their respect for scripture.

So she explained to her students that this admittedly primitive, somewhat immoral teaching was corrected in the Sermon on the Mount—an intervention that offended the views of people who do not see the Old Testament (hereafter OT) as primitive or immoral. (On being questioned, the teacher recalled no objection from members of the class.)

Another teacher abstained. He reported that his method of helping students to grow and of avoiding a charge against him of bias about the Bible was to remain aloof in discussions of values. Thus he would not influence his students, and they might arrive at their own moral judgments.

Therefore, he refrained from commenting when his students unanimously condemned as reprehensible the actions of God in the early stories of Genesis. Adam and Eve, they concluded, were punished unjustly for doing wrong when they didn't know right from wrong. They agreed that God showed unjustified favoritism to Abel and discrimination against Cain. The flood cruelly and unjustly destroyed innocent children and animals. And, they felt, the people at Babel were improperly punished for wanting to build a tower for what the students saw as a seemingly worthy desire to reach God's heaven. This, then, was an unjust and immoral God!

Not a word from the teacher; no countervailing interpretations. That would be indoctrination and would violate his own basic philosophy of education. And teaching the Bible called especially for complete objectivity on his part. (When pressed by the audience to whom he was recommending this method of dealing with the Bible, he reluctantly admitted that he had finally reassured his students. They would find a more enlightened morality later in the book, as people [and God?] became more sensitive ethically.)

Here we have two extremes. Intervention can lead to partisan religious indoctrination that imposes the teacher's bias. Extreme laissez-faire can encourage antireligious skepticism or reinforce a bias in a student whose simplistic prejudices are not challenged with alternative viewpoints.

These well-intentioned but misguided and misinformed teachers did not understand that what they were doing was offensive to certain religious traditions. Yet the problem remains for every teacher.

Suppose that the teacher neither indoctrinates nor remains aloof. Should he or she invite religiously naive students to discuss, judge, and even question such biblical phenomena as holy war and a psalm that asks for enemies to be "dashed to pieces"? the condemnation of some people to an eternity of torment in hellfire and brimstone? the relevance of the Beatitudes to contemporary religious institutions?

Should the teacher ask young students to express their opinions about the Bible's teaching regarding election and chosenness and missionary evangelism? about miracles? about motives expressed or implied by God—in the "sacrifice" of Isaac or at the beginning of Job?

Here are some questions taken from a textbook (*A Literary Survey of the Bible*, Logos, 1973) that is offered for use by young people in public school literature classes:

> Can you prove or disprove the historicity of the biblical account [of Eden] [of the miraculous elements in Jonah]? . . . Do you think the description [of Solomon's wealth] is an exaggeration? . . . Explain, in accordance with your own beliefs and philosophy, the killing of one thousand men with the jawbone of an ass. . . . Why did God allow Satan to test Job? . . . Which view [of the Song of Solomon] do you think the author had in mind [man and bride, God and his people, Christ and the church]? . . . Argue the case for and against [Psalm 22] [Isaiah 42] [Jeremiah 23:5-8] [Micah 5:2-4] being "messianic, prophetic of Jesus Christ." . . . What was the purpose of the transfiguration? . . . What does Jesus mean when he tells his disciples to eat his body and drink his blood? . . . Did Jesus think that he was the Son of God?

Answers to such questions are matters of serious concern and disagreement for religious authorities, biblical scholars, and the parents of students. How many of these people are satisfied to have children wrestle with them without guidance?

Let us return to our earlier question. When a literature class is studying the Bible, should the teacher focus on goals that foster moral and spiritual values or those that lead to literary appreciation? Here it seems that we have a clear mandate to avoid the two pitfalls illustrated by the two anecdotes recorded above:

1. For teachers to draw morals from the biblical text and then apply them to the way students should view the world and live their lives is flirting with the First Amendment's separation of church and state. This is true even if the purpose is "secular"—to broaden students'

minds and spirits—and even if the teacher believes that the Bible's teaching merely reinforces secular values.

2. Similarly, for teachers to go out of their way to invite students themselves to make uninformed value judgments about the moral and theological issues raised by biblical stories and teachings is asking for trouble.

Consider some of the questions often asked about a piece of literature: What kind of person is the main character, and what do you think of him or her? What is the point—the meaning or the message—of the play, poem, or story? What statement is the author making about the human condition, and is it valid? What values does he or she express? Do you agree with the author's values, and why or why not? Does the author do a good job of presenting the issues and his or her values?

Now apply these and similar questions to the Bible. Remember that the main character of the book is God. Remember that it is sacred literature—in subject matter and intention. Remember also that its meaning, both as to interpretation and as to its authority for people's lives, is (as this handbook attempts to clarify in Part II) a subject of controversy and of ultimate concern for many people.

For many, the concern goes beyond a matter of life and death; it is a matter of the salvation or damnation of their eternal souls. This consideration recently persuaded the Supreme Court to exempt certain parents from sending their children to "worldly" high schools, even though the children were not yet at the legal school-leaving age and no alternative formal education was provided.

Which set of goals, human or literary, should have primary emphasis in a language arts class that studies the Bible? The answer, it seems clear, is that the teacher should not, either explicitly or as hidden agenda, use the biblical text primarily as a vehicle for moral instruction or even for value clarification. It is better to put the *main* focus on analyzing the content of the passage, its literary craftsmanship, and their relationship to each other. Students must know the content—what is in the book—and how that content is expressed.

Of course, examining the content of a piece of literature for its literary values does not entirely avoid talking about its issues and human values. This is especially true of the Bible, whose content constantly involves the religious beliefs of the characters. The Bible's people, places, and plots include God, angels, and devils as actors; heaven and hell as settings; and miracles and visions as events. Its subject matter, in the stories as well as in the teachings, includes ethical and theological ideas.

How does one avoid stirring up religious antagonisms without evading controversial subjects? We suggest as a general rule that teachers of the Bible should refrain from *initiating* a discussion and evaluation of those ideas. A teacher need not restrain students themselves from raising such questions. They often ask about the historicity of some event in the Bible and about the moral and religious issues involved in the passage they are studying—even volunteer judgments about what the Bible teaches or seems to them to teach. If they do, and if the teacher decides that it is pedagogically valuable at that point for the discussion to ensue, then the teacher accepts a responsibility. *The teacher has an obligation to see that as many denominational, as well as nonreligious, points of view are fairly presented as is practical.* (See Part II, chapter 6, below.)

In sum, when a literature class studies the Bible, the teacher should try to avoid (and to be seen to avoid) fostering either irreligion or religion (or any specific religious viewpoint). The teacher will probably be more successful in this attempt if he or she pursues the second, more specifically literary set of goals than the first, which centers on building character.

Nevertheless, the choice is there for the teacher to make, and it need not be considered between absolutes. The two sets of goals, human and literary, represent a polarity that cannot be completely separated. In the study of literature, human and literary educational ends are inextricably intertwined. It is a question of focusing the attention of the class on one aspect or the other. The teacher will choose which side to approach biblical literature from and also what overall emphasis to give the entire course or unit. The literary pole appears the safer; but whichever the choice, the instructor must stand upon a firm commitment to pluralism in our society.

Manner and Matter: The What, the How, and the Why

Using the Bible as a text presents further problems, even within the pursuit of mainly literary goals. Literary analysis takes many paths. A common and convenient way of looking at a piece of literature is first to distinguish between manner and matter and then to see how the two are related to each other and how they constitute an artistic whole.

One of the most important characteristics of a great work of literary art is the striking appropriateness of its manner to its matter, the extent to which the way it is expressed enhances what is expressed. Virtuoso use of literary technique is superficial unless it supports the idea or emotion that the author is expressing. An outstanding work of literary art must consist of more than a series of set pieces. Conversely, without some artistry of expression, the mere statement of a fact or an idea does not constitute good literature.

From which end shall the class begin its analysis? One option is to begin the critical examination of the play, poem, or prose selection by asking students questions about its literary craftsmanship. What is remarkable about the characterization, method of narration, point of view, structure, setting, style, or tone? Where is there use of irony, foreshadowing, coincidence, symbolism, allusion, recurrent motifs, archetypal pattern, and the rest of our armory of bloody weapons—or trayful of surgical instruments?

Alternatively, the teacher may ask students to start with the facts: details of who, when, where, what happened, who is speaking, what kinds of words and sentences the author uses. Even such "content" as the ideas, issues, and main idea or theme may be included (though we shall make a distinction below between two kinds of content).

The class is free to launch its attack, or dissection, from either end—manner or matter. The choice depends mainly on the teacher's own predispositions and purposes, the demands of the piece of literature or of the course, and the kind of students in the class.

Not only do manner and matter constitute alternative ways into a piece of literature; they also offer themselves as possible emphases for the entire process of critical analysis. Teachers may choose to concentrate on, or even limit the activity to, either the work's literary techniques or its substance.

For one teacher, one selection, one course, or one set of students, only a word or two about the literary techniques and devices—how it is written—will more than suffice. Nearly all the time and attention will be devoted to looking at the subject matter. In other situations, less frequent but not unusual, the teacher is more interested in developing the students' awareness of literary craftsmanship, their skills in recognizing technical devices. In such a lesson, subject matter may be only secondary.

Here again we have what nearly all teachers of literature would probably agree is not a dichotomy but a polarity in their teaching, both for an initial approach and for a main emphasis. Manner and matter complement each other and are merely abstractions drawn for the convenience of literary analysis. To teach only for form, manner, literary artistry, or esthetic surface does develop some reading skills. As an end in itself, however, it is a sterile exercise. At the other extreme, to teach only for subject matter, story, ideas, or meaning may engage students' attention; but it ignores the English teacher's obligation to develop students' reading skills. It does not advance their esthetic discrimination. It blurs the distinction between literary criticism and the discussion of ideas.

For students to understand Crane's literary achievement in *The Red Badge of Courage,* they must have the facts clearly in hand. Under what circumstances did Henry Fleming acquire his red badge—his head wound? From what motivation, if any, and with what ultimate result did Henry lead the successful charge? Those are bits of the story's content.

Students must also see Crane's technique. He uses irony when he refers to the bandage, over Henry's ignominiously received wound, as a "badge of courage." They must see that the utter mindlessness of that successful "heroic" charge—of its motivation and its result—is a symbol for the mindlessness of the war and of War. Irony and symbolism are literary devices. Literary analysis demands attention to both facts and technique, matter and manner. We are free to choose, however, where to start the class's analysis and which aspect of the work to emphasize.

In the examination of narrative, our twofold division into matter and manner can bear further refinement. It is useful to distinguish between two kinds of matter, the facts and the ideas behind them—the issues the facts represent.

Facts about characters, setting, plot, and language are the content —*what* is said. In addition, the narrative is about issues and ideas, one or more of which may stand out as a main idea or theme of the story. (Here the word *theme* is used to mean the author's statement about his or her subject.) In a carefully written novel or play, the author's main idea or theme gives the story a broader meaning, generalized into an observation about some aspect of the human condition. It furnishes a reason *why* the author has selected the particular facts of setting, character, and plot for the particular story. The theme also justifes and is supported by the narrative's manner or form—*how* the story is told.

Theme explains or makes sense of both content and craftsmanship. Which of them comes first, chronologically, logically, or psychologically, is the author's business. What is important is that together the three elements—facts, technique, and main idea—make an artistic whole.

Not every novel or play breaks down neatly into these aspects: content, form, and theme—the what, how, and why. Alan Paton's *Cry, the Beloved Country*, already mentioned, is an eminently teachable example of Bible-related literature. It also offers both a good illustration of the harmony among the three elements discussed above and of teaching the Bible *in* literature (see chap. 3, below).

We have suggested that a theme is a statement about the subject, generalized from the specific facts of the story. The subject of this novel may be expressed as the troubles of South Africa. That is what the book is "about," in general terms, as distinct from the particular problems of the main characters of the story. One of its identifiable themes is that the troubles of South Africa may be overcome by the biblical ideal of love. Both in Paton's own comments about the book, quoted in Lewis Gannett's introduction, and within the novel itself we find fairly obvious allusions to I John 4:18: "There is no fear in love; but perfect love casteth out fear."

Let that stand for the novel's why. Now a look at how it is written.

One of Paton's literary devices is the use of the *recurrent motif* of fear, which appears on nearly every other page. The blacks fear the whites; the whites fear the blacks. On five occasions various characters are described in almost identical words: "Have no doubt it is fear in the eyes"; and once we find "Have no doubt it is fear in the land." At his trial, young Kumalo says that he carried a gun on the robbery "to frighten the servant of the house," and he shot Arthur Jarvis because "I was afraid." On Stephen Kumalo's nightlong vigil before his son's execution at the end of the book, he meditates on the white man's fear of the natives and thinks, "Such fear could not be cast out but by love." This recurring motif of fear is explained by, and reinforces, Paton's theme, expressed in the words of the Epistle of John.

Another aspect of the novel's craftsmanship is the *point of view*—the narrator's and the reader's. The latter results from both the characterization and the method of narration. As suggested earlier, nearly all the characters are two-dimensional. Even though the "good" people have foibles and the "bad" ones are understandable, the *characterization* is symbolic.

Some of the characters, black as well as white, represent the attitude that the troubles of South Africa should be solved by power. The elder Harrison and other white voices speak with suspicion about attempts to deal gently with the blacks. They call for stricter laws and stricter enforcement. Stephen Kumalo's brother John and his fellow leaders of the futile strike want black power.

Opposed to the use of power are others, notably the white Arthur Jarvis and Father Vincent and the black Reverend Msimangu and Stephen Kumalo. Their solution is Christian love. To emphasize and to prejudice the conflicting ideals, Paton characterizes John Kumalo, whose goal is power, as an utterly contemptible and immoral person while his brother Stephen, advocate of love, is almost a saint. These characterizations influence the reader's point of view.

Paton also takes advantage of a more subtle literary technique calculated to enlist the reader's sympathies with Stephen—the *method of narration*. In the main, the narrator intrudes into the consciousness of only Stephen. But the intrusion is often deliberately ambiguous and fuzzy. There are passages where it is impossible to tell whether the narrator is effaced or present, whether we are getting Stephen's direct thoughts and feelings or the narrator's report of them. At times the narrator seems to coalesce into Stephen's consciousness and identify with him, drawing the reader along in the process. The reader's point of view coincides with that of the narrator and of the protagonist. Thus, almost subliminally, Paton urges the reader to accept Stephen's values, among them the value of love as the answer to South Africa's troubles.

Yet another technique that reinforces Paton's biblical theme is his use of *allusion*. Effective biblical allusions abound in the book, from the opening description of the white owner's rich land, "Stand unshod upon it, for the ground is holy," to Stephen Kumalo's closing reenactment of the Eucharist on the morning of his son's execution, "And he gave thanks, broke the cakes and ate them, and drank of the tea."

One biblical allusion, however, is extended, and it is central to the book. The name of Stephen's wayward son is Absalom. Like his biblical namesake, he abandons the ideals and land of his father, who is the spiritual leader of the tribe; he violates the law; and he dies hanging. In Stephen's vigil on the mountain, he cries out, "My son, my son, my son." Just so, David "went up to the chamber over the gate, and . . . said, O my son Absalom! my son, my son Absalom! would God I had died for thee, O Absalom, my son, my son!" (II Sam. 18:33).

Paton uses the *recurrent motif* of fear. He shapes the reader's *point of view* through *characterization* and *method of narration*. Thus he enlists the reader's sympathy for the biblical ideal of love that casts out fear. Paton also uses biblical *allusions* to enrich the biblical atmosphere of the story and to connect this story directly to a biblical episode that ends in a lament that is loving and forgiving.

Another facet of the book's content and craftsmanship that is useful for this analysis of the relationship among the what, the how, and the why of the book is Paton's use of language, his *style*. Compare, for example, three pieces of writing: (a) the opening and closing paragraphs of the novel; (b) the newspaper account of the murder of Arthur Jarvis, in chapter 11; and (c) the biblical story of David and Absalom, excerpted from the King James Version (hereafter KJV) which is the source of Paton's quotations.

The style—diction and syntax—of the opening and closing of the novel is demonstrably close to that of the Bible story. They are alike in their use of many rhythmic repetitions and of relatively simple syntax. They state facts clearly and use active verbs and short words.

Both the biblical story and the novel's opening and closing stand in great contrast to the style of the newspaper account of the murder. This piece of writing is full of passive verbs, polysyllables, and expressions that indicate that the narrator is not sure of his facts. None of these characteristics appears in the other two, which are further connected by the biblical allusions and dependence upon God.

After assembling these facts, one might ask students to learn three quite simple lessons. First, since Paton wrote both the newspaper story and the opening and closing paragraphs of the novel and can write in at least two quite different styles, he can choose among various styles whichever one suits his purpose (often an astonishing revelation to students). Second, the style of the greatest portion of the book is like that of the opening and closing rather than like that of the newspaper account. Third, one may legitimately conclude that Paton wrote the book mostly in a biblical style as a deliberate choice. The teacher may then suggest, or lead students to discover, that the effect (and probably the purpose) of Paton's biblical style is to enhance his biblical theme.

To recapitulate, we have examined various aspects of the novel: recurrent motif, point of view as affected by method of characterization and of narration, allusion, and style. In each instance the relation among content, technique, and theme gives evidence of careful, artistic writing.

Repetition of the words *fear* and *afraid* throughout the book; the narrator's selective reports of the actions, words, and thoughts of the characters; the many expressions taken from the Bible and the parallels with the biblical Absalom; the simple diction and direct syntax that pervade the book—all these are the content of the story, *what* is said.

The use of such techniques as a recurring motif; slanted methods of characterization and narration to manipulate the reader's point of view; biblical allusions; and a biblical style—all these are the novel's craftsmanship, *how* the content is expressed. And the theme that the troubles of South Africa may be overcome by the biblical ideal of love, offers an explanation of *why* the author has used that content and those literary devices. Content and form support, and are justified by, theme.

This brief analysis of the novel by no means exhausts its excellence. One may uncover other themes and their related content and techniques. For example, the book's structure, together with another of its recurrent motifs, the land, might support and be justified by the theme that the troubles of South Africa may be overcome by renewing the land. (It is useful for students to learn that a well-written novel may have more than one theme.)

Or one might examine the archetypal night journey followed by both Stephen Kumalo and James Jarvis, with its possible relationship to the theme that the troubles of South Africa may be overcome only after its people have become aware of the evils and change their direction. (For another look at this novel, see Roland Bartel's discussion in *Biblical Images in Literature,* a companion volume in the series of which the present book is a part.)

As suggested at the outset, not all literature lends itself to this three-part analysis, into technique, facts, and ideas. Often, it is unproductive to insist on separating the matter into facts and ideas. One cannot always distinguish between the content and theme of a formal essay (or of some novels of ideas). The content, what is said, includes many explicit statements of the writer's views about his or her subject. Theme is an integral part of content. Conversely, some imagist poems have no theme. In such instances the conventional twofold division, into subject matter and form, is more appropriate. But in a narrative one may, perhaps should, distinguish betweeen the specific facts of the story and the ideas of which the story is an instance, between the particular conflict and the more general issue that it represents.

What difference does all this make to a teacher when the literature under examination comes from the Bible? Most of the biblical selections will be stories. With secular narratives, the teacher has the choice of asking students to begin their analysis with any one of the story's aspects, its facts or its literary techniques or its issues. Likewise, in the overall treatment of a secular story, the teacher may feel free to emphasize any one of these three elements. In deciding on the approach and main concern, the teacher takes into consideration his or her own educational philosophy and purpose, the kind of student in the class, and the nature of the piece of literature.

Does the fact that the stories come from the Bible weigh more heavily in those considerations? We suggest that it should, because the ideas that Bible stories exemplify, the values to which they point, and the issues with which they are concerned are religious since the values come from God. It seems advisable that teachers should not focus students' attention, especially at the outset, on the religious ideas expressed or implied by the stories.

This suggestion applies as well to biblical teachings as it does to biblical narratives. Teachings also have their manner and matter. The esthetic form of the Ten Commandments and the Beatitudes, for example, is poetic. Their content does include people and events as part of the setting. The content, however, consists mainly of religious ideas. Yet students must become familiar with what they say. With teachings as well as narratives, then, the class might best approach a biblical text by looking at its facts and its craftsmanship. Discussion of values and issues may come later.

After all, just getting the facts straight can be a problem at times. Examination of contrasting commentaries and a variety of translations will show the difficulties involved in determining what the Bible is actually saying. Consider two nonnarrative examples, one from the OT and one from the New Testament (hereafter NT).

In the Revised Standard Version (hereafter RSV), Psalm 22:16 reads, "They have pierced my hands and feet." Christian tradition views the passage as prefiguring the crucifixion. The Jewish Bible (Jewish Publication Society, 1917) has for the same passage, "Like a lion, they are at my hands and my feet." No prefiguring here. Which is correct? It depends on which ancient manuscript the translators use.

In the Common Bible, an edition of the RSV acceptable to most Protestants and Catholics, John 1:1 reads, "In the beginning was the Word, and the Word was with God, and the Word was God." Christian tradition considers "the Word" to be a title for Jesus; among many denominations it points to his role as the Second Person of the Trinity. In the Inspired Version, sacred to one branch of the Latter Day Saints

(Mormons), John 1:1 reads as follows: "In the beginning was the gospel preached through the Son. And the gospel was the word, and the word was with the Son, and the Son was with God, and the Son was of God." No trinity here. Which is correct? It depends on how one interprets, and how freely one translates, the original Greek text.

If there are such serious difficulties about what the text says, it is even more controversial to try to formulate with certainty what ideas are being expressed or implied when the text does hold still. Does the OT prefigure the NT? Is there conclusive evidence in the Bible for the trinitarian or unitarian view of God? In what manner should a person be baptized, and wherein lies salvation? What does "This is my body" mean? When is the Bible speaking literally and when metaphorically or even, in some cases, "mythically"?

Such questions seem to send a message to teachers who are organizing a course or unit for the first time. Until they have a fairly firm grasp of their material (and the purpose of this handbook is to furnish some help in that direction), they might well start with the narrative facts and how they are expressed, rather than with the ethical and theological issues and values. Furthermore, an inexperienced teacher, with a limited background, should not emphasize religious ideas as the main focus of the ensuing literary analysis.

Teachers need not, nor should they, completely avoid explicit or implicit ideas in biblical stories and teachings, especially when students raise questions about them. What teachers must keep in mind is that ideas involve meaning, meaning involves interpretation, interpretation involves clashing religious sensibilities, and the clashing of religious sensibilities worketh suffering.

A healthy respect for the complexities is useful. There are possible alternatives of textual language, meaning, and interpretation at nearly every step along the way. Teachers should know where to find authoritative statements of the alternatives.

Understanding the text and making value judgments, as has been noted, tend to flow into each other. The teacher has to ask whether he or she is properly prepared to handle, in a manner appropriate to a pluralistic society, a rounded discussion of the value-laden issues expressed or implied in a biblical passage.

One way of making a decision about which aspect of the Bible to begin with and/or to emphasize is to consider and choose among the various alternative approaches to studying the Bible in a literature course, a subject we look at next.

Alternative Approaches to the Bible

Most secondary school courses or units are called "The Bible as Literature." In fact, they rarely treat Bible selections primarily as pieces of carefully crafted literature, as good writing suitable for a critical analysis of the how and why of their artistry.

That omission is not necessarily bad. There are legitimate alternatives to teaching the Bible *as* literature. Nor is it necessarily a reason for changing the course's title, which may be inaccurate but politically useful. Recognizing that the title of the course is a misnomer is often the first step toward analyzing precisely what the teacher will be, or is, actually doing in the class. It will help expose the alternative approaches among which to make conscious and informed decisions.

The Bible *as* literature is only one of at least four broad but distinguishable ways of introducing the Bible into a literature class. The four are abstractions from what occurs in practice. Like all constructs, they rarely, if ever, appear in pure form. A teacher may be doing a little bit of all four kinds of teaching, at any one time using one or another of these approaches. A combined approach may be just what a particular classroom situation calls for.

The abstractions are useful, however. They expose principles for selection—among approaches, curricular materials, and teaching methods. They offer a controlling focus for a course. The basic question for the teacher to answer is, Around which primary focus is my course or unit (to be) organized?

The four major kinds of approach that we discern are: (1) the Bible *as* literature, (2) the Bible *in* literature, (3) the Bible *and* literature, and (4) the Bible and its *contexts.* So that these terms will have some immediately recognizable, though as yet incomplete, meaning, let us look at some representative examples. They illustrate how a teacher would deal with the book of Job within each of the four kinds of approach.

For the Bible *as* literature, the main activity would consist of analyzing the framing, characterization, recurring images and motifs, and the irony—verbal and situational—in the book of Job itself.

For the Bible *in* literature, the reading would consist of the book of Job and, for example, MacLeish's *J. B.* The class would analyze both, perhaps with an emphasis on the latter, and discuss the relationships between the two selections.

For the Bible *and* literature, the class might compare the book of

Job with another literary treatment of the subject of unmerited suffering, such as Wilder's *The Bridge of San Luis Rey* or Voltaire's *Candide*.

For the Bible and its *contexts*, one might relate the book of Job to the historical and cultural climate of postexilic Israel, when many scholars think the book was put into its present form. We shall argue later that it is more appropriate for the English teacher to choose one of the first three approaches as the primary focus rather than the fourth.

Sometimes decisions among these four kinds of approach rest heavily upon the practicalities of what classroom materials are available and what methods a teacher finds comfortable. These factors are important, but let us concentrate here on the literature itself.

The examples given above for Job represent choices not only among the four kinds of approach but also those within each category. Let us now explore the categories in some detail.

The Bible *as* Literature

As suggested above, most secondary school teachers do little with literary analysis of the Bible *as* literature, regardless of the title of their courses. In some instances, the class reads the Bible selection only because of its relevance to other pieces of literature. In others, it is a taking-off point for a discussion of its issues or its cultural contexts, ancient or modern.

In most cases teachers have simply had little or no guidance in analyzing the craftsmanship and literary artistry of the biblical text. Scholars who have specialized in either the Bible or literature have provided both precedent and cause for this neglect, although the picture is changing.

On the one hand, ***biblical scholars*** have traditionally directed their "literary" energies where literary critics were not interested. For literary specialists, the term *literary criticism* means (in an oversimplified definition) the analysis of the formal techniques and structures of a piece of writing and of their relationship to its content. Literary critics examine the piece as a work of art, usually in relation to some theory of literature. (See "Literary Criticism," Part II, chap. 6, below.)

For biblical scholars, *literary criticism* has, until recently, meant source analysis: How have various traditions been successively conflated, glossed, and shaped into the final redaction? In the past, they rarely treated the book of Judges and the Gospel of Matthew, or even shorter passages, as literary units for esthetic examination. Even with their new and exciting interest in true literary analysis, biblical scholars are of little direct help to the teacher of English. They work in the original languages, and their main impulse is exegesis. (See "Scholarly Approaches to the Bible," Part II, chap. 6, below.)

On the other hand, the traditional neglect of the purely literary aspects of the Bible is not to be charged exclusively to biblical scholars. *Literary critics,* with some significant exceptions, have usually laid aside their critical apparatus upon approaching the Bible. Perhaps the book seemed too sacred or too emotionally charged for them to read and analyze as they would secular literature. In addition, literary scholars are often intimidated because they do not control the original languages, and many do not know much of the historical-cultural background of the text.

If the secondary school teacher has taken a Bible literature course in a college English department, he or she probably found that the instructor generally slighted the Bible's literary craftsmanship and dealt with its content (the facts and ideas of the stories and teachings) and its contexts (what it meant to people in ancient times and what it means to people today). These courses have begun to change, but not greatly.

When they come to literary qualities of the Bible, such courses have ordinarily acknowledged the power and eloquence of the KJV and its influence on our language and literature. They have identified some technical devices—parallelism in Hebrew poetry, concrete imagery, symbolism, structure, irony. They have put little stress on the artistic effect of those technical devices. And, like the biblical scholars, the newer literary critics who are truly working with literary criticism of biblical literature have published little that is of direct help for the secondary school classroom teacher.

In addition to literary and biblical specialists, *theologians* in the tradition of Augustine and the rabbis and Luther study the Bible. Their energies, however, are mainly devoted to hermeneutical commentary: What does the Bible mean for the lives of believers? Their work is usually remote from courses taken by prospective teachers of literature in their liberal arts or professional training curricula.

The influence of such religious thinkers may filter through to teachers in their early religious training or in their other contacts with religion, perhaps even in a college Bible course. If the teacher does have access to the commentaries themselves and wants to use their observations about the craftsmanship of the text, the religious biases that may interfere with the work of a literary critic must first be filtered out.

Secondary school teachers cannot hope to absorb all this scholarship from biblical exegetes, literary critics, and theologians. Neither can they easily bridge the gap between scholarship and the practicalities of the classroom. How much scholarship do teachers need, and how much should they pass on to students? There are no precise rules. Practical decisions will vary with the teacher, the students, and the piece of literature.

These are matters for compromise, never completely satisfying either the scholarly specialist or the classroom teacher. The former may feel that it encourages superficiality and distorts and violates the piece of literature if students do not understand as much as possible about it. The latter may feel that to insist too much on scholarly background will cause students to think that reading skills consist of solving puzzles one by one and/or that literary analysis requires special knowledge outside the text. Either result will discourage many students from enjoying reading.

Biblical scholarship presents one special kind of problem for the secondary school teacher of literature. Must teachers know the ancient languages, the original documents, the religious commentaries, and the history of scholarship before they can engage in literary analysis? We suggest that they may venture forth, checking along the way with scholars, to make sure that their own observations do not obviously contradict the results of scholarship.

They are not required to explain to their students the Hebrew and Greek behind the text and the meaning of all the concepts in their ancient contexts, valuable as this information may be on occasion. (See Part I, chap. 5, below.) We suggest that students may be allowed to go ahead with the text, with only enough glossing to see that they don't get into serious trouble.

The problem is similar to what teachers face with *Oedipus, The Canterbury Tales, Macbeth, Paradise Lost,* and even a novel of Jane Austen's. Scholars know more than schoolteachers, and teachers transmit only a part of their own knowledge to their students. The problem is also dissimilar, because the Bible is for many people the Holy Book. Incomplete information may offend religious sensibilities.

The book is holy only in the religious sense, however. One need not regard literary analysis of the Bible as a sacred mystery, to be engaged in only by those initiated into the congregation of scholars.

It is no wonder that few secondary school teachers build their courses around critical analysis of the Bible *as* literature. They have not encountered such analysis in their normal literature courses in college, in most cases. Their ignorance of and respect for both religious sensibilities and biblical scholarship inhibit their own efforts at literary analysis.

Furthermore, research in the critical literature will turn up meager results should the harried teacher have the time and energy to engage in it. Only a few widely scattered articles or isolated chapters in books analyze biblical literature from the point of view of the literary critic in a manner accessible and useful to the average teacher of English.

Few classroom anthologies or their related teacher's manuals offer much. School anthologies are including more Bible readings among their secular selections: a psalm among the poems, a biblical narrative with the short stories. Even then, exercises and questions generally direct the student to the factual content and the issues of the biblical passage rather than to its craftsmanship and artistry.

To understand more specifically what we mean by the Bible *as* literature and to encourage teachers to try this approach in their classrooms, we present several examples.

The Creation Stories

(What follows is an example of translating the work of a literary scholar into classroom material. The original analysis is by Kenneth R. R. Gros Louis, in *Literary Interpretations of Biblical Narratives.* It is arranged for use by secondary school students in Ackerman and Warshaw, *The Bible as/in Literature.*)

In the classroom text, we have broken down this block of material into three passages: (a) part one of the creation story (Gen. 1:1–2:4*a*), (b) part two of the creation story (2:4*b*-25), and (c) the Eden story (3:1-24). The two accounts of creation are called "parts" to avoid commitment either to the two-source theorists or to traditionalists, for whom source theory is objectionable. That controversy, however interesting, is not vital to a purely literary analysis of the text, at least for a public secondary school class—although not necessarily to be avoided for that reason when a student raises the question.

We have separated the creation story from the Eden story for practical reasons. The Eden story abounds with so many provocative literary techniques and themes and has inspired so many excellent pieces of secular literature that students ought to be allowed to consider it separately. True, most scholars regard it as a continuation of the second (part of the) creation story; but that connection can be made effectively at the proper time. (See "Literary Units," Part II, chap. 6, below.)

Gros Louis calls attention to the language and structure of the first part of the creation story: the kinds of verbs whose subject is the word *God,* the formulaic repetitions, the parallels and the progressions of the six days of creation. He makes the point that *the orderliness of the creation process is reinforced by the orderliness of the form in which creation is presented,* and both enhance the picture of an orderly God. God is transcendent, omniscient, omnipotent, majestic. The universe is previously thought out, patterned, and hierarchical. God creates a static universe in the first three days; in the next three days God sets it in orderly motion that is to continue according to plan. Humankind, made in God's image, is God's vice-regent on earth; and by implication, people should also be orderly, conservatively following a preset pattern.

Thus we start with an examination of the facts and the literary devices in the text. We proceed to a recognition of the close relationship between those devices and the facts and ideas. Finally, we gain an appreciation of the literary artistry of the story: Form and content coalesce into the ideas. And the ideas turn out to be nothing less than the nature of God, the nature of the universe, and the nature and purpose of humankind.

In the classroom text we follow these same steps. We ask students to assemble the facts—to make lists of each day's creations, repetitive phrases, and verbs describing God's actions. We then ask them to speculate about these lists: Is there any logic to the order, the repetitions, and the parallels? How is the form of the statements related to the facts being stated? Finally, we ask students to draw inferences about the nature of God, about God's relation to the world and its creatures, and about what it means to be created in God's image—as presented or implied by the text. (Naturally, there are enough other questions to avoid limiting the imagination; we are not offering a regimented series of questions leading inevitably to our own vision.)

In the second part of the creation story, the Lord God is not depicted as a remote, disembodied voice. The Creator has a new title and is described in human metaphors. The Lord God creates a world in which the creator is immanent, a world in which the rationale of creation seems to be the satisfying of the human beings' needs as they become evident in time.

The Lord God experiments and allows Adam to participate in the experiment by naming the creatures. (In the Eden story we shall see that the Lord God questions Adam and Eve, insisting that they assume responsibility for their actions.) By analogy, human beings are to be not only orderly and conservative, as suggested by the first part of the creation story. Like the Lord God, they must also create, experiment, and question—responsibly.

In the classroom text, once again we ask students for lists and for inferences from them: about the order of creation, the nature of God and of the world as implied by the text, and the role of human beings. Finally, the student is asked to contrast the two parts of the creation story: What are the differences, and how might one explain them? These last questions are completely open-ended and permit answers from all kinds of religious traditions and at all levels of maturity, knowledge, and intellectual and imaginative ability. The answers are less important than the process of arriving at them. Students have to consider both what the text says and how it is said. The invitation to use their imaginations does not come out of the blue; it is tied to what the students have been digging out of the text.

How far the teacher chooses to lead students to a really sophisticated literary analysis will vary. Perhaps all but the top students may need some help in seeing that form and matter intertwine artistically. The way the story is told in each case is suited to what is being told and what is being implied; the result is two excellent and complementary works of literary art. The structure and style of the first part of the creation story reflect the idea of the conservative orderliness of God, the universe, and humankind. The contrasting structure and style of the second part help elaborate the idea of the dynamic potential for creative change in all three.

As suggested above, one may consider the Eden story a continuation of the second part of the creation story. The setting, especially the tree, ties them together. More important, the picture of the two human beings, of the Lord God, and of their relation to one another is similar—and quite different from what is presented in the first chapter of Genesis.

The Eden story has its own multiple motifs and literary devices. Let us consider one device mentioned previously. The serpent (whether Satan, in the Christian tradition, or not) is the creature that pulls Eve, and Adam, away from the Lord God. The polar relationship between the serpent and the Lord God is reinforced by the fact that both of them ask questions of the human beings, questions to which the questioner already knows the answer. And in both cases the purpose of the questions is to involve the people and force them to accept responsibility.

These similarities in manner and purpose of address emphasize their differences. The serpent wants Eve to accept responsibility for the decision to disobey the Lord God, and he is successful. The Lord God, rather than lecture Adam and Eve, wants them to admit responsibility for their action; but he gets evasive answers. Failing this more important moral test, Adam and Eve must learn the hard way and feel the consequences—physical pain and banishment from the paradise they do not deserve.

Again, the teacher can ask students to list the questioners, questions, and answers. Having assembled the facts, the students are invited to see how each group is similar and how the groups differ from each other: the serpent's questions and Eve's unspoken answer conrasted with the Lord God's questions and the answers of Adam and Eve. Finally, the teacher puts the question: How might one explain these similarities and differences? Once more, students wrestle with the wedding of content and form. They are learning readings skills by analyzing carefully crafted literature.

The Tower of Babel

(The following is an example of translating the work of a biblical scholar into material usable in the classroom. The original insights come from Isaac M. Kikawada's chapter in *Rhetorical Criticism: Essays in Honor of James Muilenberg,* Jared J. Jackson and Martin Kessler, eds., Pickwick Press, 1974.)

The story told in Genesis 11:1-9 (RSV) is so short that it might be called an anecdote, but it repays close attention to its literary artistry. (The format has been altered here).

1. Now the whole earth had one language and few words.
   2. And as men migrated from the east, they found a plain in the land of Shinar and settled there.

   3. And they said to one another, "Come, let us make bricks, and burn them thoroughly." And they had brick for stone, and bitumen for mortar.
      4. Then they said, "Come, let us build ourselves a city, and a tower with its top in the heavens, and let us make a name for ourselves, lest we be scattered abroad upon the face of the whole earth.

5. And the Lord came down to see the city and the tower, which the sons of men had built.

6. And the Lord said, "Behold, they are one people, and they have all one language; and this is only the beginning of what they will do; and nothing that they propose to do will now be impossible for them.

7. Come, let us go down, and there baffle [RSV reads "confuse"] their language, that they may not understand one another's speech."

8. So the Lord scattered them abroad from there over the face of all the earth, and they left off building the city.

9. Therefore its name was called Babel, because there the Lord baffled [RSV reads "confused"] the language of all the earth; and from there the Lord scattered them abroad over the face of all the earth.

The medieval scholars who divided the OT into verses and numbered them were not always so felicitous as in this instance. The nine verses exactly fit the story's structure. It is symmetrical, the first four verses dealing with the people and their ambitions, the last four reporting the Lord's frustrating of those ambitions.

The plot line is pyramidal, following the rise and fall of the tower. The apex of the pyramid is the middle verse, when the Lord comes down to see what the people have done. As in many plays of Shakespeare the turning point in the fortunes of the protagonists occurs in the geographical center of the story. And as in classic tragedies, the reason for their downfall lies in their own nature, their improper ambition or pride or hubris.

The detail of the symmetry goes further. The first two verses balance the last two. Verses 1 and 2 are strictly narrative, telling about the people of the earth and what they did. Verses 8 and 9 are also limited to narration, telling what the Lord did to those people on their earth. Beginning and end are further tied by movement into and out of Shinar.

Verses 3 and 4 balance 6 and 7. The use of dialogue makes the link between these two pairs of verses. Verses 3 and 4 report what the people said, revealing their growing ambition. Verses 6 and 7 neatly balance these two with the words of the Lord about that ambition.

The relationship between the people's pride and the Lord's sure and swift retribution is reinforced by the balancing of the first half of the story and the second. The symmetry calls attention to the relationship of the form of the sin and the form of its penalty. With poetic justice the punishment fits the crime.

The people wanted to "make a name for ourselves, lest we be scattered abroad upon the face of the whole earth." The Lord confuses their language not only to separate them but also so that they cannot make any name for themselves that one another will understand. The linguistic diffusion accompanies the physical dispersion; without a land and a language they cannot be a people.

They have come together to Shinar without dependence on God and without his even taking an interest. They use man-made brick instead of nature's stone, to live in a man-made city instead of out in God's nature. They want to reach the heavens, by their own efforts and for their own glory, without the help of God. God punishes them by driving them out of their city, ignominious, with their tower unfinished and unnamed in the story. Symmetry of form parallels symmetry of content.

They had "one language" and "few words," the first verse tells us—in few words. There is much play on words in this short narrative, some of it lost in English. But we can appreciate the use of repetition, emphasizing the power of what can be done with "few words."

For just one example, consider the phrase *"Come, let us."* First the people say it "one to another," consulting before they act. Next, they merely announce what they will do, without consultation, and immediately act. (One thinks of the widening communication gap between Macbeth and his wife with each of Macbeth's successive murderous decisions.) Finally, the words have a resonant, cumulative, and ironically opposite significance when the Lord says, "Come, let us go down."

Even in translation the choice of language is a pervasive enhancement of the content of the story—a story of how the diversity of languages began and of how language, the instrument of communication that brings people together, was used to punish prideful people and to divide them by becoming a barrier to communication. Irony piles on irony, reinforced by symmetrical structure and by repetition.

One may carry the analysis of the Babel story further by relating it to its context within the Bible. (See "Literary Units," Part II, chap. 6, below.) For example, the separation of humankind from one another and from God that is recorded in the story of the tower is the climax of a process begun in Eden, as James Ackerman has suggested.

Adam and Eve separate themselves from God by disobeying his command about the forbidden fruit and by hiding from him. They withdraw from each other by hiding their nakedness. Adam further estranges himself from both his wife and God by blaming her for his sin, and God for giving her to him.

They try to restore their unity by "knowing" each other but produce Cain. Their sons try to restore human harmony with God by offering sacrifices but produce the first murder. The growing distance among people is epitomized in Cain's isolation as an outcast. The breach between God and humankind widens in Noah's generation. Finally, in the story of Babel, the people not only ignore God but even compete with him by trying to reach heaven through their own efforts. They end up completely separated from one another by language and distance.

The story of Babel is also pivotal in the context of the entire book of Genesis, from the creation through the patriarchs. God created by separating: light from darkness, the waters from the waters, the terrestrial waters from the dry land, the man from the earth, and the rib from Adam. God created the separate kinds of light, the differentiated species of animals and vegetables, and man and woman.

God also created by uniting and completing: gathering the waters together; filling the air, water, and land with creatures; rounding out the hierarchies of the universe and creatures with vice-regents; and giving the man a wife, with whom he would become one flesh. A harmony makes everything "good." The separation that occurs at Babel is bad for humanity because there is no underlying harmony. The destructive and growing separation recorded in Genesis 3–11 must be corrected.

The history of the Jews begins in the chapter following the story of the tower of Babel. The reconciliation between God and God's people starts with Abraham, reaches a climax at Sinai, and points beyond toward the eventual union of all nations with one another and with God. Thus the Babel story looks forward as well as backward. It is the extreme example of alienation, but it is also the point from which the process is reversed.

The immediately adjacent narratives, of Noah and Abraham, also furnish a foil for the story of Babel. Noah and Abraham acted in response to a call from God and were successful. The people at Babel act on their own, for their own name's sake, and they are confounded. Furthermore, the people at Babel want to join heaven and earth, but that can happen only when God is the agent—as when Moses saw God on Mt. Sinai. In Eliade's terms, without a hierophany, there can be no *axis mundi*, connecting heaven and earth.

Psalm 23

Let us take a fresh look at an old favorite from the RSV:

1 The Lord is my shepherd, I shall not want;
2   he makes me lie down in green pastures.
   He leads me beside still waters;
3   he restores my soul ["renews life within me," NEB].
   He leads me in paths of righteousness ["the right path," NEB]
      for his name's sake.

4 Even though I walk through the valley of the shadow of
         death ["dark as death," NEB],
     I fear no evil;
   for thou art with me;
     thy rod and thy staff,
     they comfort me.
5 Thou preparest a table before me
     in the presence of my enemies;
   thou anointest my head with oil,
     my cup overflows.

6 Surely goodness and mercy shall follow me
     all the days of my life;
   and I shall dwell in the house of the Lord for ever ["my whole
     life long," NEB].

Note the structure as it is rendered above, dividing the poem into three stanzas that represent stages in the psychic progress of the speaker. Verses 1-3 are an extended metaphor: The speaker is a sheeplike ward of the Lord, who is like a shepherd. This image, familiar in ancient literature, has rarely been used with more appropriateness or greater effect than here. The first stanza stresses innocent trust: The speaker has the unquestioning complacency of an untroubled sheep. The sheep is also part of a flock, the community, in which the individual draws warmth from being part of the group.

The second part, consisting of verses 4 and 5, is distinguished by two departures from the first three verses. In this stanza the speaker thinks about things that threaten—death and enemies (in later translations *death* is softened to *darkness,* but the notion of danger remains). Second, the speaker now turns to the Lord and addresses the Lord directly as "thou."

The sheep/shepherd image continues for verse 4 but disappears in verse 5. Midway in this second stanza the sheep becomes a person, who now eats at a table rather than in a pasture. The trust remains, but it is now less sheeplike—neither innocent nor so carefree that the speaker can look away from the Lord as he (or she) expresses confidence. He passes from innocence to experience, to use Blake's categories. He enters on a night journey or a rite of passage. He looks at and to the Lord, as if for confirmation of his trust, and is reassured. Now a human being, he is not only defended but also made triumphant by the Lord, with a banquet and overflowing cup. The anointing empowers and exalts him.

Verse 6, constituting the third stanza, shows a return to the unthreatened, serene confidence of part one. The archetypal crisis is over, so that the speaker need not seek reassurance in the immediacy of the Lord's presence. No longer menaced, he refers to "the Lord," using the third person, and drops *thou.*

We can see movement and development as the poem progresses. The speaker's trust has undergone a change. So has the imagery. In the first stanza the Lord provided physical sustenance and guidance for the here and now. In part two, the Lord protected the speaker from threats of death and enemies, over whom he exulted. In the third stanza, the speaker's trust is spiritualized and projected beyond the present.

A sheep is given green grass, water, and restored vigor; the man looks forward to goodness and mercy. The sheep lives among green pastures and by still waters; the man lives in the house of the Lord. The innocent sheep's comforts meet his immediate needs; the man of experience thinks of all the rest of his life.

(At least one scholar sees the *house of the Lord* and *for ever* as eternal life in God's celestial abode, which would further extend the man's horizons beyond the rest of this life and would betoken a further development in the poem. But this interpretation does seem inconsistent with early Jewish notions of immortality.)

Underscoring the contrasting relationship between the beginning and the end of the poem, the expression *the Lord* appears only at the opening and close, as an "inclusio." The device forces the careful reader to think back and see the development of the speaker's trust in the Lord, from innocence through experience to a deeper serenity. For the speaker, *the Lord* is the beginning and the end.

When literary analysis of a poem uncovers the use of technical devices that subtly reinforce, and are justified by, its meaning, we must acknowledge the poem's literary artistry. This kind of analysis is one of the main reading skills the teacher of English would like his or her students to learn. Surely Psalm 23 is as valid a piece of literature for such a lesson as any other.

I Corinthians 13

(The following is based on the work of NT scholar Donald Juel in *Introduction to New Testament Literature*. The RSV is particularly felicitous for many details of this analysis. The format has been slightly altered here.)

Verse   *Line*

1   If I speak in the tongues of men and of angels,
        but have not love,
            I am a noisy gong or a clanging cymbal.

2   And if I have prophetic powers,
        and understand all mysteries and all knowledge,   5
        and if I have all faith, so as to remove mountains,
            but have not love,
                I am nothing.

3   If I give away all I have,
        and if I deliver my body to be burned,   10
            but have not love,
                I gain nothing.

4   Love is patient and kind;
        love is not jealous or boastful;

5   it is not arrogant or rude.   15
        Love does not insist on its own way;
        it is not irritable or resentful.

6   It does not rejoice at wrong,
        but rejoices in the right.

7   Love bears all things,   20
        believes all things,
    hopes all things,
        endures all things.

8   Love never ends;
        as for prophecies,   25
            they will pass away;
        as for tongues,
            they will cease;
        as for knowledge,
            it will pass away.   30

9   For our knowledge is imperfect
         and our prophecy is imperfect;

10   but when the perfect comes,
         the imperfect will pass away.

11   When I was a child,   35
         I spoke like a child,
         I thought like a child,
         I reasoned like a child;
         when I became a man,
         I gave up childish ways.   40

12   For now we see in a mirror dimly,
         but then face to face.
         Now I know in part;
         then I shall understand fully,
         even as I have been fully understood.   45

13   So faith, hope, love abide,
         these three;
         but the greatest of these is love

Paul's familiar hymn to love is divided above into three stanzas: verses 1-3, 4-7, and 8-13.

In the first stanza, Paul (or the speaker in the poem) contrasts the importance of love *(agape)* with that of the gifts of the spirit *(charismata)*. He says that the gifts amount to nothing without selfless love. The stanza itself is divided into three parts, which exhibit movement and variety as well as thematic coherence. They move from a physical gift by which one is possessed, to conscious gifts of the mind and heart, to intentional actions that issue from those gifts.

The imagery that the speaker uses in each case also changes with the movement. Verse 1 looks at ecstatic speaking in tongues. A gift that one can hear, it is aptly compared to a gong or cymbal. Verse 2 talks of increasingly nonphysical powers—prophecy, understanding and knowledge, and spectacular faith. It links them with personal identity ("I am nothing"), which is also an abstraction. In verse 3, generosity and martyrdom are gifts that express active commitment to the last named, faith. Activities should accomplish something, but these achieve no result ("I gain nothing").

The three verses vary in form as well as content, and they move in logical sequence, accompanied by appropriate imagery. Underlying the three verses is a singleness of view that is emphasized by the repetitive formula: "If I . . . but have not love, I . . ."

In the second stanza, the speaker, having put the other gifts into their proper subordinate position, proceeds to define the basic virtue: love. Here too he makes a threefold division. In the first two statements the speaker again uses the mode of contrast. He describes love, now personified, by the way it acts and does not act.

Verses 4 and 5 say that love is selfless, not self-centered; they balance a positive attribute of love against four opposite ones. Verse 6 is a second contrast, but it varies the pattern by using the same verb for both halves of the statement (as does the Greek). In addition, it reverses the order, starting with a negative description followed by an affirmative one. Thus we have a chiastic contrast to the statement that just preceded it, which began with the affirmative and ended with the negatives.

As a climax to this stanza, verse 7 breaks free of the series of contrasts between love and its opposites. It lists love's properties in an effective series of four positive statements. Yet a touch of division remains: The series begins with *bears* and ends with *endures*, similar ideas that enclose and somewhat contrast with another pair of similar verbs: *believes* and *hopes*.

The third stanza brings the first two stanzas together. In the first stanza, the speaker examined the relationship between love and gifts of the spirit. The second stanza ended with endurance, belief, and hope as the identifying aspects of love. Now he contrasts three gifts of the spirit with three virtues.

Prophecies, speaking in tongues, and knowledge are impermanent (v. 8), because they are imperfect (v. 9), immature (v. 11), unclear (v. 12), and incomplete (v. 12). By contrast, faith, hope, and love are abiding. As the stanza begins, so it concludes: Love never ends; and of the three lasting virtues, it is the greatest.

Time is the test. When the time of perfection comes, people will lose their childish speech, thought, and reason; their blurred vision; and their deficiency of understanding. The speaker implies that his reader should contrast the seemingly important gifts of the transient present with the perfect, permanent future. People may value these showy spiritual gifts, but they have no substance of their own. Their independence is only apparent; they depend on love, the essential eternal virtue.

By itself, the poem is a work of art. As with many other excerpts from the Bible, it also gains in significance when considered in context. Paul uses contrast throughout the poem to reinforce an ironic theme. The effect of irony is to shock the reader or hearer into seeing that appearance has been mistaken for reality. This is Paul's main purpose in his Letter to the Corinthians and in this passage.

Chapter 13 falls in the middle of three chapters (12–14) that deal with spiritual gifts. Within this section, Paul is at pains to show that the Corinthians have mistaken the importance of the ostentatious gifts of tongues and prophecy. For them, the two gifts are paramount and prestigious, supreme proofs of their true Christian status.

In fact, says Paul, tongues is one of the least valuable gifts because it helps only the possessed. Furthermore, true Christianity, based on selfless love, leads to cooperation by members of a community, not to its Corinthian opposite—competition as to whose gifts are the most valuable. In chapters 12 and 14, Paul discusses spiritual gifts themselves; the central chapter compares them unfavorably with love.

Within the wider context of the second half of the Epistle (chaps. 7–16), in which Paul is answering the specific questions raised by the Corinthians' earlier letter to him, the three chapters containing the hymn to love occupy a pivotal position. First he deals with a group of questions about religious practice and morality (chaps. 7–11). Then he discusses spiritual gifts (chaps. 12–14). This arrangement of topics suggests that correcting the Corinthians about the true relationships among the spiritual gifts is the climax of his advice on specific issues of behavior. They need love.

Finally, he goes on to answer their questions about Jesus' resurrection and the contribution of the saints (chaps. 15–16). Paul seems to imply that a proper understanding of spiritual gifts and the nature of love must precede an understanding of the seeming defeat of the crucifixion and real victory of the resurrection as well as of the role of the saints. Thus, the inversion of values discussed in chapter 13 is at the bottom of all the Corinthians' other problems. If they only had love (and faith and hope), they could resolve their disharmony within the community and act properly as Christians (chaps. 7–11) and understand the mysteries of their religion (chaps. 15–16).

The ironic content and form of the hymn to love also have relevance within the context of the first half of the Letter (chaps. 1–6). There Paul deals with factionalism in the matter of Paul's authority as God's spokesman. Some complain that he is not as effective a preacher and evangelist as they would like. Paul replies that they mistake appearance for reality, just as they confuse worldly wisdom and success with Jesus' real wisdom and only seeming defeat. Their factionalism indicates that they do not love one another and do not understand the gospel. Their dissatisfaction with Paul, God's spokesman, shows that they do not have faith in, nor love for, God and his message. Their criticism ironically shows their own failings.

All these aspects of irony, which pervade the Letter and are accented in the hymn to love, are foreshadowed in Paul's ironic, not to say sarcastic, opening complimentary address to the congregation. He gives thanks to God "that in every way you were enriched in [Christ Jesus] with all speech and all knowledge . . . not lacking in any spiritual gift"(RSV). The Corinthians pride themselves on these gifts. Imagine their chagrin as they read further. Paul undertakes to prove to them that the opposite is true: Their gift of speech is unimportant, their knowledge is mistaken, and they lack the one essential spiritual gift: love.

Biblical Style

In its simplest definition, *style* is the result of the choice and order of words and sentence structure. Two characteristics of biblical style that are often pointed out are its concrete imagery and its use of parallelism. We may not review here the many excellent scholarly analyses and comments dealing with parallelism. (A good source is T. R. Henn's *The Bible as Literature,* Oxford, 1970.)

Identifying instances of concrete language and of the various classes of parallelism is only the first step in a critical analysis of the artistic function of literary devices. The further question is, What do these stylistic characteristics contribute to the piece of literature?

For example, having identified parallelisms in a piece of Hebrew poetry, what does a teacher do with them? (Among other things, he or she may profitably go on to an exercise in writing balanced sentences.) Many teachers feel that for most of their secondary school students poetic parallelism may be lumped with English prosody as an interesting but irrelevant embellishment to the poem. It is fair to ask, then, what parallelism adds to the poem. How does it enhance the ideas being expressed? Conversely, what kinds of ideas may the poet express more effectively through the use of parallelism?

Among other things, the device highlights comparisons. As with other kinds of balanced sentences, parallelism in Hebrew poetry helps to dramatize striking analogies among ostensibly dissimilar things or striking contrasts among apparently similar ones. Thus the class might examine how effectively the Bible uses parallelism to express a comparison, adding force to similarities or differences.

For an example of the artistic use of parallelism to reinforce both a series of analogies and a climactic contrast, let us look at a gem from Proverbs (30:18-19 RSV):

> Three things are too wonderful for me;
>   four I do not understand:
> the way of an eagle in the sky,
>   the way of a serpent on a rock,
> the way of a ship on the high seas,
>   and the way of a man with a maiden.

The device used in the first two lines is not unusual in biblical poetry (see, for example, the first two chapters of Amos). Ordinarily, the "three" and "four" do not necessarily imply a contrast between the first three items and the fourth. The "four" normally reinforces the "three."

In this instance, however, the "three" and "four" seem to have an additional function. They draw the attention of a close reader both to the similarity among the four elements and to a difference between the first three and the fourth. Line 2 is seemingly only a slightly altered and emphatic restatement of line 1. But the three things are "too wonderful," whereas with the addition of the fourth thing there is an inability to "understand."

The speaker can only passively observe the wonders of the world of nature—in the sky, on land, at sea. But the speaker is more involved when it comes to human nature; so he or she tries to understand. Alas! in vain. Human nature is out of this world of physical nature. The parallel structure of lines 1 and 2 calls attention to the differences between the two thoughts.

Then we note that the first two lines are general and abstract, while the next four are concrete. In a sense, the last four lines balance the first two, repeating the general thought with specific examples and also repeating the pattern. Line 2 took the same form as line 1 but offered a contrast. Similarly, the concrete instance in line 6 is in the same form as the preceding three concrete instances in lines 3-5. The effect is to highlight the difference between physical nature and human nature.

Thus, we may see a final parallelism of thought, which can be expressed as a proportion: as line 2 is to line 1, so line 6 is to lines 3-5. The three things of line 1 that are too wonderful are the eagle in the air, the serpent on the rock, and the ship on the high sea. They are concrete images that represent all of nature. The fourth thing, which in line 2 renders the speaker unable to understand all four, is human nature, epitomized by the way of a man with a maiden. As an example of the effective use of parallelism, the proverb is perfect.

Part of the power of the proverb derives from its concrete language, another notable characteristic of biblical style. One identifies parallelism with Hebrew poetry, but concrete imagery adds force in prose passages as well (in particular the teachings, of which the parables of Jesus are outstanding examples).

George Orwell, in his essay "Politics and the English Language," provides a classroom exercise that deals specifically with the Bible's concreteness. He quotes from Ecclesiastes 9:11:

> I returned, and saw under the sun, that the race is not to the swift, nor the battle to the strong, neither yet bread to the wise, nor yet riches to men of understanding, nor yet favor to men of skill; but time and chance happeneth to them all.

Orwell then offers a parody in "modern" English:

> Objective consideration of contemporary phenomena compels the conclusion that success or failure in competitive activities exhibits no tendency to be commensurate with innate capacity, but that a considerable element of the unpredictable must invariably be taken into account.

He then goes on to teach a lesson on the evils of retreating from straightforward, concrete language into immoral irresponsibility expressed in abstract euphemism—or, more concretely, turning one's back on truth by not calling a shovel a shovel.

Another language lesson presents to the students four pieces of writing: Genesis 1:1-8 (KJV, 1611); the opening two sentences of the translators' dedication to their king (KJV, 1611); a Shakespearean prose passage from *Macbeth* (ca. 1606) or from *Hamlet* (ca. 1600); and a paragraph or two from William Bradford's *Journal* (1620). (See Part II, chap. 9, of this handbook, below.)

Aside from the wonder that all these seventeenth-century writers were contemporaries, students might learn something about style, audience, the influence of Wycliffe's language in a baroque age, and the history of letters. The concreteness of the verses from the Bible, preserving the concreteness of the ancient Hebrew, is emphasized in this exercise in comparisons, and the style still strikes us as effective today.

A course drawing only on the Bible *as* literature will find enough selections of literary excellence in the Bible, but it will take some effort to work out the critical analyses. The examples discussed above show that teachers can get some ideas from the scholars—of both literature and the Bible, especially in the more recent articles and books. Research, adaptation, and original analysis can supply an industrious teacher enough biblical literature to fill out a course or unit. One may organize the material according to its occurrence in the Bible, or by genre, or by subject. The Bible has representative examples of many genres and of nearly every human concern.

The primary focus of the Bible *as* literature is on its craftsmanship and artistry. The teacher approaches the biblical selection as a piece of good writing and emphasizes its literary aspects.

If a teacher does not want to be limited to passages from the Bible, he or she may include secular literature that is related to biblical selections. One of the most common, and rewarding, approaches is the Bible *in* literature, which is the subject of the next chapter.

The Bible *in* Literature

CHAPTER 3

To paraphrase Falstaff, not only is the Bible good writing in itself; it is the cause that good writing is in others. One could say much about the influence of biblical style, especially of the KJV, on the English language and on the writings of English and American authors. Here, however, we are interested in works that depend on the Bible's content, its stories and teachings.

If a teacher decides that his or her course or unit will focus on studying the Bible and its effects on other literature—the Bible *in* literature—there still remain several options within that category, suggested by the following questions:

How closely will the class analyze the Bible story to which the secular literature alludes? Will the students, as has most often been the case, examine the Bible passage mainly for the content, theme, and images that link it to the secular selections? Or will they explore its literary techniques as well—consider the Bible itself as literature? Will the students read Bible stories before or after the related literature?

Will the teacher use only those pieces of secular literature that rely centrally on the Bible? Or will the teacher give some attention to those that contain less crucial, or even only passing, allusion and references to biblical persons, events, and sayings? Finally, to what extent, if at all, will the teacher ask students to venture beyond the Bible in literature, into the humanities—music, art, and other modes of human expression?

These questions suggest that the house has many mansions among which to wander. The first step is to decide on the goals, scope, and major focus of the course or unit. Such decisions depend partly on the nature of the students, of the school and its administration, of the community, and of the person teaching the course. Second, there are the alternatives presented by the kinds of Bible-related secular literature. Within the broad field of teaching the Bible *in* literature, there are at least three major options and three lesser ones.

Filling in the Bible Story

Some Bible-related literature expands the original story, retaining the biblical setting, characters, and events. Taking advantage of the Bible's cryptic style, the author both supplies the missing psychology for the characters and invents additional details or incidents. Just so, the Greek dramatists reworked the old legends from Homer and Hesiod that were so familiar to their audiences.

Every genre furnishes instances. Hundreds of poems are set in the garden of Eden or at the cross. The names of poets who engaged in this activity with regularity and success come to mind: Benét, Browning, Byron, Crashaw, Dickinson, Eliot, Masefield, Milton, Muir, and Shapiro.

In drama there are the medieval mystery plays and miracle plays. More modern examples are Oscar Wilde's *Salomé* and Christopher Fry's *The Firstborn*—the latter telling of Moses and Pharaoh and their families.

In nonfiction prose, Kierkegaard speculates on Abraham's thoughts on his way to Mt. Moriah, in *Fear and Trembling.* One also thinks of the many fictionalized lives of Jesus, Joseph, Moses, David, and others, by such authors as Sholem Asch, Taylor Caldwell, Thomas Costain, Elmer Davis, Lloyd C. Douglas, Irving Fineman, Friedrich Hebbel, Dan Jacobson, Thomas Mann, Frank Slaughter, and Morris West—all accessible to secondary school students of varying levels of reading ability, maturity, and perceptivity. (For more extensive lists, see *Bible-Related Curriculum Materials: A Bibliography* in the present series.)

Reading the biblical account together with such modern treatments enhances both one's understanding of the Bible and one's appreciation of the related secular literature. Each reinforces the other. On the one hand, the reader is invited to share the author's imaginative response to the Bible and thereby gain a deeper insight into biblical literature. On the other hand, the author expects the reader to have some background in the Bible out of which to respond creatively and with greater understanding to the new retelling of the Bible story.

A public school literature course limited to this mode of retelling the Bible story, in its original setting and with the original cast of characters, usually focuses on the differences among the various modern authors' recreation of the original and the differences between the modern versions and the biblical account. What new characters and events does the author invent, and what do they add to the story? How convincing and illuminating is the psychology—the characters' motivations and reactions? How do these modern treatments make the story new, and sometimes quite different? What literary devices do the secular authors use, and to what effect?

If the class also subjects the biblical passage itself to literary analysis, so much the better. The more common practice has been to limit such inquiry to the secular literature, largely because of the teacher's diffidence when confronting the job of applying a thoroughgoing literary analysis to the Bible. One hopes that this will change. It is not necessary, however, to limit the Bible *in* literature to this "filling-in" type of Bible-related play, poem, or prose fiction. Teachers will probably want to go further afield in selecting secular pieces, some of which we examine below.

Modernizing the Bible Story

Another kind of Bible-related literature useful for a Bible *in* literature course is equally tied to the biblical narrative but leaves the original setting behind and recreates the situation in the modern world. In like manner, Joyce brings the Odyssey to twentieth-century Dublin and replaces Odysseus and Telemachus with Leopold Bloom and Stephen Dedalus.

The controlling biblical story, image, or motif may or may not be immediately perceivable on the surface. Nevertheless, it is central and pervasive. Biblical reverberations and resonances echo throughout the secular piece. Without them the timbre of the new work would be greatly diminished, if not lost.

In Hardy's *The Mayor of Casterbridge,* Michael Henshard and Donald Farfrae reenact the story of Saul and David, episode after episode. Henshard is the tallest man in the village; Farfrae charms everyone with his singing. Donald, a protégé of Mayor Henshard, rises in position and wealth and, without guile, eventually takes over Henshard's grain business, house, fiancée, and municipal office. Meanwhile, Henshard, consumed by a deadly hatred toward the upstart, forbids his daughter to continue her friendship with Farfrae, tries to kill him, and finally ruins himself.

Yet of Hardy's many literary allusions in the book, only two refer to the book of Samuel—and of those two one is quite obscure. When, in desperation, the once-powerful man visits the disreputable local prophet, Henshard feels "like Saul at his reception by Samuel" at Endor. The second allusion is more subtle. Farfrae, at his first appearance, is described as "ruddy and of a fair countenance," the exact words used in the KJV to describe the young David before he wins the hearts of the people of Israel with his dramatic victory.

In Hemingway's *The Old Man and the Sea*, biblical imagery is more obvious, but the case is at the same time more complex. Its biblical image shares attention with another, nonbiblical image that is equally central to the story.

Two seemingly conflicting aspects of the old man's struggle create a tension. Hemingway strongly indicates that his protagonist not only is an amoral "champion" who pits his strength, expertise, and luck against nature and fate but is also in some, perhaps ironic, sense a Christ figure.

The old man's stigmatic wounds on palms and forehead, his three-day "agony," his cry at the appearance of the sharks ("a noise such as a man might make, involuntarily, feeling the nail go through his hands and into the wood"), his recapitulation of the walk up to Calvary at the end—these and other less obtrusive allusions demand that the careful reader think of the Passion.

These are only two examples of this kind of central biblical image, taken from novels that transfer a Bible story to a modern context—novels that often appear in the secondary school English curriculum. Teachers will undoubtedly think of others. As a matter a fact, a course in the Bible *in* literature could never exhaust the possibilities of poetry, drama, and fiction that transfer the biblical situation to modern life. (For teachable examples, see Bartel, *Biblical Images in Literature.*)

The Crucial Biblical Allusion

Some Bible-related pieces of literature depend less centrally on a Bible story; they do not retell it either in its original setting or in a modern one. Yet they use biblical allusion at some important point to underscore the work's main idea or theme—what the author is saying about his or her subject. In such instances the Bible story is a less pervasive presence, but no less crucial to an appreciation of the author's intent.

More subtly, but with equal dependence, such Bible-related secular literature assumes that the reader has a religious or humanistic tradition that includes the Bible. The author counts on the reader's knowledge of and attitude toward the biblical account to add a dimension to the modern poem, drama, or piece of fiction. Reading good literature, as with any artistic experience, is a creative act to which the artist asks the reader to contribute out of his or her own background.

This type of critical biblical allusion may be only the title. Sassoon calls his war poem "Golgotha"; Miller's drama of lost innocence is entitled *After the Fall.* Such a title makes an important difference.

The allusion may be elsewhere. Steinbeck wants his reader to catch the biblical connection between his novella *The Pearl* and the parable of the pearl of great price. Yet he signals it only once, in the epigraph, "If this story is a parable, perhaps everyone takes his own meaning from it." Keats is forlorn when he hears the nightingale. He conveys the depth of his feeling to his reader by evoking a biblical image, with his memorable reference to the "sad heart of Ruth when, sick for home, she stood in tears amid the alien corn." As suggested earlier, Paton makes effective use of an extended biblical allusion in *Cry, the Beloved Country.*

In Harper Lee's *To Kill a Mockingbird,* young Scout hears her father and uncle discussing her father's decision to defend a black man charged with rape in the bigoted town:

"You know, I'd hoped to get through life without a case of this kind, but [Judge] John Taylor pointed at me and said, 'You're It.'"
"Let this cup pass from you, eh?"
"Right. But do you think I could face my children otherwise?"

The reader understands that Scout's father accepts his coming crucifixion by the town, that he must drink the bitter cup alone, and that he must do it for the sake of the souls of his children. The agony of that decision is crucial to the theme of the book.

One of the central concerns of Melville's *Typee* is the corrupting influence of (Christian) civilization. Until white strangers interfered, Melville felt, the people on the island were as innocent as Adam and Eve before they tasted the fruit of the tree of knowledge. His publisher prevented him from directly charging that Christians, including missionaries, had corrupted the South Seas natives. Melville continually urged his point, however, by allusion to the garden of Eden:

> The penalty of the Fall presses very lightly upon the valley of Typee [as yet inaccessible to corrupting Christians]; for with the solitary exception of striking a light, I scarcely saw any piece of work performed there that caused the sweat to stand upon a single brow.

Other examples of literature that make extended or crucially important use of biblical allusion will come to any teacher's mind. It is clear that they are many and that if a teacher wishes, he or she can easily combine them with those that retell the Bible story more closely. These are the major options.

The Bible *for* Literature

A less direct way of teaching the Bible *in* literature is to separate the study of the Bible from the study of secular literature that refers to it. If the teacher feels a need for a completely aseptic approach, free of all controversy, the students may be asked to read the Bible in a course or unit whose sole purpose is to make them familiar with the book's contents. They thus acquire background for some later unit or course in which they will be able to recognize biblical allusions in secular literature. During such an insulated Bible course the teacher may avoid nearly all questions of biblical interpretation, asking only that students know what is in the book.

In such an approach, the teacher will probably want to use the KJV, so that students can recognize quotations as well as personalities and stories. Most writers quote the language of the KJV (see "Classroom Text: Bible," Part II, chap. 6, below).

By means of study questions and quizzes (see Part IV of this handbook), the teacher may call to the attention of the students—whose biblical illiteracy will ordinarily be enormous—which people, which narrative details, and even which lines are most likely to appear in secular literature. One may emphasize and firmly set these passages in the students' minds by all sorts of techniques: vivid instances from our culture and everyday life in which the Bible appears or has an influence, creative projects that fasten the biblical information in their memories, and just plain drill.

Though aseptic, the course need not be anemic. Art, music, advertisements, newspaper and magazine items, and cartoons—as well as original student creations, verbal or other—can make memorizing also memorable.

This approach, the Bible *for* literature, may seem to reduce the Bible to merely a sourcebook, a storehouse of famous names, stories, and sayings. The method is, however, eminently appropriate for some teaching situations. In the first place, it confronts squarely and most efficiently a deplorable gap in students' knowledge of their cultural heritage, their lack of the simplest acquaintance with what is in the Bible. It is a gap that few teachers of literature have not had occasion to bemoan. Second, it is useful for a teacher who is not sufficiently knowledgeable about the Bible and about its religious context or who faces an overly suspicious public or an overly cautious administration.

Once the students have this minimal biblical background, the teacher can, if desired, go on to secular literature that will draw upon and reinforce their new knowledge. The teacher may now feel easier about using one of the other approaches to the Bible *in* literature with less fear of inadequacy or harassment. The Bible unit is over; the class is no longer studying the Bible itself.

With the secular literature, the teacher may lead students, through ingenious Socratic questioning (of course!) to discover the biblical layer in a particular poem, play, or prose piece. The climactic question is, How does the biblical image or allusion affect the piece of literature? More important even than where and how the author uses the Bible is the question of why. What point is the author trying to make? How appropriate to that point is the biblical passage to which allusion is being made?

These may develop into sticky questions of meaning, but the teacher can now proceed to discuss the meaning of the biblical content in a less pressured atmosphere. An English class that is studying secular literature can usually deal with the reason for the biblical layer of that literature with less heat and at least a chance for more light than in the context of a Bible course or unit. Teacher and students are freer to discuss the meaning of the piece of literature and the contribution of the biblical allusion to that meaning.

Only the pressure is relieved, however. In avoiding a controversy during the insulated Bible unit, we have not evaded the obligation to deal responsibly with the biblical component of the secular literature when we come to it.

For example, once we have established that Hemingway's Old Man is in some sense a Christ figure, we must ask why the author alluded to the Passion. What is the artistic justification for that literary device, in terms of some central theme? Such a question, raised by the demands of literary analysis, forces us to probe further. In what sense is Santiago a

Christ figure? And finally, what does it mean to be a Christ figure? What is the meaning of the life, death, and resurrection of Jesus? Here is plenty of room for controversy.

The controversy has been postponed. The class has not had to confront such a question while studying the Bible *for* literature. But the question, however fraught with religious burdens, cannot be avoided if one is to pursue the literary implications of the author's use of literary allusion.

That does not mean that all restraints are off, however. The point of postponing such a question is that in some teaching situations it will raise fewer eyebrows and temperatures to discuss the various "meanings" attributed to Jesus as the Christ/messiah when that discussion is part of the literary analysis of a secular novel than it will within courses or units formally devoted to the study of the Bible and so labeled.

The teacher still has obligations to present factual information about the Bible and its many versions and interpretations; to display and encourage sensitivity to a variety of religious and nonreligious sensibilities; and to adhere to a strong commitment not to use the opportunity to engage in religious indoctrination or subversion.

These obligations apply regardless of the context in which the class disucsses theological and ethical ideas found in the Bible. The Bible *for* literature does free the hesitant teacher from some of the more obvious occasions for anxiety but not from the professional responsibilities surrounding sensitive material.

The Bible as Footnote

In many cases a biblical allusion in literature is purely incidental to a main theme. It need be acknowledged, if at all, with only a bare footnote to the students. In other instances the allusion demands a bit more. While neither pervasive nor crucial, it may be important enough in its local context to warrant time out for some examination of the Bible story in order to enrich the work of literary art being studied.

Consider some biblical allusions in *Hamlet.* It may suit a teacher's purpose to ignore the allusion in the "special providence in the fall of a sparrow." "If you call me Jephthah, my lord, I have a daughter" could use a brief summary of the story of Jephthah; but will the interruption be worth it to the class? Again, "It out-Herod's Herod" might take some explication, but the allusion most often carries English teachers beyond the Bible and into the mystery plays.

In each of these three instances, one could possibly make a case for a deeper significance of the allusion than appears on the surface and for a wider application than to the immediate speech. Hamlet trusts God's providence at last; Polonius characteristically devalues his son and daughter, as well as others; Claudius is another Herod. But perhaps few teachers of secondary school English would go so far, considering the time available. At all events, a teacher may ignore these allusions or give them minimal footnotes, as he or she wishes, without greatly lessening the students' understanding or appreciation of the play.

Some other biblical allusions in *Hamlet* may warrant more attention. Claudius reveals his consciousness of his sin as "the primal eldest curse." Hamlet echoes that image at the graveyard, with "How the knave jowls it to the ground, as if it were Cain's jawbone." Many teachers do stop to point out these allusions, which link the kneeling Claudius and the grave. Students might well learn not only the Bible story of Cain and Abel but also something of its significance to people as biblically aware as the play's Danish (i.e., Elizabethan) court and many God-fearing people. Shakespeare seems to be asking his audience to remember the heinousness of Cain's sin.

On three occasions Hamlet rages about his mother's incest. A biblical footnote may explain to students why Gertrude's marriage was considered incestuous. More important, it helps them understand the intensity of Hamlet's revulsion. The religious sanction against the unnatural sin of incest, obviously very much on Hamlet's mind, is added to the more readily recognizable horror of a son whose mother remarries so soon after the death of his greatly admired father. Hamlet is more concerned with hell and damnation than with death, for himself and for Claudius, as he reveals in his soliloquies. His mother's damnable sin must bother him as much as her o'er-hasty marriage. And if, as Ernest Jones suggests, there is an Oedipal problem, incest, condemned by religion, increases its weight.

Teachers may well consider such biblical glosses as the story of Cain and the laws of incest to be important for an understanding and appreciation of the play. Surely, they are more important than the mere footnoting of an obscure reference that occurs only once and that may be of only momentary significance, however illuminating for the nonce.

On the other hand, these glosses are far less central to the artist's structure and theme than when the author is more dependent on a Bible story. Shakespeare never expands an original biblical story *in situ,* nor does he transfer it to a modern setting or use it as a controlling and organizing image.

Footnoting and glossing are the Bible *in* literature with a considerable difference. We are no longer in a Bible-oriented unit or course. Yet this approach to the Bible has its ideological proponents. Some people feel quite strongly that religious literature and religion should not be brought into the public school curriculum except where they are absolutely necessary for an understanding of the "main" subject matter of the course as described within a traditional, discrete discipline.

The Bible in the Humanities

Once more there are options within options. As is the case with straight literature courses, some humanities courses introduce Bible selections only incidentally, to broaden the range of material. Others use the Bible centrally, as the organizing focus for the course.

In addition, definitions of "humanities" courses, their concerns and subject matter, cover a spectrum. Some study the fine arts, music, and literature. Others take a panoramic view of cultural artifacts, activities, and institutions. Still others consider the enduring questions of meaning and purpose, goals and standards, values and norms, that each person and culture must ask anew about the individual, society, and the universe. Many courses are not so neatly categorized, combining these varied interests in different ways. One can readily see, however, at what points the Bible might legitimately be included in each of them.

For example, the Bible is relevant at the more abstract end of the range of subject matter for the humanities, that of the enduring questions. Such a course will study the answers given to these value questions by the humanistic philosophers. It should also study the many answers of religion, some of which are in or based on the Bible.

At the other end of the spectrum, when a humanities course focuses on artifacts, the Bible makes its contribution in nearly every human activity. Literature provides only one instance of the influence of the Bible throughout our culture and our everyday life. A Bible-centered humanities course, therefore, may cover broad areas beyond literature and be richly rewarding.

The teacher may want to demonstrate, or lead students to discover, how pervasively and to what significant effect the Bible has shaped people's lives, thought, institutions, and cultural products. Further, students may engage in creative projects on their own, linking the Bible to art, music, secular literature, mythology, ancient history and ancient cultures, and current events. (Part III, chap. 9, of this handbook lists specific suggestions for such student projects.)

Using only *paintings* and *graphics* that have biblical subjects, one can teach the history of Western art—at least for the past seventeen centuries—as well as of Western cultures and world views as they are reflected in that art. Artists have expressed themselves in biblical art throughout, from the murals of the Roman catacombs and the mosaics of the ancient Near East; through Michelangelo, Dürer, Rembrandt, and Doré; to Dali's illustrations for The Jerusalem Bible and Ensor's bitter satires.

It is similar to the other two branches of what are most narrowly defined as "the fine arts." Through the ages the Bible has inspired much of the time, effort, and money expended on *architecture* and its associated *sculpture*. People have built churches in the form of various kinds of crosses and in the shape of a fish and even of a dove. Like church murals and altarpieces, church sculpture tells Bible stories that serve as silent sermons in stone.

Biblical texts appear in choral *music,* from majestic medieval and modern masses to contemporary country-and-western hits, from Palestrina to popular protest song. Church music may serve merely as background for the sacred text, or it may distort the words all out of recognition in the composer's attempt to convey musically the meaning and feeling that the text expresses or inspires. In secular music the names of biblically related operas, oratorios, and spirituals spring to mind. As with art, the Bible has permeated music over the centuries to such an extent that one might successfully survey most of the history and geography of Western music by studying pieces influenced by the Bible.

Considering the early relationship between religion and *dance,* it should not be surprising to see parts of the liturgy being choreographed and even performed in churches. The regular repertoires of modern-dance companies increasingly include Bible stories; Martha Graham, for example, has created many of them.

Dance leads to *mime,* whose leading exponent, Marcel Marceau, has put on film his engaging portrayal of the conflict of David and Goliath (in which he takes both parts). Live and videotaped *performances* of biblical or Bible-related plays and pageants broaden still further the field of these more or less fugitive artistic activities. Some performances are preserved on *films,* a medium that has also fostered original creations in biblically oriented cinema—of varying degrees of excellence.

In addition to becoming acquainted with such examples of the Bible in our formal culture, secondary school students in a humanities course may be made more aware of the part the Bible plays in our everyday world. *Newspapers* and *magazines* use familiar biblical allusions in headings for news items and editorials to catch the knowing eye and to add overtones to a story or an essay.

Political *cartoons* and comic strips—think of "Peanuts"—often depend on the reader's biblical knowledge for quick recognition and sometimes for an understanding of the deeper implications of the cartoonist's message. Commercialism has not ignored the advantages of people's familiarity with the Bible. *Advertisements* feature Samson hairpieces, Salome dancing on a Magee carpet, and Eve offering Adam any of a number of tempting products. Our very *language* abounds in metaphor and simile based on biblical people: "I'm a Jonah"; "She has the patience of Job"; "He's as wise as Solomon"; "You Judas!"

Popular culture has become important to social scientists. In some institutions of higher learning one can earn a degree in the field. Secondary school social studies courses pay more and more attention to the popular aspects of our society. Biblical allusion in popular culture is a valid dimension of a Bible-centered humanities course.

In summary, the Bible *in* literature as an organizing principle for a course or unit offers teachers a wide variety of choices. Biblical selections may be the main ingredients or the seasoning in the feast. Bible stories and teachings may be essential to an understanding and appreciation of the individual pieces of secular literature or peripheral. One may isolate the Bible-related secular component from a Bible-*for*-literature course, or one may combine it with other Bible-related contributions from the humanities.

This general kind of approach makes an easy transition from what is familiar to teachers and students (and administrators and parents). Language art teachers already use many works that would fit into a course in the Bible *in* literature. It is not surprising that many Bible-as-literature courses include many Bible-related secular pieces, despite the title of the course. Quite often, a teacher who wants to introduce the Bible into his or her teaching will start with a few incidental Bible passages relevant to what the class is already reading, and then move on to a greater emphasis on biblical literature.

The process may go in the other direction, however. From secular literature that alludes to the Bible, the teacher may move to secular literature that is related to the Bible only because it is in the same genre or has a similar theme but has no biblical imagery or allusions. This is our third kind of approach to the Bible in secondary school literature classes and is the subject of the next chapter.

The Bible *and* Literature

We have discussed two kinds of approach to the Bible in secondary school English courses. The Bible *as* literature primarily engages in critical analysis of the craftsmanship and literary artistry of the Bible. The Bible *in* literature combines the Bible with Bible-related literature. The third literary approach, the Bible *and* literature, combines the Bible with secular literature that does *not* depend upon the Bible.

There are two more or less recognizable ways of organizing a course in the Bible *and* literature—by genre and by theme—and some special variants. As with all these cases of theoretical distinctions, one may keep them separate or mix them together in actual practice.

Genre

Commentators have pointed out that nearly all the usual literary genres are represented in the Bible. Some critics consider the Gospels, and certain other forms, as genres of their own. Most teachers, however, are satisfied to fit biblical selections into their familiar broad divisions: poetry, prose fiction, nonfiction, and drama. These genres, of course, have their varieties.

(A few overzealous analysts identify subsubdivisions—hemisemi-demiquaver categories far too refined for the ears of secondary school students to distinguish. Others impose inappropriate classifications upon Hebrew poetry. Two early examples have recently been reprinted: E. W. Bullinger, *Figures of Speech Used in the Bible* [Baker Books, 1898/1969], which identifies 202 *kinds* of biblical figures of speech and many more subspecies; and Richard G. Moulton's *The Literary Study of the Bible* [AMSCO Press, 1899/1970], which, among other things, professes to find sonnets in the Bible. These are scholarly books, in contrast to a contemporary example offered as a secondary school classroom text. Alton C. Capps's *The Bible as Literature* [McGraw-Hill, 1971], asks students to recognize 8 different kinds of lyric poetry in the Bible and calls the book of Ruth epic history, as part of the story of Jesus—a literary categorization that constitutes an unacknowledged sectarian interpretation.)

Anthologies and syllabi for secondary school English classes today quite often include biblical *poems* in their poetry units. Psalms are usually the first choice, but other poems of literary merit abound. Whether the literature unit is Bible-centered or not, teachers of poetry have effectively used the songs of Moses and of Deborah; powerful excerpts from Job and the Song of Solomon; passages from Proverbs, Ecclesiastes, and Isaiah; and the Beatitudes and Paul's poem on love.

Purely as *short stories,* some biblical selections stand up well with the best of secular writing, both in their technical achievement and in their thought-provoking treatment of human experience. Jonah and Ruth are demonstrably among the most excellently wrought short stories in Western literature. The story of Joseph is as carefully structured as a modern novella. The account of Samson by itself is an artistic whole; it is also a fine climactic episode in the book of Judges. (The Gros Louis book, *Literary Interpretations of Biblical Narratives,* in our series, may be helpful in pointing to the subtleties of the craftsmanship of these four selections.) The books of Esther, Judith, and Susanna are also examples of well-constructed stories that students enjoy. Whether to edit these three stories is a question for the teacher to decide; shortened versions may be found in Ackerman and Warshaw, *The Bible as/in Literature.*

With some cutting for convenience, the Song of Solomon becomes good *drama* for platform performance. So does the book of Job. For one teacher a student wrote a part for a fourth miserable comforter, significantly named Mort. The class videotaped the thus-revised drama, with results described by Ruth Hallman in Bartel's *Biblical Images in Literature.*

In addition to using biblical and secular literature within these traditional genres, teachers often combine *epic cycles* in the Bible with the legends of Greek heroes and those of other civilizations. The individual episodes in the lives of Abraham, Jacob, Moses, David, and Jesus combine to form epics that invite a study of similarities and contrasts within the genre. Some teachers have mini-units on the *epigrammatic* sayings of many cultures, juxtaposed with biblical Wisdom Literature. Biblical and secular *fables* and *parables* go well together.

Some courses or units are unified by the thread of *tragedy*, a "genre" of substance as much as of form. Saul serves as an instance of the classic tragic figure for inclusion in such a study. The tragedy of Moses is more subtle, as suggested by Hillel Barzel in the Gros Louis book.

When considering tragedy as a genre, one naturally thinks of the types of literature described by Northrup Frye, who finds the Bible a prime case of every phase of his schema. One may find every kind of writing in the Bible: romantic, satiric-ironic, tragical, comical, pastoral, historical—enough to content even Polonius.

Theme

(Here we shift: We use the term *theme* in its sense of a more or less universal or archetypal human situation or preoccupation.) A Bible-oriented course that includes secular literature related to biblical passages only by theme presents a special problem. Nearly every human theme appears in some part of the Bible. Therefore, nearly every piece of literature is related to the Bible in some respect and is a candidate for inclusion in such a course.

A teacher might reasonably want to narrow the field of choice to those themes that are rather obviously central to the biblical selection. One should not stretch the Bible selection to cover the theme of some favorite piece of literature whose relevance to the biblical passage is only peripheral.

Nor is it advisable, at least at the secondary school level, to focus students' attention on recondite themes of a Bible selection. For example, one textbook (F. Parvin Sharpless, *The Myth of the Fall*, Hayden, 1974) ties various pieces of secular literature to the "myth" of the Fall through the themes of youth (because Adam and Eve were innocent) and redemption (because of the notion of the "fortunate Fall"). There are enough more obvious and less controversial themes in the Eden story without stretching the text so far.

As a matter of fact, the first three chapters of Genesis are among the most fertile in human themes: the fall from innocence, sexual awareness, disobedience and punishment, consciousness of guilt, the relation of humankind to animals and the environment, the relationship of man and woman, creativity and orderliness, the thirst for knowledge, nostalgia for a lost golden age, and the quest for a new one. More specifically metaphysical and theological themes include God's immanence in, versus his transcendence of, this world; the existence of evil and the nature of sin; humankind's relationship to God; and order and purpose in the universe.

All of these themes suggest pieces of literature of interest to adolescents that a teacher may clearly link to the stores of Genesis 1–3. (See also Warshaw and Miller, *Bible-Related Curriculum Materials.*) Furthermore, a unit that centers on one of these themes might also include other Bible passages with similar thematic links. Babel, Ecclesiastes, Job, the Epistles, and Revelation all pick up motifs introduced in the creation stories.

Other themes, which run through several biblical passages, could properly form the core of a unit or course that studies the Bible *and* literature. *Sibling rivalry* would include Cain and Abel, Jacob and Esau, and Joseph and his brothers. The younger or weaker son is favored over the older or stronger in still other stories: Isaac, Ephraim, David, Solomon, and the prodigal son.

A unit or course on *women* might use the stories of Deborah and Jael, Ruth, Esther, Susanna, and Judith. One teacher expanded this theme to a full year course, starting with Eve; adding Sarah, Rebecca, Leah, and Rachel, as well as Tamar, Rahab, and Delilah along the way; and ending with Mary, Mary Magdalene, and Paul's pronouncements on women. For *fathers,* one thinks of Abraham and Ishmael, Abraham and Isaac, Isaac and his two sons, Jacob and his children, Saul and his children, David and his children, Mattathias and the Maccabees, and the father of the prodigal son.

A unit on *social justice* could include passages from Amos, Hosea, and Micah; Luke's parables of the good Samaritan and of the rich man and Lazarus; and epistles of John on brotherly love. One aspect of this theme is *ethnic prejudice,* in which case students might read the stories of Jonah, Ruth, Esther, and the good Samaritan, among other selections.

Teachers may easily find secular literature of interest to secondary school students that will fit these Bible-related themes—and others, such as innocence and experience, symbolic death and resurrection, human pride versus God or nature, fathers and sons, crime and punishment, and war and peace.

Some Special Cases

Theoretically, the items in this subdivision are not entirely separate from the preceding two. In practice, however, the following special cases often function as organizing "genres" or "themes," and they do have distinguishing features.

For example, *mythology,* as the term is ordinarily applied, is not really secular literature except to people who do not share the view of its original believers. Its thematic relationship to biblical stories, especially those in Genesis 1–11, is of a somewhat different kind than that, say, of *Candide* to Job. The myth is a religious response to a subject that is also found in the Bible; it is independent of our tradition. Voltaire's story not only is a philosophical or esthetic response to a subject found in the Bible, but it is also composed within our culture—a culture of which the Bible itself is an important part.

Some teachers have a unit on the creation stories of many cultures, from the familiar Greek and Scandinavian accounts, through those of the tribes of Africa and the American Indians, to the less well known ethnic stories of Asia and Europe. Secondary school classes often read the Epic of Gilgamesh with the early Bible stories. They have similar motifs: creation, loss of paradise and peace, the temptress, the evils of civilization, a flood—all common threads in the traditions of many cultures. Theodor H. Gaster, in *Myth, Legend, and Custom in the Old Testament* (Harper, 1969), lists some thirty different flood stories from all over the world and through the ages.

Within Greek mythology alone, one may profitably compare Eve with Pandora, Noah with Deucalion, Samson with Hercules, David and Jonathan with Damon and Pythias, and Abraham and Sarah with Baucis and Philemon. Reliefs carved on early Christian sarcophagi bear witness to the long history of connections that Christians have made between their own religion and Hellenistic culture. One sarcophagus shows, amid Christian motifs, Odysseus tied to the mast and sailing past the Sirens, as analogous to Jesus on the cross or to the Christian tied to his or her faith and avoiding worldly blandishments. Another depicts Dionysus, in his role as god of death and rebirth, as a symbol of the resurrection and salvation expected for the dead Christian occupant of the sarcophagus. More recently, W. B. Yeats has made an interesting connection between Leda and the swan and Mary and the dove.

A word of caution: The popular connotation of the word *myth* implies the lack of literal truth. We suggest that a teacher is better off not calling Bible stories myths—or legends, for that matter. Try as one may to define *myth* as having a kind of "truth" and as a response to the universe or to the human experience, most secondary school students will probably not erase the conventional definition from their own, or their parents', minds.

Furthermore, even this latter kind of definition implies that the myth is a human creation, an attitude toward Bible stories that is offensive to many sects. Thus, a unit that deals with the Bible *and* mythology ought not to come across as the Bible and *other* mythology. A teacher should not even appear to assume that one takes the same attitude toward the Bible and mythology merely because their subject matter is similar. (This caution applies equally to other "special cases" described below. One would not, for example, call an elective "The Bible and Other Science Fiction.")

A related problem arises when the teacher takes nonbiblical literature from a living religion. It would be inappropriate, for example, to compare corresponding sections of the Bible and the Koran with the intention of showing how much "better," in artistry or in content, the biblical account is.

Folklore and *legends* are often the focus of a special unit or are included in courses in mythology. Here again, the teacher may either add the Bible or make it serve as the organizing core. Episodes from the life of David or from the various judges go well thematically with those of the legendary heroes, aside from the epic cycle parallels mentioned in the discussion of genres, above.

Biblical miracle stories, fables, and parables bear a relationship to secular folk tales in many respects. Both *Snow White* and *Humpty Dumpty* add a fillip to the Eden story. Younger siblings often triumph in fairy tales, as they do in the Bible.

Within Jewish and Christian traditions there are collections of nonbiblical stories about Bible characters. Louis Ginzberg's *Legends of the Jews* (7 vols., Jewish Publication Society, 1920/1969; 1 vol. abridged, Harper) is one such storehouse. Teachers might also consider the "Cherry Tree Carol" and the legends of the true cross and of the holy grail.

Science fiction is also something of a special case. Its recent vogue has resulted in specialized electives and units in secondary school language arts departments. Several textbook publishers offer science fiction anthologies, to which a teacher might add biblical selections at appropriate points.

(Some science fiction uses biblical imagery. For example, Robert A.

Heinlein's *Stranger in a Strange Land* has a clear echo of the crucifixion at the end. Isaac Asimov's short story "The Last Question" ends climactically with a quotation from the opening of Genesis.)

Many parts of the Bible, taken at face value, imply the suspension of the "normal" order of physical nature as we experience it, especially in the early chapters of Genesis, in the miracles, and in the visions. For some people they are the result of the intervention of God: The biblical account is a literal and accurate report. Others attempt to explain such phenomena naturalistically. Still others see them as metaphors or as "myths," in a special sense of that word. The explanation becomes a blend when a modern author seriously describes Ezekiel's chariot as an early unidentified flying object from outer space, a chariot of the gods. Yet all the supernatural incidents of the Bible stimulate writers and readers of science fiction, so that some teachers are successfully, if cautiously, combining the two kinds of writing into a course or unit.

Some of the more thoughtful pieces of science fiction are similar to the Bible thematically whether or not they have an overt central biblical image. David Ketterer's *New Worlds for Old* (Indiana University Press, 1974; Doubleday Anchor Books) is subtitled *The Apocalyptic Imagination, Science Fiction and American Literature.*

The author mentions many pieces of general literature other than science fiction that would go well with the book of Revelation (or other apocalyptic passages, such as Mark 13, Isaiah 24–27, or Daniel 7). Such stories and apocalyptic visions go well together in courses or units that are either related by direct allusion (the Bible *in* literature) or associated thematically (the Bible *and* literature). Ketterer says, however, that the apocalyptic imagination "finds its purest outlet in science fiction."

Drawing on Ketterer's book, Scott Sanders of Indiana University suggests titles of recent science fiction that have certain apocalyptic motifs that a teacher may easily combine with biblical apocalypses:

a) A vision of world doom—in Ray Bradbury's *Fahrenheit 451* and Walter Miller's *A Canticle for Leibowitz,* or an account of the destruction of the self, as reflecting an external world catastrophe—in D. H. Lawrence's *Women in Love* and Doris Lessing's *Golden Notebook.*

b) Beasts and dragons (either literal or as a projection of man's evil nature) from the sea, the earth, or the bottomless pit—in William Golding's *Lord of the Flies,* or films like *Godzilla* and *Them.*

c) A prophecy of judgment and revenge against the evil ones—in D. H. Lawrence's *Apocalypse* and Arthur Clarke's *Childhood's End*— together with the salvation of the elect.

d) A vision of a new world, a utopia or dystopia, either radically new and optimistic or a pessimistic and reiterative beginning on the same road to yet another destruction—in Kurt Vonnegut's *Player Piano* and Albert Camus' *The Plague.*

e) An interest in cosmic and metaphysical questions about man's origins, nature, and destiny—questions that most of the rest of contemporary fiction, philosophy, and scientific activity seem to avoid nowadays.

The teacher who starts a science fiction course or unit with biblical apocalypses as archetypes will find a wealth of science fiction to match their motifs.

Related to science fiction but recognizably different is *utopian* literature, which supplies the theme for some elective courses or units. The utopian theme runs through the Bible: the physical and spiritual quest for a homeland, for peace, for deliverance or salvation, for God's kingdom on earth as well as in heaven.

Abraham and Jacob journey physically to the promised land. The exodus, from Egypt to Sinai to Canaan, is the archetypal experience: By the waters of Babylon the exiles weep for Zion. Old men dream dreams and young men see visions: Isaiah and Micah yearn for the peaceable kingdom; Daniel and Malachi end in prophecies of deliverance. Ezekiel envisions a utopia, in chapters 34–48. John the Baptist preaches that the kingdom of heaven is at hand. Jesus and Paul hold forth the hope of salvation, for the individual and for mankind. The early Christians experiment with a utopian community where "all who believed were together and had all things in common, and they sold their possessions and goods and distributed them to all, as they had need." John on Patmos describes the new city.

And as Frye suggests, in keeping with traditional Christian thought, the Bible as a whole, from Genesis to Revelation, may be looked on as one long utopian quest. The impulse toward a kingdom of heaven or a peaceable kingdom—toward some paradise, whether a New Jerusalem or the old Garden—certainly fits well with secular utopian literature. Once more, the teacher may choose to use biblical selections merely as adjuncts or as the taking-off point for a unit on utopias.

The Bible *and* literature as a way of using the Bible in secondary school literature courses is a fertile field. Whether the organizing interest is genre, theme, or one of the special cases, there is enough material to separate this kind of approach from the Bible *in* literature and the Bible *as* literature.

On the other hand, it is just as obvious that the approaches may be combined. Teachers may organize the biblical selections for a Bible *in* literature or Bible *as* literature course according to genre or theme instead of following the order of their appearance in the Bible. Similarly, pieces of secular literature that are related to the Bible only by reason of genre or through some universal theme may just as well go with the Bible *in* literature or even be added to the Bible *as* literature. (Our classroom text, *The Bible as/in Literature,* takes this approach.)

The three general kinds of approach to the Bible for a secondary school literature course that we have discussed thus far offer many suitable alternatives either by themselves or in some combination. It soon becomes clear that the problem is not where to find material but how to limit the field. (Lists of appropriate student and teacher readings and audio-visual items for each kind of approach appear in *Bible-Related Curriculum Materials,* in this series.)

Most textbooks, syllabi, and actual classroom activities do not fit neatly into any one category, much less into any subcategory, that we have identified above. The purpose of the categorization has been to analyze the alternatives so that teachers may consciously and intelligently choose a primary emphasis or organizing principle for their course. Whichever a teacher chooses as basic for his or her course will probably be supplemented with the other alternatives.

Beyond these classroom materials and methods, there is still another valuable, even essential, resource for the teacher. The teacher should have a fairly solid grounding in the ancient and modern contexts of the Bible—information that will be needed on occasion, to supplement a strictly "literary" approach to the book. This is our next subject.

CHAPTER 5

The Bible and Its *Contexts*

To read any piece of literature intelligently, one ought at least to know what the words mean, or meant, both denotatively and connotatively. That implies some familiarity with the culture within which the work was produced and to which it was originally addressed.

When a modern poem contains words that are new to students, the teacher ordinarily glosses the words or sends the students to a dictionary. If that is true of a contemporary poem, it is especially important for literature of a different language, time, and culture.

It is even more crucial in the case of the Bible, of which we have many early and variant versions but no first edition and about which there is such strong feeling. Even if one accepts an authorized canon and even if one believes the book to have been written for all time, one must acknowledge that the language of the early texts is ancient. The reader needs help from its ancient cultural and linguistic context, which is not easily available to most students.

The modern context of the Bible contributes equally thorny implications for the meaning of the text. Some sects today insist that one cannot read the Bible properly except in their own sectarian versions or except through the eyes of their own sectarian interpreters and commentators.

Furthermore, a comparison of even our ecumenical contemporary translations against the familiar seventeenth-century KJV or Douay reveals not only different language in the newer versions but also new shades of meaning imposed on the text. Often the new translations result in completely different interpretations.

Scholars are constantly reexamining and revising their understanding of the original texts in their ancient context as new discoveries and theories unfold. They also take note of the developing shifts of connotation, denotation, and usage in our own language. And they try to fit together both the advances in scholarship and our changing English language to create valid new translations—which nevertheless often conflict with one another in some important details.

For a public school teacher, the existence of these textual and contextual problems is important (not that the teacher must keep up with all the latest developments). Even if the approach to the Bible is strictly "literary," within the three categories described above (the Bible *as* literature, the Bible *in literature, the Bible and* literature), questions will arise in class about authorship, historicity, meaning, and interpretation.

Consider these actual, and quite representative, student questions: Who wrote the Five Books of Moses? When were the Gospels written? Why are the Protestant, Catholic, and Jewish Bibles different? Is there some scientific explanation of what happened at the Red Sea? How is it that people lived for hundreds of years in those days? Just how did Saul die; which story is right? Does Psalm 22 foretell the crucifixion? How do we know that Jesus lived? Why wasn't Cain's sacrifice accepted? Why did God allow the Jews to suffer so much in Egypt? Why don't Jews accept Jesus as the messiah that was foretold by Isaiah and the others? Why does Jesus threaten "everlasting fire and punishment" if you're supposed to love your enemies? (The questions have not been edited except to arrange them roughly in an order of increasing embarrassment for the teacher.)

How does the teacher handle such questions? Unequivocal answers in the text cannot be found—except from a faith position. For a public school class in a pluralistic society, we suggest, the answers should all begin with "Well, *some* people say . . . , and *others* say . . ."; and they should not end with "but the best explanation is . . ." (expressed or implied).

Does the teacher in fact know what "some people" say and what "other people" say? And if so, should the teacher introduce the Bible course by first providing some background in biblical scholarship and in sectarian beliefs?

If this were a social studies class in which religious literature was being studied mainly for its relation to an ancient or modern culture, such an approach would have a high priority. But we are talking about a literature course. How long can a teacher delay the reading of the literature itself? How much time can or should be devoted to an introductory block of background material?

Sooner or later, however, students will raise their questions. No matter how much preliminary background the teacher has offered, some questions will be new, or seem so to the students.

We suggest that, at the very least, a teacher should know, and be ready to direct students to, the sources where some alternative answers to such questions may be found—the critical and the sectarian commentaries. At the minimum, the school library should have on its reference shelves the books listed in Part III, chapter 8, of this handbook. Further, the teacher should not neglect the obligation to send students to their own religious leaders for their denomination's interpretation of controversial passages when the occasion warrants.

Sending students to sources, of course, is not invariably the most appropriate way of dealing with a difficult passage. The classroom situation may call for some other method. As a rule, the teacher will probably consider, in advance or on the spot: Shall I stop the class to discuss the question in depth? Shall I postpone the issue until we have covered more ground? Shall I send them to a source and have them report? Shall I call in a resource person?

The situation is not unique. The teacher has probably often faced the problem of how to handle students' sticky questions with other literature. In this instance, we suggest that the teacher should solve it in his or her usual professional manner, pedagogical considerations taking precedence. The basic questions are the same: What will best advance the progress of the class and help this individual student? What are my obligations to the literature, to education, and to the community?

Surely a teacher cannot spend much time in a literature course giving students enough introductory background for them to be able to handle, on their own, all questions of the kind quoted above, whenever they may arise. Neither can the teacher, as the course proceeds, gloss every difficult or controversial passage that students read. After all, how much of a Shakespearean text gets explicated? One of the best compromises is to offer contextual information as a supplement to literary study when necessary to avoid serious misunderstanding, but otherwise mainly to respond to questions that arise in class.

Then, out of such questions and responses, students must learn two very important lessons: (1) *Nearly every question about the Bible has alternative answers,* and (2) *no religious (or nonreligious) position is to be ridiculed.*

These two lessons are essential not only when students read the Bible itself but also when they read Bible-related secular literature. When students come to biblical allusions in secular literature, they may find that the allusions issue from a particular interpretation of the Bible. Students should learn to accept the author and the text as givens. They should understand an allusion to Lucifer as referring to the devil; and the question of who or what Isaiah 14:12 "really" means is interesting but irrelevant. It may be ignored—unless a student expresses curiosity and the teacher wants to stop the class.

In a piece of modern literature, a narrator or character may express disbelief in the historicity of the biblical account of creation or of the virgin birth of Jesus. The student should accept that disbelief as part of the characterization, not as an occasion to condemn the author. Students should not feel called upon, or be allowed, to lead their classmates either in cheers or in prayers for their souls.

The Ancient Context

If the teacher of English has taken a secular college course in the Bible but not within the literature department, he or she has probably been exposed to the concerns of biblical scholarship. Such courses introduce one to the historical and cultural setting of the Bible in ancient Israel and early Christianity, to textual problems, and to putative sources and analogues. These and other areas of scholarship help the teacher understand the book he or she is now teaching to secondary school students.

Scholarly background exposes questions (and suggests some answers). What did *covenant* mean to Abraham, to Moses, to David, to the prophets, to early Christians? What did *anointed* (messiah) mean at various points in the OT and in the NT? Is there a relation between the "wisdom" that is personified in Wisdom Literature and the "Logos" of John? How shall one harmonize the ministry of Jesus as reported by the various evangelists, and in the Gospel of Thomas? The ministry of Paul as reported in Acts and as it appears in the Epistles? How are the NT and rabbinic literature to be related to the OT and to each other? Of what value are such tools as literary criticism (source analysis), form criticism, and redaction criticism—their strengths and limitations?

Such background information is extremely valuable for a teacher to have available, whether he or she accepts the conclusions of critical scholars or those of more conservative scholarship. Lacking a solid college course, teachers might consider some such introductory books as Ackerman's *Teaching the Old Testament in English Classes* and Juel's *An*

Introduction to New Testament Literature. These books generally represent the view of critical scholarship. Other resources are more tradition-oriented and/or sectarian. (See Part II, chap. 6, below.)

It must be emphasized that these college courses and/or books are recommended mainly for the teacher's own background. We suggest strongly that one's syllabus for a secondary school class not be an attempt to replicate the college course or such books as Ackerman's and Juel's and their equivalents.

It is a normal and understandable tendency of teachers, especially teaching a new course, to pass on what they learned in college. Teachers must always resist this temptation, but particularly in a Bible-centered language arts course. Except for strict exegesis for glossing on occasion, most of what college courses and introductory books deal with is more appropriate as primary subject matter for a social studies class rather than an English class.

For example, compare the literary critic's analysis of the tower of Babel story, in chapter 2, above, with the critical biblical scholar's treatment in the Ackerman book. The latter mentions a possible Babylonian background, the ancient tradition of holy mountains, the etymology of the word *Babel,* and the probable purpose of the hypothesized Yahwist source. Teachers have found this kind of scholarly information most helpful when questions arise in class. (If a teacher does offer Ackerman's critical analysis to students, however, he or she should complement it with divergent explanations provided by the more conservative Catholic, Jewish, and evangelical Protestant traditions, among others, that are available in many authoritative books.)

A digression to consider some exceptions to what we have been saying: In a few instances, the teacher should supply background information for a Bible passage before students read it. The reason is not so much that the students might misread the text, though that is important. The main consideration is that the text might tend to foster or reinforce student prejudices against other people. Part II, chapter 6, of this handbook discusses two instances where the teacher should intervene: In "The World of the NT," the issue is anti-Semitism. In "Prophecy Fulfillment," the issue is the christologizing of the OT.

We suggest that a third such case is the Sermon on the Mount, in particular Matthew 5:21-48. Jesus' words are often taken to contrast early Christianity with the Judaism of that period, to the detriment of the latter. More important, many people have accepted that contrast as being characteristic of the two religions (and their adherents) today. As a matter of fact, the implied contrast was not true at the time nor is it true today. Nearly every reinterpretation of earlier Jewish law attributed to Jesus in the NT is also found in rabbinic writings that are roughly contemporary with early Christianity. Modern Judaism continues the tradition of rabbinic Judaism. Before students read that passage from the Sermon on the Mount, their teachers should explain these facts.

To resume: In ancient history classes within the social studies curriculum, the Bible offers valuable source material for such subjects as the fertile crescent, covenant, charismatic leaders, transition from tribal league to monarchy, the impact of Hellenism and of the Roman Empire on the ancient Near East, and the nature and influence of mystery cults. Such issues are subordinate, if not peripheral, to the main concerns of an English course.

To suggest that these questions are more properly the concern of social studies classes is not to insist upon the compartmentalization of disciplines in secondary school. When questions arise in the literature class or when the teacher feels that it would serve the main literary purpose of the course, he or she may very well introduce contextual information from the ancient Near East by whatever method suits the occasion. The teacher of English and his or her colleagues in the social studies department may wish students to make connections between their Bible-centered literature course and their ancient history course—in both directions. A student project might consist of a report that will satisfy both an English course and one in social studies.

The Modern Context

Few people in our culture can approach the Bible free of preconceptions and feelings, whether out of their religious or their humanistic traditions. For many, the emotional load is so heavy that the mere idea of reading the Bible in a secular setting and for a secular purpose is disturbing. Teachers must be conscious of what they themselves bring to a Bible-centered literature class in this respect. They must also be aware of and show respect for the assumptions and attitudes that students bring with them.

Beyond these considerations lies the question of the teacher's obligation to those religious or nonreligious traditions that are not represented in the class—or even in the community. Should the teacher feel relief that the class has no fundamentalists or no Jews or no atheists or no Catholics—or at least none who seem to object to a "majority culture" approach? Or does that mean that the relatively homogeneous group is even more in need of exposure to alternatives?

One must keep reminding students, by word and gesture, that, as far as possible, they should keep their religious or irreligious attitudes out of their reading of the Bible *as* literature (and of Bible-related secular literature). This applies even more strongly to their behavior in class.

It becomes a constant juggling act for the conscientious teacher. On the one hand, to accept the world of the Bible with its supernatural elements and its seeming contradictions, some students require a suspension of disbelief. On the other hand, to study the Bible in the context of an a-religious literature class, other students have a much more difficult requirement: a temporary suspension of belief, if that belief inhibits literary pursuits. In this latter instance, however, the teacher's request that students take a literary approach—to consider the bare text stripped of faith interpretation—should not threaten their belief.

The basic premise should be the givenness of what the Bible says: What did God say and do, according to the text? What miracles did Jesus perform? What did the prophet see in his vision? What are the two accounts of this event? The main point is that believer and skeptic should agree on what the text says or the texts say.

Equally important, but more difficult, is the matter of discussing the text's "meaning." Class discussions must also aim at being "literary," even when they involve students' answers to questions about the text.

That implies limits. Believers must not attempt to use class discussion as an opportunity to evangelize. Skeptics must not attempt to discredit beliefs expressed in the literature or by fellow students. The teacher must establish rules and set the tone by example. He or she ought constantly to see that students get a fair hearing but do not go too far. In sum, preconceived attitudes toward the Bible and the demands of a pluralistic society complicate the teacher's job.

A second fact that forces teachers to face the problem of the contemporary context is the students' great interest in Bible-related religious questions that have relevance to their own experience and their society. What do you/others believe about the Bible? Shall we visit some churches, synagogues, mosques? Have some clergymen in? Exchange information about my eucharist and your seder? (An aside: Dancing an Israeli *hora* or eating chopped liver in a Jewish home do not, despite suggestions from two teachers, constitute learning about Judaism.)

Where in the Bible do people find justification or a mandate for opposition to birth control, blood transfusions, joining unions or political parties, saluting the flag, swearing oaths, using tobacco or liquor, and worldliness?

Whence come baptism, circumcision, confession, Easter, Epiphany, the Eucharist, Hanukkah, holy orders, the Lord's Day, Palm Sunday, Passover, Pentecost, Purim, Rosh Hashanah, the Sabbath, Sukkoth, and Yom Kippur? (Note that these lists are alphabetical and incomplete.)

Where does one find the biblical origin of the names of certain sects: Amanah, Apostolics, Baptists, Brethren, Episcopalians, Evangelicals, Friends, Gideons, House of David, Jehovah's Witnesses, Jews, Millennialists, Pentecostals, Presbyterians, Sabbatarians, Salvation Army, Seventh-day Adventists, Spiritualists, Trinitarians, Unitarians, and Universalists?

What biblical texts are related to such concepts as anointing, celibacy and chastity, church organization (congregations and hierarchies, bishops, deacons, elders, kohanim, levites, priests, rabbis, rectors), election, excommunication, faith healing, foot washing, immaculate conception, justification by faith and by grace, kosher foods, millennium, missionary work and evangelism, natural law, original sin, pacifism, purgatory, resurrection, salvation, second coming, snake handling and the drinking of poison, speaking in tongues, tithing, vegetarianism, and vow of poverty?

Some of these questions fascinate youngsters (and answers to most of them are in Part II, chap. 7, of this handbook). Teachers themselves may be irresistably drawn to follow their students' curiosity (after all, how often do students become so eager to learn?). Also, here is an opportunity to strike a blow for democratic pluralism and for brotherhood by making students aware of other people's religious beliefs.

As in the case of the ancient context, teachers make decisions about what, when, and how to teach about the contemporary American context of the Bible. We offer a guiding principle: If the course is within the literature curriculum, a teacher might best consider questions about the context as secondary to the main business of the course.

If a teacher chooses to ignore that advice, at least the choice should be a deliberate decision—to take the class into a realm that is beyond literary concerns but valuable for other reasons. As a reference book, in addition to this handbook, a good introduction to contemporary religious contexts of the Bible is *The Bible Reader,* by Abbott et al. (Chapman-Bruce-Macmillan, 1969).

To repeat, the place of the Bible in contemporary life is important primarily to a class studying the religious configuration or the values of our national culture or of some group. True, many social studies textbooks and teachers bypass such issues because they are controversial. (How many pictures of typical towns, in elementary-grade social studies textbooks, dare to include one of the most characteristic buildings—a church or synagogue?) That failing, however, seems to be the responsibility of the social studies teacher, rather than the English teacher, to correct.

And correct it they should. How can students in a social studies course understand, if not sympathize with, opposing positions on issues like abortion, contraception, divorce, euthanasia, evolution, the flag salute, inoculation, school prayer, textbook censorship, and a host of others without some knowledge of the biblical background for certain strongly held attitudes? How can they understand our present culture without some knowledge of the recent spread of Bible-centered charismatic and pentecostal groups?

These issues, however, are not essential to the literary study of the Bible or of Bible-related literature in an English class—except when a secular piece of literature refers to such a controversy and then needs explication. Otherwise, they are for the most part only incidental to language arts.

Down Through History

The Bible and religious beliefs and practices stemming from it have affected Western civilization throughout history. This fact opens possibilities for yet another approach to the Bible as a classroom text or resource that intrigues some teachers—and, in some cases, their students. On what basis, biblical and political, did Rome become the center of Catholicism? What were the issues of biblical interpretation in all those cases of heresy in the early church?

In more modern times, how central was the Bible to Luther's Reformation? Can one understand Calvinism without some knowledge of the Bible? Or understand the persecution of sects that split off on points of Bible-related beliefs and practices, such as the sacraments and one's relationship to temporal authority? What biblical grounds have some people found for anti-Semitism? for racial superiority? for missionary colonialism?

In America, John Winthrop felt that his settlers were establishing the New Jerusalem. Cotton Mather called Winthrop the American Nehemiah, leading his people from Babylon to the promised land. Colonial history shows biblical idealism. It is also shot through with religious intolerance, much of it based on competing views of the Bible's teachings.

Early (and continuing) state laws regulating marriage were based on the Puritan commitment to the rules of consanguinity found in Leviticus. Restrictive laws against sexual bestiality and homosexuality came from the same book of the Bible. Statutes making illegitimate children inferior before the law originate in Deuteronomy. Article III, Section 3, of the U.S. Constitution, protecting the children of a deceased traitor, also comes from Deuteronomy. Laws against "unnatural" acts took their label from the Epistle to the Romans. (See Leo Pfeffer, *God, Caesar, and the Constitution,* Beacon Press, 1975.)

Conversely, history has had an effect upon the Bible. The story of translations, into Latin and other vulgar tongues, is full of social, political, and legal controversy, danger, and even violence—to the translator and to the establishment. Consider what happened to people who translated the Bible into English—Protestants under a Catholic monarch, Catholics under a Protestant.

More recently, right-wing Protestants objected to the Revised Version and produced the American Standard Version. In the last century, Catholics rioted in New York against the exclusive use of the KJV in public schools for daily devotions, and the state officially sanctioned the Douay as an alternative.

For certain pieces of secular literature, the influence of the Bible on history and history's impact on the Bible may be valuable background information on occasion. As a major focus of a unit, however, this field, like the ancient and modern contexts of the Bible, seems more properly to be the concern of the social studies department.

The Bible as Religious Literature

We have previously skirted another approach to, or use of, the Bible in secondary schools: studying the Bible as religious literature. While this emphasis is not strictly contextual, nevertheless it seems similarly to be more suitable to social studies courses than to English classes. A course or unit on the Bible as religious literature focuses on the study of religion. It juxtaposes Christian and Jewish beliefs and practices with each other and, in some instances, with other religions.

Studying the Bible as a religious document in a religion studies course within the social studies curriculum is different from studying it as a piece of literature in the language arts curriculum. The former activity asks how the Bible functions as the record, content, and/or source of people's religion. The latter asks how the Bible functions as a piece of literature, both as a work of artistic craftsmanship and as an insight into important human issues. The two approaches are related—and sometimes confused—because people's religion is an important human issue (and because some people define all important human issues as religious). But the distinction lies in the priorities both of purpose and of methodology in the two pursuits. In one, the Bible is religious literature; in the other, it is literature that is religious.

Naturally, each course in religious literature is different, using the Bible in a variety of ways. *Religious Literature of the West,* by Whitney and Howe (Augsburg Press, 1971), is an example of a fine textbook for this kind of course. The thrust both of the book's selection of texts and of its student exercises and questions is to present representative portions of: (a) the Hebrew Bible; (b) the apocryphal, rabbinic, and NT writings; and (c) the Koran, so that students will understand the contexts and the meaning of each group of writings. Text and comment focus neither on the religions for which the literature is sacred nor on the purely literary aspects of the literature. The book's preoccupation with the meaning and interpretation of the literature emphasizes the literature's religious content—the theology and the God-centered ethics, the beliefs and practices.

The Whitney and Howe book in itself might serve either as background for a study of the religious component of a culture being examined by a social studies class or as an introductory primary source for a course or unit in comparative religions. As a matter of fact, however, it is offered for English courses because of a restrictive mandate of the Pennsylvania legislature, under whose sponsorhsip it was produced. The book's student questions are of only incidental importance to the normal concerns of secondary school teachers of English. Language arts teachers who are interested in a literary approach to literature may use accompanying booklets, which deal mainly with the Bible *in* literature. By itself, it is of quite limited usefulness to English classes, despite its many other excellences.

Whether it uses this secular textbook or another or none, a course that is exclusively or primarily interested in the strictly religious content of the Bible, its theology and related ethics, is at best omitting an essential part of the English curriculum. At worst, it flirts with indoctrination or the violation of religious sensibilities.

Courses "about" religion, based on readings in religious literature, do exist—some pedagogically sound and some not. Some use textbooks far more religion-oriented than the Whitney and Howe book, emphasizing denominational attitudes and practices rather than the theological and ethical concepts of the literature. These courses get into the English curriculum, when they do, usually because the texts, particularly those with biblical excerpts, have the word *literature* in their title or perhaps because the English teacher is interested in religion.

The "religious literature" approach may take many forms. Some courses limit themselves to Judaism and Christianity or to the "Judeo-Christian tradition" (which is a different thing). Others broaden out to include Eastern religions or even "such secular religions as Communism," according to one teacher's description.

Some carefully avoid any attempt at comparison. Others make charts of beliefs and practices. Still others try to abstract some definitions and to generalize about the concept "religion" in terms of its common phenomenology, functions, and/or main concerns. Some are centered on religious literature; others emphasize the experiential dimension.

The validity and propriety of all these pedagogical alternatives have been hotly debated on both empirical and theoretical grounds. Regardless of one's attitude toward such curricula, however, it seems clear that none of them should be the major interest or central focus for the study of the Bible in a course in language arts.

We have suggested that the teacher have some knowledge of the Bible's contexts—what it has meant to people from ancient times to the present. An understanding that the Bible is primarily a religious book is equally important for the teacher to have, to keep constantly in mind, and to bring to the students' attention on occasion.

As a main approach to the Bible in secondary school, however, it seems more appropriate to the social studies class. The teacher of literature has enough scope among the literary approaches to biblical literature for his or her students within the options provided by the Bible *as* literature, the Bible *in* literature, and the Bible *and* literature.

PART II
RELIGIOUS
SENSIBILITIES

In Part I we described various kinds of approaches and emphases open to teachers who use the Bible in a secondary school literature course. We suggested that teachers might best focus primarily on literary goals and on literary aspects of biblical literature.

In making such a recommendation, we do not ignore the "human" goals of education, the issues raised by the literature, the cultural contexts of the Bible, or the variant religious responses to the Bible. Rather, it is a matter of priorities and practicality. If the teacher concentrates the attention of the class on these less specifically literary concerns, the students may never get around to the main business of a secondary school language arts course, the reading skills needed for literary analysis and appreciation. Moreover, the teacher may be asking for trouble, whereas he or she might more prudently deal with controversial issues of biblical literature as they arise naturally from student comments and questions.

Having said that, however, we must acknowledge that sooner or later the teacher who uses the Bible as a text must be prepared for problems related to religious sensibilities. Only the teacher can decide when and how to handle them. On such occasions the teacher may find some help from the two chapters that constitute this part of the handbook. The first is an alphabetically arranged list of possible classroom problems. The second is a list of religious beliefs and practices arranged according to their biblical sources.

The material in Part II may seem to invite teachers to raise questions of religious sensibilities with their students in order to pursue the "human" goals of education. Nevertheless, we reiterate the position we took in Part I. It is generally better for the teacher to consider these materials as essential background for his or her own attitudes and actions and to draw upon them as course content only as supplementary to the main concerns of a literature course.

CHAPTER 6

Possible Classroom
Problems

Much of this handbook is devoted to presenting alternatives: of approaches and emphases in using the Bible in literature classes (Part I), of sectarian beliefs and practices based on biblical texts (Part II, chap. 7), of teaching materials and methods (Parts III and IV), and of the meanings of words (Part V). Many of these matters have been the subject of controversy, both outside the classroom and within it.

In this chapter we single out a few areas of religious or ethnic differences that may pose special problems for teachers. In some instances we suggest solutions; in others, only the issues. In either case, we hope that making teachers aware of sensitive areas also makes teachers better able to deal with them, or to avoid them.

Uncovering spheres of agreement and similarity among the various religious traditions and ethnic components of our country is socially beneficial. We all need to be reminded to increase our appreciation of what people have in common. It is also an intellectually satisfying pursuit: Aristotle said that genius consists of making connections among seemingly disparate things.

On the other hand, Plato said that it is even more important to see how the one is many, to analyze rather than to synthesize, to discriminate where things seem the same. As worthwhile as it is to recognize that we Americans share a common heritage, it is equally, if not more, valuable to understand and to accept our differences.

Most teachers acknowledge the value of cultural pluralism. In their classrooms they understand the right of students to be self-respecting members of varied traditions and to interpret the Bible according to their group's religious or humanistic convictions. For some teachers, however, their own religious beliefs convince them that there is only one right way to interpret the Bible and that they must evangelize whenever and wherever they discuss the Bible. That is an understandable impulse; but such people should not, and in most cases do not, use the Bible as a textbook in public school.

In general, our inability to handle classroom problems satisfactorily arises from our lack of awareness of alternatives. We are unaware of what is going on in the consciousnesses of our students that makes them hear our words or read the text, and to react, in a way we have not foreseen. This is most certainly true of Bible study. Our difficulties rarely stem from not caring or from deliberately ignoring or denigrating other people's religious or humanistic traditions. We simply do not realize how differently others read the Bible, especially where it appears to us to be unequivocal or uncontroversial.

What we need is information. How do various people feel about the Bible as a whole and about individual passages? What expressions, ideas, and attitudes offend their beliefs or sense of worth? How do their own attitudes toward the Bible affect their reading of the assigned text? What practicalities are involved in being suitably "objective" or fair? Such information this chapter attempts, however imperfectly, to provide.

By way of background, we might reflect that ours is an open society. Cultural pluralism is not only a fact but also an ideal. It is expressed in the history of the free-exercise and no-establishment clauses of the First Amendment to the U.S. Constitution. Only in America is the separation of church and state so strongly guarded.

In other societies, to varying degrees, the state controls religion or is itself under the influence of religious interests. Members of the majority can either deny the religious claims and sensibilities of minorites through law or ignore them through indifference: Minorities are either dangerous subversives or merely inoffensive nonconformists. Most people from those societies wonder at the seemingly absurd extremes to which our constitutional commitment to freedom of religion and freedom from religion sometimes brings us.

Even in our own country some members of the national or local majority feel hampered at times by the necessity of making what appear to them to be annoying or harmful, often merely hairsplitting, concessions to divergent minorities. They wish—even go so far as to act—to deny or ignore the claims and sensibilities of religious minorities.

Our open society, however, demands respect for and concessions to atheists and agnostics as well as theists, to oriental as well as Western religions, to Judaism as well as Christianity, to other Christian variants in addition to Catholicism and Protestantism, and to extremes of fundamentalism and liberalism as well as the wide realm between.

This handbook does not see these demands as inhibiting teachers from venturing beyond what is safe and uncontroversial. In fact, the handbook is an attempt to respond to those demands. It seeks to sensitize teachers and to encourage them to broaden their own perspectives and, where appropriate, those of their students.

Generally speaking, the more that students know about their own and other religious (or humanistic) traditions, the better. In addition to their literary pursuits, which are the primary function of a literature class, they may be introduced to basic reference books on the Bible in the school library: concordances, biblical dictionaries and encyclopedias, differing versions and commentaries. An assignment or two across versions and traditions may be useful, no matter how aseptic the teacher's approach and goals. Beyond that, students can pursue questions of meaning and interpretation in the library; they may also be referred to their own clergy or other spiritual advisers.

At the very least, teachers (and, where the classroom situation calls for it, students) should be aware that certain terms mean different things—factually and emotionally—to different groups. Teachers have an obligation to inform themselves, as far as possible, as to the content of those differences, even though the immediate classroom situation may not often require or lend itself to student discussion of such differences.

Many of the subjects treated here are quite complex and have been ruthlessly simplified to provide only a minimum of information for use in the average classroom circumstances. Please consult authorities where you feel cheated.

Note: Words in SMALL CAPS are cross-references to items within this chapter. Some biblical citations are marked with an asterisk (*); the passages cited appear in Part II, chapter 7, of this handbook. For brief definitions of technical terms, see the Glossary, Part V.

Under the subheading of ACCURACY, AUTHORSHIP, AND AU-THORITY we will have something to say about labels. There are no completely satisfactory labels for religious points of view, but we do need to distinguish at least two generally conflicting kinds of attitudes toward the Bible. *Conservative* is a fairly acceptable term for one recognizable attitude. The other has been called "liberal," "critical," and "scholarly." All three words give offense: Most people to whom the label refers don't like the connotations of *liberal,* and people within the "conservative" range object to the exclusion implied by the other two terms. We have chosen to call the second group "critical scholars," begging the pardon of conservatives who are critical and scholarly, and hoping that they will sympathize with our agony and accept our choice of labels with charity if not love.

The opinions expressed here are certainly neither inerrant nor authoritative. We hope that readers will tell us when we have said the wrong thing or have said things incompletely or have omitted what we should have included. We sincerely solicit comments.

List of Entries

Accuracy, Authorship, Authority (of the Bible). The three related terms accuracy, authorship, authority, evoke different questions. *Accuracy:* To what extent does our present version of the Bible reflect historical facts and the original "message"? *Authorship:* Who wrote the Bible and under what circumstances? *Authority:* What makes the book authoritative, and how far does its authority extend into people's lives—their beliefs and actions? Answers to the questions about accuracy and authorship determine one's answers to the questions about authority.

In all three of these respects, positions vary. Here are some diverse and fuzzy, often confused, labels: fundamentalist, traditionalist, orthodox (among Jews), evangelical (among Christians), conservative, critical, liberal, humanistic, skeptical. The labels are neither clear nor distinct. In a hazy continuum, then, here are four groupings, from Right to Left:

1. God, or the Holy Spirit, wrote, dictated, revealed, or inspired the Bible through the writers whose names are attached to its books. In its original form, or in its present (sectarian) form, it is infallible. That is to say, it is inerrant and authoritative—textually without error and historically accurate as well as binding upon the minds, hearts, and actions of people in order for them to achieve salvation. Because people are intellectually limited, they must accept what they cannot rationally understand or scientifically verify.

2. Our present Bible is the work of fallible writers who may have inaccurately transmitted the original inspired message. The present, or even the original, versions are not inerrant; scholarship may peel away errors; but the traditions are by and large authentic. The Bible and officially sponsored interpretations and/or versions are accepted as authoritative, both as to origin and as a guide to salvation.

3. The Bible is a response to, and interpretation of, formative events in a people's history. Its controlling "inspiration" lies in the efforts of its ancient Jewish and Christian writers over the centuries to remain true to their religious tradition and to apply it to changing circumstances. It is a proper subject for critical scholarly investigation. The Bible contains profound insights into the nature of reality, which, if appropriated, can become authoritative for people in their efforts to find meaning in, and guidelines for, their lives.

4. The Bible is a record of ancient Jewish and Christian traditions that are fallible—factually, logically, and morally. Judged by modern science, literary standards, and humanitarian ideals, it contains a lot

of fairly primitive morality, superstitions, myths, and legends as well as much that is of value. Its authority today should be no greater than that of any other book; its past influence has been both good and bad. The reader should subject it to rational, empirical, and moral criticism and reject as untrue or without value what is unacceptable by these humanistic tests.

Each of these categories is broad and includes some estranged bedfellows. Teachers, especially in public school, must be constantly aware of positions within this spectrum of attitudes: their own; their students'; those of various groups in the community; and, within reason, those of still other groups. Teachers must show no disrespect for any of these positions or their adherents and ought to discourage students from expressions of disrespect.

Apocrypha: Protestant and Catholic. The thirty-nine books that are common to Protestant, Catholic, and Jewish Bibles (see BIBLE) are called "protocanonical" by Catholics. In addition, the Catholic OT includes eleven books or parts of books that are not in the Protestant or Jewish canon. Catholics consider them to be equally inspired, but for purposes of identification call them "deuterocanonical."

These eleven items appear in the Septuagint (the earliest Greek versions) but not in the Masoretic text (the Hebrew canon). Protestants adhere to the Hebrew canon and exclude the eleven deuterocanonical works. Following Luther, they have called them "Apocrypha" (hidden, spurious). In this category are also included three other writings that are not in the Catholic Bible: I Esdras, II Esdras (Catholic titles: III and IV Esdras), and the Prayer of Manasseh (Manasses).

These fourteen books or parts of books were often bound within Protestant Bibles and labeled Apocrypha, usually between the OT and the NT. This was true of KJV Bibles until the nineteenth century. Protestants consider them valuable sources of religious teaching and/or history, although noncanonical. Recent ecumenical Bibles resume this practice of inserting the Apocrypha after the Protestant canon of the OT or after the NT.

Catholics, however, apply the term *Apocrypha* only to those books that were considered by the early church to be neither protocanonical nor deuterocanonical. These include the last three items of the Protestant Apocrypha (III and IV Esdras and the Prayer of Manasses) and a long list of others that are generally agreed to be uninspired and in many cases falsely attributed to biblical personages. Like Protestants,

Catholics consider their Apocrypha valuable but noncanonical.

This long list of books in the Catholic Apocrypha is technically called by Protestant scholars "Pseudepigrapha" (false ascriptions), to distinguish them from the fourteen items of the Protestant Apocrypha. For most lay Protestants, however, the term *Apocrypha* includes both the fourteen and the Pseudepigrapha.

Many pseudepigraphic books are characterized by (a) evidence of the hope of Jews, around the time of Jesus, for a future that would answer their present despair, and (b) evidence of the faith of Christians—especially in NT apocryphal writings—that Jesus supplied the answer.

Attribution. Some traditions accept the names of the books of the Bible as those of their authors. Others would say that the question of attribution is unimportant (Did Bacon write *Hamlet* ?); what matters is the text.

Critical scholars, however, are very much interested in this issue. Generally, they see a writer setting down an oral tradition that may have been reshaped in the process of transmission. In applying this critical view, they differ from traditionalists most markedly in such instances as the authorship of the five books attributed to Moses (the Pentateuch/Torah); Ecclesiastes (written, say most scholars, in the third or second century B.C.E.) attributed to Solomon (tenth century B.C.E.); Gospels attributed to original apostles; some Epistles attributed to Paul and those attributed to James and Peter.

Most critical scholars also find evidence in the Bible to support a theory that at some points redactors have conflated material from more than one source or that editors have added comments to an earlier, lost source. In the Pentateuch, for example, they label the hypothetical sources *J* (or Yahwist), *E* (Elohist), *P* (priestly), and *D* (deuteronomist). Similarly, critical scholars theorize that Matthew and Luke both drew upon Mark and upon a hypothetical *Q* source, in addition to their own individual traditions, labeled *M* and *L* respectively.

In a few places such scholars see at work a previously acceptable literary device that is unusual in our post-Gutenberg day: the anonymous author's presentation of new material as old and his attribution of authorship to a great name of the past. Examples here are the nine narratives and visions edited, according to most scholars, in the second century B.C.E. under the name of Daniel; various parts of the book of Isaiah; and the books of the Pseudepigrapha.

Fundamentalists, as well as many conservatives of all faiths to whom the Bible is sacred, accept none of these theories of editorial tampering, conflation of sources, and false ascriptions. Some other conservatives take a middle view—that the actual recorders accepted the stories as received. Such scholars often stop there and focus on the content, to examine how it is used as biblical witness; for them, what is important is the theological and moral message that must be dug out of the text.

Teachers of literature would also do well to accept the text as it now exists rather than worry about its provenance. The business of a secondary school class is literary criticism, not literary scholarship.

(Related to the issue of attribution is another departure of critical scholars from tradition. Some early Bible stories are viewed as narrating tribal histories rather than individual biographies. According to this theory, Noah's son Shem and the sons of Jacob are not the eponymous ancestors of, respectively, the Semites and the tribes of Israel as the Bible stories relate. Instead, they are legendary characters who have become, in the course of oral tradition, personifications of those tribes. Thus, the tribe preceded the hero as we know him. He has become clothed in his descendants' histories. In a sense, the Bible reverses history, in this view: The history of the tribe retroactively becomes part of the life of the founder.)

Audio-Visual Teaching Aids. Bible-related pictures, music, and other objects are useful and proper teaching materials. When they are assembled in certain ways or used in certain contexts, however, they not only illustrate and illuminate but also suggest value judgments and religious points of view. Their effect can often be more powerful than the printed or spoken word. A film prepared for use in Sunday schools or a focus on nativity scenes at the Christmas season will carry too heavy an affective sectarian load for a public school classroom.

Teachers have the responsibility for avoiding explicit or implicit bias in their own use of the basic audio-visual elements. They should also reject in its entirety any film, filmstrip, or slide-tape that even in small part or only very subtly fosters a special religious attitude toward the Bible that is unacceptable to any group of believers or nonbelievers. Here we are suggesting more rigorous criteria of acceptability than with secular textbooks (see CLASSROOM TEXT: BIBLE-CENTERED). A teacher can usually counteract or have students skip short sections of unsuitable printed matter, but audio-visual materials are a much "hotter" medium and are much more difficult to excerpt.

In point of fact, few audio-visual materials now available—whether produced by religious or secular organizations—are appropriate for public schools. Proceed with caution.

B.C., A.D.; B.C.E., C.E. A.D. and B.C. stand for *anno Domini* ("in the year of our Lord") and "before Christ"; both express faith in Jesus as Lord and Messiah. Many scholars prefer to use C.E.("common/Christian era") and B.C.E. ("before the common/Christian era"). These latter abbreviations, while they may sound peculiar at first, might well be introduced into the classroom conventions.

Bible: Protestant, Catholic, Jewish. The number, order, and names of the books of the Bible all vary for Protestants, Catholics, and Jews. Certain religious groups have still other differences that make them reject what any of the major traditions accept as the Bible (see SECTARIAN INTERPRETATIONS).

For Christians, the Bible includes both OT and NT. Many Christians, following conservative tradition, see much of the former as prologue and/or prophecy for the latter. The Catholic OT has forty-six books while the Protestant has thirty-nine. Most Catholic Bibles use Greek personal names.

For Jews, the word *Bible* refers to thirty-nine books in three divisions. It is conventional but imprecise to call the Jewish Bible the OT because Jews do not recognize a NT and because the Jewish scriptures differ in important respects from even the Protestant OT. For example, the book of Malachi (which ends with a prophecy of the coming of Elijah and the day of the Lord and is used by most Christians as a bridge to the NT) is not the last book, as in the Christian OT, but the twenty-sixth. The book of Ruth, important to most Christians for its genealogical relevance to David and, more especially, to Jesus, does not follow Judges as a prelude to the story of David but is included under Writings as one of the five "scrolls." (See chart below.)

Bible Versions (Translations). The best known English translation, the *King James Version* (KJV), also called the *Authorized Version* (AV), was produced in 1611 by a group of translators appointed by King James I of England. It was a new translation and also a revision of the first Protestant translation into English, that of William *Tyndale* (1525) as completed by Miles *Coverdale* (1535). The language of the KJV preserves as an act of reverence the old language and plain style of Tyndale and Coverdale, in contrast to the rather ornamental mode of

JEWISH BIBLE

Pentateuch
(The Law)
(Torah)

1. Genesis
2. Exodus
3. Leviticus
4. Numbers
5. Deuteronomy

Prophets
(Former, or early, prophets)

6. Joshua
7. Judges
8. I Samuel ⎤
9. II Samuel ⎦ +
10. I Kings ⎤
11. II Kings ⎦ +

(Later, major prophets)

12. Isaiah
13. Jeremiah
14. Ezekiel

PROTESTANT OLD TESTAMENT

(Pentateuch)#

1. Genesis
2. Exodus
3. Leviticus
4. Numbers
5. Deuteronomy

(History)

6. Joshua
7. Judges
8. Ruth
9. I Samuel
10. II Samuel
11. I Kings
12. II Kings
13. I Chronicles
14. II Chronicles
15. Ezra
16. Nehemiah
17. Esther

CATHOLIC OLD TESTAMENT

1. Genesis
2. Exodus
3. Leviticus
4. Numbers
5. Deuteronomy
6. Josue
7. Judges
8. Ruth
9. I Kings (I Samuel)
10. II Kings (II Samuel)
11. III Kings (I Kings)
12. IV Kings (II Kings)
13. I Paralipomenon (I Chronicles)
("parts omitted," supplement)
14. II Paralipomenon (II Chronicles)
15. I Esdras (Ezra)
16. II Esdras, alias Nehemias
17. Tobias* (Tobit)
18. Judith*
19. Esther** (10:4–16:24, and passim)
20. Job‡
21. Psalms
22. Proverbs‡

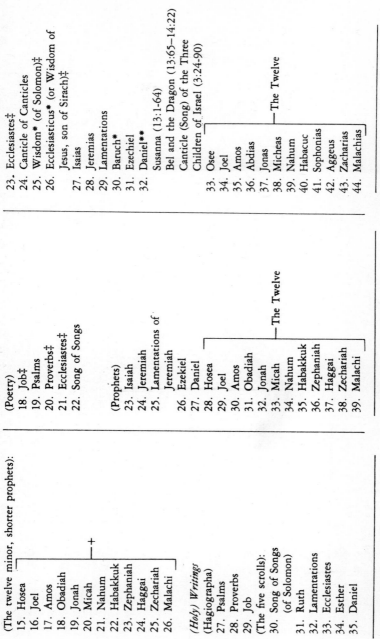

(The twelve minor, shorter prophets):
15. Hosea
16. Joel
17. Amos
18. Obadiah
19. Jonah
20. Micah
21. Nahum
22. Habakkuk
23. Zephaniah
24. Haggai
25. Zechariah
26. Malachi
+

(Holy) Writings
(Hagiographa)
27. Psalms
28. Proverbs
29. Job
(The five scrolls):
30. Song of Songs (of Solomon)
31. Ruth
32. Lamentations
33. Ecclesiastes
34. Esther
35. Daniel

+ Originally 1 book

(Poetry)
18. Job‡
19. Psalms
20. Proverbs‡
21. Ecclesiastes‡
22. Song of Songs

(Prophets)
23. Isaiah
24. Jeremiah
25. Lamentations of Jeremiah
26. Ezekiel
27. Daniel
28. Hosea
29. Joel
30. Amos
31. Obadiah
32. Jonah
33. Micah — The Twelve
34. Nahum
35. Habakkuk
36. Zephaniah
37. Haggai
38. Zechariah
39. Malachi

#Divisions are informal
‡Wisdom Literature

23. Ecclesiastes‡
24. Canticle of Canticles
25. Wisdom* (of Solomon)‡
26. Ecclesiasticus* (or Wisdom of Jesus, son of Sirach)‡
27. Isaias
28. Jeremias
29. Lamentations
30. Baruch*
31. Ezechiel
32. Daniel**
   Susanna (13:1-64)
   Bel and the Dragon (13:65–14:22)
   Canticle (Song) of the Three Children of Israel (3:24-90)
33. Osee
34. Joel
35. Amos
36. Abdias
37. Jonas
38. Micheas — The Twelve
39. Nahum
40. Habacuc
41. Sophonias
42. Aggeus
43. Zacharias
44. Malachias

*Books
**Parts of books included in Protestant Apocrypha

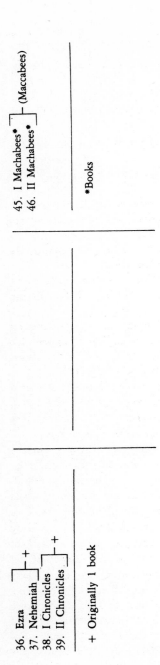

36. Ezra ⎤ +
37. Nehemiah ⎦
38. I Chronicles ⎤ +
39. II Chronicles ⎦

45. I Machabees* ⎤ — (Maccabees)
46. II Machabees* ⎦

*Books

+ Originally 1 book

literary prose that was current in the early seventeenth century (see Part III, chap. 7, below).

The translators of the KJV used Tyndale's sources:

1. The German translation by *Luther* (1522, 1534), who had advised the exiled Protestant, Tyndale
2. A Greek version of the NT, which had recently been made available by the Dutch *Erasmus* (1516)
3. The first and most popular English translation, by John *Wycliffe* (1380, 1382)
4. The Hebrew *Masoretic* texts of the OT, vocalized by the Masoretes in the eighth century from texts of the Jewish Bible, which was standardized late in the first century C.E.
5. The Latin *Vulgate* of Jerome (late fourth century), still used today (somewhat revised) in many Catholic churches
6. The Greek *Septuagint* (LXX), copies of which we now have dating from the third and second centuries B.C.E., the oldest existing versions of the OT

While the KJV was in process, Catholic translators were completing their own new English version. Produced by English refugees—this time fleeing a Protestant monarch—in France (1580, 1610), it is called the *Douay* (or Douai, sometimes the Rheims-Douay) Bible.

New scholarship in many fields, the discovery of hitherto unknown ancient and medieval manuscripts (e.g., recently, the Dead Sea Scrolls), and the need to replace English archaisms with contemporary idiom—all these combine to demand ever-newer translations.

The Douay has been revised most notably by *Challoner* in the eighteenth century. More recent Catholic translations are those by Bishop *Knox* in England, *The Jerusalem Bible* (JB, originally in French and retranslated in 1966 for its English edition), and the *New American Bible* (NAB 1970). This last, published by the Confraternity of Christian Doctrine (CCD), replaces an earlier CCD version; has many excellent notes and concessions to ecumenicity; uses Masoretic names of people and books; and acknowledges theories of recent critical scholarship, whether acceptable to Catholicism or not—all of these features representing a departure from previous Catholic practice.

The most widely accepted English translation since the KJV among Protestants (and many others) is the *Revised Standard Version* (RSV) of 1952, recently ecumenicized with Catholic cooperation in the *Common Bible* (1973). The *New English Bible* (NEB 1970), from England, is another popular recent translation, a bit freer than the RSV. Even later is *Today's English Version* (TEV), called the Good News Bible (1977).

The standard Jewish version in English in this country has been that of the *Jewish Publication Society* (JPS) of 1917. Its current new version began with the *Torah* (1962) and continues book by book. Synagogues often use the *Soncino* Bible, which includes commentary.

The standard conservative/fundamentalist Protestant versions are the *Scofield Reference Bible* (1909), and the *New American Standard Bible* (NAS 1971). *The Living Bible* (TLB 1971), a popular paraphrase, has conservative annotations.

There are other versions that serve sectarian, literary, or scholarly purposes (see SECTARIAN INTERPRETATIONS). Some are interfaith efforts; e.g., the multivolumed *Anchor Bible* is being produced by scholars from several different traditions. Some Bibles contain only the text. Reference Bibles include citations that relate passages to one another (often typologically; see TYPOLOGY); some Bibles add concordances, maps, and other aids for the reader. Some are annotated/study Bibles: e.g., the RSV in the *Oxford Annotated Bible* (with Apocrypha, 1965) and in the more conservative *Harper Study Bible* (1964); also the NEB in the *Oxford Study Edition* (1976). In some, the exegesis and commentary take more space than the biblical text: e.g., the *Anchor*, the *Soncino*, and *The Interpreter's Bible*.

Generally, the Protestant and Jewish versions have followed the Hebrew Masoretic texts of the OT where they differ from the Greek Septuagint, whereas Catholic versions have followed the latter in points of conflict (see BIBLE). The OT was written originally in Hebrew, with some Aramaic; the NT was written in Greek and shows some Semitic/Aramaic background in its locutions. Critical scholars largely agree that Jesus probably spoke Aramaic, a sister language to Hebrew. Many conservative Christians maintain that he spoke Greek and that the NT records his actual words as he pronounced them. Some fundamentalist Protestants accept only the KJV as the Word, and language, of God.

Black/White Inferiority. Some people believe that the Bible establishes black or white inferiority. Here are some examples that such people point to:

Based on scripture and on currently accepted traditions, Mormons saw the dark skin of the American Indians and the flat nose and dark skin of Negroes (black people of African ancestry) as the "mark of Cain" (Gen. 4:15), which God set on him after he killed his brother Abel.

In addition, black people are considered by some groups to be suffering the "curse of Canaan" (Gen. 9:25), uttered by Noah against Ham's son Canaan, that he should serve Ham's brothers. (To Mormons, Ham's wife, Egyptus, was a descendant of Cain.) After the flood, Africa was allotted to Ham. Thus, according to this tradition, black people originating in Africa are "sons of Ham" and are said to bear the curse.

Finally, many Afrikaners in South Africa justify their right to rule the country (i.e., the native blacks) through Psalm 105:43-44.

On the other hand, some black people believe that the Bible proves that white skin is the leprous heritage of the curse placed upon the descendants of Gehazi. He was punished with a white, diseased skin because he took money unscrupulously from Naaman the Syrian after Elisha cured Naaman's leprosy (II Kings 5:27). (See also Num. 12:9.) The Black Muslims under the late Elijah Muhammed believed in black superiority on the basis of other religious traditions.

Many black people take pride in their special connection with various biblical passages and traditions. Black Ethiopians are considered by some to be descendants of Solomon and the Queen of Sheba. According to the KJV, Zipporah, wife of Moses, was an Ethiopian, as was the eunuch whom Philip converted to Christianity. Simon of Cyrene and Augustine of Hippo—both places are in Africa—are pointed to as black heroes of Christianity.

"Borrowed" Material. Many Bible stories, names, and religious beliefs and practices are similar to those of other ancient cultures. Most critical scholars agree that much was borrowed by Jews and Christians from the indigenous cultures: e.g., stories of the garden of Eden, the flood, the birth of Moses, some Mosaic laws and customs, parts of Daniel, nativity stories, the healing of the Gerasene demoniac.

A more conservative interpretation takes the similarities not as evidence of direct influence but of cultural affinity developing in parallel and separate lines, or else of common access to prototypes. Such interpreters would focus on superior ethical and theological aspects of the Judeo-Christian tradition.

Still others see pagan myths and legends, philosophy, and history as unconscious prefigurings, influenced by the Holy Spirit, of the Judeo-Christian revelation and experience. For example, Odysseus, tied to the mast as he passed through the dangerous waters and resisted the sirens, prefigures Jesus on the cross after he had resisted the temptations of Satan. The connection is made early in Christianity. Such a sculpture of Odysseus appears on an ancient Christian sarcophagus. At least one modern theologian says the hand of God linked both events.

Catholic/Roman Catholic. Without the modifier, *Catholic* usually implies "Roman" as a neutral matter of course, though not always. The term *Roman Catholic* is often a reminder (sometimes with emotional overtones) that others (e.g., Episcopalians, Lutherans, and Eastern Orthodox) believe in "one holy catholic [literally, universal] church" which is not Roman. Attitudes of speaker and hearer determine whether *Catholic* or *Roman Catholic* is appropriate for easy conversation. As a related issue, Protestants object to calling the Catholic Church after the Reformation "the Church."

Censorship. Some people feel that no child should be exposed to the Bible except through sectarian interpretation or guidance. Others feel that some children are too young to be exposed to theological doctrine that varies from their own tradition. It seems clear that if parents feel strongly enough in such matters, their children should be excused from a course that will offend their religious sensibilities—or even threaten their salvation.

Alternatively, the teacher may wish to use a less controversial approach, provided that he or she is serving a positive and honorable academic purpose. If the purpose and effect of changing the syllabus is only censorship by pressure groups, however, then it is better not to use the Bible at all.

A related problem is the objection by some people to certain Bible passages that they feel are inappropriate for young students, in particular those episodes that describe violence and (illicit) sex. Objectors are especially concerned when such actions have the explicit or implicit sanction of God: e.g., holy war (Deut. 1:30*), everlasting punishment (Matt. 12:32*), the story of Judah and Tamar (Gen. 38). (The asterisk indicates that the passage cited appears in the next chapter.)

If the teacher avoids such passages, is he or she evading responsibility or following the path of discretion that is the better part of valor? If the teacher includes the passages and permits discussion without intervening, is he or she presenting challenging issues or encouraging students to question the morality of the Bible and God? If the teacher offers explanations, is he or she presenting alternative interpretations or defending a particular, sectarian interpretation of the Bible?

It seems that here, as elsewhere, the teacher must make decisions based on awareness and thoughtful consideration of the issues, the alternatives, and the contexts. With what kind of students, school, and community does the teacher work? What academic goals does the teacher aim at? Will the glare of titillation or controversy blind the students to the main concerns of the course or the literature?

In choosing secular literature for classes to study, there is no infallible, universally accepted test that results in lists of approved and forbidden texts. When it comes to biblical literature, the problem is complicated by the importance of religion in people's lives. We suggest, nevertheless, that if students indicate that what they read strikes them as strange, offensive, or even repulsive, they ought to be given some explanation that will allow them to see the text from the point of view of the writer, to enter the world of the text; and the explanation should be so labeled. (See WORLD OF THE NT.)

Student discussions are especially treacherous waters. The teacher must avoid the Scylla of partisan intervention, of expressing or approving student value judgments that may be offensive to others (whether they are present in the classroom or not), or disapproving positions that others hold sacred. Charybdis is to withdraw oneself from the discussion completely, allowing the class to arrive at a consensus regardless of the cost to the quiet or browbeaten minority.

Christian. *Christian* means Protestant, Catholic, and others. "Others" include, for example, most Eastern Orthodox churches, Quakers, Jehovah's Witnesses, and Latter Day Saints (Mormons). It is no more proper to omit these "others" (a condescending term, but conventional and intended here as neutral) from Christianity than it is to say or imply that America is a Christian country or that all Americans are either Christians or Jews. There are many other religious groups in the United States: Consider the membership of Islam; of Baha'i; and, especially in Hawaii, of the many oriental religions. It might also be well to remind students that atheists, whether secular humanists or not, are full, and generally honorable, citizens of the country.

Christian Scientists. See SECTARIAN INTERPRETATIONS for biblical implications.

Classroom Text: Bible. The Bible version used in the classroom should depend on the teacher's purpose. (See BIBLE VERSIONS.)

The KJV's language is most often quoted (see John Bartlett, *Familiar Quotations,* Little, Brown). It is quite successful in matching the concreteness of the original, and it has many partisans for its beauty. (It is also the only acceptable version for some religious groups, but that is true of other versions and other sects.) On the other hand, some of its language is archaic or obsolete; and, according to critical scholars, it is based on poorer Hebrew and Greek manuscripts than are the more modern translations. To Jews, since it contains the NT and certain other polemical details in the OT, it is a Christian book and should be so labeled.

The teacher may legitimately gloss or update archaisms, even if the overall approach to biblical literature is otherwise completely aseptic. Such glosses are rarely a matter of religious interpretation; an informed teacher or an unabridged dictionary is usually sufficient authority. Some KJV Bibles contain lists of words that have changed their meaning.

Many teachers prefer the language of the RSV as being more accessible to students and more accurate. Its recent updating and ecumenical approval make it acceptable to most Catholics and Protestants (although some scholars and conservative religious groups object to certain passages). As for Jews, liberals and conservatives find little objection to the notes in the Oxford annotated edition of the RSV's OT; Orthodox Jews for the most part read the text in Hebrew.

Accessibility of language and compatibility with contemporary scholarship are also considerations for teachers who use The New English Bible and/or the New American Bible. The Good News Bible (whose title emphasizes the New Testament) is attractive to many students. If one's purpose is merely to make students familiar with the Bible's stories and characters, especially for less able readers, there are simplified Bibles; many of them, however, have been prepared for Sunday schools and contain sectarian editorial materials.

Some teachers ask students to bring their own Bibles, the teacher adding still other versions to round out the collection. This allows students to compare translations, to learn something about language, and to become aware of other people's Bibles. In this situation teachers should be prepared to deal with some student questions: Why are there differences? Which translation/word is closer to the Hebrew, Aramaic, or Greek? What difference does the variance in translation make? Are those differences matters of scholarship (greater knowledge of the original meaning), of our own changing language, of literal versus freer translation, or of religious perspective? A variety of resources, both books and people, will be helpful.

As for abridgments, see the appendix to *Teaching the Old Testament in English Classes*. It may not be necessary to give students a Bible for the biblical passages. Some of the Bible-centered classroom texts (see following item) contain generous portions of the Bible.

If the teacher uses only one version, he or she should enlighten the students about the alternatives and the reasons for the choice.

Classroom Text: Bible-Centered. Here are some criteria for a teacher to consider when selecting and using a Bible-centered student textbook designed for use in a literature class:

1. *Freedom from bias.* (a) Are the editor's comments, questions, and principles of selection free of *religious* bias, both as to sectarian beliefs and as to the authorship and historicity of the Bible? (Most often, the bias is Christian and conservative.) (b) Are they free of *literary* bias? (Some books are so wedded to a critical theory that they distort biblical literature to fit the theory.)

2. *Appropriateness of approach.* (a) Is the book's approach to the biblical literature appropriate to a *literature* class? (Often one finds an almost exclusive interest in the Bible's ancient context or in the ethical and theological ideas and message of the biblical selections, with little attention to their literary craftsmanship.) (b) Is it appropriate to *your* literature class? (If you are emphasizing the Bible *as* literature, or the Bible *in* literature, or the Bible *and* literature, what is the organizing principle of the textbook?) (See Part I of this handbook.)

3. *Pedagogical competence.* (a) *Scholarship:* Does the editor seem familiar with biblical scholarship? Does the editor show evidence of literary scholarship, perceptivity, and taste? (b) *Classroom effectiveness:* Have the experiences of many and varied teachers and classes contributed to the book? Are there informative glosses for the biblical passages? Are the "thought" questions open-ended? (Unfortunately, many secular Bible-centered textbooks fail some of these tests.)

No book will perfectly fit any individual situation. Choosing a less than perfect textbook with care, however, helps teachers to decide where they will have to compensate for its imperfections—and where they and their students are free to be creative.

Some textbooks that are primarily addressed to teachers or to college students reflect a bias. Before transmitting to secondary school students the information and observations contained in such books, the teacher must either filter out evidences of bias or else supply points of view that have been omitted. The books should be put into the hands of public school students only after proper preparation, if at all. Among such books we include our own volumes on NT and OT scholarship and on literary analysis, as well as nearly all those of other writers. (See JESUS/CHRIST.)

Clergy and the Public School. The relationship between clergy and the public school should be one of mutual respect for each other's competences, integrity, and areas of professional activity. The clergy and/or religious groups should not become involved in inaugurating or conducting a course in biblical literature, and public schools should resist any such efforts. Furthermore, inviting professional religionists to teach the course or unit puts too great a strain on a pluralistic approach and the separation of church and state. For their part, public school teachers who propose to teach biblical literature have a serious obligation to acquire background in biblical knowledge and religious sensibilities and to be as fair as possible in the classroom.

The public school teacher should welcome classroom observation by the clergy, should then ask whether anything that went on in the class was incorrect or offensive, and should be happy to correct errors caused by ignorance or thoughtlessness. The teacher might choose to set aside a session for students to ask the clergy, or other knowledgeable religious representatives, about sectarian interpretations of certain biblical passages that the students and the teacher have been struggling with and could not resolve through research.

The clergy should not expect the right to approve, amend, or reject the curriculum or even to be consulted in advance. Nor should they go public with any complaints unless they have observed the class and talked with the teacher. Then they must decide whether the objectionable practice is legal: If one objects to exposing one's children to a fair presentation of alternative and unacceptable versions or interpretations of the Bible—which is legal—that calls for a warning within one's congregation; and the school should recognize the right of parents to withdraw children on those grounds. If the objection is to a biased offense against one religion—which is illegal—and if the teacher will not cooperate, then the objector's next step is to go to the school administration. See CENSORSHIP.)

Convention vs. Confession. How does one determine when convention becomes confession? It is conventional to write *God* for the

Judeo-Christian deity and *god* for other people's, but atheists might object. Some writers capitalize all pronouns referring to God (He, Who); some, only the personal pronouns and not the relative pronouns; others (including most Bibles) capitalize none. Ordinarily, these are not sensitive issues, though they might be. Consider modern efforts to soften the masculine "bias" in the Bible.

One person's harmless conventional practice, however, may be another's irritating or offensive confessional practice. Is it Old Testament, Hebrew Scriptures, or Jewish Bible? B.C. or B.C.E., nativity or Nativity, passion or Passion, Matthew or St. Matthew? Where the responsible teacher or author thinks that sensibilities may (or should) be involved, he or she makes deliberate decisions, gives a forthright statement of the alternatives and the reasons for the choices, and follows a consistent pattern.

But is an initial disclaimer enough to make up for a consistently offensive practice, especially when students soon forget the textbook's or the teacher's introductory remarks? Considering the lack of sophistication of most students, probably not. At the least, there should be periodic reminders, acknowledging that the teacher or textbook has chosen a specific convention among alternatives.

In areas where sensibilities may be involved, teachers and authors cannot rely entirely on their own experience and intuition, both of which are necessarily limited. Nor can they rely on theory, gained from learning and logic, to decide in advance which of the seemingly innocuous conventions will not give offense to people they have not met. Neither can one hope to offend absolutely no one in every idiosyncratic interpretation within every sect. "One person, one vote" would lead either to chaos or immobility. In deciding which conventions to follow and which confessional locutions to avoid, the teacher should weigh who are the responsible spokespersons for religious points of view; and the more inclusive the teacher is in his or her considerateness, the better. (See JESUS/CHRIST.)

Crucifix/Cross. Crucifix includes the body (corpus); the cross is bare. For many people the distinction is important, one term emphasizing the crucifixion, the other the resurrection. Some Christian denominations insist on either the one or the other as a central symbol in their church.

Explaining Supernatural Events. Students may seek, and teachers may wish to offer, an "explanation" of biblical miracles and other interventions of God into the world of nature. If a discussion is to take place at all, what constitutes a satisfactory explanation of the Bible's supernatural elements?

People have offered at least four kinds of explanations for these stories:

1. The explanation is found in the literal truth of scripture. The events really happened as part of history. If God can create the universe, he must be able to affect its course. The entire world was flooded, and God told Noah to build the ark.

2. The explanation lies in natural phenomena. The account is the result of human interpretation or misinterpretation. The delta's waters devastated the land and traumatized the people; it is quite possible that only one family escaped.

3. The explanation lies in folklore and myth. Such accounts are found in many ancient cultures, usually among people who live near a flood plain. The stories reflect a people's experience and express their values, their view of physical nature and of human nature. The flood was a pivotal and moral event in human history, exemplifying the people's relationship to God.

4. The explanation lies in its imperative for human beings. Whether the account is historical, invented, or "mythic" is relatively unimportant. Readers must seek its meaning for their own lives. The flood resulted in a new covenant of laws for humanity, and it opened the way to salvation.

Some religious or humanistic traditions may insist on only one "explanation" of supernatural events in the Bible. Teachers in a public school, however, should not encourage students to feel that the school sponsors any one explanation—or indeed that there must be only one correct explanation. One must avoid both bias and reductionism.

After all, these four kinds of explanation are not necessarily mutually exclusive. Most people would approve more than one. The flood may have been a judgmental and saving act of God as well as an unusual glacial phenomenon. The story may coincide with accounts from other ancient cultures and fit into the ancient Hebrew world view; yet it may also have been recorded as a lesson for humanity.

Here, as elsewhere, the teacher must be aware of alternatives. And if there is to be discussion, the teacher must make the students aware not only of alternatives but also of the possibility that more than one explanation is satisfactory.

Harmonizing the Gospels. Both conservatives and critical scholars explain the differences among the four Gospels as matters of emphasis and point of view among the four evangelists. For conservatives, all of the Gospels are direct revelations from one source; therefore, a single perspective harmonizes the differences. Critical scholars account for the different points of view by interposing between the life of Jesus and the writing of the Gospels distances both of time and of the cultural situations of the individual evangelists. (See *Introduction to New Testament Literature.*)

Islam. A public school teacher who uses stories from the Koran should be very careful not to make value judgments in comparing either the content or the style of the Koran with that of the Bible. (See SECTARIAN INTERPRETATIONS.)

Israel/Holy Land/Palestine. America has recognized the state of Israel; so a public school teacher may legitimately use that modern geographic and political term. Teachers should know, however, that the three terms generally reflect the differing attitudes of Jews, Christians, and Arabs (Christian or Moslem).

For most Jews, the state of *Israel* fulfills a long-awaited return to their ancient homeland. Most Arab countries do not recognize the state of Israel and consider the land part of Arab *Palestine.* Most Christians are more interested in the religious connotations of the *Holy Land* of Jesus and the early church than in its political aspects.

Teachers should be careful not to urge a partisan Jewish, Christian, or Arab position when speaking of the biblical area in its modern context. The land, the ancient patriarchs, and the Bible are sacred to all three groups. When the subject arises, students should be exposed to all three attitudes.

Jehovah. The Hebrew Scriptures have many names for the deity. One group clusters about the root *El* (usually translated "God") and another about the four consonants (tetragrammaton) YHWH (usually translated "the Lord"). The Hebrew word for a secular lord is *adon,* and a form of this word, *Adonai* (my Lord), is substituted by Jews as the oral rendition of YHWH, to avoid even trying to pronounce the ineffable name of the deity.

This oral substitution, protecting the name of the deity, was partially incorporated into some modern Hebrew texts. The YHWH consonants have been "clothed" with roughly equivalent vowel sounds from the word *Adonai.* (Written vowels to help the inexpert read the ancient Hebrew consonantal language were added around 800 C.E.) Thus, the formerly unpronounceable and forbidden name is now often pronounced and spelled Jehovah. Some people add different vowels to the YHWH to form the word *Yahweh,* which, it is believed, originally meant "he causes to be" or "he creates."

Jehovah's Witnesses insist upon Jehovah as the name of God. Orthodox and Conservative Jews will say only *Adonai* and prefer as a translation "the Lord" to either Jehovah or Yahweh. Critical scholars generally use the tetragrammaton or Yahweh, a word that now appears in some English Bibles.

Note that the names of people and places include the two roots in various forms: El—, —el; Je—, Jo—, —jah, —iah, —ias (Greek form). Uriel, Uriah, Urias, and Urijah all mean "God {or the Lord} is my light" or else "the light of God {the Lord}." What *Israel* means etymologically is unclear; but with this explanation of roots, students should never misspell it.

Jehovah's Witnesses. See SECTARIAN INTERPRETATIONS for biblical implications.

Jesus/Christ. The OT does not mention Jesus by name. The NT definitely refers to Jesus as Jesus Christ or as Christ, especially in Acts and the Epistles.

In the Gospels, the "world of the text" is a bit complicated. Evangelists introduce their Gospels as the story of Jesus Christ (Matt. 1:1; Mark 1:1; John 1:17) or assume that Jesus is the Christ. Within the story of the life of Jesus, however, the narrator does not use that title and always refers to him as Jesus. Within the story, people ask whether Jesus is the Christ/messiah, Son of God; they taunt him with the titles; but only once does Jesus state that he is the Christ.

Thus, the objective critic has a variety of milieus. The critic finds: (a) literary justification for referring to Jesus Christ or to Christ when the context is the world of the text of Acts or Epistles, (b) no literary justification within the world of the OT text, and (c) some distinctions to acknowledge with regard to the world of the Gospels. (See WORLD OF THE NT.)

Nevertheless, literary justification for the use of *Christ* or *Jesus Christ* as names for Jesus in normal classroom discourse comes into conflict with other demands upon a public secondary school teacher in our society. *Christ,* applied to Jesus, is a confessional term: It carries with it the belief that Jesus is the Christ/messiah anointed by God as the savior.

Will the teacher be able to make clear and will the students understand that whenever the teacher uses the term *Christ* to refer to Jesus, it is done within the world of the text rather than within the teacher's (and their own) religious tradition? One may assume that the students (if not their parents, to whom they may report) will not understand the subtle distinction. (See CONVENTION VS. CONFESSION.)

Say *Jesus* and avoid misunderstanding.

Attitudes toward Jesus' messiahship run a gamut. Many Christians make a distinction: When expressing their faith in Jesus as the messiah, they say *Christ;* in stressing his humanity, they say *Jesus.* Other Christians define Jesus' messiahship only figuratively, a view that is antipathetic to those who believe that Jesus was not only *the* Christ but also the Son of God. Many critical scholars suggest that Christology did not develop until after Jesus' death. People who see Jesus not as a messiah but as simply a man consistently use only the term *Jesus.* For a public school teacher to call him Jesus is not to reject Jesus' messiahship but to use the least controversial term.

The point being made here seems to be one of the most difficult for some authors and teachers to accept. The unfootnoted term *Christ,* or *Jesus Christ,* appears as a synonym for *Jesus* in many textbooks recently offered for public school students: e.g., *The Bible as Literature,* by Alton Capps (McGraw-Hill, 1971); *A Literary Survey of the Bible,* by Joyce Vedral (Logos, 1973); *The Myth of the Fall,* by F. Parvin Sharpless (Hayden, 1974); and *The Enduring Legacy,* by Douglas Brown (Scribner's, 1975). In all these books, whatever excellences the last two may have in other respects, they contain additional evidences of Christian bias. (See CLASSROOM TEXT: BIBLE CENTERED.)

The same holds true for books offered as teacher aids and as college texts: e.g., *The Literature of the Bible,* by Leland Ryken (Zondervan, 1974), an otherwise fine book. Here, the caution is that the teacher should compensate for the bias of the textbook when transmitting its insights to students—as we recommend for our own books.

Jewish/Christian Differences. Most Americans are familiar with the broad outlines and main beliefs and practices of Christianity. The largest non-Christian group is the Jews, who also regard the Bible as sacred (see BIBLE). Since many Christians are uninformed or misinformed about this group, it seems proper to point out some special problem areas.

Generally speaking, Jewish attitudes toward the ACCURACY, AUTHORSHIP, AND AUTHORITY of their Bible run the same gamut as do those of Christians toward theirs (see BIBLE). Jewish attitudes toward the NT are apt to coincide with those of critical scholars rather than those of conservative Christianity.

Here are some Jewish/Christian differences:

Covenant. The concept changes throughout Jewish scriptures, but Jews do not see the NT (new covenant) as a higher development. (See *salvation,* below.)

God. Most Orthodox and some Conservative Jews write the word *G–d* for several reasons: (a) the traditional biblical practice of writing in consonants only, especially in the case of the tetragrammaton YHWH; (b) the rabbinic injunction against pronouncing the name of the deity; and (c) the desire to guard against desecration of the holy name if the paper is destroyed. Most members of the same groups will not speak the name *Yahweh* nor write it. In prayer, they say *Adonai;* in secular speech, *Adoshem,* a further euphemism whose last syllable means "name."

History. Many people, quite without thinking, often refer to the Bible as the history of "the Jews and the early Christians." From this, one might infer that the Jews have had little noteworthy history or religious development since OT times—an attitude that is reinforced by the absence of Jews from most of the medieval and modern history textbooks. Better say "ancient Jews and early Christians." Similarly, the Hebrew language is not properly called only an "ancient language"; it is alive and well in Israel and elsewhere.

Holidays. Although they occur at the same season, Hanukkah is not the Jewish Christmas. Hanukkah commemorates events recounted in I Maccabees; Christmas, the birth of Jesus.

Likewise, though Easter may in some sense be the Christian Passover, Passover is in no sense the Jewish Easter. Passover commemorates the exodus from Egypt and does not, for Jews, foreshadow the resurrection of Jesus at Easter.

Just as most Christians see Passover as prefiguring Easter, they see a foreshadowing relationship between the Jewish and Christian Pentecosts (see PENTECOST, below).

Jews view their history and religion as self-contained, not as prefiguring the Christian experience (see PROPHECY FULFILLMENT). They are understandably unhappy, therefore, when Christians see their celebration of these and other holidays as though they commemorate the "providential preservation of Israel so that Jesus Christ might appear to his people," as one no doubt well-meant message of congratulations and fellowship put it to a Jewish community.

The Law and the Prophets. This expression, used by Jesus, probably referred to the two parts of the Hebrew Bible that were then accepted as sacred: *Torah* and *Nebi-im.* Jews today do not call the Five Books of Moses "the Law" in English, but prefer either Pentateuch [Greek: five books] or Torah [Hebrew: instruction, law]. In Jewish tradition there is the "written Law" (the entire Jewish Bible) and the "oral Law" (embodied in rabbinic literature and beyond). In both phrases, the Hebrew word for "Law" is *Torah.*

Incidentally, Daniel and Lamentations are included among the "Prophets" in Protestant tradition but not in Jewish divisions. And the Jewish Bible ends with II Chronicles not with Malachi, a Christian arrangement that Jews see as an attempt to link the OT to the NT. (See BIBLE.)

New Testament. Not only is the NT not a part of the Jewish Bible, but it is regarded ruefully by many Jews because it has been used so often through history to perpetuate unpleasant prejudice. Its title is looked on as polemical, implying that it updates, and offers the proper viewpoint for understanding, an "old" and partially outdated scripture—which Jews call their Bible.

Moreover, some Christian sects emphasize the view that the NT supersedes the laws of the OT, as directed by the Holy Spirit to translators of the Septuagint (accounting for the differences from the Masoretic text) and as stated in passages like Romans 8:3-4.* In the latter instance, the implication is that those who do not accept Jesus as the Christ "walk after the flesh," not after the spirit.

Parts of the NT strongly criticize Jews who did not accept Jesus as the messiah, encourage evangelism among Jews, and impose christological typology on the Hebrew Scriptures (see WORLD OF THE NT). Instead of reading its scripture through the lens of the NT, Jewish tradition interprets the Jewish Bible through the rabbinic writings, some of which are contemporary with the NT and contain commentaries that are exactly parallel to most of the ethical teachings of the NT.

Pentecost. For Jews, this is a holiday occurring fifty days (seven weeks) after the second day of Passover and is more commonly called the

Feast of Weeks, or Shavuot. It celebrates both the wheat harvest and the giving of the Law on Mt. Sinai and was one of the three pilgrimage holidays.

For Christians, the holiday commemorates the descent of the Holy Spirit/Ghost upon the apostles fifty days after the resurrection, with its gift of tongues and instruction to use them to preach to the world. The occasion is sometimes referred to as the birthday of the church and is called by some Whitsunday (when Anglican clergymen wore white). It is of central importance for Pentecostal traditions in America.

It is interesting, and probably not purely coincidental, that the first clear reference to the giving of the Law in connection with the Jewish holiday dates from the third century C.E. At the time when the Pentecost was taking on its new meaning for Christians, according to some critical scholars, the Jewish community was also adding a new significance to what had been only an agricultural holiday.

Similarly, the ritual of the Passover feast was first set down in the *Haggadah* at the time when the holiday came to be identified by Christians with Easter. One of the impulses behind this reinterpretation and formalization of these holidays, in addition to the loss of the temple and its cult, may have been a concern that some Jews still feel today—the need to protect themselves from a Christian "takeover" of their holidays. But this is part of the much larger issue of assimilating a dominant culture.

Personal names. A Jew's first name is not his or her "Christian name," as officially in England and often unofficially in this country. Neither is a Jewish child "christened"; boys are traditionally given their names at circumcision, and girls at the first Torah service following the birth.

Pharisees. In Jewish tradition, the Pharisees are remembered with respect; in Christian tradition, with scorn.

Historically, the term describes a loosely defined group within the Jewish community at the time of Jesus. They were characterized by: (a) an emphasis on the holy daily life, as opposed to the worldliness of the Sadducees and the asceticism of the Essenes; (b) commitment to the idea of a developing religious tradition rather than the inflexible dependence on holy writ, to the exclusion of oral Law, insisted upon by the Sadducee establishment; and (c) belief in a messiah, in the resurrection of the dead, and in a day of judgment.

Pharisees varied. Some were very slow to accept additions to the oral Law. They were looked upon as too conservative, even as reactionary, by the more progressive Pharisees, who freely continued to add humanitarian interpretations to scripture and tradition and to build what became normative rabbinic tradition. Progressive Pharisee rabbis of the period (as recorded in what is now the Talmud, and elsewhere), like Jesus (in the NT), attacked as narrow-minded, legalistic, and "hypocritical" those Pharisees whom they accused of observing only the letter rather than the spirit of both the written and oral Law.

Thus, for Jews today the term *Pharisees* refers to those progressives who established the mainstream of Jewish tradition and emphasized the humanitarian aspects of Judaism. For most Christians, who know only the NT, and in most literary allusions, the term is pejorative, largely because Jesus, in attacking the reactionary, pietistic Pharisees, makes no allowance for those who saw eye to eye with him as a teacher.

Furthermore, after the destruction of the temple and expulsion of the Jews from Jerusalem in 70 C.E., the Sadducees lost their base of power and the Pharisees became the leaders of the Jewish community in Judea. One of their main concerns was to preserve their religious tradition, from which Christians were increasingly diverging. By the time Christianity became a separate sect and the NT was being composed, the hostility between Christians and all Pharisees became especially bitter. The NT reflects that mutual hostility.

Prejudicial stereotypes. As is the case with most societies, Christian group loyalty and/or chauvinism, compounded of many elements, has often been directed against divergent traditions. At times, this bias has drawn support from biblical texts and has been expressed in overt or unconscious overemphasis on certain aspects of the Bible: (a) the part played by Jews in the trial of Jesus, (b) attacks upon Jews in the Gospels of Matthew and John and in some Epistles, and (c) belief in the superiority of the NT over the OT. The result has been that some Christians have attributed to modern Jews certain harsh values represented in the OT (and by no means missing from the NT). They exclude other values, also in both testaments, that are more congenial to most people (including Jews) today. Here are two examples:

Retributive justice and fear of a fierce God are often seen (and portrayed in literature) as peculiarly Jewish values in such a stereotype—as opposed to love, mercy, and social justice among

Christians and in their deity. As a matter of fact, both the compassionate and the wrathful aspects of God appear in both the OT and the NT; and Jews and Christians as individuals seem to be equally diverse in their human virtues and vices.

Chosenness is often seen as making Jews narrowly separatist, somehow mysterious, and arrogantly elitist—as opposed to the democratic universality of Christianity. Again, both OT and NT, both Christianity and Judaism, both Christians and Jews, contain elements of election and of universalism.

For their part, Jews are apt to emphasize only the God of love and the humanitarianism and universalism of the Prophets and rabbinic literature to the exclusion of harsher passages of the OT. They are apt to oppose these more attractive values to an exaggerated emphasis upon Christian condemnation of Jews, the Christian doctrine of exclusive salvation through Jesus as the Christ, and the related drive to evangelize (especially when it is directed toward Jews or accompanied by force—physical or other). Jewish history of the twin threats of oppression and assimilative extinction has led some Jews to withdraw into their own community and to generalize their fears into an unpleasant stereotype of all Christians as conscious or unconscious anti-Semites—as unfortunate a stereotype as that against which they defend themselves.

In America, of all places, our ideal should be to expose, understand, and educate against such prejudices. Before deciding whether and/or how to do so in the context of using the Bible in a literature class, however, teachers have to do a lot of thinking about themselves, their students, and their communities.

Salvation/Savior. In the normative Jewish view these terms are not associated with the kingdom of God in the Christian sense. As used in the OT, they related more directly to deliverance from oppression. Originally, the word *messiah,* when it pointed to the future, referred only to political and social deliverance. Its spiritual meaning for Jews developed later. Even so, their spiritual redeemer, savior, or deliverer was God; the messiah was to be a herald or a symbol of God's peaceable kingdom.

Many Christians see the entire Bible, Old and New Testaments, as a continuing series of God's saving acts. They begin with creation and Eden; end in the second coming; and climax in the life, death, and resurrection of Jesus. As this great plan of history becomes increasingly evident, according to this interpretation, people's understanding of God, salvation, and religion grows. The new covenant/testament refines and supersedes the old.

This reading of biblical history reinforces the theory of the (foreordained) gradual transition from a primitive Jewish religion to a more enlightened Christian one. It is further supported by the fact that in Greek, Latin, and English versions of the Bible the same word is used for both OT and NT, Jewish and Christian, concepts—in the case of *salvation* and *savior* as well as *covenant*.

Obviously, Jews resent such ideas and point to the breadth of OT theology and ethics and to the continued development of postbiblical Judaism as negating this reductive reading of the OT and of Judaism.

Jews, Hebrews, Israelites, Israelis; Jewish, Yiddish. Scholars use the terms *Jews, Hebrews,* and *Israelites* to designate specific stages in the history of the people: *Hebrews,* Abraham through Joseph: *Israelites,* exodus through exile; *Jews,* since the diaspora (postexilic dispersion). (See time line, Part III, chap.8 of this handbook.)

Today, American Jews commonly use the word *Hebrew* to designate only the language and its literature; *Israelite* to speak of ancient tribal people; *Israeli* (noun), inhabitant of the modern state of Israel or (adjective) pertaining to that country. Everything and everybody else, in common American parlance today, is "Jewish" or "Jew": Jewish person, history, religion (back to Abraham, the first Jew)—not Hebrew or Israelite. A Jew prefers not to be called a Hebrew or an Israelite.

Sensitivities vary with place and change with time. In Mexico, for example, Jews are politely called *israelitas* and pejoratively *judios.* A few generations ago in the United States, Jews often referred to themselves in print as Hebrews. (Compare *colored,* then *Negro,* and now *black* ; also the change of such originally scornful terms like *Quaker* and *Methodist.*) It has always been inappropriate to use the word *Jew* as an adjective (instead of *Jewish,* as in "Jew food") and offensive to use the word as a verb ("to Jew").

Yiddish is primarily a language, composed of High German, Hebrew, and Slavic elements. It also refers to the culture of people who speak the language. "Yid" [German: Jude] is usually offensive in the speech of non-Jews.

"Just like Shakespeare." Teachers of literature are legitimately entitled to examine with their students the literary craftsmanship of the Bible, as

they would with Shakespeare. It is also valuable pedagogy, with Shakespeare as with the Bible, not to insist on any one interpretation of the text.

But to "treat the Bible *just* like Shakespeare" is a shibboleth. It is not a matter of life and death if teachers of Shakespeare condemn or never mention the Oedipal interpretation of Hamlet's motivations. In contrast, for teachers of the Bible to condemn (or omit justifications for) holy war, for example, is an entirely different thing. By the spoken or silent disapproval of holy war they are espousing or encouraging in their students an attitude toward God and the Bible that is seriously partisan. It is more than a matter of life and death; it is a matter of the possible eternal salvation or damnation of their students' souls, in the view of some people.

It is necessary for a teacher not to push his or her own interpretation and values, but it is not sufficient. The teacher has the further obligation to solicit, elicit, or supply varying interpretations when a classroom discussion is one-sided, to protect minority traditions and/or adherents from scorn.

Furthermore, one cannot make a neat distinction between *literary* and *confessional* statements about the Bible. If one starts from the confessional assumption that the entire Bible was written under the influence of the Holy Spirit, then TYPOLOGY is literary foreshadowing by the "author."

For example, suppose a teacher asks students to speculate about why Isaac is not mentioned as accompanying his father away from Mt. Moriah after the "sacrifice." May the teacher rule out—as confessional and therefore not literary—the suggestion that Isaac may have died and later been revived, foreshadowing the resurrection of Jesus, as some believers infer from Hebrews 11:19? Such an answer is as permissible as speculating that Isaac was shocked and remained on the mountain to recover—provided that the students understand that the typological response to a literary question is based on a confessional view of the Bible's authorship. The teacher cannot insist that students accept a less conservative view.

Latter Day Saints (Mormons). See SECTARIAN INTERPRETATIONS.

Literary Criticism. The term *literary criticism* has two meanings. Literary scholars have used it to mean the analysis of literary techniques and devices and of their relationship to subject matter, often according to some theory of literature. Biblical scholars have, until recently, used the term to mean source analysis: examination of the development and writing down of biblical literature. Occasionally biblical scholars observed that the Bible was well written in some passages—a "good read" that sometimes used concrete imagery, symbolism, irony, and structure effectively; but these were in most instances peripheral judgments or enthusiasms rather than the disciplined criticism of literary specialists.

More recently, both groups of scholars have been paying more attention to biblical books and shorter passages as literary units. They examine the esthetic surface of the original texts with tools and expertise that have been used on secular literature. One group of biblical scholars calls its work "rhetorical criticism." Many scholars try to fit biblical literature into one or another theory of literature.

Some biblical scholars are engaged in "structural criticism," which probes beneath the esthetic surface of the original text. This approach is based on linguistic models (e.g., of Saussure and Chomsky) and on anthropological models (e.g., of Lévi-Strauss). But none of this ferment is of much immediate use to the average teacher of English, who has little Hebrew and less Greek and who would in any event have to do a lot of work to transmute scholarly investigations into classroom activities. (See "The Bible as Literature," in *The Interpreter's Dictionary of the Bible,* Supplementary Volume, Abingdon, 1976.)

As for literary criticism as source analysis, public school teachers who emphasize such scholarship as an approach to biblical literature risk two problems: antagonizing many religious conservatives and dissipating the piece of literature that is before the students. The study of sources and analogues to the *Merchant of Venice* may be literary scholarship, but it is not literary criticism and is not what goes on in most secondary school literature classes. Even if the biblical story is a conflation, it is being read in the final form in which it was set down. The source theory is useful, however, as one of the possible explanations of textual problems when they arise—a relatively rare circumstance in secondary school English.

Critical analysis, therefore, is best pursued in the tradition of the literary specialists. We must, however, offer an important warning. With biblical literature, to talk of the *author's* use of literary devices and how well he (or she) has reinforced meaning with technique is to take a stand on questions about the Bible's authorship: By what/whom was the "author" inspired and in how great detail? How free was the writer to choose the content and method of narration? How much credit can we give to the writer for artistry and imagination? To what extent can we attribute a purpose and meaning to the writer?

One avoids unnecessary controversy about such matters by examining how the *story*, not the *author* or *writer*, works. It is better to talk about what *effect* the story's technical devices have than what the author/writer's *purpose* and achievement were. It is preferable to speak of the literature rather than of the author or writer, the narrative rather than the narrator—even though several books do have a first-person narrator or do mention a speaker or writer.

One should ask, If this passage is ironic, what does it do to the rest of the story? Not, Is the author/writer being ironic here; and if so, why? It is preferable to ask, What is the effect of the repetition in the story? Not, Why do you suppose the author/writer repeats so many phrases? The difference is small but important as an indication of attitude.

Literary Units of the Bible. Faulkner wrote "The Bear" as a short story. When he incorporated it into the novel *Go Down, Moses,* it took on a richer, even different meaning. From the perspective of the family history unfolding in his other novels, it changes again. Yet one may properly read and appreciate it at any of these levels. One may do the same with certain chapters excerpted from Steinbeck's *Grapes of Wrath,* even though they were not published separately. On the other hand, an author may have a private vocabulary, as did Blake and Yeats. In such cases, it is not only enlightening but crucial to study some of the poems in the context of the poet's other works.

What of selections taken from the Bible? Can they be studied alone, or must we include other passages, adjacent or removed? And if so, what constitutes an appropriate textual context for a biblical passage?

For example, is it proper to study Mark's account of Peter's denial (14:66-72) as a separate story? It takes on more meaning when linked with Jesus' prophecy that Peter would deny him (14:26-31). And the meaning of Peter's lapse expands again when it is combined with Judas' defection (14:10-11) and betrayal (14:43-45), together with the desertion of the other apostles (14:50).

We add still another meaning to the story of Peter's denial when we read it in the context of the verses that immediately precede and follow it (14:53-65; 15:1). They describe Jesus' trial by the Jewish council. Peter's denial of Jesus interrupts the account of the trial, as a device for contrasting two simultaneous and critically related events. Both Peter and Jesus are being tried, or tested, at the same time, and Peter's trial is also a test of Jesus' right to be called a prophet. At the same moment when Jesus is being mocked as a false prophet, his prophecy about Peter's denial is coming true. The juxtaposition implies that his prophecy concerning the three days, about which the council questions him, will also come true. (For a more detailed discussion, see *Introduction to New Testament Literature.*)

Can the story of Peter's denial stand alone without doing it an injustice? If not, which passages must the teacher include?

Consider the story of Jonah (see chap. 10 of Gros Louis, *Literary Interpretations of Biblical Narratives*). Shouldn't the teacher tell students that the Bible says elsewhere that Nineveh epitomized evil and was a hated enemy and that Jonah was a strongly nationalistic prophet? Should the teacher then go on to explain that, by juxtaposing other biblical passages, one may read the story as an intentional allegory about the exile? And should the teacher add the typological interpretation given by Jesus (Matt. 12:40)?

Similarly, the story of Judah and Tamar (Gen. 38) may be read as a separate literary unit. But its meaning grows when it is a foil for the Joseph story, which it interrupts, especially in contrast to the tale of Potiphar's wife (Gen. 39) that immediately follows. The Judah-Tamar episode is part of a pattern of the preservation of the clan, which is a central theme of the Joseph story. (For more on this theme, see chap. 5 of the Gros Louis book.)

Some literary and biblical scholars go beyond the Joseph story and find even broader contexts in the Bible. The unusual sexual relationship of Judah and Tamar takes on another meaning when it is seen as part of a deep structural pattern that includes Lot and his daughter (Gen. 19) and Ruth and Boaz. Ruth, descendant of Lot's son Moab, and Boaz, descendant of Judah and Tamar, were united in a manner that many scholars find ambiguous. They are the ancestors of David, whose heir is the son of Bathsheba, whom David married under abnormal conditions. Continuing along traditional Christian lines, the unusual circumstance of the birth of Jesus becomes a part of this pattern. It now encompasses Judah, Boaz, and David, as well as the women: Lot's daughter, Tamar, Ruth, Bathsheba, and Mary. The last four are the only women Matthew's genealogy mentions. Such esoteric literary analysis, however, will probably distract nearly all high school students away from their appreciation of the great literary achievement of either the story of Joseph or the book of Ruth rather than enhance it.

The question of what constitutes a literary unit of the Bible can, on the one hand, be a threat for some teachers. They may feel that they cannot make all the possible connections between a particular story and the rest of the Bible and may fear that they will distort its meaning or show a sectarian bias. On the other hand, some teachers may see this question as an opportunity to support a special religious interpretation of the text, particularly in the case of TYPOLOGY.

The first reaction is not necessary; the second is improper. Students (and teachers) may read a story at whatever level their background information and their perceptiveness allow them to understand it, provided that the teacher is honestly pursuing literary goals with the class. When the addition of contextual passages involves obvious confessional differences—as with typology that links the OT to the NT—then the teacher must plainly label the larger context as confessional and controversial.

Otherwise, there is no reason for limiting the scope of a literary unit, other than good pedagogy within the purposes of the course. Nor is there any compulsion to go beyond a brief, coherent episode.

Myth. Regardless of stipulated definitions by scholars or classroom teachers, the term *myth* in popular understanding almost always excludes the idea of historical accuracy. Calling the Bible stories myths, therefore, brings connotations that are unacceptable to most conservatives. The word *legend* carries a similar onus. Students will probably remember only that the teacher spoke of Bible myths and legends and will forget the teacher's special definitions, however sensibly or elaborately presented. Their parents may then resent what they interpret as the teacher's treating the Bible as if it were in the same category as, say, Greek mythology. Say *story* and save energy.

Old Testament Books. See BIBLE.

Prophecy Fulfillment and Typology (especially linking the OT to the NT). Early Christians could understand the OT only in terms of Jesus, and Jesus only in terms of the OT. Many Christians today similarly see OT prophecies of a deliverer fulfilled in Jesus as the Christ/messiah. An OT passage is understood either to prophesy and foretell or to prefigure and "typify" (i.e., to foreshadow or act out in advance) a person or event in the NT.

Some of these linkages are openly stated or hinted at in the NT: The

NT event is said to be the fulfillment of an OT prophecy or the reenactment of an OT event. It is the "antitype" of the OT "type," or model. Other linkages are less clear, being interpreted as such by later commentators.

In all instances, such linkages are seen as throwing light on episodes and/or characters of both the OT and the NT. Conservative Christians hold that the links are deliberate acts of God or the Holy Spirit. They believe that the OT prophecy is fulfilled and the significance of the OT prefigurings is revealed in Jesus, regardless of the conscious intention of the OT writer or "witness." Augustine, reading the Bible allegorically, says, "In the Old Testament the New lies hid; in the New Testament the meaning of the Old becomes clear."

Unsurprisingly, opinions as to the validity of these linkages differ considerably between critical scholars and conservatives. Most critical scholars see such linkages as later human, hermeneutical interpretations of the OT traditions, as religious communities struggled with the meaning of the text and its application to their lives and faith. (Similarly, the rabbis and also the writers of the Dead Sea Scrolls reinterpreted the OT in their own ways.)

Critical scholars see still other forces at work. For example, OT and NT stories that resemble one another may simply be reworkings of similar traditional folk materials, as in the birth stories of Sargon, Oedipus, Moses, and Jesus. Alternatively, apparent similarities between OT and NT stories may be based on the fact that they express some common archetypal theme: of physical nature (death and rebirth of vegetation), of human nature (learning through suffering), or of literature (the night journey). A third theory is that the linkages may be a deliberate polemical attempt by the NT writers or by later commentators to show Jesus as the messiah expected by many Jews.

When the class is studying the Bible *as* literature, questions may arise: How does one account for these explicit or implicit linkages between the OT and the NT? Are they implanted by the Holy Spirit, explained culturally, or artificially imposed? To handle such questions properly, the teacher needs both sensitivity and knowledge. The teacher needs background information concerning the christologizing of the OT, both within the NT and by later commentators. The teacher also needs information about ecclesiologizing by the church fathers, who saw the church and ancient Israel as almost interchangeable in the OT text.

When the class is studying the Bible *in* literature, typology becomes much more important. Quite often, in secular literature, in music, and in art, a reference to an episode of the OT implies an allusion to the NT as well. It assumes as a matter of course the validity of such prophecy fulfillment and typology. Handel's *Messiah* opens with a passage from Isaiah. Christian art before the Renaissance contains almost no OT subject matter that is not clearly intended to point to an episode in the life of Jesus. Teachers should make their students aware of the writer's or artist's assumptions where they are important.

People have used several arguments to validate their typological interpretations of the OT:

1. The OT itself practices it. A story is shown to fulfill a prophecy recorded earlier or to reenact an earlier, similar event. Lamentations 2:17 says that Israel's punishment fulfills God's earlier words (I Kings 9:6-9). Sometimes the reference to the earlier episode is indirect, through a repetition of language. Genesis 9:1 repeats Genesis 1:28;* thus Noah is the new "first man." Noah in turn foreshadows Moses: the word for his vessel, translated as "ark," reappears only once in the OT, in the story of the infant set adrift in an ark; the two deliverances are meant to be compared.

2. Jesus himself explains his crucifixion to disciples on the way to Emmaus using this method. "Beginning at Moses [("the books of Moses," in later versions] and all the prophets, he expounded unto them in all the Scriptures the things concerning himself" (Luke 24:27). Thus the OT is said to contain the hidden story of Jesus.

3. The Gospels make several specific links between Jesus and the OT. Some are explicit: "that it might be fulfilled which was spoken [by] the Lord [through] the prophet"; "as Moses lifted up the serpent in the wilderness"; "as Jonah was three days in the whale's belly." The language used by the translators of the KJV, quoted here throughout, especially tends to reinforce the typological attitude of traditional conservative Christianity—an important reason for some conservatives' preference for that version.

Some links are implicit, using language from the OT passage in the NT to help the reader recall the former as a prefiguring "type." Mark's account of the trial and crucifixion uses many expressions taken directly from Psalms and other OT writings.

4. The Epistles use forms of the word *typos* for the reenactment kind of typology: Adam is a "figure [*typos*] of him that was to come" (Rom. 5:14). Israel's experiences in the exodus "were our examples [*typoi*]"

(I Cor. 10:6). "All these things happened unto them for [examples] *{typicos}* " (I Cor. 10:11). The tabernacles are "figures *{antitypoi}* of the true" holy places (Heb. 9:24). Noah's family was "saved by water. The like figure *{antitypon}* whereunto even baptism doth also now save us" (I Pet. 3:20-21).

Sometimes the Greek word is *parabole.* The high priest's atonement in the holy of holies is a "figure *{parabole}* for the time [of Christ]" (Heb. 9:9). Abraham "offered up his only begotten son. . . . God was able to raise him up, even from the dead; from whence also he received him in a figure *{parabole}* ["figuratively," in later versions]" (Heb. 11:17). (Thus, some people speak of the "sacrifice of Isaac," though the OT says he was not sacrificed.)

Here are some of the most commonly encountered examples of typology, in which OT people or events are understood as appearing again in NT "antitypes" that either repeat (Jesus as the new Moses) or reverse (Mary as the new and compensating Eve) the OT "type." Unless otherwise noted below, the correspondences are to the life of Jesus. In cases where the NT explicitly makes the linkage, the text is cited in parentheses.

Creation ("in the beginning") and the incarnation. *Adam* (Rom. 5:14). The *fall* vs. the crucifixion. *Eve* vs. Mary. The *sacrifice of Isaac* (Heb. 11:17). *Moses*—especially his infancy and exile from society for a period. The *Passover* and the Last Supper; the *deliverance* through the Red Sea and baptism; the *Ten Commandments* and the Sermon on the Mount; the *brazen serpent* and the cross (John 3:14). *David,* God's anointed king and "son." *Elijah* and John the Baptist (Mark 8:28). *Elisha's* raising the dead, multiplication of loaves, and healing the sick. *Israel* and the Christian Church, especially as represented in Psalms. *Isaiah,* especially the Suffering Servant and the Prince of Peace. *Ezekiel's* visions and those in Revelation. *Daniel*—saved from the lion's den, and the deliverance of the Jews from the fiery furnace; *Noah's* deliverance from the flood; and *Jonah's* deliverance from the whale (Matt. 12:40). The *blood of the covenant* and the wine at the Last Supper (Matt. 26:28). And many others.

As always, teachers of literature must be careful about "objectivity," sensibilities, and just plain accuracy of information. When teaching a biblical story (the Bible *as* literature or *for* literature), if it has typological features, the teacher should know (or know where to find) what linkages have been made, both in the NT and by its commentators. (The reference column or footnotes in conservative "study Bibles" are a useful tool.) Which ones are students most likely to meet in art and literature? What are the alternative interpretations of the linkages?

For the Bible *in* literature, in addition to these questions, the teacher must consider one more. What did the secular author of the literary work being studied probably mean to imply about the NT (if anything) when he or she alluded to the OT? The answers to all these questions provide valuable background information for teachers. Teachers also have to work out some principles and policies about whether and how to introduce such typological information into their teaching.

Sabbath/Lord's Day. For Jews and for Christian Sabbatarians—Seventh-day Adventists, 7th Day Baptists, Lord's Day Alliance, Church of God and Saints of Christ, Worldwide Church of God, Church of God (Seventh Day), and others—the holy day (of rest) is Saturday, based on the creation story and the commandment to "remember the sabbath" and because, for these Christians, no NT text contradicts that tradition.

For others, the sabbath is Sunday, the Lord's Day—based on the resurrection on the first day of the week, on early Christian gatherings held on Sunday, and on a historic urge to distinguish Christianity from Judaism. In some countries (e.g., France) the weekly calendar shows Sunday as the seventh day, bringing the two biblical traditions together. By contrast, the word for the day we call Saturday derives, in most other Western languages, from the word *sabbath* (see Part III, chap. 8).

Satan/Serpent/Devil/Dragon. In Christian tradition, the serpent in the garden of Eden is identified with Satan; and Satan is identified with the devil and the dragon, based on Revelation 12:9 and other passages. This permits the view that the OT (and the whole Bible) is a struggle between God and Satan, between the forces of good and evil—even between the spiritual world and the demonic material world.

Indeed, one classroom textbook, *The Temple and the Ruin,* by Alvin A. Lee and Hope Arnott Lee (Harcourt, Brace, 1973), is bound to this polarized view of the OT, as well as to a special theory of literature, both of which present problems for the teacher who wants a secular textbook that is free of religious and literary bias (see CLASSROOM TEXT: BIBLE-RELATED).

Critical scholars generally agree that the OT concept of the Satan does not warrant its identification either with the serpent or with the devil within the world of the OT text. In Western literature, however, allusions to the serpent in Eden usually follow the Christian tradition and imply an allusion to Satan as well.

Scholarly Approaches to the Bible. At least three kinds of scholars may be distinguished among those who study and theorize about the Bible: literary critics, biblical scholars, and theologians (or hermeneutical commentators). The insights of each group often help the others. Nevertheless, however much their interests and insights may overlap or interact, their disciplines define different kinds of activity.

The characteristic role of the *literary critic* is to read the Bible as he or she does other literature, primarily to savor it as a work of art. How does its craftsmanship work as an esthetic performance? How do its surface techniques and deep structures serve, and affect, the work's meaning, its main idea or theme? How does the piece fit into, or alter, various theories of literature? The literary critic needs the work of biblical scholars, without whose expertise the critic might misread or misunderstand the text.

Good literature results in large measure from a writer's aptitude with the means of expression. Good writers are also particularly sensitive to physical nature and to human nature. The literary critic asks how the artistry of the piece of literature enhances the reader's perception and understanding of human experience. In this pursuit, the literary critic finds the work of hermeneutical commentators useful. They suggest ways in which the text makes the human condition meaningful.

The *biblical scholar's* primary role has been to throw light on the text by examining the historical and cultural traditions out of which it came and the long history of scholarly attempts to unlock its original meaning. Biblical scholars today increasingly acknowledge the fruitfulness of the methods and theories of literary criticism. Literary critics throw new light on the text: Their concern with literary units leads to new questions and suggests new answers, which close exegesis might have overlooked.

Theologians may also furnish valuable hints for biblical scholars: Augustine reads the text very closely, as do the rabbis, and they suggest meanings that may have been in the minds of the original writers of scripture. But the biblical scholar distinguishes between the pursuit of the original meaning of the text and attempts to find its meaning for today, between exegesis and hermeneutical commentary.

The special role of the *theologian* is to discover the text's message for the reader: What shall one believe, and how shall one act? Hermeneutical commentary interprets or reinterprets the original text to find its meaning for believers today. In this activity, theologians try to get close to the original intent of the text, for which they need the work of biblical scholars. They also examine creative secular literature for its authors' imaginative responses to biblical stories and teachings. In examining both the secular and the biblical literature, theologians find the work of literary critics useful.

All three disciplines examine aspects of the text's meaning: as part of a literary whole, as part of its ancient background, and as part of one's own life. Each has its own focus, tools, expertise. Language arts teachers must be aware of the interdependence of the three kinds of activity; but, above all, they must distinguish among them in the classroom, where the main approach and emphasis is literary.

Sectarian Interpretations of the Bible. (Note: The word *sect* is used here, and throughout this handbook, as synonymous with *religious group* or *denomination*. It includes mainline and traditional communities as well as minor or schismatic groups. Some people use the term *sect* condescendingly, to designate only groups that diverge from the mainstream. Similarly, the word *cult* may be used with or without such overtones. Teachers should consider their audience, in the classroom and elsewhere, before using these terms. Incidentally, the word *nonsectarian* is often improperly used when one really means "interdenominational Christian.")

Many religious groups that accept the authority of the Bible insist that it should not be read by itself and cannot be properly understood except through the interpretation given it by their own particular sacred literature, commentators, and tradition. Here are a few such instances:

According to *Jewish* tradition, the Hebrew Bible *(Tanak)* must be read in the light of later rabbinic writings which—often considered revealed truth, as is the Bible—are authoritative in interpreting what the Bible really meant or means. This "oral Law" is especially binding on Orthodox and most Conservative Jews.

Similarly, in most *Christian* traditions, the Hebrew scriptures are to be understood only as interpreted by and rearranged for the NT. Both OT and NT are considerd to be divinely revealed and to constitute one continuous book.

Many *Protestant* sects, even when they consider the Bible the Word of God, hold that it should be interpreted according to their own doctrines (Acts 8:31*). For example, most *Lutherans* believe in the Bible as interpreted by Luther's *Book of Concord,* the three ecumenical creeds (Apostles', Nicene, and Athanasian), and various confessions (e.g., Augsburg) and catechisms. Most *Methodists* interpret the Bible in the light of Wesley's sermons, his notes on the NT, and his Articles of Religion.

Eastern Orthodox churches accept the Bible as interpreted by "holy tradition" and by the first seven ecumenical councils of the church—before the split with Rome.

Roman Catholic tradition adds certain church doctrines to those of the Bible, supplementing or interpreting the Bible and having equal authority with it.

Seventh-day Adventists and *Jehovah's Witnesses,* like many other groups, consider the Bible inerrant and the final authority but insist on special interpretations. The former say that the Bible must be interpreted according to the writings of their prophet, Ellen G. White. The latter group has two instruments of similarly authoritative and exclusive interpretation: official pronouncements of the Watchtower Society's leadership and its own New World Translation of the Bible (although other translations are permitted to be used).

Christian Scientists, Latter Day Saints (Mormons), and *Moslems* go further. They too say that the Bible can be interpreted only through their own later, sacred writings: respectively, *Science and Health with Key to the Scriptures,* the writings of Joseph Smith, and the Koran. These writings, however, not only tell what the Bible really meant, but they also correct or supplement it in places where they say it is defective. In contrast to positions described above, these groups consider divine revelation to be completely inerrant only as recorded in these later writings. Succeeding Mormon presidents have added new revelations to those of Joseph Smith. (One branch of Mormonism, the Reorganized Church, has its own Inspired Version of the Bible, incorporating Joseph Smith's emendations and additions.)

These are only a few prominent instances of official interpretations of the Bible that originate with sages or prophets or pontiffs whose words are accepted by their followers or co-religionists as authoritative and, in most cases, inspired. They constitute yet another reason for public school teachers to respect the complexity of discussing the meaning and interpretation of Bible passages.

Awareness of alternatives is crucial to all education. It frees the minds and emotions—of teachers as well as students—both *from* unexamined assurances and *for* making judgments. Thus, knowledge of alternatives is both stimulating and risky.

Teachers of the Bible must explore alternatives and take the risk for themselves. If the teacher decides to ask students to take the risk of confronting alternatives when questions arise in class, he or she is undertaking a serious responsibility, which constitutes another risk for the teacher.

Seventh-day Adventists. See SECTARIAN INTERPRETATIONS.

Starting Off. Teachers should decide on norms in advance: (a) What aspects of the Bible will be the main focus of the course, and what aspects will be irrelevant or ignored? (See Part I of this handbook.) (b) What kinds of behavior toward biblical literature and toward various religious (or irreligious) positions and their representatives will be permitted or encouraged, and what kinds of behavior will be unacceptable?

Having made these decisions, teachers should see that their students learn, and internalize, these lessons at the outset of the course or unit. Each teacher has his or her own way of telling, showing, and/or leading students to discover the rules that will govern their study of the Bible in the classroom.

Many students will come to the class with assumptions and expectations that are not appropriate to what the teacher wants them to learn and to the tone he or she hopes will prevail in the class. Some, with a fair biblical background, may think they won't have to work because it will be a repeat of their Sunday school classes. Others will want only to find proof texts to reinforce their beliefs. Still others will expect the course to be a forum for discussion of theology and morality, where they can work out their problems. Some come to evangelize, others to challenge belief. The teacher should find out early.

If students continue to misunderstand the approach to biblical literature and/or the proper behavior beyond the first session or two, the teacher may have to deal with an explosion later on.

Teacher Preparation. Courses in biblical literature at colleges and universities usually reflect an underlying set of either conservative or liberal assumptions about the authorship, historicity, and authority of the Bible. When such a course is one of the regular offerings of a religion or literature department, as part of a theology or liberal arts degree program, the state should not question these assumptions, especially if they are overt and acknowledged.

On the one hand, for example, a state college may legitimately offer courses that approach the Bible as a humanistic document, as in the *Calvary Bible* v. *Board of Regents* (1968). On the other hand, it is equally legitimate for a church-related college to offer courses in biblical literature that presuppose that the Bible is the Word of God and that students cannot really understand the Bible unless it is approached from a faith perspective.

The situation is different, however, when any college offers a biblical literature course that may be taken for credit toward a career in public education. Students are being prepared and certified to teach biblical literature in a public school, where neither the humanist/liberal nor the religious/conservative assumption may control the teaching.

The Supreme Court says that any state-supported practice must not have a purpose or a primary effect that either advances or inhibits religion. Given the classroom situation, with its special teacher-pupil relationship, we need to go further: Public school teaching should not tend to advance or inhibit any religious, or irreligious, point of view, primarily *or secondarily.* The public school teacher must make a strong effort not to urge, openly or subtly, particular attitudes toward the Bible's authorship, historicity, or authority.

Therefore, a college or university that prepares teachers for state certification to teach biblical literature—or, for that matter, to use the Bible in a religion studies course or unit—has a special obligation. That obligation does not require that the college course be taught "objectively," which is impossible in any case. But it does mean that the college must go beyond merely acknowledging whatever assumptions underlie its biblical literature course.

In its preservice and in-service teacher training program, the college must actively sensitize its students to the diversity of religious and nonreligious sensibilities. It must also make clear that the college students' own future teaching in public schools must be both pluralistic and impartial.

This obligation applies whether the college is state-operated, church-sponsored, or private and unaffiliated. It applies whether the biblical literature course is given within a department or school of education, the English or comparative literature department, or a department or school of religion. The determining factor should be whether or not a student may use the course for credit toward a teacher-certification program.

The Teacher's Beliefs. Sooner or later, some student will probably say, "Yes, but what do *you* believe?" Some teachers offer the information early in the course. Others postpone the answer until they feel they have earned credibility as evenhanded and as respectful of all points of view. Less often (and perhaps less justifiably), a teacher will answer the question only outside of class.

If students know at the outset, will they discount the teacher's protestations of fairness and think, "But, of course, the teacher doesn't really believe that" or "Of course, he (or she) is pushing his (or her) own beliefs"? If students are put off, will they spend too much energy trying to find out? In either case, what the teacher believes may get in the way of what he or she is trying to teach.

A teacher's decision about *when* to announce (or admit) his or her religious or humanistic attitudes toward the Bible's authorship, accuracy, and authority depends on the classroom situation, particularly the relation between teacher and students. More important is *how* to do so.

It seems advisable to combine an honest answer with a convincing display (by word and action) that the teacher's beliefs are irrelevant to the teaching/learning experience. As far as is humanly possible, what the students learn about the Bible in a literature class should not be affected by the teacher's beliefs.

Ten Commandments. The Decalogue appears, somewhat differently, in both Exodus and Deuteronomy. The former is more commonly known and quoted. Aside from problems of translation (is it "kill" or "murder"?), a teacher cannot with confidence expect students to give a uniform answer to the question, Which is the first commandment?

Their religious traditions may specify quite different numberings of the verses in Exodus 20. And someone is bound to come up with the "first and great commandment" of Jesus. For teachers, again, the awareness is all. Incidentally, pictorial representations of the writing on the two tables vary: Some religious communities divide them into three and seven, some into five and five; some have the first five on the left, some on the right to simulate the Hebrew style of writing.

Typology. See PROPHECY FULFILLMENT.

Values: Religious and Secular. Some people, following Tillich and others, define any concern for questions of ultimate values as a religious activity. Most people, however, would agree with the convention that calls the Bible religious literature and *Moby-Dick* secular, even though both books are concerned with ultimate values. This conventional, more restricted definition of religion and religious activity is helpful for secondary school teachers of literature, but there remain certain other problems arising from the competing definitions.

In our American tradition, the conventional definition of religion has included a belief in a supreme being, a consequent code of moral behavior, membership in a sect, and cultic practices. This traditional definition has been gradually broadened, especially in recent times so that now many hold that an individual's belief in a purely personal, humanistic set of ethical values is his or her religion.

The older definition was considered too restrictive. It tended to exclude nontheist Eastern religions, agnostic Ethical Culturists and Secular Humanists, and such nonconforming American deists as Benjamin Franklin and Abraham Lincoln. The newer, expanded definition of religion also presents difficulties. Few fundamentalists are happy to share the umbrella of religious respectability with even virtuous atheists—many of whom for their part reject such a shelter.

The problem of the narrow versus the broad definition is especially acute in our country. The Supreme Court has reviewed the scholarship in the field on several occasions and regularly tried to avoid setting objective criteria for religion. In considering a tax exemption for an unconventional sect, it said, "The true test of religion is belief: that which is believed to be religiously true is religion" (*U.S.* v. *Ballard* 1944).

When forced to take a stand, the Court has not followed a logically consistent theory. In granting a man a religious exemption from compulsory military service, it used the broad definition. The Court said that the man's purely personal pacifist beliefs, derived solely from readings in history and sociology, were religious (*Welsh* v. *U.S.* 1970). The Court used the narrower definition, however, when it said that for a person to obtain a religious exemption from compulsory school attendance, he or she would have to belong to a recognized religious sect (*Wisconsin* v. *Yoder* 1972). (For a more detailed discussion of these two

FIVE NUMBERINGS OF THE TEN COMMANDMENTS (KJV LANGUAGE)

ref	Episcopal	Catholic	Lutheran	Jewish	Protestant (other)
1	I am the Lord thy God. . . . Thou shalt have no other gods before me.	Thou shalt have no other gods. . . . Thou shalt not make . . . my commandments.	Thou shalt have no other gods. . . . Thou shalt not make . . . my commandments.	I am the Lord thy God, . . . house of bondage.	I am the Lord thy God, . . . house of bondage.
2	Thou shalt not make unto thee any graven image . . . my commandments.	Thou shalt not take the name of the Lord thy God in vain; for . . . vain.	Thou shalt not take the name of the Lord thy God in vain; for . . . vain.	Thou shalt have no other gods. . . . Thou shalt not make . . . my commandments.	Thou shalt have no other gods before me.
3	Thou shalt not take the name of the Lord thy God in vain; for . . . vain.	Remember the sabbath day, to keep it holy. Six days . . . hallowed it.	Remember the sabbath day, to keep it holy. Six days . . . hallowed it.	Thou shalt not take the name of the Lord thy God in vain; for . . . vain.	Thou shalt not make unto thee any graven image . . . my commandments.
4	Remember the sabbath day, to keep it holy. Six days . . . hallowed it.	Honor thy father and thy mother: that thy days . . . God giveth thee.	Honor thy father and thy mother: that thy days . . . God giveth thee.	Remember the sabbath day, to keep it holy. Six days . . . hallowed it.	Thou shalt not take the name of the Lord thy God in vain; for . . . vain.

#					
5	Honor thy father and thy mother: that thy days . . . God giveth thee.	*Thou shalt not kill.	Thou shalt not kill.	Honor thy father and thy mother: that thy days . . . God giveth thee.	Honor thy father and thy mother: that thy days . . . God giveth thee.
6	Thou shalt not kill.	Thou shalt not commit adultery.	Thou shalt not commit adultery.	Thou shalt not kill.	Thou shalt not kill.
7	Thou shalt not commit adultery.	Thou shalt not steal.	Thou shalt not steal.	Thou shalt not commit adultery.	Thou shalt not commit adultery.
8	Thou shalt not steal.	Thou shalt not bear false witness against thy neighbor.	Thou shalt not bear false witness against thy neighbor.	Thou shalt not steal.	Thou shalt not steal.
9	Thou shalt not bear false witness against thy neighbor.	Thou shalt not covet thy neighbor's wife.	Thou shalt not covet thy neighbor's house, . . . nor his . . . neighbor's.	Thou shalt not bear false witness against thy neighbor.	Thou shalt not bear false witness against thy neighbor.
10	Thou shalt not covet thy neighbor's house, thou . . . thy neighbor's.	Thou shalt not covet thy neighbor's house nor his . . . neighbor's goods.	Thou shalt not covet thy neighbor's wife.	Thou shalt not covet thy neighbor's house, thou . . . thy neighbor's.	Thou shalt not covet thy neighbor's house, thou . . . thy neighbor's.

*Some LXX change order to: 5—adultery, 6—steal, 7—kill.

(based on *The Bible Reader*)

cases, see Warshaw, *Religion, Education, and the Supreme Court,* Abingdon, forthcoming.)

This latter instance may have signaled a retreat from the recent tendency of the Court to broaden the definition of religion. Yet there may be another, equally persuasive, interpretation. The criterion in both *Welsh* and *Yoder* may have boiled down to the practical consequences of a definition of religion.

Too narrow a construction in *Welsh* would have tended to end all religious exemptions or destroy our selective service system. Limiting the privilege of exemption exclusively to members of religious sects who believe in a supreme being would have given approval to an unconstitutional advancement of religion over irreligion. Too broad a construction in *Yoder* would have tended to destroy our public school system by granting exemptions to anyone whose values were opposed to the philosophy of the local schools. Theoretical consistency and definitional purity seem to have given way to practical considerations—a valuable lesson for teachers.

The result of this confusion about what is meant by religion presents a dilemma for the teacher of literature. Teachers may—and should, say the Supreme Court and most states—foster moral values; but they may not promote religion or a religion. But what if the two are synonymous, religion being defined as any set of moral values? Or if the two are separate, how does one talk about sanctions for moral values without either mentioning religious sanctions or, by ignoring them, favoring humanism?

It is normal for a secondary school teacher, in discussing the content of a piece of literature, to invite student response to its human issues and its expressed or implied values, in order to help students to experience the literature, to expand their intellectual horizons, even to raise their moral consciousness.

Is the teacher, in such circumstances, engaged in secular or religious activity? And how strongly may the teacher uphold a moral value? If the teacher wishes to espouse, for example, the "universal brotherhood of man" (or "siblinghood" of people), must he or she withhold opinion because it is a divinely sanctioned religious value as well as a secular value? Must the teacher refrain from the endorsement because according to some definitions any ultimate sanction for a moral value is religious and to sponsor such a value would be religious indoctrination? Either definition can paralyze the teacher.

As a practical matter, most teachers rightly uphold the value of the universal brotherhood of man. When challenged to defend the value in class, they should cite—and label—various sanctions, among them that of religion. Within the context of a discussion of secular literature, the dilemma is not difficult to resolve.

The horns of the dilemma become antlers when the piece of literature under consideration is from the Bible. The Bible is a religious book, sacred to many people; its main character is God; most of its themes are theological or divinely sanctioned moral imperatives. If the teacher expresses approval or disapproval of the values taught by the biblical text, the opinion may be seen as the teacher's judgment upon the Bible (or on a sectarian interpretation of it) rather than an exercise in "fostering moral values."

The situation is not the same as with secular literature. With the Bible, it is a much more serious matter. How is the teacher to separate religious indoctrination from moral education in such a context? What values may the teacher foster, beyond respect for one another's opinions and traditions—if that?

Certainly, it is necessary to distinguish between religious and secular activities when discussing questions of (ultimate) values with students in the context of studying the Bible. Making the distinction will not solve this dilemma (which may be impossible), but it is a necessary preliminary rumination. A teacher is well advised to be aware of the problem before entering the classroom. If not with fear and trembling, he or she will approach the discussion of values with at least caution and respect.

The World of the New Testament. When one studies any piece of literature, its world becomes a given, even if that demands from the reader a temporary suspension of disbelief—or of belief. Ordinarily, it is not especially crucial, or even stressful, for students to meet that demand—to withhold criticism of the world of the story so that they can enter it. Teachers may have to remind students on occasion, but it is a basic reading skill.

When the text is the Bible, such a restraint is particularly advisable for both students and teachers. The Bible's importance in many people's lives makes criticism of its content particularly threatening, as we have seen in the discussion of CENSORSHIP. Nevertheless, at least one aspect of the world of the NT, its anti-Semitism, seems to be an exception to the rule of "teacherly" abstinence, because of its heavy emotional load.

The Jews are the villains in John's account of the trial and crucifixion of Jesus. Matthew reports that "all the people" accepted the blame "on us and on our children." Jesus reviles the Pharisees (Matt. 23), whom Jews today revere for their contributions to rabbinic Judaism.

To ask young people to suspend their emotions while they enter the anti-Semitic episodes and aspects of the world of the NT is in most cases unrealistic. Without preparatory background or perspective furnished by the teacher, the world of the text will tend to reinforce anti-Semitism for some Christian students and attack the self-respect of most Jews. (If there are no Jews in the class, only the latter condition is alleviated.)

On purely literary grounds it does a disservice to the piece of literature to put such highly colored filters between the students and the text. The teacher has other than literary obligations, however. Because we have a pluralistic society, because this is a public school, and because these are young people, the students as well as the literature should be protected against prejudice—their own and that of others.

We suggest that the teacher introduce the historical and cultural background out of which Christianity grew and in which the NT was written. The teachers should discuss the first-century antagonisms within the Jewish community that lie behind some of the polemical language of the NT, according to critical scholars.

This is not a new problem for teachers who do not wish to rule out all literature that contains anti-Semitism or racism. Many teachers want their students to become acquainted with Shylock, Fagin, and Uncle Tom—stereotypes though they may be. With such literature, sensitive teachers usually feel an obligation to go outside the world of the text into its cultural context. It is no disrepect to Shakespeare, Dickens, and Stowe to point out that they were influenced by the prejudices of their times. Rather, it shows respect for the literature and for one's students.

The World of the Old Testament. Studying the OT without reference to the NT might be defended as being faithful to the conscious intention of the OT writers or to the world of the OT. Strictly adhered to, this practice can avoid some sticky questions of interpretation.

But it presents three problems: First, it does an injustice to conservative Christian sensibilities; second, in certain obvious instances—Psalm 22 and Isaiah 9:6, for examples—it leaves students with unanswered questions or unquestioned answers; and third, it ignores those works of Western literature and art that assume that the OT has meaning mainly in terms of the NT.

No answers will hold in all situations. In determining how far to go in relating the OT to the NT (if at all), teachers must consider their students and the purpose of the course. As elsewhere, we suggest two general guidelines: (1) Don't push any one interpretation. (2) Solicit or supply competing traditional and critical interpretations.

More specific guidelines are less certain. If the approach and emphasis of the course are on the Bible *as* literature, where the main focus is on the biblical text, one might openly choose to discuss the links with the NT only where a student raises a question. (See LITERARY UNITS OF THE BIBLE.) If the approach and emphasis are the Bible *in* literature and/or the humanities, then the secular writer's or character's tendency, if any, to view the OT through the lens of the NT becomes more important.

These two kinds of approach—the Bible *as* literature and *in* literature—are a bit more clear-cut than in the case of the Bible *and* literature. Here the class is focusing on Bible stories and secular literature that are related only by theme or genre. The issue becomes more complex: Is the Eden story an example of the struggle between God and Satan over the soul of a human being? Only if we accept a confessional interpretation of the biblical passage.

There seem to be plenty of less obtrusively sectarian themes to choose from in relating secular literature and the Bible, though labeling the theme of any biblical passage is open to argument. In the end, teachers will have to fall back on the two general guidelines suggested above, plus one more—common sense.

CHAPTER 7

Biblical Sources of Some Religious Beliefs and Practices

This is a list of biblical passages that have special and important meanings for American religious groups, mainstream and "divergent" (both called sects here). Its purposes are—

1. to inform teachers about the biblical sources of some sectarian beliefs and practices and to serve as a quick reference for such information;
2. to show the significance that some people attach to biblical passages that might not seem remarkable to the casual reader;
3. to impress teachers with the sheer number of the biblical passages and diversity of interpretations that various religious communities feel quite strongly about;
4. to suggest possible resonances of these passages, both for writer and for reader, when the passages are referred to in literature.
   Let us also note the limitations of this list, in order to forestall disappointment and soften criticism:
1. *Practices and beliefs.* Obviously, one might add to the list hundreds of other religious doctrines and rites that are based on the Bible. Part of the selectivity stems from our idea of what is most relevant to American culture in general and to literature in particular. Part lies in the limits imposed on our research. Most of the general sources are incomplete, and it is beyond the scope of this book to solicit from each of the hundreds of American sects either their suggestions for inclusion or their comments on the finished list before publication.
2. *Bible citations.* For those beliefs and practices that are on the list, the Bible passages that we cite are intended to be representative but not exhaustive. Additional texts might be adduced in most instances, as any reference Bible will suggest. Some people might object that the omission of these citations amounts to a reductive distortion. Many items do have brief notes that point to other passages or expand on

sectarian differences. Those passages that are quoted elsewhere in this list are marked with an asterisk (*). But comprehensiveness in that direction would not serve the purpose of this book.

3. *Explanations.* The bare quotation and its related belief and practice, without further explanation of the relationship between them, may not fully satisfy the curiosity of some readers and may not do justice to the complex reasoning behind a sectarian interpretation of a biblical text. Again, to explain all the religious positions represented in this list would call for a separate book, and perhaps several. The reader may find more information about some of these beliefs and practices in Part II, chapter 6, of this handbook and in the Glossary, Part V.

4. *Sects.* For many items on this list, the number of denominations mentioned to which they apply is far from complete. On the one hand, we have noted the names of only one or two representative sects that have a special interest in a particular text or religious position, where many other sects might be included. In review, there seems to be no consistent objective principle of selection. Certainly, inclusion or omission does not betoken our sponsorship or disapproval, though it may indicate our ignorance.

On the other hand, some beliefs are so widespread or so familiar to the majority of Americans that they appear to need no sectarian names attached to them. In such anonymous instances one must remember, however, that no doctrine or ceremony is universally accepted and that many of the unacknowledged interpretations applied to these biblical passages are even vehemently opposed by some sects. Further, the omission of the name of any sectarian sponsor for a belief or practice should not obscure the fact that no Jewish position is based on any text from the NT, which is the source of 65 percent of the citations.

5. *Subordinated areas.* Many whole classes of beliefs and practices based on the Bible are merely hinted at in this list: only two examples of church symbolism and art; only one explicit example of the christological reading of the OT; no attempt to include every item in the official creeds, catechisms, and articles of faith. Finally, some Bible-centered sects have certain prohibitions that are distinctive precisely because they are not tied to a biblical text; for example, some sects permit no instrumental music in worship services because they consider it unscriptural.

In sum, while the list attempts to be reasonably accurate and inclusive, we make no claim to definitive scholarship. Its purposes, as noted above, are practical, with the classroom teacher in mind.

In any particular community a teacher may never meet a person who represents a specific religious position listed here, especially if it is held by a group with only a few hundred members. Conversely, the teacher may be disappointed not to find a belief, practice, biblical passage, or religious group that is truly important in his or her local situation. In such instances—and in the inevitable cases of errors—we sincerely solicit suggestions for a possible future revised edition.

We use the term *sect* throughout the list. It is intended to be neutral, synonymous with *religious group* or *community, denomination,* or *church.* Quotations are from the KJV, whose very language has influenced the wording or form of some beliefs and practices. Generally, we follow the spelling in the American Bible Society edition, with some updating and Americanization of the punctuation. Principal references have been Frank S. Mead, *Handbook of Denominations* (Abingdon, 1975); Walter M. Abbott S.J., et al., *The Bible Reader* (Chapman, Bruce, 1969); and Leo Rosten, *Religions of America* (Simon and Schuster, 1975); as well as the usual dictionaries, encyclopedias, and commentaries.

Gen. 1:5. <u>Day starts and ends at sunset</u> (e.g., Jews, Baha'is)
The evening and the morning were the first day.

Gen. 1:5ff. <u>Names of days of week: First Day, Second Day, etc.</u>
(e.g., Quakers, the Hebrew language)
The evening and the morning were the first day.
(Note: For Quakers, the months are also named by ordinal
numbers, beginning with January as First Month.)

Gen. 1:28. <u>Opposition to birth control</u> (many sects; also basis
of many laws in the U.S.)
Be fruitful, and multiply.
(Note: See also Gen. 38:9, 10.*)

Gen. 1:29. <u>Vegetarianism</u> (e.g., Jesus movement, House of
David*)*
*Behold, I have given you every herb bearing seed, which is
upon the face of all the earth, and every tree, in the
which is the fruit of a tree yielding seed; to you it
shall be for meat [food].*

Gen. 1:31. <u>Nonreality of material world of evil and pain</u>
(Christian Scientists)
*God saw every thing that he had made, and, behold, it was
very good.*

Gen. 3:6. <u>Prelapsarian evil inclination/seed in man's nature</u>
(Jews, Two-Seed-in-the-Spirit Predestinarian Baptists)
*When the woman saw that the tree was good for food, and that
it was pleasant to the eyes, and a tree to be desired to
make one wise, she took of the fruit thereof, and did eat,
and gave also unto her husband with her; and he did eat.*
(Note: One group says the tendency comes from God; the
other, from the devil. See also Gen. 6:5 and 8:21.)

Gen. 3:6. <u>Doctrine of Original Sin / Fall of Man</u> (many Christian sects)
*She took of the fruit thereof, and did eat, and gave also
unto her husband with her; and he did eat.*
(Note: See also Rom. 5:12* and Ps. 51:5.)

---

*Quoted in this chapter

144

Gen. 3:19. Work ethic (Puritan/Protestant)

In the sweat of thy face shalt thou eat bread.

Gen. 3:19. Holy day: Ash Wednesday, first day of Lent (e.g.,
Catholics)

Dust thou art, / and unto dust shalt thou return.

(Note: Palms from Palm Sunday are burned and their ashes
put on the communicant's forehead, with this reminder.)

Gen. 6:18. Sect name (Covenanters) and doctrine of chosenness/
election (e.g., Orthodox and Conservative Jews, Calvinists)

With thee will I establish my covenant.

(Note: This is merely the first occurrence of the word in
the Bible. See also Rom. 11:55.*)

Gen. 11:9. Settling in America by refugees from Babel (Book of
Mormon)

*From thence did the Lord scatter them abroad upon the face
of all the earth.*

Gen. 17:10,12. Rite of circumcision (e.g., Jews, Moslems)

*This is my covenant, which ye shall keep, between me and
you and thy seed after thee; Every man child among you
shall be circumcised. . . . He that is eight days old
shall be circumcised.*

(Note: See also Lk. 2:21.* Moslem boys are circumcised
later than eight days old.)

Gen. 18:32. Quorum of ten for a congregation/public worship/
minyan (Jews)

I will not destroy it [Sodom] for ten's sake.

(Note: Ruth 4:2 and Num. 14:27 are also cited.)

Gen. 29:28. Plural marriage (some Mormons)

*He [Laban] gave him [Jacob] Rachel his daughter to wife
also.*

(Note: This is the earliest explicit case in the Bible.
See also Ex. 21:10.*)

Gen. 38:9-10. Opposition to birth control

*Onan knew that the seed should not be his; . . . he spilled
it on the ground, lest that he should give seed to his brother.*

And the thing which he did displeased the Lord: wherefore he slew him.

(Note: Other texts are cited; e.g., Gen. 1:28.*)

Ex. 3:5. <u>Sect name: Kodesh</u> (Kodesh Church of Immanuel)
The place whereon thou standest is holy [Hebrew: kodesh].
(Note: This is merely the first occurrence of the word in the Bible. For Immanuel, see Is. 7:14.*)

Ex. 14:13. <u>Sect name: Salvation</u> (Salvation Army)
See the salvation of the Lord.
(Note: This is merely the first mention of the word in the Bible, where it appears in a military context. The word "army" in the name derives from the founder's metaphor of crusaders, to save souls rather than to recover the sepulcher.)

Ex. 14:24. <u>Sect name: Pillar of Fire</u> (Pillar of Fire Church)
The Lord looked unto the host of the Egyptians through the pillar of fire.

Ex. 19:6. <u>All believers are priests</u> (e.g., Plymouth Brethren)
Ye shall be unto me a kingdom of priests.
(Note: See also Jn. 15:16,* Acts 14:23,* and I Cor. 12:11.*)

Ex. 20:4. <u>Prohibition against sacred pictures and sculpture</u>
(e.g., Jews)
Thou shalt not make unto thee any graven image.
(Note: Eastern Orthodox churches distinguish between sculpture, which is forbidden, and pictures, which are not. At various periods, Jews have taken this passage—and others, notably Deut. 4:16-18—to forbid all art, secular and religious; at other times, only representational art or only representations of human beings and animals, the minimal prohibition remaining against human representations within the sanctuary. The Bible describes sculptured cherubim and oxen in Solomon's temple. Moslems have no pictures at all in their mosques.)

Ex. 20:4, 5. <u>Opposition to the flag salute</u> (e.g., Jehovah's Witnesses)

Thou shalt not make unto thee any graven image, . . . thou shalt not bow down thyself to them.

Ex. 20:7. <u>Opposition to swearing oaths</u> (e.g., Quakers, Amish)

Thou shalt not take the name of the Lord thy God in vain.

(Note: See also Mt. 5:34.*)

Ex. 20:8-10. <u>Saturday as the sabbath</u> (e.g., Jews, Seventh-day Adventists, other Sabbatarians)

Remember the sabbath day, to keep it holy. Six days shalt thou labor, and do all thy work: but the seventh day is the sabbath of the Lord thy God: in it thou shalt not do any work.

(Note: See also Mt. 28:1* and Gen. 2:3. Adventists also cite the examples of Jesus and of his followers: Lk. 4:16 and Lk. 23:56.)

Ex. 20:13. <u>Pacifism; conscientious objection to military service</u>

Thou shalt not kill.

(Note: See also Deut. 20:8,* Mt. 5:44, and Jn 18:36.* The Bible version makes a difference here: some translations say "murder," leading people to except some instances of killing.)

Ex. 20:13. <u>Condemnation of suicide</u>

Thou shalt not kill.

(Note: Other passages are cited; e.g., 1 Jn. 3:15.)

Ex. 20:13. <u>Condemnation of abortion</u>

Thou shalt not kill.

(Note: See also Ex. 21:22, 23.*)

Ex. 21:10. <u>Plural marriage</u> (e.g., some Mormon sects)

If he take him another wife, her [the first one's] *food, her raiment, and her duty of marriage, shall he not diminish.*

(Note: See also Gen. 29:28.*)

Ex. 21:22-23. <u>Condemnation of abortion</u>

If men strive, and hurt a woman with child, so that her
fruit depart from her, and . . . if any mischief follow,
then thou shalt give life for life.
(Note: See also Ex. 20:13.*)

Ex. 22:18. <u>Condemnation of witches and witchcraft</u>
Thou shalt not suffer a witch to live.

Ex. 23:19. · <u>Objection to mixing foods: milk products and meat</u>
(e.g., Jews, some Sabbatarians)
Thou shalt not seethe a kid in his mother's milk.
(Note: This is a dietary law of kosher food.)

Ex. 26:33. <u>Use of iconostasis (icon-covered partition) between</u>
<u>altar and main church</u> (e.g., Eastern Orthodox)
The veil shall divide unto you between the holy place and
the most holy.

Ex. 28:1. <u>Priesthood of Aaron</u> (e.g., Mormons, Jews)
Take thou unto thee Aaron thy brother, and his sons with
him, from among the children of Israel, that he may minis-
ter unto me in the priest's office.
(Note: Some Jews today--often named Cohen [Hebrew: priest]
--have certain religious distinctions as descendants of
Aaron; so do others--often named Levy/Levine--who are considered members of the tribe of Levi. For notes on Christian priests, see Ex. 19:6* and Acts 14:23.*)

Ex. 34:18, 22-23. <u>The three pilgrimate holidays</u> (e.g., Jews, some
Sabbatarians)
The feast of unleavened bread [Passover] shalt thou keep.
. . . And thou shalt observe the feast of weeks [Pentecost],
. . . and the feast of ingathering [Tabernacles]. . . .
Thrice in the year shall all your men children appear be-
fore the Lord God.
(Note: See also Lev. 23:5,* Lev. 23:16,* and Lev. 23:34*
for each of the three festivals.)

Lev. 11:2-3, 7, 9, 13, 29. <u>Clean and unclean animals for food</u> (e.g., Jews, some Sabbatarians)

These are the beasts which ye shall eat. . . . Whatsoever parteth the hoof, and is cloven-footed, and cheweth the cud. . . . The swine, though he divide the hoof, and be cloven-footed, yet he cheweth not the cud; he is unclean. . . . These shall ye eat of all that are in the waters: whatsoever hath fins and scales. . . . And these are they which ye shall have in abomination among the fowls: . . . the eagle, and the ossifrage [vulture]. . . . These also shall be unclean unto you among the creeping things; . . . the weasel, and the mouse, and the tortoise.

(Note: These are dietary laws of kosher food. See also Deut. 14. Most Reform Jews do not observe them.)

Lev. 17:10; Acts 15:20. <u>Opposition to blood transfusions</u> (e.g., Jehovah's Witnesses)

I will even set my face against that soul that eateth blood.

Abstain from . . . blood.

Lev. 17:14-15. <u>Ritual slaughter of animals</u> (e.g., Jews, some Sabbatarians)

Ye shall eat the blood of no manner of flesh; . . . or that which died of itself, or that which was torn with beasts.

(Note: This is a dietary law of kosher food.)

Lev. 18:6ff. <u>Laws of consanguinity</u> (many sects; also laws in the U.S.)

None of you shall approach to any that is near of kin to him, to uncover their nakedness.

Lev. 18:22-23. <u>Condemnation of homosexuality and bestiality</u> (many sects; also laws in the U.S.)

Thou shalt not lie with mankind, as with womankind: it is abomination. Neither shalt thou lie with any beast to defile thyself therewith: neither shall any woman stand before a beast to lie down thereto: it is confusion.

(Note: See also Rom. 1:26* and 1 Cor. 6:9-10.)

Lev. 23:5-6. <u>Observance of the Passover/Pesach</u> (e.g., Jews, some Sabbatarians)

In the fourteenth day of the first month [Nisan] at even is the Lord's passover. And on the fifteenth day of the same month is the feast of unleavened bread unto the Lord: seven days ye must eat unleavened bread.

(Note: In the postexilic Jewish calendar, the spring lunar month of Nisan became the seventh month. See Ex. 34: 18.*)

Lev.23:16, 21. <u>Observance of the Pentecost/Feast of Weeks/</u> Shavuot (e.g., Jews, some Sabbatarians)

After the seventh sabbath [from the Passover] shall ye number fifty days. . . . And ye shall proclaim on the selfsame day, that it may be a holy convocation unto you.

(Note: See Ex. 34:18* and Acts 2:1.*)

Lev. 23:24. <u>Observance of New Year/Rosh Hashanah</u> (Jews)

In the seventh month [Tishri], in the first day of the month, shall ye have a sabbath, a memorial of blowing of trumpets, a holy convocation.

(The autumn lunar month of Tishri became the first month of the year in the postexilic Jewish calendar.)

Lev. 23:27. <u>Observance of Day of Atonement/Yom Kippur</u> (Jews)

On the tenth day of this seventh month [Tishri] there shall be a day of atonement: it shall be a holy convocation unto you; and ye shall afflict your souls.

(Note: See Lev. 23:24.*)

Lev. 23:34. <u>Observance of Tabernacles/Booths/Sukkot</u> (Jews)

The fifteenth day of this seventh month [Tishri] shall be the feast of tabernacles for seven days unto the Lord.

(Note: This holiday was the prototype for the original Puritan--not the present secular American--holiday of Thanksgiving. See Ex. 34:18* and Lev. 23:24.*)

Lev. 27:30, 32. <u>Tithing</u>

All the tithe [tenth] of the land . . . is the Lord's. . . . And concerning the tithe of the herd, . . . the tenth shall

be holy unto the Lord.
(Note: Other passages are cited; e.g., Mal. 3:8-11.)

Num. 15:38. <u>Use of prayer shawl/tallit</u> (Jews)
*Bid them that they make them fringes in the borders of
their garments, throughout their generations, and that they
put upon the fringe of the borders a ribband of blue.*
(Note: Orthodox Jews wear a "small tallit" under their
garments every day.)

Deut. 1:30. <u>Holy war</u> (e.g., many conservative sects)
*The Lord your God which goeth before you, he shall fight
for you.*
(Note: Many other passages refer to holy war; e.g., see
Judg. 7:18.* Today, the concept is applied literally mainly
in cases of "just wars"; otherwise, it is usually taken
metaphorically, if no less seriously.)

Deut. 6:4. <u>Confession of faith:</u> Sn'ma (Jews)
Hear, O Israel: The Lord our God is one Lord.
(Note: The Jewish formulation ends "the Lord our God, the
Lord is one.")

Deut. 11:20. <u>Use of encased scroll on doorpost: mezuzah</u> (Jews)
Thou shalt write them [Moses' words] *upon the doorposts of
thine house, and upon thy gates.*
(Note: The parchment scroll is inscribed with Deut. 6:4-9;
11:13-21.)

Deut. 20:5-8. <u>Exemption from military service</u>
*The officers shall speak unto the people, saying, What man
is there that hath built a new house, and hath not dedicated it? . . . Hath planted a vineyard, and hath not yet
eaten of it? . . . Hath betrothed a wife, and hath not taken
her? . . . Is fearful and faint-hearted? let him go and return unto his house.*
(Note: See also Ex. 20:13.*)

Deut. 23:2. <u>Inferior status of illegitimate children</u> (basis
for many such laws in U.S.; also for practices among some
sects)

A *bastard shall not enter into the congregation of the Lord.*

Deut. 24:16. <u>Protection of a deceased traitor's children</u> (basis for Article III, Section 3, of U.S. Constitution)
The fathers shall not be put to death for the children, neither shall the children be put to death for the fathers.

Judg. 7:18. <u>Sect name: Gideon</u> (Gideons)
Blow ye the trumpets also on every side of all the camp, and say, The sword of the Lord, and of Gideon.
(Note: See also Judg. 8:23.)

1 Sam. 26:23. <u>Sect name: Amanah</u> (Amanah Church Society)
Faithfulness. [Aramaic; Hebrew: emunah]
(Note: This is merely the first appearance of this form of the Hebrew word in the Bible.)

1 Sam. 28:14. <u>Materialization of spirits</u> (e.g., some Spiritualists)
She said, An old man cometh up; and he is covered with a mantle. And Saul perceived that it was Samuel.
(Note: See also Mt. 17:3,* Mt. 28:7,* and Lk. 1:28.*)

2 Sam. 5:7. <u>Sect name: Zion</u> (e.g., United Zion Church)
David took the stronghold of Zion: the same is the city of David [i.e., Jerusalem].
(Note: This is merely the first occurrence of the word in the Bible.)

1 Kgs. 18:19. <u>Name of order of friars: Carmelites</u> (Catholic)
Gather to me [Elijah] all Israel unto mount Carmel.
(Note: This is merely the first passage in the Bible that connects Elijah to Mt. Carmel. According to tradition, Elijah founded the order at Carmel.)

Esth. 9:26-27. <u>Observance of the Feast of Lots/Purim</u> (Jews)
They call these days Purim. . . . The Jews Ordained, and took upon them, and upon their seed, . . . that they would keep these two days . . . every year.

Ps. 51:1. Name of anthem: Miserere (e.g., Catholics, Episcopalians)

Have mercy upon me, O God. [Latin: Miserere mei, Deus]

Ps. 90:3-5. Funeral liturgy (e.g., Episcopal Book of Common Prayer, Jews)

Thou turnest man to destruction;/ and sayest, Return, ye children of men. For a thousand years in thy sight / are but as yesterday when it is past / and as a watch in the night. / Thou carriest them away as with a / flood; they are as a sleep.

Ps. 90:4. Days of creation are many years long (many sects)

A thousand years in thy sight are but as yesterday when it is past, and as a watch in the night.

Ps. 100:1. Name of hymn: Jubilate Deo

Make a joyful noise unto the Lord.

(Note: "Old Hundredth," an early melody for this psalm, is now used for the Protestant doxology "Praise God from whom all blessings flow.")

Ps. 110:4. Priesthood of Melchizedek (e.g., Mormons, Church of Illumination)

Thou art a priest for ever / after the order of Melchizedek.

(Note: Mormons consider the order of Melchizedek higher than their priesthood of Aaron, Jesus being the priest here promised, according to Christian tradition. One branch of Mormons, the Strangites, choose their high priest on this tradition. See also Heb. 5:9, 10* and Gen. 14:18.)

Ps. 130:1. Prayer for the dead: De Profundis

Out of the depths [Latin: de profundis] *have I cried / unto thee, O Lord.*

Ps. 148:1. Name of prayer: Lauds (Catholic)

Praise ye the Lord. [Latin: Laudate Deum]

(Note: Psalms 148, 149, and 150, all beginning with this expression, were part of this second, or dawn, prayer/office; today, it is usually combined with the first office, Matins, shortly after midnight.)

Is. 7:14. <u>Sect name: Immanuel/Emmanuel</u> (Kodesh Church of Immanuel, Emmanuel Holiness Church)

Call his name Immanuel [Hebrew: God (is) with us].
(Note: Christians traditionally apply the term to Jesus;
see Mt. 1:23. For Kodesh, see Ex. 3:5.*)

Is. 34:14. <u>The female demon and night monster, Lilith</u> (e.g.,
Jewish mystics)

*The screech owl [Hebrew: lilith; RSV: night monster] also
shall rest there, and find for herself a place of rest.*

Is. 43:12. <u>Sect name: Witnesses</u> (Jehovah's Witnesses)

Ye are my witnesses, saith the Lord [New World Translation:
Jehovah]*, that I am God.*
(Note: Other passages are cited.)

Jer. 7:18. <u>Title for Mary: Queen of Heaven/Regina Coeli</u>
(Catholics)

*The children gather wood, and the fathers kindle the fire,
and the women knead their dough, to make cakes to the queen
of heaven.*

(Note: Application of the title to Mary reinterprets this
context.)

Jer. 49:11. <u>Opposition to life insurance</u> (e.g., some Amish)

*Leave thy fatherless children, I will preserve them alive;
and let thy widows trust in me.*

Dan. 8:13-14; Dan. 9:24-25. <u>Date of day of judgment</u> (e.g.,
Adventists)

*How long shall be the vision concerning the daily sacri-
fice, and the transgression of desolation, to give both the
sanctuary and the host to be trodden under foot? . . . Unto
two thousand and three hundred days; then shall the sanctuary be cleansed.*

*Seventy weeks are determined upon thy people and upon thy
holy city, to finish the transgression, and to make an end
of sins, and to make reconciliation for iniquity, and to
bring in everlasting righteousness, and to seal up the vision and prophecy, and to anoint the Most Holy. Know*

> *therefore and understand, that from the going forth of the
> commandment to restore and to build Jerusalem, unto the
> Messiah the Prince, shall be seven weeks, and threescore
> and two weeks.*

(Note: Other passages are also cited. Sects interpret
these passages differently and disagree on the calculation
of the date; see Rev. 2-6.*)

Dan. 12:4. <u>Explosion of science as sign of the end of time/
last days</u> (e.g., some Adventists)

> *The time of the end: many shall run to and fro, and knowl-
> edge shall be increased.*

(Note: Another sign of the end is that this increased
technology will be accompanied by moral decay, as described
in 2 Tim. 3:1-9, and elsewhere.)

Zech. 8:19. <u>Fast of Ab</u> (Jews)

> *The fast of the fourth month, and the fast of the fifth.*

(Note: Zechariah is only listing the fast days here. The
ninth of Ab, the fifth month, is the traditional date of the
destruction of the first temple. The holiday commemorates
the destruction of the second temple as well.)

Mal. 4:5. <u>Christological reading of the OT</u> (Christian tradition)

> *Behold, I will send you Elijah the prophet before the com-
> ing of the great and dreadful day of the Lord.*

(Note: The christological reading consists of using this
passage as a link to the Gospel of Matthew, which follows
it in Christian Bibles, and in equating John the Baptist
with Elijah. This is merely one representative OT passage
among many that are interpreted in the NT or by Christian
commentators as foreshadowing the advent of Jesus as the
Christ/Messiah.)

2 Esd. 2:34,35. <u>Name of prayer: Requiem</u>

> *He shall give you everlasting rest. . . . Be ready to the
> reward of the kingdom, for the everlasting light shall
> shine upon you for evermore.*

(Note: The prayer differs slightly from the Bible. Latin:

Requiem aeternam dona eis, Domine; English: "Give
eternal rest to them, O Lord, and let everlasting light
shine on them." This prayer is the opening of the Introit
in the Latin mass for the dead.)

2 Macc. 10:5-8. <u>Observance of Feast of Dedication/Hanukkah</u>
(e.g., Jews, some Sabbatarians)
*The five and twentieth day of the same [ninth] month, which
is Chislev. . . . They kept eight days with gladness . . .
and sang psalms unto him that had given them good
success in cleansing his place [the temple]. They ordained also by a common statute and decree, That every year
those days should be kept of the whole nation of the Jews.*

2 Macc. 12:45. <u>Doctrine of purgatory</u> (e.g., Catholics)
*He made a reconciliation for the dead, that they might be
delivered from sin.*
(Note: Eastern Orthodox churches believe in a state prior
to and intermediate between heaven and hell, but not purgatory. See also 1 Cor. 3:11-15.)

Mt. 1:6-16. <u>Jesse window/tree</u> (many Christian sanctuaries)
*Jesse begat David the king. And David the king begat Sol-
omon. . . . And Jacob begat Joseph the husband of Mary, of
whom was born Jesus, who is called Christ.*
(Note: See also Is. 11:1 and Lk. 3:23-32.)

Mt. 1:16. <u>Sect name and doctrine:</u> Christ (e.g., Churches of
Christ)
*Jesus, who is called Christ [Greek: annointed; Hebrew: mes-
siah].*
(Note: This is merely the first occurrence of the term in
the Bible.)

Mt. 1:18. <u>Doctrine of the virgin birth</u>
*When as his mother Mary was espoused to Joseph, before they
came together, she was found with child of the Holy Ghost.*
(Note: See also Mt. 1:25 and Is. 7:14.)

Mt. 1:25. <u>Observance of Christmas, Jesus' birthday</u>

She had brought forth her firstborn son: and he [Joseph]
called his name Jesus.

(Note: See also Lk. 2:7, for other details of the nativity. Various sects celebrate the holiday on different
dates: some churches still use the Julian calendar, e.g.,
Armenian, on Jan. 6, and Russian Orthodox, on Jan. 7.)

Mt. 2:11. <u>Observance of Epiphany</u>

[The wise men] saw the young child with Mary his mother,
and fell down, and worshipped him.

(Note: The holiday commemorates three manifestations to
the world of Jesus' messiahship: to the wise men; at the
baptism--see Mt. 3:16,* and at Cana--see Jn. 2:11.*)

Mt. 2:16. <u>(Holy) Innocents' Day/ Childermas, Dec. 28</u> (e.g.,
Catholics, Episcopalians)

Then Herod, when he saw that he was mocked of the wise men,
was exceeding wroth, and sent forth, and slew all the chil-
dren that were in Bethlehem, and in all the coasts thereof,
from two years old and under.

Mt. 2:23. <u>Sect name: Nazarene</u> (Church of the Nazarene)
He came and dwelt in a city called Nazareth.

Mt. 3:11. <u>Opposition to infant baptism</u> (e.g., Baptists, Mennonites)

I indeed baptize you with water unto repentance.
(Note: Mt. 18:15-18* is also cited, making commitment to
discipline as well as repentance a part of baptism.)

Mt. 3:11. <u>Sect name: fire-baptized</u> (Fire-Baptized Holiness
Church; Pentecostal Fire-Baptized Holiness Church)
He shall baptize you with the Holy Ghost, and with fire.
(Note: See also Mt. 28:19* and Acts 2:34.)

Mt. 3:16. <u>Baptism by immersion</u> (many Christian sects)
Jesus, when he was baptized, went up straightway out of the
water.
(Note: See also Mt. 28:19* and Acts 8:38. For the idea
that baptism is like death and resurrection, see 2 Col. 2:
12* and Rom. 6:4.)

Mt. 3:16-17. <u>Observance of Epiphany</u>
Lo, the heavens were opened, . . . and lo a voice from
heaven, saying, This is my beloved Son.
(Note: See also Mt. 2:11* and Jn. 2:11.*)

Mt. 4:23. <u>Sect name and doctrine: gospel/evangel</u> (e.g., Evangelical churches)
Jesus went about all Galilee, teaching in their synagogues,
and preaching the gospel [Anglo-Saxon: good news; Greek:
evangelion] of the kingdom.
(Note: This is the first occurrence of the word in the
Bible. In the U.S., evangelicism is a conservative Christian position; in Europe, it refers to churches that stem
from Luther and that are distinct from the "reformed"
churches.)

Mt. 5:1. <u>Sect name: disciples</u> (Disciples of Christ)
His disciples came unto him.
(Note: This is merely the first appearance of the word in
the NT. It has been taken to apply to the 12 apostles, to
the 70 mentioned in Lk. 10:1, and to all followers of Jesus.)

Mt. 5:34. <u>Objection to taking/swearing an oath</u> (e.g., Quakers,
Amish)
Swear not at all.
(Note: See also Ex. 20:7* and Jas. 5:12. For the substi-
tution of affirming, see Tit. 3:8.)

Mt. 6:13. <u>Inclusion of the doxology in the Lord's Prayer/Our</u>
<u>Father</u> (Protestant and Eastern sects)
For thine is the kingdom, and the power, and the glory,
for ever.

Mt. 7:1. <u>Objection to jury duty</u> (some conservative Christians)
Judge not, that ye be not judged.
(Note: This position resulted in a case before the Minne-
sota supreme court.)

Mt. 7:12. <u>Christian formulation of the Golden Rule</u>

*All things whatsoever ye would that men should do to you,
do ye even so to them.*

Mt. 7:7; Rev. 3:20. <u>Sect name</u>: <u>open door</u> (Light of the Way
Open Door Church Fellowship, International)
Knock, and it shall be opened unto you.
*I [Jesus] stand at the door, and knock: if any man hear my
voice, and open the door, I will come in to him.*

Mt. 8:7-8; Mk. 7:29. <u>Healing at a distance</u> (e.g., Christian
Scientists)
*Jesus saith unto him, I will come and heal him. The cen-
turion answered and said, Lord, I am not worthy that thou
shouldest come under my roof: but speak the word only, and
my servant shall be healed.*
*He said unto her, For this saying go thy way; the devil
is gone out of thy daughter.*

Mt. 9:6. <u>Healing by enlightenment</u> (Christian Scientists)
*That ye may know that the Son of man hath power on earth to
forgive sins, (then saith he to the sick of the palsy,)
Arise, take up thy bed, and go unto thine house.*
(Note: Mrs. Eddy, founder of the sect, said that this story
inspired her to form her doctrines; the emphasis is on
enlightenment rather than on faith. See also Gen. 1:31.*)

Mt. 9:18,25. <u>Healing by laying on hands</u> (e.g., Pentecostals)
*There came a certain ruler, and worshipped him, saying, My
daughter is even now dead: but come and lay thy hand upon
her, and she shall live. . . . He went in, and took her
by the hand, and the maid arose.*
(Note: See also Mk. 16:17-18.*)

Mt. 9:20-22 <u>Healing by faith</u> (e.g., Pentecostals)
*A woman, which was diseased, . . . said within herself, If
I may but touch his garment, I shall be whole. But Jesus
turned him[self] about, and when he saw her, he said,
Daughter, be of good comfort; thy faith hath made thee
whole.*

Mt. 10:1,2. <u>Ruling council of twelve apostles</u> (e.g., Mormons)
When he had called unto him his twelve disciples, he gave
them power. . . . Now the names of the twelve apostles are
these.
(Note: See also Eph. 4:11.*)

Mt. 10:2. <u>Sect name: apostolic</u> (e.g., Apostolic Evangelical
Christian churches)
The twelve apostles.
(Note: This is merely the first appearance of the word in
the Bible. For "evangelical," see Mt. 4:23.*)

Mt. 10:9-10. <u>Vow of poverty</u> (e.g., Catholic monks)
Provide neither gold, nor silver, nor brass in your purses;
nor scrip for your journey, neither two coats, neither
shoes, nor yet staves.

Mt. 12:32; Mt. 25:46; Rev. 21:8. <u>Doctrine of eternal pun-</u>
<u>ishment</u> (many conservative Christian sects)
Whosoever speaketh against the Holy Ghost, it shall not be
forgiven him, neither in this world, neither in the world
to come.
These shall go away into everlasting punishment: but the
righteous into life eternal.
The fearful, and unbelieving, . . . shall have their part in
the lake which burneth with fire and brimstone: which is
the second [i.e., eternal] death.
(Note: Some sects define the "unforgivable sin" as failure or refusal to repent, which must precede forgiveness.)

Mt. 13:45-46. <u>Name of sacred book: The Pearl of Great Price</u>
(Mormons)
The kingdom of heaven is like unto a merchantman, seeking
goodly pearls: who, when he had found one pearl of great
price, went and sold all that he had, and bought it.
(Note: The book, by Joseph Smith, has equal authority with
the <u>Book of Mormon</u>.)

Mt. 16:18-19. <u>Primacy of the papacy</u> (e.g., Roman Catholics)
Thou art Peter, and upon this rock I will build my church;

and the gates of hell shall not prevail against it. And I
will give unto thee the keys of the kingdom of heaven.
(Note: Jn. 21:15-17 is also cited.)

Mt. 16:19.   Remission of sins (e.g., Catholics)
Whatsoever thou shalt bind on earth shall be bound in
heaven; and whatsoever thou shalt loose on earth shall be
loosed in heaven.
(Note: See Jn. 20:21-23.)

Mt. 17:1-2.   Feast of the Transfiguration, August 6 (e.g.,
Catholics)
After six days Jesus taketh Peter, James, and John his
brother, and bringeth them up into a high mountain apart,
and was transfigured before them.

Mt. 17:3.   Materialization of spirits (e.g., some Spiritualists)
Behold, there appeared unto them Moses and Elijah talking
with him.
(Note: See also 1 Sam. 28:14,* Mt. 28:7,* and Lk. 1:28.*
For some Spiritualists, Jesus is considered a medium con-
trolled by the spirits of Elijah, Moses, and John the Baptist.)

Mt. 18:15-16, 17-18.   Brotherly responsibility to others (e.g., Mennonites, Hutterites)
If thy brother shall trespass against thee, go and tell
him his fault between thee and him alone: if he shall hear
thee, thou hast gained thy brother. But if he will not
hear thee, then take with thee one or two more, . . . but if
he neglect to hear the church, let him be unto thee as a
heathen man and a publican. Verily I say unto you, Whatso-
ever ye shall bind on earth shall be bound in heaven; and
whatsoever ye shall loose on earth shall be loosed in
heaven.
(Note: See also Acts 2:44* and Jn. 3:17. This passage is
taken to define a person's obligation both to help others
and to submit to the discipline of the group. Acknowledg-

ment of these obligations is cited as an argument against infant baptism. See Mt. 3:11.*)

Mt. 18:20. <u>Quorum for a public worship service</u> (e.g., many Christian sects)
Where two or three are gathered together in my name, there am I in the midst of them.
(Note: See Num. 14:27.)

Mt. 18:20; Mt. 28:20. <u>Freedom of individual conscience and thought</u> (e.g., the Liberal Catholic Church, Quakers)
Where two or three are gathered together in my name, there am I in the midst of them.
I am with you alway, even unto the end of the world.

Mt. 18:35. <u>Laboring in love with an erring brother</u> (e.g., most Mennonites)
From your hearts forgive . . . every one his brother their trespasses.

Mt. 19:6. <u>Sacrament/ordinance of matrimony</u> (e.g., many Christian sects)
They are no more twain, but one flesh. . . . God hath joined [them] together.
(Note: See also Gen. 2:24 and Eph. 5:22ff.*)

Mt. 19:6. <u>Opposition to divorce</u>
What therefore God hath joined together, let not man put asunder.
(Note: See also 1 Cor. 7:10-11.)

Mt. 19:9. <u>Prohibition against marrying a divorcee guilty of fornication</u> (e.g., some Christian sects)
Whoso marrieth her which is put away [for fornication] doth commit adultery.

Mt. 19:12. <u>Vow of celibacy/chastity</u> (e.g., Catholic priests, monks, and nuns)
There be eunuchs, which have made themselves eunuchs for the kingdom of heaven's sake.
(Note: See also 1 Cor. 7:1, 8, etc.)

162

Mt. 22:21. <u>Obligation to be law-abiding citizens</u>
Render therefore unto Caesar the things which are Caesar's.
(Note: See Acts 5:29.*)

Mt. 23:8-10. <u>Opposition to clerical titles</u> (e.g., Jehovah's
Witnesses, some Brethren)
*Be not ye called Rabbi; for one is your Master, even
Christ; and all ye are brethren. And call no man your
father upon the earth: for one is your Father, which is in
heaven. Neither be ye called masters: for one is your
Master, even Christ.*

Mt. 24:29,30-31. <u>End of the world, second coming/Parousia, and
judgment day/doomsday</u> (many Christian sects)
*Immediately after the tribulation of those [last] days
. . . they shall see the Son of man coming in the clouds of
heaven with power and great glory. And he shall send his
angels with a great sound of a trumpet, and they shall
gather together his elect.*
(Note: This is merely the first mention of these ideas in
the NT. See also Acts 1:11 and 1 Thess. 4:14.*)

Mt. 26:28. <u>The NT as God's new covenant with Israel</u>
This is my blood of the new testament.
(Note: See Jer. 31:31 and Heb. 7:22.)

Mt. 27:29. <u>Symbolism of tonsures</u> (e.g., some monks)
They had platted [woven] a crown of thorns.

Mt. 28:1; Acts 20:7. <u>Sunday as the Lord's Day</u>
*In the end of the sabbath, as it began to dawn toward the
first day of the week, came Mary Magdalene and the other
Mary to the sepulchre.*
*Upon the first day of the week, when the disciples came
together to break bread, Paul preached unto them.*
(Note: For some sects, the Lord's Day has become the sabbath; see Ex. 20:8.* Article I, Section 7, of the U.S.
Constitution acknowledges that Sunday is a special day, as
have many state and local blue laws. See also Rev. 1:10*
and 1 Cor. 16:2. Sunday was decreed a public day of rest
and worship under the Roman Emperor Constantine.)

Mt. 28:5-6. <u>Celebration of the resurrection of Jesus: Easter</u>
The angel answered and said unto the women, Fear not ye:
for I know that ye seek Jesus, which was crucified. He is
not here: for he is risen, as he said.
(Note: For all sects, the date is movable, depending on
the lunar calendar. Eastern churches follow the Nicean
formula (325 CE); Catholics and Protestants, the Triden-
tine (1562 CE)--the council that also changed from the Julian to Gregorian calendar. Some Eastern churches adopted
the Gregorian and share the West's fixed-date holidays--
e.g., Christmas--yet differ for Easter.)

Mt. 28:7. <u>People living on in the spirit world</u> (e.g., some
Spiritualists)
He is risen from the dead.
(Note: See also 1 Sam. 28:14,* Mt. 17:3,* and Lk. 1:28.*)

Mt. 28:19. <u>Evangelism/missionary work</u> (a strong and general
Christian emphasis)
Go ye therefore, and teach all nations.
(Note: This is also a sect name: Missionary Church.
Church missionary work is generally classified as either
"foreign" or "home"—American.)

Mt. 28:19. <u>Sacrament/ordinance of baptism</u>
Go ye therefore, and teach all nations, baptizing them.
(Note: Sects differ about the method and meaning of this
ceremony; see Glossary. See also Jn. 3:5.*)

Mt. 28:19. <u>Doctrine of the Trinity</u>
Baptizing them in the name of the Father, and of the Son,
and of the Holy Ghost.

Mt. 28:19. <u>Trine/triune/triple immersion at baptism</u> (e.g.,
Brethren/Dunkers, Eastern Orthodox)
Baptizing them in the name of the Father, and of the Son,
and of the Holy Ghost.
(Note: See Mt. 28:19.* Dunkers baptize while the communicant is kneeling in water and then dunk the body three
times.)

Mk. 6:13. <u>Sacrament/ordinance of anointing the sick/ (extreme)</u> <u>unction</u> (many Christian sects practice one or both)
They [the apostles] . . . anointed with oil many that were
sick, and healed them.
(Note: See also Jas. 5:14.* For Catholics, unction for the dying, formerly "extreme unction," is now considered an instance of anointing the sick.)

Mk. 15:42. <u>Holy day: Good Friday</u>
[The day of the Crucifixion] was the preparation, that is,
the day before the sabbath.

Mk. 16:17,18. <u>Snake handling, drinking poison</u> (e.g., some Holiness Pentecostals)
These signs shall follow them that believe; In my name
shall they cast out devils; they shall speak with new
tongues; they shall take up serpents; and if they drink
any deadly thing, it shall not hurt them; they shall lay
hands on the sick, and they shall recover.

Lk. 1:28. <u>Messages from the spirit world</u> (e.g., some Spiritualists)
The angel came in unto her.
(Note: See also 1 Sam. 28:14,* Mt. 17:3,* and Mt. 28:7,* as well as other references to angelic messengers.)

Lk. 1:28. <u>Name of a devotion: Angelus</u> (Catholics)
The angel came in unto her, and said, Hail.
(Note: The angelic salutation of the annunciation gives its name to this prayer, traditionally announced by the "Angelus bell.")

Lk. 1:28. <u>Doctrine of immaculate conception of Mary</u> (e.g., Catholics)
Hail, thou that art highly favored [Douay: full of grace].
(Note: The inference from "full of grace" is that Mary herself was conceived without sin.)

Lk. 1:28; Lk. 1:42. <u>Name of prayer: Ave Maria/Hail Mary</u> (e.g., Catholics)

Hail [Mary], *thou that art highly favored* [Douay: full of grace], *the Lord is with thee; blessed art thou among women.*

Blessed art thou among women, and blessed is the fruit of thy womb [Jesus].

Lk. 1:31. Festival of the Annunciation/Lady Day, March 25 (e.g., Catholics)
Behold, thou shalt conceive in thy womb, and bring forth a son, and shalt call his name Jesus.

Lk. 1:46. Name of song/canticle: Magnificat
My soul doth magnify the Lord.
(Note: In Latin, the first word of the song is "magnificat.")

Lk. 1:68. Name of song/canticle: Benedictus
Blessed be the Lord God of Israel.
(Note: In Latin, the first word of the song is "benedictus.")

Lk. 1:69. Sect name: house of David (House of David)
[He] hath raised up a horn of salvation for us / in the house of his servant David.

Lk. 2:13-14. Singing of Christmas carols
Suddenly there was with the angel a multitude of the heavenly host praising God, and saying, / Glory to God in the highest.

Lk. 2:14. Greater Doxology/Angelic Hymn
Glory to God in the highest,/and on earth peace,/ good will toward men.
(Note: There are various versions of the hymn; in any case, it is differentiated from the Lesser Doxology/Gloria Patri, which begins "Glory be to the Father, and to the Son, and to the Holy Ghost.")

Lk. 2:21. Feast of the Circumcision/Holy Name Day (e.g., Catholics, Eastern Orthodox)
When eight days were accomplished for the circumcising of the child, his name was called Jesus.

(Note: For Catholics, it falls on January 1 and is a
holy day of obligation, commemorating Jesus' circumcision.
Eastern churches celebrate it as Holy Name Day. Circumcision, the Jewish naming day, gave way to christening.)

Lk. 2:22; Lk. 2:32. <u>Festival of the Purification and the Presentation: Candlemas, February 2</u>
*When the days of her purification according to the law of
Moses were accomplished, they brought him to Jerusalem, to
present him to the Lord.*

*A light to lighten the Gentiles,/and the glory of thy
people Israel.*

(Note: Catholics combine the celebration of the presentation of Jesus in the temple and blessing of candles with
that of the purification of Mary. Eastern churches add
commemoration of the meeting with Anna and Simeon. German
immigrants, settling near Punxsatawney, Pa., brought their
tradition of Groundhog Day, adapted from a medieval Scottish rhyme: "If Candlemas be fair,/ There'll be two win-
ters in the year." Scottish scansion was askew.)

Lk. 2:29. <u>Name of anthem: Nunc Dimittis</u>
Lord, now lettest thou thy servant depart in peace.
(Note: In Latin, the first words of this song of Simeon
are "nunc dimittis.")

Lk. 8:21. <u>Sect name: brethren</u> (Brethren, Christadelphians)
*My brethren are these which hear the word of God, and do
it.*
(Note: Several other passages apply; e.g., see Mt. 23:8.*
Christadelphos is Greek for "brother of Christ.")

Lk. 10:18; Is. 14:12. <u>Name for Satan/Devil: Lucifer</u>
I beheld Satan as lightning fall from heaven.
*How art thou fallen from heaven, O Lucifer [Latin:
light bearer], son of the morning!*

Lk. 16:22; Lk. 23:43. <u>Doctrine of Limbo</u> (e.g., Catholics)
*The beggar died, and was carried by the angels into Abra-
ham's bosom.*

Verily I say unto thee, Today shalt thou be with me in paradise.

Lk. 18:1. <u>Central role of prayer</u> (many Christian sects)
Men ought always to pray.

Lk. 22:19-20. <u>Sacrament/ordinance of Communion/Eucharist/Lord's Supper/Mass</u>
He took bread, and gave thanks, and brake it, and gave unto them, saying, This is my body which is given for you: this do in remembrance of me. Likewise also the cup after supper, saying, This cup is the new testament in my blood, which is shed for you.
(Note: The name of this ritual, its meaning, and its practices vary among sects. See Glossary.)

Lk. 24:44. <u>Christian acceptance of the full Jewish Bible</u>
All things . . . which were written in the law of Moses, and in the prophets, and in the psalms, concerning me.
(Note: In this view, "psalms" represents the Writings, the third section of the Jewish Bible. It also generalizes from OT prophecies about Jesus to all the teachings of the OT. For some sects, however, the NT nullifies some Mosaic laws.)

Jn. 1:9. <u>The inner voice/inner light</u> (e.g., Quakers, Salvation Army)
The true Light, which lighteth every man that cometh into the world.

Jn. 1:14. <u>Doctrine of the incarnation</u>
The Word was made flesh.
(Note: Other passages are cited.)

Jn. 1:29. <u>Name of prayer: Agnus Dei/Lamb of God</u>
Behold the Lamb of God!

Jn. 2:11. <u>Observance of Epiphany</u>
This beginning of miracles did Jesus in Cana of Galilee, and manifested forth his glory.
(Note: See also Mt. 2:11* and Mt. 3:16.*)

Jn. 3:3. <u>Doctrine of regeneration as necessary for salvation</u>
(e.g., Evangelical and "born again" Christians)
Except a man be born again, he cannot see the kingdom of
God.
(Note: The expression is usually interpreted as "accept-
ing Jesus Christ as personal Lord and Savior.")

Jn. 3:5. <u>Institution of sacrament/ordinance of baptism</u>
Except a man be born of water and of the Spirit, he cannot
enter into the kingdom of God.
(Note: See Mt. 28:19.*)

Jn. 10:11. <u>Sect name: good shepherd</u> (Church of the Good Shepherd)
I am the good shepherd: the good shepherd giveth his life
for the sheep.

Jn. 12:12-13. <u>Observance of Palm Sunday</u>
When they heard that Jesus was coming to Jerusalem [they]
took branches of palm trees, and went forth to meet him.

Jn. 13:4-5. <u>Observance of the love feast</u> (e.g., most Mennonites, some Brethren)
He riseth from supper, and laid aside his garment; and took
a towel, and girded himself. After that he poureth water
into a basin, and began to wash the disciples' feet, and to
wipe them with the towel wherewith he was girded.
(Note: See also Acts 2:42.*)

Jn. 13:14. <u>Ordinance of foot washing</u> (e.g., some Baptists,
some Methodists, some Mennonites)
Ye also ought to wash one another's feet.
(Note: See also Jn. 13:4-6,* Acts 2:42,* and Jn 13:10.
For some sects, this is not an ordinance but a practice.)

Jn. 13:34. <u>Observance of Maundy Thursday</u>
A new commandment [Latin: mandatum novum—► maundy] *I give*
unto you, That ye love one another.
(Note: The Gospels agree that the Last Supper occurred on
Thursday: the "day" of the Passover meal, according to the
Synoptics; but according to John, it was the day of prepa-
ration, presumably the day before the Passover meal, when

the paschal lamb was being slaughtered. Humble foot washing is thus connected with Maundy Thursday, as a symbol of
the "new commandment," as in Jn. 13:4-6.* By extension, it
is an occasion for giving charity to the poor.)

Jn. 13:34-35. <u>Doctrine of noncreedal, nonsectarian, pacifist
fellowship</u> (e.g., the Christian Congregation)
*Love one another, as I have loved you, that ye also love
one another. By this shall all men know that ye are my
disciples.*

Jn. 14:16; Jn. 14:26. <u>The Holy Spirit/Ghost as the promised
Comforter/Paraclete</u> (e.g., Disciples of Christ)
*I will pray the Father, and he shall give you another Com-
forter [Greek: paraclete], that he may abide with you for
ever.*

*The Comforter, which is the Holy Ghost, whom the Father
will send in my name, he shall teach you all things.*
(Note: Mary Baker Eddy described the "science of Christ"
as the Comforter promised here.)

Jn. 15:15. <u>Sect name: friends</u> (Society of Friends/Quakers)
*Henceforth I call you not servants; for the servant knoweth
not what his lord doeth: but I have called you friends; for
all things that I have heard of my Father I have made known
unto you.*

Jn. 15:16. <u>All witnesses for Christ are ordained ministers</u>
(e.g., Jehovah's Witnesses)
*Ye have not chosen me, but I have chosen you, and ordained
you.*

Jn. 16:13. <u>Belief in holy tradition</u> (e.g., Eastern Orthodox
churches)
*When he, the Spirit of truth, is come, he will guide you
into all truth.*

Jn. 17:19. <u>Sacrament/ordinance/rite of confirmation</u> (e.g.,
Catholics, Episcopalians, Lutherans)
*For their sakes I sanctify myself, that they might be sanc-
tified through the truth.*

(Note: Use of this passage makes a relation between confirmation and sanctification. The ceremony usually confirms an earlier baptism, though some sects combine the two; see Mt. 28:19.* See also Acts 8:15* and Acts 1:8.)

Jn. 18:36. Objection to political parties (e.g., Jehovah's Witnesses, Christadelphians)

My kingdom is not of this world: if my kingdom were of this world, then would my servants fight.

(Note: This passage is also cited by pacifists. See also Acts 5:29.*)

Jn. 19:17. Stations/way of the cross/via dolorosa

He bearing his cross went forth into a place called the place of a skull, which is called in the Hebrew Golgotha.

(Note: Nine of the 19 Catholic stations are biblical, and 5 are based on tradition. The first station is Jesus' condemnation to death by Pilate, the next 8 occur on the way to Golgotha/Calvary, and the last 5 take place at the cross and end with the entombment.)

Jn. 19:25. Name of hymn: Stabat Mater [Latin: the mother was standing]

There stood by the cross of Jesus his mother.

Jn. 20:23. Institution of the sacrament of penance/reconciliation (e.g., Catholics)

Whosesoever sins ye remit, they are remitted unto them.

Acts 1:9. Observance of Ascension Day/Holy Thursday (some Christian sects)

While they beheld, he was taken up; and a cloud received him out of their sight.

(Note: The holiday occurs 40 days after Easter.)

Acts 1:11. Doctrine of the second coming/Parousia (e.g., Adventists, Pentecostals, most Evangelicals)

This same Jesus, which is taken up from you into heaven, shall so come in like manner as ye have seen him go into heaven.

(Note: See also Mt. 24:29-31* and 1 Thess. 4:14.*)

Acts 1:20.   <u>Sect name: episcopal</u> (Episcopalians)

>   *His bishopric* [Greek: episcopē=overseership] *let another take.*

>   (Note: See also Acts 14:23.*)

Acts 2:1-4.   <u>Sect name and orientation: pentecostal</u> (Pentecostals, pentecostalism)

>   *When the day of Pentecost was fully come, they were all with one accord in one place. And suddenly there came a sound from heaven as of a rushing mighty wind, and it filled all the house where they were sitting. And there appeared unto them cloven tongues like as of fire, and it sat upon each of them. And they were all filled with the Holy Ghost, and began to speak with other tongues, as the Spirit gave them utterance.*

Acts 2:1.   <u>Observance of Pentecost/Whitsunday</u> (many Christian sects)

>   *When the day of Pentecost was fully come, they were all with one accord in one place.*

>   (Note: See also Lev. 23:16.*)

Acts 2:3.   <u>Sect name: fire baptized</u> (Fire-Baptized Holiness Church; Pentecostal Fire-Baptized Holiness Church)

>   *There appeared unto them cloven tongues like as of fire, and it sat upon each of them.*

>   (Note: See also Mt. 3:11.*)

Acts 2:4.   <u>Speaking in tongues: glossolalia</u> (e.g., Pentecostals)

>   *They were all filled with the Holy Ghost, and began to speak with other tongues, as the Spirit gave them utterance.*

>   (Note: The "spiritual gift of tongues" mentioned elsewhere is usually understood as the sudden ability to speak ecstatic words or sounds that are incomprehensible and that need interpreting. The context here suggests that the apostles suddenly had the ability to speak foreign languages.)

Acts 2:17. <u>Baptism by pouring/infusion</u> (e.g., Catholics)

I will pour out of my Spirit upon all flesh.

(Note: This passage quotes Joel 2:28. Other passages are also cited. See also Mt. 28:19.*)

Acts 2:42. <u>Observance of love [Greek: agape] feast</u> (e.g., most Mennonites, some Brethren)

They continued steadfastly in the apostles' doctrine and fellowship, and in breaking of bread, and in prayers.

(Note: See also Jn 13:4-6.*)

Acts 2:44. <u>Communal living</u> (e.g., Hutterites)

All that believed were together, and had all things common.

Acts 5:29. <u>Obeying human laws only when they do not conflict with God's laws</u> (e.g., Jehovah's Witnesses)

We ought to obey God rather than men.

(Note: See also Mt. 22:21* and Jn. 18:36.*)

Acts 6:3. <u>Church organization: deacons</u>

Look ye out among you seven men of honest report, full of the Holy Ghost and wisdom, whom we may appoint over this business.

(Note: The actual word "deacon" first appears in the Bible at Phil. 1:1. See also Acts 14:23.*)

Acts 8:15-17. <u>Ceremony of confirmation</u>

When they were come down, [Peter and John] prayed for them [the new converts], that they might receive the Holy Ghost: (for as yet he was fallen upon none of them: only they were baptized in the name of the Lord Jesus.) Then they laid their hands on them, and they received the Holy Ghost.

(Note: This ceremony is practiced and interpreted differently by various sects; see Glossary. See also Jn. 17:19.*)

Acts 8:31. <u>Dependence upon sectarian interpretation of the Bible</u>

How can I [understand what I read] except some man should guide me?

Acts 9:36,39. <u>Dorcas societies: sewing for the needy</u>
Dorcas . . . was full of good works and almsdeeds which she
did. . . . All the widows stood by him weeping, and show-
ing the coats and garments which Dorcas made, while she was
with them.

Acts 11:26. <u>Sect name: Christian</u> (Christian churches)
The disciples were called Christians first in Antioch.

Acts 12:3,4. <u>Celebration of Easter</u>
(Then were the days of unleavened bread.) And when he [Her-
od] had apprehended him [Peter], he put him in prison, . . .
intending after Easter to bring him forth to the people.
(Note: This is the only place in the KJV where the Greek
word <u>pascha</u> is translated as "Easter." The date differs
among Western and some Eastern Orthodox sects. See also
Mt. 28:5, 6.*)

Acts 14:23. <u>Sect name: presbyter</u> (Presbyterians)
They had ordained them elders [Greek: presbyteros].
(Note: See next entry.)

Acts 14:23. <u>Church organization and officials: congregational</u>
<u>polity and priestly leadership</u>
They had ordained them elders in every church.
(Note: The Greek word is "presbyter." It is translated
"elders" in the KJV and elsewhere, "congregation" in Tyndale's Bible and elsewhere, "older men" by Jehovah's Witnesses, "presbyters" and "priests" in various Catholic versions. Thus sectarian organization varies: Prebyterians
and others have elders; Congregationalists and others make
the congregation predominant; Catholics, Episcopalians, and
Eastern sects have priests. Elsewhere, as in Phil. 1:1,
the word "episcopos"—overseer—is used, giving rise to
bishops in some sects. See Glossary. Here is merely the
alphabetical beginning of an incomplete list of church
titles: abbess, abbot, acolyte, apostle, apostolic delegate,
archbishop, archdeacon, archimandrite, archpriest—most of
which claim biblical origin. See also Mt. 10:1,2;* Acts 1:
20;* and Acts 6:3.*)

Acts 14:23. <u>Sacrament/ordinance of orders/ordination</u> (e.g., Catholics, Eastern Orthodox, Episcopalians)

When they had ordained them elders in every church, and had prayed with fasting, they commended them to the Lord, on whom they believed.

(Note: Other passages are also cited; e.g., Acts 6:3-6.)

Acts 15:6. <u>Ecumenical (and other) church councils</u>

The apostles and elders came together for to consider this matter.

(Note: This council at Jerusalem is the prototype for future such gatherings to decide church doctrine and procedures.)

Acts 17:23. <u>Name for attitude toward God:</u> Agnosticism

I found an altar with this inscription, To the Unknown God [Greek: Agnoste Theo]. Whom therefore ye ignorantly worship, him declare I unto you.

(Note: The term was coined by Thomas Huxley, who is said to have based it on the inscription quoted here.)

Acts 17:26. <u>Doctrine of the brotherhood of man</u>

[God] hath made of one blood all nations of men.

(Note: This is the principal passage cited for the doctrine by most Christians. Jews generally refer to Lev. 19:18 and Mal. 2:10.)

Acts 17:26-27; Acts 10:34-35. <u>Racial equality within a sect</u> (e.g., Jehovah's Witnesses)

[God] had made of one blood all nations of men for to dwell on all the face of the earth, and hath determined the times before appointed, and the bounds of their habitation; that they should seek the Lord, if haply they might feel after him. Though he be not far from every one of us.

God is no respecter of persons: but in every nation he that feareth him, and worketh righteousness, is accepted with him.

Rom. 1:26-27. <u>Sexual "crimes against nature"</u> (many sects: also laws against "unnatural sex acts" in the U.S.)

For this cause [worshiping and serving "the creature more than the Creator"] *God gave them up unto vile affections* [passions]: *for even their women did change the natural use into that which is against nature: and likewise also the men, leaving the natural use of the women, burned in their lust one toward another; men with men working that which is unseemly.*

(Note: See also Lev. 18:22,23*.)

Rom. 3:23-24. <u>Justification by grace</u> (a traditional Protestant accent)

All have sinned, and come short of the glory of God; being justified freely by his grace through the redemption that is in Christ Jesus.

(Note: "Justification" usually means freeing from guilt and the penalty of a serious sin, as here. Sometimes it means being judged innocent, acquitted.)

Rom. 3:28. <u>Justification by faith</u> (a traditional Protestant accent)

We conclude that a man is justified by faith without the deeds of the law.

(Note: See also Gen. 15:6 and Rom. 1:17. Compare with Jas. 2:24,26.)

Rom. 5:12. <u>Doctrine of Original Sin</u> (many Christian sects)

As by one man sin entered into the world, and death by sin; and so death passed upon all men, for that all have sinned.

(Note: See also Gen. 3:6* and Ps. 51:5.)

Rom. 8:3. <u>New Testament supersedes the Old</u>

What the [old] *law could not do, in that it was weak through the flesh, God sending his own Son in the likeness of sinful flesh, and for sin, condemned sin in the flesh.*

(Note: Many other passages are cited.)

Rom. 11:5. <u>Doctrine of election</u>

At this present time also there is a remnant according to the election of grace.

(Note: Other passages are cited. See Gen. 6:18.*)

Rom. 12:2. <u>Rejection of materialistic values/"worldliness"</u>
(e.g., Old Order Amish Mennonites, some Brethren)
Be not conformed to this world.
(Note: Other passages are cited; e.g., see 2 Cor. 6:14.*)

Rom. 16:16. <u>Kiss of peace/brotherly love</u> (e.g., Catholics,
Brethren, some Mennonites)
Salute one another with a holy kiss.
(Note: Other passages apply. In some sects, members kiss
one another; in others, they kiss an image of Jesus or some
other object.)

1 Cor. 1:10; 1 Cor. 1:13. <u>Opposition to all sectarianism</u>
(e.g., some Brethren, some Church of God sects)
*Now I beseech you, brethren, by the name of our Lord Jesus
Christ, that ye all speak the same thing, and that there be
no divisions among you.*

Is Christ divided?

1 Cor. 2:9; 1 Cor. 13:12. <u>The nature of heaven</u> (Catholic doctrine)
*Eye hath not seen, nor ear heard,/neither have entered into
the heart of man,/the things which God hath prepared for
them that love him* [i.e., we know only that heaven exists].

Now we see through a glass, darkly, but then face to face.

(Note: That is, heaven, as a state of being, is seeing God
face to face, in this interpretation.)

1 Cor. 5:13. <u>Excommunication</u>
Put away from among yourselves that wicked person.
(Note: See also Ezra 10:8.)

1 Cor. 6:7. <u>Refusal to defend oneself in court</u> (e.g., Amish,
some Brethren)
*There is utterly a fault among you, because ye go to law
one with another. Why do ye not rather take wrong? Why do
ye not rather suffer yourselves to be defrauded?*
(Note: See also Mt. 5:39.)

1 Cor. 6:19; 1 Cor. 3:17. <u>Opposition to tobacco and liquor</u>
(e.g., Adventists, Mormons, Salvation Army, Church of God)
Know ye not that your body is the temple of the Holy Ghost
which is in you, which ye have of God?

If any man defile the temple of God, him shall God destroy;
for the temple of God is holy.

1 Cor. 10:16; 1 Cor. 11:26. <u>Sacrament/ordinance of Communion/</u>
<u>Eucharist / Lord's Supper/Mass</u>
The cup of blessing which we bless, is it not the communion
of the blood of Christ? The bread which we break, is it
not the communion of the body of Christ?

For as often as ye eat this bread, and drink this cup, ye
do show the Lord's death till he come.

(Note: These terms often apply to the specific practice,
to the service in which it occurs, and to the elements--
bread and wine--themselves. See also Lk. 22:19* and the
other Gospel accounts of the Last Supper. The expression
"the Lord's supper" occurs at 1 Cor. 11:20.)

1 Cor. 11:3; Tit. 2:4-5. <u>Subordination of the wife</u> (e.g.,
Mennonites)
The head of the woman is the man.
Teach the young women to be . . . obedient to their own
husbands.

1 Cor. 11:5-6. <u>Covered heads, long hair for women</u> (e.g., Amish, Catholic women in church)
Every woman that prayeth or prophesieth with her head un-
covered dishonoreth her head . . . . It [is] a shame for a
woman to be shorn or shaven.

1 Cor. 11:11. <u>Marriage for time and eternity</u> (Mormons)
Neither is the man without the woman, neither the woman
without the man, in the Lord.
(Note: Mormons interpret this to apply to heaven as well
as earth.)

1 Cor. 12:4ff. <u>Emphasis on spiritual gifts [Greek: charismata]</u>
(e.g., Pentecostals and charismatic sects)

There are diversities of gifts.

(Note: In this passage the list includes wisdom, knowledge, faith, healing, miracles, prophecy, discerning spirits, divers tongues, and interpretation of tongues. See
also Rom. 12:6-8; Paul's lists vary slightly. The Greek
word "pneumatikos" [spiritual things/gifts] is also used,
elsewhere, in the sense of charismata. See also Is. 11:2.)

1 Cor. 12:11; Rom 12:6-7. <u>No official church organization or
ordained clergy</u> (e.g., Plymouth Brethren)
All these [gifts] *worketh that one and the selfsame Spirit,
dividing to every man severally as he will.*
*Having then gifts differing according to the grace that is
given to us, whether prophecy . . . or ministry.*

1 Cor. 15:29. <u>Vicarious baptism of/for the dead</u> (Mormons)
What shall they do which are baptized for the dead?
(Note see also 1 Pet. 4:6.* Mal. 4:5,6 and 1 Pet. 3:18 are
also cited.)

1 Cor. 15:44; 1 Cor. 15:50. <u>Spiritual, not bodily resurrec-
tion</u> (e.g., Presbyterians)
[The seed] *is sown a natural body, it is raised a spiritual body.*
Flesh and blood cannot inherit the kingdom of God.

2 Cor. 6:14,17. <u>Opposition to intermarriage; also to joining
unions, world corporations, and secret societies</u> (e.g., Amish, some Adventists)
*Be ye not unequally yoked together with unbelievers. . . .
Be ye separate.*

Gal. 6:7. <u>Doctrine of inevitable compensation</u> (e.g., Church of
Illumination)
Whatsoever a man soweth, that shall he also reap.
(Note: This doctrine denies special rewards and punish-
ments at the hands of God. Other passages apply; e.g.,
Prov. 28:10.)

Eph. 1:21; Col. 1:16. <u>Hierarchy of angels</u>

[Christ is] *far above all principality, and power, and might, and dominion.*

By him were all things created, that are in heaven, and that are in earth, visible and invisible, whether they be thrones, or dominions, or principalities, or powers.
(Note: See Glossary.)

Eph. 4:5. Doctrine of the exclusiveness of truth (e.g., Jehovah's Witnesses)
One Lord, one faith, one baptism.

Eph. 4:11. Form of church government: apostles (e.g., Mormons, Catholic Apostolic Church)
He gave some, apostles; and some, prophets; and some, evangelists; and some, pastors and teachers.
(Note: See also Mt. 10:1,2* and Acts 14:23.*)

Eph. 5:22, 25. Sacrament/ordinance of matrimony
Wives, submit yourselves unto your own husbands. . . . Husbands, love your wives.
(Note: See also Mt. 19:6.*)

Col. 2:12. Baptism by immersion
Buried with him [Christ] *in baptism, wherein also ye are risen with him.*
(Note: This passage is particularly cited by Mormons. See also Mt. 3:16,* Mt. 28:19,* and Rom. 6:4.)

1 Thess. 4:11-12. Objection to welfare and pensions (e.g., Amish)
Work with your own hands, as we commanded you; . . . that ye may have lack of nothing.

1 Thess. 4:14; 2 Thess. 2:1-2; Heb. 9:27-28. Second coming and resurrection of the dead (e.g., Adventists)
If we believe that Jesus died and rose again, even so them also which sleep in Jesus will God bring with him.
Now we beseech you, brethren, by the coming of our Lord Jesus Christ, and by our gathering together unto him, that ye be not soon shaken in mind.
As it is appointed unto men once to die, but after this the

judgment: *so Christ was once offered to bear the sins of many; and unto them that look for him shall he appear the second time without sin unto salvation.*

(Note: Other passages apply; e.g., see Mt. 24:29-31* and Acts 1:11.*)

1 Tim. 2:9. <u>Objection to personal adornment for women</u> (e.g., Amish, some Baptists, Church of God)
Women [should] adorn themselves in modest apparel, with shamefacedness and sobriety; not with braided hair, or gold, or pearls, or costly array.

(Note: See also 1 Pet. 3:3. Similar restrictions apply to men—not to live according to the flesh; e.g., Rom. 8:5.)

1 Tim. 4:14; 2 Tim. 1:6. <u>Sacrament/ordinance of ordination/ holy orders and laying on of hands</u>
Neglect not the gift that is in thee, which was given thee by prophecy, with the laying on of the hands of the presbytery.

I put thee in remembrance, that thou stir up the gift of God, which is in thee by the putting on of my [Paul's] hands.

(Note: See also Acts 14:23.*)

2 Tim. 3:15-16. <u>Inspiration and authority of scripture</u> (a traditional Protestant accent)
From a child thou hast known the holy Scriptures, which are able to make thee wise unto salvation through faith which is in Christ Jesus. All Scripture is given by inspiration of God, and is profitable for doctrine, for reproof, for correction, for instruction in righteousness.

(Note: See also 2 Pet. 1:21.)

Heb. 5:9-10. <u>Chosen ones in the priestly line of Melchizedek</u>
(e.g., Church of Illumination, Mormons)
Being made perfect, he [Christ] became the author of eternal salvation unto all them that obey him; called of God a high priest after the order of Melchizedek.

(Note: See also Ps. 110:4,* Gen. 14:18, and Heb. 7:1-26.)

Heb. 6:1-2. <u>Sect name: six principles</u> (Six Principle Baptists)

Leaving the principles of the doctrine of Christ, let us go on unto perfections; not laying again the foundation of <u>repentance</u> from dead works, and of <u>faith</u> toward God, of the doctrine of <u>baptisms</u>, and of <u>laying on of hands</u>, and of <u>resurrection of the dead</u>, and of <u>eternal judgment</u>.

Heb. 10:22. <u>Baptism by sprinkling</u> (e.g., Methodists)

Let us draw near with a true heart in full assurance of faith, having our hearts sprinkled from an evil conscience. (Note: See blood sprinkling in the OT; e.g., Lev. 8:30. See also Mt. 28:19.*)

Jas. 1:5. <u>Revelation to a modern prophet</u> (Mormon Joseph Smith)

If any of you lack wisdom, let him ask of God, that giveth to all men liberally, and upbraideth not; and it shall be given him.

Jas. 5:14. <u>Sacrament/ordinance of anointing the sick/(extreme) unction</u>

Is any sick among you? let him call for the elders of the church; and let them pray over him, anointing him with oil in the name of the Lord.

(Note: See also Mk. 6:13.*)

Jas. 5:15. <u>Miraculous healing of sick by prayer</u> (e.g., Assemblies of God)

The prayer of faith shall save the sick, and the Lord shall raise him up.

1 Pet. 4:6. <u>Posthumous baptism and salvation</u>

For this cause was the gospel preached also to them that are dead, that they might be judged according to men in the flesh, but live according to God in the spirit.
(Note: See also 1 Cor. 15:29.* Mal. 4:5,6 and 1 Pet. 3:13 are also cited.)

1 Jn. 2:18. <u>Doctrine of the Antichrist</u>

Ye have heard that antichrist shall come.
(Note: The Antichrist is usually identified biblically as

the Beast of Revelation and historically as any powerful
opponent of Christianity.)

Rev. 1:10. Observance of Sunday as the Lord's Day
I was in the spirit on the Lord's day.
(Note: See also Lk. 24:1,* Acts 20:7, and 1 Cor. 16:2.)

Rev. 3:12. Sect name: new Jerusalem (Church of the New Jerusalem, Swedenborgian)
*The city of my God, which is new Jerusalem, which cometh
down out of heaven.*
(Note: See also Rev. 21:2,10.)

Rev. 10:7. Sect's founder as the seventh messenger (House of
David)
*In the days of the voice of the seventh angel, when he
shall begin to sound, the mystery of God should be finished.*
(Note: Benjamin Parnell, founder of the sect, is believed
to have been the messenger/angel mentioned.)

Rev. 14:3. The 144,000 who will reign at the Resurrection
(e. g., Jehovah's Witnesses)
*The hundred and forty and four thousand, which were re-
deemed from the earth.*
(Note: See also Rev. 7:4.)

Rev. 16:14, 16. (Name and place of) final war: Armageddon
*They are the spirits of devils, working miracles, which go
forth unto the kings of the earth and of the whole world,
to gather them to the battle of that great day of God Almighty. . . .   And he [Satan] gathered them together into a
placed called in the Hebrew tongue Armageddon.*
(Note: See also Rev. 20:8.)

Rev. 20:2-6. Doctrine of the millennium/chiliasm (e.g., Adventists and other millennialists)
*He laid hold on the dragon, that old serpent, which is the
Devil, and Satan, and bound him a thousand years, and cast
him into the bottomless pit, . . . and after that he must be
loosed a little season. . . .   And I saw the souls of them*

*that were beheaded for the witness of Jesus . . . and they
lived and reigned with Christ a thousand years. But the
rest of the dead lived not again until the thousand years
were finished. This is the first resurrection. Blessed
and holy is he that hath part in the first resurrection:
on such the second death hath no power.*

(Note: Sects differ in interpreting the sequence of these
events—especially whether the second coming/advent/parou-
sia of Jesus, the resurrection of the dead, and the final
judgment precede the 1,000 years—premillennialists—or
follow it—postmillennialists.)

Rev. 22:3. <u>Equality of women and of all oppressed people</u> (Quakers)

There shall be no more curse [in the new Jerusalem].

(Note: See also Rev. 21:1-5. Quakers, who believe they
have entered the Kingdom now, must live according to its
rules, in which the curse of oppression is removed.)

PART III
TEACHING AIDS

This section of the handbook is an omnium gatherum, with little claim to completeness—or even coherence. The division into chapters is in many instances purely arbitrary; some of the teacher and student materials are interchangeable. We invite teachers to look on these pages as mere suggestions for their own creative efforts.

CHAPTER 8

Teacher Materials

Chronologies

Historical Time Line for the Old Testament

Note: *All* dates are approximate, and many are strongly disputed.

2000–1400: Patriarchal Period
  Abraham, Isaac, Jacob, Joseph
  Hammurabi 1725–1685

1400–1020: Egypt and Canaan
  Moses, Joshua, Judges
  Exodus 1280
  Conquest of Canaan 1250–1200
  Judges 1200–1020

1020–928: The Early Kings
  Saul 1020–1000
  David 1000–965
  Solomon 965–928
  Kingdom divided 922

925–722: The Northern Kingdom—Israel (Ephraim)
  Ahab 870–850
  Elijah and Elisha 875–825
  Hosea and Amos 760–725
  Assyria (Shalmaneser V and his son Sargon) destroys kingdom 722

925–586: The Southern Kingdom—Judah
Isaiah 740–690
Jeremiah 625–585
Josiah finds "Book of the Law" 622
Ezekiel 595–570
Babylonia (Nebuchadnezzar) destroys Jerusalem 586

586–538/516: Babylonian Exile
Ezekiel 595–570
Persia (Cyrus) conquers Babylon 538

538–332: Persian Period (postexilic)
Temple rebuilt 520–15
Ezra and Nehemiah rebuild 450–400
Greeks (Alexander the Great) conquer Palestine 332

332–165: Hellenistic Period
Under Ptolemies of Egypt 300–200
Under Seleucids of Syria 200–165
Jewish revolt under Maccabees 166–160

165–65: Independent Hasmonean Kingdom
Independent treaties with Rome 161, 142, 134
Rome (Pompey) takes Jerusalem 63

65 B.C.E.–fifth century C.E.: Roman Period
The Herodians
Julius Caesar assassinated 44 B.C.E.
Augustus Caesar 27 B.C.E.–14 C.E.
Jesus 5 B.C.E.–30 C.E.
Paul d. 64 C.E.
Rome burned 65 C.E.
Jerusalem destroyed 70 C.E.
Bar Kochba revolt 132/5 C.E.
(expulsion of Jews from Jerusalem)

New Testament Time Line

(Approximate dates)

5 B.C.E.–30 C.E.: Life of Jesus
30–70: Apostolic age

33/4: Paul converted

48/9: Apostolic conference in Jerusalem

50: I Thessalonians written by Paul

55/6: Paul arrested, imprisoned, voyage to Rome

50–58: Galatians, I and II Corinthians, Philippians, Philemon, Romans, (Col.) written by Paul

58–70: (Col.), (II Thess.) Ephesians, Mark written

66–70: Jewish war with Rome and destruction of Temple

70–125: Post–Apostolic age (or sub–apostolic age, in which case *post-Apostolic* refers to the period after 125 C.E.)

70–100: (II Thess.), Matthew, Luke, John, II Timothy, Hebrews, James, Revelation, (I Pet.), (Titus), (I–III John) written

100–125: (Titus), (I Pet.), (I–III John), I Timothy, Jude, II Peter written

150–200: Muratorian canon: Four Gospels, Pauline Epistles, Catholic Epistles

367: Athanasian canon (present NT)

The Writing of the Hebrew Scriptures

Most critical scholars think that nearly all scripture was first handed down orally, then circulated in writing, then edited, and finally officially closed. This last step is not always the same as canonization, which is official recognition of the edited work as sacred, not to be touched by hand. These scholars say that Hebrew Scriptures were *closed* in three sections:

1. *Pentateuch* (Hebrew: *Torah,* also called the Law), some time between 550 and 400 B.C.E. This is the first five books of our present Bible.
2. *Prophets* (Hebrew: *Nebi-im*), between 400 and 200 B.C.E. This section consisted of two parts, each with four books: the Former Prophets (Joshua, Judges, Samuel, and Kings) and the Latter Prophets (Isaiah, Jeremiah, Ezekiel, and The Twelve—"minor" prophets). Some of these books were later split.
3. *Writings* (Hebrew: *Ketubim*), 150 B.C.E.–90 C.E. There are three groups: poetry (Psalms, Proverbs, Job), the five scrolls (Song of Songs, Ruth, Lamentations, Ecclesiastes, and Esther), and three histories (Daniel, Ezra/Nehemiah, Chronicles).

The "Hebrew" name for the complete Jewish Bible is *TaNaK,* an acronym formed from the initial letters of the Hebrew names of the three sections.

No two lists of dates for the development of the Hebrew Scriptures agree. Not only do conservatives and critical scholars differ about such things as *authorship* and *attribution* (see Part II, chap. 6); critical scholars themselves vary as much as two hundred years in some instances. Therefore, all dates used here are to be considered approximate at best and unacceptable to fundamentalists and most conservatives.

Many critical scholars agree that the oldest writing in the Bible dates from about 1200–1100 B.C.E. and includes the Song of Deborah (Judges 5) and some other poems. The latest writing of the Jewish Bible is often dated at 175–150 B.C.E., with Daniel considered the last book written down. Within these termini, here are a few dates:

1000–850 *J* materials written and edited in Southern Kingdom (Judah)

875–722 *E* materials written and edited in Northern Kingdom (Israel, Ephraim).

D materials collected and partially written; also stories of the four Former Prophets books

768–60 Amos, Hosea, Isaiah 1–39, Micah written and edited

700 *J* source and *E* source combined and edited; probably appears only in Genesis, Exodus, and Numbers

622/1 Book of the Law (major part of Deuteronomy) found and *canonized*

622–540 *D* document and the four Former Prophets books (also called deuteronomic history because influenced by *D* document) edited

Jeremiah, Ezekiel, Isaiah 40–55, Habakkuk, Obadiah, Naham, Zephaniah, and Lamentations written and edited

P materials collected and probably written

540–400 *JE* + *D* + *P* edited; Pentateuch closed and *canonized*

Haggai, Zechariah, Isaiah 56–66, Joel, Malachi, Ezra, Nehemiah, Ruth, Jonah, and probably Job written and edited

400–150 Rest of books compiled and edited

250 Prophets *canonized*

Pentateuch translated into Greek (Septuagint)

170 Ecclesiasticus, or Ben Sirah, written (not canonized by Jews)

125 First Maccabees written (not canonized by Jews)

90–100 C.E. Writings *canonized*

Reference Books

Basic List for Teachers

Bibles
  New American Bible
  New English Bible with Apocrypha, Oxford Study Edition
  Oxford Annotated Bible with Apocrypha (RSV)
  Harper Study Bible (RSV)
  King James Version, with references and concordance

Annotated Abridgments
  Abbott, W. M., et al. *The Bible Reader* (RSV). Chapman Bruce (paper).
  Chamberlain, R. B., et al. *The Dartmouth Bible* (KJV). Houghton Mifflin (paper).

Commentaries
  Black, M., et al., *Peake's Commentary on the Bible.* Nelson, OR
  Laymon, C. M. *The Interpreter's One-Volume Commentary on the Bible.* Abingdon.
  Brown, Raymond, et al. *The Jerome Biblical Commentary.* Prentice-Hall, OR
  Fuller, Reginald C., et al. *A New Catholic Commentary on Scripture.* Nelson.
  Cohen, A. *Soncino Books of the Bible.*
  Guthrie, D., et al. *The New Bible Commentary Revised.* Eerdmans.

Dictionary, Encyclopedia
  Buttrick, G. A., et al. *The Interpreter's Dictionary of the Bible.* Abingdon. 5 vols.
  The Family Bible Encyclopedia. Curtis (accessible to students). 22 vols.

Atlases
  Aharoni, Y., et al. *The Macmillan Bible Atlas,* OR
  May, H. G. *Oxford Bible Atlas,* OR
  Wright, G. E., et al. *The Westminster Historical Atlas to the Bible.*

Concordances
  Young, R. *Analytical Concordance to the Bible.* Eerdmans (KJV), OR
  Cruden's *Concordance to the King James Version* (paper).
  Ellison, John W. *Nelson's Complete Concordance of the Revised Standard Version.*

Teacher Texts
  Ackerman, J. S., et al. *Teaching the Old Testament in English Classes.*

Indiana University (paper). See pp. 447ff for additional bibliography and annotations.

Juel, Donald, et al. *Introduction to New Testament Literature.* Abingdon (paper).

Bartel, Roland, et al. *Biblical Images in Literature.* Abingdon (paper).

Gros Louis, Kenneth R. R., et al. *Literary Interpretations of Biblical Narratives.* Abingdon (paper).

Warshaw, Thayer S., et al. *Bible-Related Curriculum Materials.* Abingdon (paper).

Ryken, Leland. *The Literature of the Bible.* Zondervan.

Student Texts

Ackerman, J. S., and Warshaw, T. S. *The Bible as/in Literature.* Scott, Foresman (paper).

Life Series: *The Bible; Religions of Man.*

For others, see CLASSROOM TEXT, Part II, chapter 6, above.

General Articles in Several Bible Commentaries

Peake

The Authority of the Bible

The Bible as Literature

The English Versions of the Bible

The Geography of Palestine

Weights, Measures, Money, and Time

The Archeology of Palestine: I. Prehistoric and Early Phases; II. The Biblical Period

The Archeology of the Ancient Near East

The Languages of the Old Testament

Chronology of the Old Testament

Canon and Text of the Old Testament

The Ancient Versions of the Old Testament

The Literature of the Old Testament

Form Criticism of the Old Testament

Israel's Neighbors: I. Mesopotamia; II. Egypt; III. The Levant

History of Israel: I. To the Exile; II. Post-Exilic

The Social Institutions of Israel

The Religious Institutions of Israel

The Theology of the Old Testament

The Religion of Israel

Introduction to the Pentateuch

The Language of the New Testament

The Textual Criticism of the New Testament

The Early Versions of the New Testament

The Literature and Canon of the New Testament

Form Criticism of the New Testament

The Jewish State in the Hellenistic World

The Development of Judaism in the Greek and Roman Periods

The Roman Empire in the First Century

Contemporary Jewish Religion

Pagan Religion at the Coming of Christianity

The Doctrine of the Church in the New Testament

The Constitution of the Church in the New Testament

The Chronology of the New Testament

The Life and Teaching of Jesus

The Synoptic Problem

The Theology of the New Testament

Jerome

Introduction to the Pentateuch

Israel and Her Neighbors

Introduction to Prophetic Literature

Hebrew Poetry

Post—Exilic Period: Spirit, Apocalyptic

Introduction to Wisdom Literature

Synoptic Problem

Modern New Testament Criticism

A Life of Paul

New Testament Epistles

Inspiration and Inerrancy

Canonicity

Apocrypha; Dead Sea Scrolls; Other Jewish Literature

Texts and Versions

Modern Old Testament Criticism

Hermeneutics

Church Pronouncements

Biblical Geography

Biblical Archeology

A History of Israel

Religious Institutions of Israel

Aspects of Old Testament Thought

Aspects of New Testament Thought

Pauline Theology

Johannine Theology

New Bible

The Authority of Scripture

Revelation and Inspiration

The History of Israel

Old Testament Theology

History of Literary Criticism of the Old Testament

Moses and the Pentateuch

The Poetry of the Old Testament

The Wisdom Literature of the Old Testament

The Apocryphal and Apocalyptic Literature

Between the Testaments

The Fourfold Gospels

The Pauline Epistles

Soncino

See the index for the *Chumash* volume, by Abraham Cohen; supplemented by the index to J. H. Hertz: *The Pentateuch and Haftorahs.*

Interpreter's

The History of Biblical Interpretation

The Historical Study of the Bible

The Theological Study of the Bible

The Unity Between the Testaments

The Word of God

The Fertile Crescent and Its Environment

The People of the Old Testament World

The History of Israel

Greece and Rome in the Biblical World

The Greco-Roman Background of the New Testament

The Early History of the Church

Archaeology

The Dead Sea Scrolls

The Hebrew Community and the Old Testament
The Literary Forms of the Old Testament
The Compiling of Israel's Story
The Law Codes of Israel
The Prophetic Literature
The Wisdom Literature
The Apocalyptic Literature
The Intertestamental Literature
The New Testament and the Christian Community
The Literary Forms of the New Testament
The Literary Relations Among the Gospels
The Letters of Paul
Noncanonical Early Christian Writings

The Religion of Israel
The Kingdom of God in the Old Testament
The New Testament Interpretation of Jesus
The Kingdom of God in the New Testament
The New Testament and Christian Origins

The Languages of the Bible
Writing in Biblical Times
The Making of the Old Testament Canon
The Making of the New Testament Canon
The Transmission of the Biblical Text
The Bible in English
The Bible in Every Tongue

The Impact of the Bible on History
The Bible and Preaching

Teaching the Bible to Children
Teaching the Bible to Youth and Adults

New Catholic
The Bible in the Life of the Church
The Formation and History of the Canon (OT and NT)
The Languages, Texts, and Versions of the Bible
History of the English Versions of the Bible
The Inspiration of Scripture
The Interpretation of the Bible
The Geographical Setting of Biblical History
The History of Israel
Archaeology and the Bible
Measures: Weights, Money, and Time
The Apocrypha of the Old and New Testaments

The Critical Study of the OT
The Religious Institutions of Israel
The Gentile Neighbors
The Chronology of the OT

The Text of the NT
The Jewish World in NT Times
The Pagan World in NT Times
Pagan Religious Movements and the NT
The Critical Study of the NT
The Forms of NT Literature
The Synoptic Problem
Jesus Christ in History and Kerygma
The Mother of Jesus in the Scriptures
Tradition and Theology in Apostolic Times
The Life of St. Paul
The Chronology of NT Times

Note: All these commentaries have tables and maps.

English Words and Expressions
Familiar Expressions and Words from the Bible

"In the beginning" (Gen. 1:1; John 1:1)

A tohu-bohu (Gen. 1:2)
"Saw the light" (Gen. 1:4; Acts 9:3)

"The lesser light" (Gen. 1:16)
"In his own image" (Gen. 1:27)
The garden of Eden (Gen. 2:8)
Forbidden fruit (Gen. 3:1-6)
Original sin (Gen. 3:6)
Adam's apple (Gen. 3:6)
The Fall of Man (Gen. 3:19)
The sweat of your brow (Gen. 3:19)
Dust to dust (Gen. 3:19 via *Book of Common Prayer*)
Cherub/im (Gen. 3:24)
"My brother's keeper" (Gen. 4:9)
The mark of Cain (Gen. 4:15)
"The land of Nod" (Gen. 4:16)
"East of Eden" (Gen. 4:16)
The deluge (Gen. 7:10)
Dove of peace; olive branch (Gen. 8:11)
Tower of Babel (Gen. 11:4)
The promised land (Gen. 12:5)
A tithe (Gen. 14:20)
"A good old age" (Gen. 15:15)
Fire and brimstone (Gen. 19:24)
"God will provide" (Gen. 22:8)
"Sold his birthright" (Gen. 25:33)
A mess of pottage (Gen. 25:33)
Jacob's ladder (Gen. 28:12)
"Beautiful" (Gen. 29:17, coined by Tyndale)
"The fat of the land" (Gen. 45:18)
Burning bush (Exod. 3:2)
"Milk and honey" (Exod. 3:17)
"Let my people go" (Exod. 5:1)
Bricks without straw (Exod. 5:7)
The exodus (Exod. 14:22)
"The fleshpots" (Exod. 16:3)
Manna from heaven (Exod. 16:15)
The Ten Commandments (Exod. 20:1)
"Thou shalt not" (Exod. 20:4)
A "graven image" (Exod. 20:4)
Sins of the fathers (Exod. 20:5 via *Merchant of Venice*)
An eye for an eye (Exod. 21:24; Matt. 5:38)
First fruits (Exod. 23:16)
Holy of holies (Exod. 26:13)

Heart of hearts (from above construction)
Inner sanctum (Exod. 26:33)
The golden calf (Exod. 32:1)
"Long-suffering" (Exod. 34:6)
A "scapegoat" (Lev. 16:8)
"A stumblingblock" (Lev. 19:14)
"Love thy neighbor" (Lev. 19:18)
The Golden Rule (Lev. 19:18; Matt. 7:12)
Lex talionis (Lev. 24:20; Matt. 5:38)
Sabbatical year (Lev. 25:4)
Jubilee year, golden jubilee (Lev. 25:10)
"Amen" (Num. 5:22)
"What hath God wrought!" (Num. 23:23)
"Your sin will find you out" (Num. 32:23)
"Not live by bread alone" (Deut. 8:3; Matt. 4:4)
Wife of my bosom (Deut. 13:6)
A "howling wilderness" (Deut. 32:10)
"The apple of his eye" (Deut. 32:10)
Cross over Jordan (Josh. 3:15)
Walls of Jericho (Josh. 6:20)
"Hewers of wood" (Josh. 9:21)
A "shibboleth" (Judg. 12:6)
Smite "hip and thigh" (Judg. 15:8)
"Jawbone of an ass" (Judg. 15:16)
They "arose as one man" (Judg. 20:8)
A hair's breadth (Judg. 20:16)
Solomon's temple (I Kings 5:5)
Cedars of Lebanon (I Kings 5:6)
"Whither thou goest" (Ruth 1:16)
"The flower of their age" (I Sam. 2:33)
"[Ac]quit yourselves like men" (I Sam. 4:9)
"The voice of the people" (I Sam. 8:7)
"God save the king" (I Sam. 10:24)
"A man after his own heart" (I Sam. 13:14)
He "played the fool" (I Sam. 26:21)
"How are the mighty fallen!" (II Sam. 1:19)
"My son, my son!" (II Sam. 18:33)
Gird your loins (I Kings 18:46)

"A still small voice" (I Kings 19:12)

He took up the mantle of his predecessor (II Kings 2:13)

A woman's painted face (II Kings 9:30)

Set your house in order (II Kings 20:1)

The wrath of God (II Chron. 28:11)

"Weeping, and wailing" (Esth. 4:3)

"Sackcloth and ashes" (Esth. 4:3)

"Give up the ghost" (Job 3:11)

"Fear . . . and trembling" (Job 4:14; II Cor. 7:15)

By "the skin of my teeth" (Job 19:20)

"The root of the matter" (Job 19:28)

"Day of wrath" (Job 21:30)

"In the land of the living" (Job 28:13)

"To the ends of the earth" (Job 28:24)

"Songs in the night" (Job 35:10)

Morning star (Job 38:7)

So far, and no further (Job 38:11)

"Stand in awe" (Ps. 4:4)

Out of the mouths of babes (Ps. 8:2)

"His heart's desire" (Ps. 10:3)

"Loving-kindness" (Ps. 17:7)

"My cup runneth over" (Ps. 23:5)

Clean forgotten (Ps. 31:12 via *Book of Common Prayer*)

Troubled waters (Ps. 46:3)

"Took sweet counsel together" (Ps. 55:14)

"Words . . . smoother than butter" (Ps. 55:21)

"Lick the dust" (Ps. 72:9)

This vale of tears (Ps. 84:6)

"Go from strength to strength" (Ps. 84:7)

"A tale that is told" (Ps. 90:9)

A twice-told tale (Ps. 90:9)

"Threescore years and ten" (Ps. 90:10)

"Down to the sea in ships" (Ps. 107:23)

"At their wit's end" (Ps. 107:27)

"Labor in vain" (Ps. 127:1)

"Out of the depths" (Ps. 130:1)

Bind up their wounds (Ps. 147:3)

Proverbial wisdom (Prov.)

Throw in one's lot with others (Prov. 1:14)

The bitter end (Prov. 5:4)

"Go to the ant, thou sluggard" (Prov. 6:6)

"Stolen waters are sweet" (Prov. 9:17)

"Tender mercies" (ironic) (Prov. 12:10)

"The way of transgressors is hard" (Prov. 13:15)

Spare the rod and spoil the child (Prov. 13:24)

"A soft answer turneth away wrath" (Prov. 15:1)

"Pride goeth . . . before a fall" (Prov. 16:18)

"The seeing eye" (Prov. 20:12)

"Heap coals of fire" (Prov. 25:22)

Know not what the day may bring (Prov. 27:1)

"Vanity of vanities" (Eccles. 1:2)

Nothing new under the sun (Eccles. 1:9 via RSV)

There is a time to/for . . . (Eccles. 3:1)

A time and place for everything (Eccles. 3:1)

"The house of mourning" (Eccles. 7:2)

Eat, drink, and be merry (Eccles. 8:15)

"The race is not to the swift" (Eccles. 9:11)

A fly in the ointment (Eccles. 10:1)

"Cast . . . bread upon the waters" (Eccles. 11:1)

Lily of the valley (Song of Sol. 2:1)

"The voice of the turtle" (Song of Sol. 2:12)

Ivory tower (Song of Sol. 7:4)

"Let us reason together" (Isa. 1:18)

"As white as snow" (Isa. 1:18)

"Swords into plowshares" (Isa. 2:4)

"Woe is me!" (Isa. 6:5)

"I am undone' (Isa. 6:5)

Seraph/im (Isa. 6:2)

The lion and the lamb shall lie down together (Isa. 11:6)

"And a little child shall lead them" (Isa. 11:6)

"Here a little, and there a little" (Isa. 28:10)

Set your "house in order" (Isa. 38:1)

A voice crying in the wilderness (Isa. 40:3; Matt. 3:3)

"In the hollow of his hand" (Isa. 40:12)

A drop in the bucket (Isa. 40:15)

No peace for the wicked/weary (Isa. 48:22)

"See eye to eye" (Isa. 52:8)

Like "a lamb to the slaughter" (Isa. 53:7)

Rise and shine (Isa. 60:1)

"Holier than thou" (Isa. 65:5)

Can the leopard change his spots? (Jer. 13:23)

"With all your heart" (Jer. 29:13)

Sour grapes (Jer. 31:29 and Aesop)

Like "lost sheep" (Jer. 50:6)

Wormwood and gall (Lam. 3:19)

"A wheel in . . . a wheel" (Ezek. 1:16)

Wheels within wheels (Ezek. 1:16)

Scatter to the winds (Ezek. 5:10)

"The parting of the way" (Ezek. 21:21)

Feet of clay (Dan. 2:33)

The handwriting on the wall (Dan. 5:5)

"Mene, mene, tekel, upharsin" (Dan. 5:25)

Tried and found wanting (Dan. 5:27)

Naked as the day she was born (Hos. 2:3)

Sow the wind and reap the whirlwind (Hos. 8:7)

Neither a prophet nor the son of a prophet (Amos 7:14)

He that runs may read (Hab. 2:2)

"Prisoners of hope" (Zech. 9:12)

Apocryphal story (Apocr.)

Communion (Ecclus. 9:10, by Wycliffe)

"Two edged sword" (Ecclus. 21:3)

"Let us now praise famous men" (Ecclus. 44:1)

"Kindhearted" (Song of Three Children 67, by Coverdale)

"The last gasp" (II Macc. 7:9)

The Gospel truth

"Star in the east" (Matt. 2:2)

Repent! The end of the world is near. (Matt. 3:2, 13:39)

"Generation of vipers" (Matt. 3:7)

Baptism by fire (Matt. 3:11; Acts 2:3)

Separate the wheat from the chaff (Matt. 3:12)

Sermon on the Mount (Matt. 5:1)

Beatitudes (Matt. 5:1)

The meek will inherit the earth (Matt. 5:5)

"Peacemakers" (Matt. 5:9)

"Salt of the earth" (Matt. 5:13)

"Good for nothing" (Matt. 5:13)

A city on a hill (Matt. 5:14)

Hide his light under a bushel (Matt. 5:15)

Not one jot or tittle (Matt. 5:18)

His yea is yea, his nay is nay (Matt. 5:37)

"An eye for an eye, and a tooth for a tooth" (Matt. 5:38; Lev. 24:20)

Turn the other cheek (Matt. 5:39)

Go the second mile (Matt. 5:41)

The left hand doesn't know what the right hand is doing (Matt. 6:3)

The Lord's Prayer (Matt. 6:9)

"Kingdom come" (Matt. 6:10)

"Our daily bread" (Matt. 6:11)

The power and the glory (Matt. 6:13)

"No man can serve two masters" (Matt. 6:24)

"Solomon in all his glory" (Matt. 6:29)

"Ye of little faith" (Matt. 6:30)

"Sufficient unto the day" (Matt. 6:34)

"Judge not, that ye be not judged" (Matt. 7:1)

Measure for measure (Matt. 7:2 via Shakespeare)

Casting "pearls before swine" (Matt. 7:6)

"Seek, and ye shall find" (Matt. 7:7)

Do unto others (Matt. 7:12)

The straight and narrow path (Matt. 7:14)

A wolf in sheep's clothing (Matt. 7:15)

By their fruits you will know them (Matt. 7:20)

"The dead bury their dead" (Matt. 8:22)

New wine in old bottles (Matt. 9:17)

A "lost sheep" (Matt. 10:6)

Judgment day (doomsday) (Matt. 10:15)

Shout from the housetops (Matt. 10:27)

A "house divided" (Matt. 12:25)

"He that is not with me is against me" (Matt. 12:30)

The unpardonable sin (Matt. 12:32)

Fall "by the wayside" (Matt. 13:4)

Whoever has, gets (Matt. 13:12)

Small as a mustard seed (Matt. 13:31)

A "pearl of great price" (Matt. 13:46)

Prophet without honor (Matt. 13:57)

Loaves and fishes (Matt. 14:17)

The blind leading the blind (Matt. 15:14)

"Signs of the times" (Matt. 16:3)

St. Peter, gatekeeper of heaven (Matt. 16:19)

"Get thee behind me, Satan" (Matt. 16:23)

Faith moves mountains (Matt. 17:20)

Labor in the vineyard (Matt. 20:2)

"The eleventh hour" (Matt. 20:6)

The "heat of the day" (Matt. 20:12)

The first shall be last, and the last shall be first (Matt. 20:16)

"A den of thieves" (Matt. 21:13)

"By what authority?" (Matt. 21:23)

"Made light of it" (Matt. 22:5)

"Many are called, but few are chosen" (Matt. 22:14)

Render unto Caesar (Matt. 22:21)

"Weightier matters" (Matt. 23:23)

"Strain at a gnat" (Matt. 23:24)

"Whited sepulchres" (Matt. 23:27)

"Wars and rumors of wars" (Matt. 24:6)

"The end is not yet" (Matt. 24:6)

Wise/foolish virgins (Matt. 25:2)

A talented person (Matt. 25:14)

"Well done (thou good and faithful servant)" (Matt. 25:21)

The poor are always with us (Matt. 26:11)

"Thirty pieces of silver" (Matt. 26:15)

The holy grail (Matt. 26:16)

The Last Supper (Matt. 26:26)

Break bread (Matt. 26:26)

"The spirit indeed is willing, but the flesh is weak" (Matt. 26:41)

Kiss of death (Matt. 26:49)

"Blood money" (Matt. 27:6, by Coverdale)

Buried in potter's field (Matt. 27:10)

Washed his hands of it (Matt. 27:24)

"Crown of thorns" (Matt. 27:29)

Crisscross (Christ's cross) (Matt. 27:32)

"Name is Legion"/they are legion (Mark 5:9)

"In his right mind" (Mark 5:15)

A camel go through the eye of a needle (Mark 10:25)

The widow's mite (Mark 12:42)

Hail, Mary (Luke 1:28)

"No room . . . in the inn" (Luke 2:7)

Glad tidings (Luke 2:10)

Peace on earth (Luke 2:14)

"Good will" (Luke 2:14)

"Physician, heal thyself" (Luke 4:23)

Shake the dust off your feet (Luke 9:5)

"Put his hand to the plow" (Luke 9:62)

"The laborer is worthy of his hire" (Luke 10:7)

Good Samaritan (Luke 10:23)

The halt and the blind (Luke 14:21)

A cross to bear (Luke 14:27)

Prodigal son (Luke 15:13)

Kill the "fatted calf" (Luke 15:23)

"Lo, these many years" (Luke 15:29)

"They know not what they do" (Luke 23:34)

Paradise (Luke 23:43)

"The wind bloweth where it listeth" (John 3:8)

"A shining light" (John 5:35)

"The truth shall make you free" (John 8:32)

"He is of age" (John 9:21)

"The good shepherd" (John 10:14)

"Lord and Master" (John 13:14)

"Behold the man!" (John 19:5)

Maudlin (John 20:11 from Magdalene/Madeleine)

"Touch me not" (John 20:17)

To every man according to his need (Acts 4:35)

Simony (Acts 8:18)

"No respecter of persons" (Acts 10:34)

The quick and the dead (Acts 10:42)

Cretin (from Christian) (Acts 11:26)

"Turned the world upside down" (Acts 17:6)

"Live, and move, and have our being" (Acts 17:28)

God willing/Deo volente (Acts 18:21)

Burned books in public (Acts 19:19)

"More blessed to give than to receive" (Acts 20:35)

"No mean city" (Acts 21:39)

Sit at the feet of (study under) (Acts 22:3)

"Fair Havens" (Acts 27:8)

"A law unto themselves" (Rom. 2:14)

The spirit, not the letter, of the law (Rom. 2:29)

"God forbid" (Rom. 3:31)

"The wages of sin" (Rom. 6:23)

The elect (Rom. 8:33)

Hint of "things to come" (Rom. 8:38)

"Brotherly love" (Rom. 12:10)

"Vengeance is mine" (Rom. 12:19)

"The powers that be" (Rom. 13:1)

"It is high time" (Rom. 13:11)

"Fully persuaded in his own mind" (Rom. 14:5)

"Eye hath not seen, nor ear heard" (I Cor. 2:9)

"Absent in body, but present in spirit" (I Cor. 5:3)

"All things to all men" (I Cor. 9:22)

"Sounding brass, or a tinkling cymbal" (I Cor. 13:1)

"When I was a child, I spake as a child" (I Cor. 13:11)

"When I became a man, I put away childish things" (I Cor. 13:11)

"See through a glass, darkly" (I Cor. 13:12)

Faith, hope, and charity (I Cor. 13:13)

"In the twinkling of an eye" (I Cor. 15:52)

"Death, where is thy sting?" (I Cor. 15:55)

"A cheerful giver" (II Cor. 9:7)

"Rude in speech" (II Cor. 11:6)

"Suffer fools gladly" (II Cor. 11:19)

"A thorn in the flesh" (II Cor. 12:7)

Gave the right hand of fellowship (Gal. 2:9)

"Fallen from grace" (Gal. 5:4)

Whatsoever a man sows, so shall he reap (Gal. 6:7)

"Tossed to and fro" (Eph 4:14)

Christian soldier (Eph. 6:11; II Tim. 2:3)

"Work out your own salvation" (Phil. 2:12)

"Press toward the mark" (Phil. 3:14)

Passes all understanding (Phil. 4:7)

"Labor of love" (I Thess. 1:3)

Like "a thief in the night" (I Thess. 5:2)

"The feeble-minded" (I Thess. 5:14)

"Filthy lucre" (I Tim. 3:3)

Old wives' tales (I Tim. 4:7 via Shakespeare)

"The root of all evil" (I Tim. 6:10)

"Holy Scriptures" (II Tim. 3:15)

"Fought a good fight" (II Tim. 4:7)

"Kept the faith" (II Tim. 4:7)

"Unto the pure all things are pure" (Titus 1:15)

"Pilgrims on the earth" (Heb. 11:13)

"The patience of Job" (James 5:11)

"The weaker vessel" (I Pet. 3:7)

"All of one mind" (I Pet. 3:8)

Cover a multitude of sins" (I Pet. 4:8)

Busybody (I Pet. 4:8)

"Antichrist" (I John 2:18)

The Alpha and the Omega (Rev. 1:8)

"The book of life" (Rev. 3:5)

The four horsemen (Rev. 6:2)

Palm of victory (Rev. 7:9)

"Washed . . . in the blood of the Lamb" (Rev. 7:14)

The grapes of wrath (Rev. 17:4)

A scarlet woman (Rev. 17:4)

The "bottomless pit" (Rev. 20:1)

The millennium (Rev. 20:4)

Second coming (Rev. 20:5)

"New Jerusalem" (Rev. 21:2)

The pearly gates (Rev. 21:21)

Streets paved with gold (Rev. 21:21)

"Clear as crystal" (Rev. 22:1)

Crystal clear (Rev. 22:1)

Biblical Sources of Literary Allusions:

Some Epithetical, Metaphorical, and Symbolical People, Places, and Things

A son of Adam (a man): Genesis 1:26ff

The old Adam (earthy part of a man): *Book of Common Prayer*

Adam's rib (a woman): Genesis 2:21

An Ananias (a liar): Acts 5:1-10

An Antichrist (an antagonist, opponent of Christ and the church): I John 2:1ff

Armageddon (the final war, holocaust): Revelation 16:16

Tower of Babel (confusion of language): Genesis 11:1-9

A Babylon (an evil city): Isaiah 14:4, 21:9, Revelation 17:1-7

Balaam's ass (a talking, balking animal that knows more than its master): Numbers 22ff

Beelzebub (the devil): Matthew 10:25ff

A behemoth (huge beast): Job 40:14-24

Sons of Belial (satanic men): Deuteronomy 13:13

Belshazzar's feast (profane orgy): Daniel 5:1

Bethlehem (in Judah—birth of David, Jesus)

The mark of Cain (denoting an outcast, on forehead?): Genesis 4:15

To raise Cain (create commotion)

A Calvary (a place or occasion of defeat, crucifixion): Luke 23:33

Marriage (wedding) at Cana (Jesus' first miracle): John 2:1-11

Canaan (the promised land): Genesis 12:5ff

Christ-like (pure, self-sacrificing): NT

From Dan to Beersheba (the length of the land): Judges 20:1

Daniel in the lions' den (saved by God): Daniel 6

Like David and Goliath (a small man defeats a giant): I Samuel 17

Like David and Jonathan (sworn brothers): I Samuel 18:1

Brother Jonathan (Uncle Sam): II Samuel 1:26

David the sweet singer/psalmist (harpist for Saul): II Samuel 23:1

King David (main events: Goliath, Bathsheba, conqueror, dynast): I Samuel, I and II Chronicles

City of David (Bethlehem, Jerusalem): Luke 2:4, II Samuel 5:9

A Dives (a rich man): Luke 16:19

A Dorcas (sewing—society—for the poor): Acts 9:36

A dove (of peace, hope): Genesis 8:8 (with olive branch)

The dove (Holy Spirit, Holy Ghost): Matthew 3:16, etc.

(Garden of) Eden (main concepts: innocence, Original Sin, Fall of Man, the apple, the serpent—Satan, the curse, expulsion): Genesis 2-3

Egypt (events, people: slavery, exodus, Joseph, Pharaoh, Moses, Aaron): Genesis; Exodus

Elijah (vs. Ahab and Jezebel, priests of Baal, widow's curse, flaming chariot, mantle): I and II Kings

Emmaus (Jesus breaks bread, reveals himself): Luke 24:13-25

Esau (sold his birthright for a mess of pottage): Genesis 25:21

Esther (saved her people from Haman): Esther

A daughter of Eve (a woman): Genesis 3:20

Ezekiel (visions: dry bones, wheels in air): Ezekiel

Fish (Christ)

The angel Gabriel (announces coming of Jesus, end of world): Luke 1:19; Revelation

Galilee (home area of Jesus): Matthew 2:22

A Gehenna (hell): II Kings 23:10

(The garden of) Gethsemane (place of Jesus' agony): Matthew 26:36

A balm in Gilead (relief): Jeremiah 8:22

Gog and Magog (invaders at Armageddon): Revelation 20:8 (Ezekiel 38, 39)

Golgotha (see Calvary): Matthew 27:33

A Goliath (a giant): I Samuel 17:4

Land of Goshen (best place to live): Genesis 45:10

Ham (Noah's son, ancestor of black people): Genesis 5:32ff

A son of Ham, Hamite (dark-skinned person, Negro, black African)

A Herod (a cruel ruler): Matthew 2:1ff (a raging villain—mystery plays)

Mount Horeb (see Mt. Sinai)

Isaac (sacrifice of, blessing Jacob): Genesis 17:19ff

Isaiah (most quoted prophet): Isaiah

Iscariot (*see* Judas)

Israel (main notions: slavery, wilderness, children of, Kingdom, lost tribes)

An Ishmael (outcast, wanderer, ancestor of Arabs): Genesis 16ff

Jacob (main events: Esau, Laban, dream, ladder, 12 sons): Genesis 25ff

James (apostles: son of Zebedee, James the younger) (Epistle) (Jesus' brother)

Jehovah (the Lord): Genesis 2:5ff

Jephthah (sacrificed daughter): Judges 11:1

A Jeremiah (prophet of doom, weeping reproacher): Jeremiah

A Jeremiad (lamentation)

Jerusalem (capital city, site of temple, Mt. Zion): Joshua 18:28

The/a new Jerusalem (city of God, heaven on earth): Revelation 21:2ff

A Jezebel (a wicked woman; painted face in the window): I Kings 16:31

A Job (patient sufferer): Job; James 5:10

John the Baptist (forerunner of Jesus; Salome and Herod, voice in the wilderness)

John (apostle son of Zebedee, beloved; Gospel; Epistles; the Divine, Revelation)

A Jonah (bringer of bad luck): Jonah

Cross over Jordan (to promised land; to heaven): Numbers 32:5ff; II Kings 2:6

Joseph (main events: coat, dreams, brothers, Egypt, Potiphar's wife, Pharaoh, famine)

Joshua (at Jericho, sun stands still): Joshua

Judah (Jacob's son, the lion; tribe; kingdom)

A Judas (a traitor): Matthew 26:47ff

Judith and Holofernes (saved her people by beheading the sleeping man); Apocrypha

A Lazarus (risen from the dead): John 11:2

A Lazar (leper; poor man, beggar): Luke 16:20

Cedars of Lebanon (wood imported for important buildings): I Kings 5:14

A Leviathan (huge fish): Job 41:1

A Levite (priest): Numbers 18:2

Lot's wife (pillar of salt): Genesis 19:26; Luke 17:32

Lucifer (devil; fallen angel, rebel): Isaiah 14:12

Luke (author of Gospel, Acts)

Mammon (wealth): Matthew 6:24

Mark (author of Gospel)

Mary, mother of Jesus (annunciation, sorrows, assumption?)
Mary (sister of Martha; Magdalene; woman taken in adultery?)
Matthew (apostle, publican; author of Gospel)
Law of the Medes and the Persians (unalterable): Daniel 6:8
A messiah (anointed ruler, deliverer, savior): Daniel 9:25; John 1:41
A Methuselah (very old man): Genesis 5:21ff
Michael (an archangel): Daniel 10:13; Jude 9; Revelation 12:7
A Moloch (a fire-eating idol): Amos 5:26
Moses (main events: Pharaoh's daughter; burning bush; rod—serpent,
    plagues, Red Sea; wilderness—Mt. Sinai, laws, books)
Nazareth (home of Jesus, Nazarene): Matthew 2:23
A Nimrod (mighty hunter): Genesis 10:8
Nineveh and Tyre (once-great cities): Nahum 1:1
Noah (ark and Flood, drunkenness): Genesis 5ff
Olive branch (peace): Genesis 8:11
Paul (Saul of Tarsus, apostle, Epistles, Acts, missionary)
Peter (Simon, apostle, Epistles, Roman bishop, gatekeeper of heaven)
Pharaoh (with Joseph, with Moses): Genesis; Exodus
A Pharisee (self-righteous): Matthew 3:7ff
A Philistine (reactionary; anti-esthetic): I Samuel 17:8
Pilate (Roman governor at trial of Jesus): Matthew 27:2
Pisgah, Nebo (high place from which to see the future): Deuteronomy
    34:1
Red Sea (crossing by Israelites, drowning of Egyptians): Exodus 14:21
Ruth and Naomi (loyal daughter-in-law, convert): Ruth
Salome (and John the Baptist, Herod): Matthew 14:6
A good Samaritan (offers help): Luke 10:33
A Samson (strong man): Judges 13:24ff
Samson (events: vs. Philistines; Delilah): Judges 13:24ff
Samuel (priest, judge, prophet; anointed Saul, David): I and II Samuel
Satan (devil, opponent of God): I Chronicles 21:1
Saul (and Samuel; and David): I Samuel 9:2ff
Serpent (devil, Satan): Genesis 3:1; Revelation 12:9
Shadrach, Meshak, and Abednego (three children of Israel in the fiery
    furnace): Daniel 1:7
Queen of Sheba (visited Solomon; from Ethiopia?): I Kings 10:1
Shem (Noah's son, ancestor of Semites): Genesis 5:32ff
Simon (apostles: Peter and Zelotes—the Zealot) (simony)
Mt. Sinai (Ten Commandments, sacrifice of Isaac)
Like Sodom and Gomorrah (wicked cities): Genesis 13:10

A Solomon (wise; proverbs, Song of; temple, glory, wives, judgment of): II Samuel; I Kings

Stephen (first Christian martyr): Acts 6:5

Susanna and the elders (falsely accused of wantonness): Apocrypha

A doubting Thomas (apostle, doubting): John 20:27

Tophet (devil): II Kings 23:10

Zion (Jerusalem): II Samuel 5:7ff

A Few Biblical Names in Many Fields:
Some Representatives

Anatomy: Adam's apple (thyroid cartilage: where apple stuck in his throat)

Buildings: Bedlam (insane asylum: from St. Mary of Bethlehem, London)

Lazaretto (for lepers: from sores of Lazarus the beggar)

Coins: Angel (English, 1465–1634)

Angelel (half angel, English)

Angelot (French, Louis IX)

Christian d'or (Danish, 19th c.)

St. Andrew (Scottish, 14th c.)

Jacobus (British: for James I, a biblical name)

Johannes (Portugal, 1722–1835: for King John, a biblical name)

Constellations: Columba Noae (Noah's dove)

Crux (the Cross)

Dressmaking: angel's sleeve   bishop's cotton

bishop's sleeve   bishop's lawn

Food: angel food, or angel cake

hot cross buns

Gunnery: angel shot

Horse racing: Shushan (a famous horse's name)

Journalism: Balaam basket (for rejected stories describing miracles)

Medicine: angel's wing (bone growth on shoulder)

apostle's ointment (had twelve ingredients)

Metallurgy: cristobalite (from San Cristóbal)

devil's marble (a kind of granite rock)

Perfume: angel water (a generic name)

Seafaring: nun buoy (conical shape, like nun's hat)

Shells: bishop's mitre (shape)

Silverware: apostle's spoon (with figure of an apostle carved on handle)

Wine: Holy Ghost wine

jeroboam (an oversized bottle of champagne)

Lachryma Christi wine ("Christ's tear": a sweet Neapolitan wine)

Other areas in which students might pursue biblical allusions:

Titles of pieces of literature, pieces of music, modern dance, films

Names of places, famous people, plants, animals

Advertisements, stamps, news headlines

Anything they read or hear

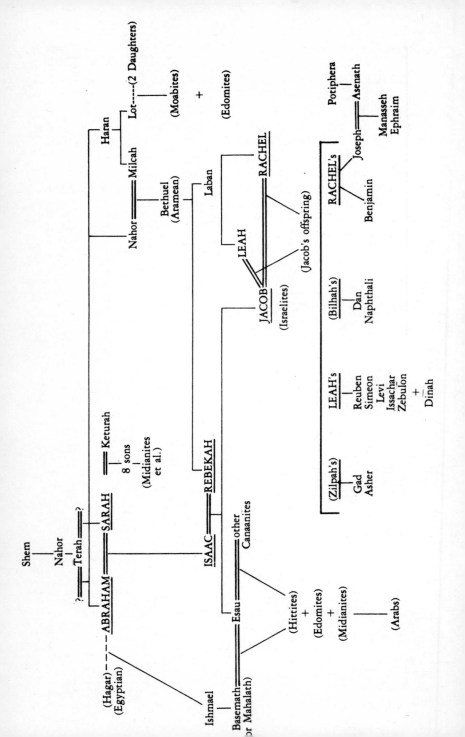

NOTES: Several generations separated Shem (son of Noah) and Nahor, Abraham's grandfather.
Abraham married his half sister. Keturah was his second wife (or concubine?).
Milcah married her uncle.
Lot had offspring by his own daughters.
Isaac married his cousin.
Esau married the daughter of his father's half brother.
Jacob married his cousins.
Both Abraham and Jacob had children by their wives' handmaids.

Herodians Who Appear in the New Testament: an abridged genealogy (from Josephus—and the NT, which conflicts at times)

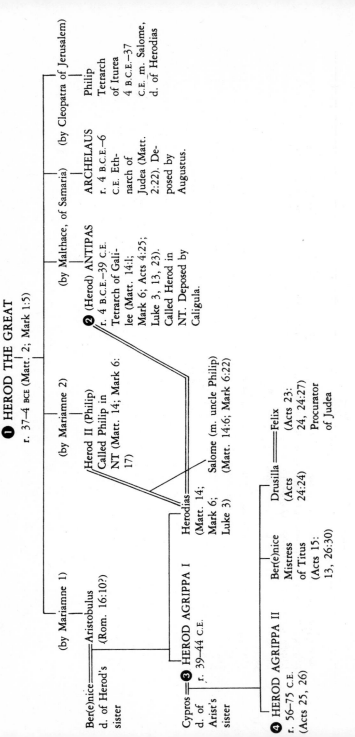

❶ HEROD THE GREAT
r. 37–4 BCE (Matt. 2; Mark 1:5)

(by Mariamne 1)

Ber(e)nice ═ Aristobulus
d. of Herod's (Rom. 16:10?)
sister

(by Mariamne 2)

Herod II (Philip)
Called Philip in
NT (Matt. 14; Mark 6:
17)

(by Malthace, of Samaria)

❷ (Herod) ANTIPAS
r. 4 B.C.E.–39 C.E.
Tetrarch of Gali-
lee (Matt. 14:1;
Mark 6; Acts 4:25;
Luke 3, 13, 23).
Called Herod in
NT. Deposed by
Caligula.

ARCHELAUS
r. 4 B.C.E.–6
C.E. Eth-
narch of
Judea (Matt.
2:22). De-
posed by
Augustus.

(by Cleopatra of Jerusalem)

Philip
Tetrarch
of Iturea
4 B.C.E.–37
C.E. m. Salome,
d. of Herodias

Herodias
(Matt. 14;
Mark 6;
Luke 3)

Salome (m. uncle Philip)
(Matt. 14:6; Mark 6:22)

Cypros ═ ❸ HEROD AGRIPPA I
d. of Arist's   r. 39–44 C.E.
sister

Drusilla ═══ Felix
(Acts   (Acts 23:
24:24)   24, 24:27)
               Procurator
               of Judea

Ber(e)nice
Mistress
of Titus
(Acts 15:
13, 26:30)

❹ HEROD AGRIPPA II
r. 56–75 C.E.
(Acts 25, 26)

Background: Antipater, Herod the Great's father, succeeded his own father, a forcibly converted Jew of Idumea, as military governor of Idumea; helped Hyrcanus II win Hasmonean throne from brother during Pompey's wars (63 B.C.E.) and retain it against revolts. Like his father, he helped Julius Caesar vs. Pompeii in Egypt (48 B.C.E.). Caesar made him a Roman citizen and procurator of Judea, with Hyrcanus as ethnarch and high priest. Antipater grew stronger, appointed one son, Phasael, governor of Jerusalem, and Herod, son by an Arabian/Nabatean wife, governor of Galilee.

Herod the Great killed father's assassin. Efficient in Galilee, made governor of Samaria (part of Syria). Cassius made him governor/procurator of all Syria. He invaded Jerusalem, ousting Hyrcanus, ruler of all Judea. Antony made him king (39 B.C.E.) and helped him kill all Hasmoneans (except wife Mariamne 1). Killed own sons. Founded Caesarea, rebuilt Jerusalem temple and palace, built many forts, Roman temples, amphitheaters. ❶ [SLAUGHTER OF THE INNOCENTS]

Herod the Great's wives numbered ten; four shown here. Mariamne/Mariamne 1 was granddaughter of John Hyrcanus (original Maccabee). Mariamne 2 was daughter of Simon the high priest.

Herod Antipas, who got one fourth of his father's kingdom, founded Tiberias, divorced his Nabatean wife to marry sister-in-law Herodias, whom he met in Rome, living apart from her husband, Philip. ❷ [JOHN THE BAPTIST; TRIAL OF JESUS]

Herod Agrippa I finally consolidated all grandfather's kingdom from other tetrarchs and ethnarchs. ❸ [IMPRISONED PETER]

Agrippa II, a minor on succession, waited six years under regency. Sided with Romans at Jewish revolt, 66 C.E. Moved to Rome with sister Bernice, 75 C.E., died at 100. Corresponded with Josephus about his book. ❹ [PAUL'S APPEAL TO ROME]

Philip (confused in NT with Herod II) founded Caesarea Philippi [Mark 8:22].

Student Materials

Bible Pretest and Answers

Bible Pretest

(First answer the questions you are sure of; then go back to the others.)

Part I—Old Testament

1. On the seventh day of creation (the sabbath) God _____.
2. Adam and Eve lived in the garden of _____.
3. Cain said, "Am I my brother's _____?"
4. Attempting to reach God's heaven, people built the Tower of _____.
5. Noah built the ark to escape the _____.
6. Lot's wife turned into a pillar of _____.
7. The cities of Sodom and Gomorrah were _____.
8. Abraham took his son Isaac up the mountain to be _____.
9. Jacob's ladder, with angels on it, extended to _____.
10. Jacob had twelve _____.
11. The coat of many colors belonged to _____.
12. Joseph was Pharaoh's governor in the land of _____.
13. The infant Moses was adopted by Pharaoh's _____.
14. God first spoke to Moses from a burning _____.
15. "Thus saith the Lord God of Israel: 'Let my people _____.' "
16. The promised land was "flowing with milk and _____."
17. To escape death, Israelites put on their doorposts blood of a _____.

18. After the Israelites crossed, the Egyptians were drowned in the _____.
19. For food in the wilderness God sent to the Israelites _____.
20. On Mount Sinai Moses received the Ten _____.
21. While Moses was gone, Aaron the priest made for the people a _____.
22. "Thou shalt love thy neighbor as _____."
23. Under Joshua the Israelites' trumpets brought down Jericho's _____.
24. In a battle God helped Joshua by making the sun _____.
25. The secret of Samson's strength was in his _____.
26. To create the first king of Israel, Samuel anointed the head of _____.
27. To soothe the king, David played the _____.
28. With a slingshot David killed the gigantic Philistine, named _____.
29. Absalom was David's _____.
30. Solomon was David's _____.
31. Hearing of his wealth and wisdom, the Queen of Sheba visited King _____.
32. Jezebel was Ahab's _____.
33. Two Old Testament books are named for women: Ruth and Queen _____.
34. Elijah was carried to heaven in a flaming _____.
35. God and Satan agreed to try the patience of _____.
36. "I am escaped with the skin of my _____."
37. "The Lord is my shepherd, I shall not _____."
38. *Hallelujah* means "Praise ye the _____."
39. Two books—Proverbs and Song of Songs—are said to be written by _____.
40. "A soft answer turneth away _____."
41. "There is no new thing under the _____."
42. "They shall beat their swords into _____."
43. "The wolf shall dwell with the lamb . . . and a little child shall _____."
44. "The voice of him that crieth in the _____."
45. In a valley Ezekiel saw a heap of dry _____.
46. The three Jews of Babylon were thrown into a "burning fiery _____."

47. At Belshazzar's feast there appeared handwriting on the _____.

48. Daniel was saved by an angel from a den of _____.

49. Daniel defended Susanna against wicked accusations of two _____.

50. Jonah spent some time inside a _____.

Part II—New Testament

51. Matthew, Mark, Luke, and John wrote the _____.

52. "In the beginning was the Word . . . and the Word was made _____."

53. Mary was told of the coming of Jesus on the occasion called the _____.

54. Jesus was born in a manger because there was no room in the_____.

55. Although Jesus was born in Bethlehem, he and his family lived in _____.

56. To escape from Herod, Joseph and Mary fled with their infant to _____.

57. Because "the kingdom of heaven is at hand," John warned people to _____.

58. Jesus went to his cousin John to be _____.

59. In the wilderness Jesus was tempted by _____.

60. Jesus' first miracle was at the wedding at Cana, where he created _____.

61. After Salome danced, she asked Herod for John the Baptist's _____.

62. Jesus fed the multitude of thousands with a few loaves and _____.

63. In one miracle Jesus raised from the dead a man named _____.

64. Jesus drove the money changers out of the _____.

65. The occasion of the Last Supper was probably the Jewish holiday of _____.

66. At the Last Supper Jesus said that the bread was _____.

67. Jesus was in agony as he prayed in the garden of _____.

68. The traitor Judas pointed out Jesus to the soldiers by _____.

69. Feeling no responsibility, Pilate publicly washed his _____.

70. The soldiers mocked Jesus and put on him a crown of _____.

71. The place where the crucifixion took place was called _____.

72. "Father, forgive them, for they know not what they _____."
73. The day of the week on which Jesus rose from the dead was _____.
74. The stories by which Jesus taught are called _____.
75. The man beaten by thieves was helped by the Good _____.
76. The man killed the fatted calf to welcome back his Prodigal _____.
77. Jesus' most famous teaching was the Sermon on the _____.
78. "Blessed are the meek: for they shall inherit the _____."
79. The Lord's Prayer begins, "Our _____."
80. "Man doth not live by bread _____."
81. "Seek, and ye shall _____."
82. "Every . . . house divided against itself shall not _____."
83. "Get thee behind me, _____."
84. "The last shall be _____."
85. "Render unto Caesar the things which are _____."
86. "Many are called, but few are _____."
87. "Behold the Lamb of _____."
88. "The spirit is willing, but the flesh is _____."
89. "Thou art Peter, and upon this rock I will build my _____."
90. On the Pentecost the disciples were filled with the Holy _____.
91. Stephen, the first Christian martyr, met his death by _____.
92. Saul saw the light, and was converted, on the road to _____.
93. The great missionary Paul wrote many _____.
94. "It is more blessed to give than to _____."
95. "And now abideth faith, hope, and _____."
96. "Whatsoever a man soweth, that shall he also _____."
97. "The love of money is the root of all _____."
98. "Washed in the blood of the _____."
99. "I have fought a good fight, I have kept the _____."
100. The four horsemen appear in the _____.

Bible Pretest Answer Sheet

1. rested
2. Eden
3. keeper
4. Babel
5. flood (storm)
6. salt
7. wicked, destroyed
8. sacrificed
9. heaven, the sky
10. sons

11. Joseph
12. Egypt
13. daughter
14. bush
15. go
16. honey
17. lamb
18. Red Sea
19. manna
20. Commandments
21. golden calf (idol)
22. thyself
23. walls
24. stand still
25. hair
26. Saul
27. harp
28. Goliath
29. son
30. son
31. Solomon
32. wife
33. Esther
34. chariot
35. Job
36. teeth
37. want
38. Lord
39. Solomon
40. wrath
41. sun
42. plowshares
43. lead them
44. wilderness
45. bones
46. furnace
47. wall
48. lions
49. elders, old men
50. great fish, whale

51. Gospels
52. flesh
53. annunciation
54. inn
55. Nazareth
56. Egypt
57. repent
58. baptized
59. Satan, the devil
60. wine
61. head
62. fish(es)
63. Lazarus
64. temple
65. Passover, Pesach
66. his body
67. Gethsemane
68. a kiss, kissing him
69. hands
70. thorns
71. Calvary, Golgotha
72. do
73. Sunday, the first day
74. parables
75. Samaritan
76. son
77. Mount
78. earth
79. Father
80. alone (only)
81. find
82. stand
83. Satan
84. first
85. Caesar's
86. chosen
87. God
88. weak
89. church
90. Ghost, Spirit

91. stoning, stones	96. reap
92. Damascus	97. evil
93. Epistles, letters	98. lamb
94. receive	99. faith
95. charity (love)	100. Apocalypse (Revelation)

Writing Assignments and Projects

Creative work by students is a particularly effective teaching/learning technique for several reasons. (a) It is adaptable throughout the entire range of ages and abilities in even the most heterogeneous secondary school classes. (b) It allows students to work individually or in groups. (c) It involves them in their own learning in ways that follow their personal interests and abilities. (d) It offers the choice of expressing themselves either by addressing only the teacher or by making a presentation to the entire class. In addition, the Bible is especially adaptable to creative student projects because of the pervasiveness of both its images and its themes in our culture.

The teacher also has the freedom and responsibility of choosing among alternatives. How often will student assignments be due: once a week, once a unit, once a semester? What limits will the teacher set on choice of topic or medium: advance approval of projects or not, only a writing exercise or broader choices, "no more collages this semester"? How much will the teacher be involved: regular progress reports, conferences, or no checkup; furnishing resources and some ideas or actually helping some students work things out? How important will the project be in determining the course grade? How, indeed, to grade: creativity, effort, difficulty or ambitiousness of the project, promptness, technical execution? How will the teacher make each student feel good about what he or she is doing and has done?

Generally speaking, student projects may be verbal or nonverbal or both. Verbal projects may be imaginative or expository, and either kind may be written or oral—even a performance. Nonverbal projects may be worked in the usual arts and crafts media or more elaborate audio-visual techniques. As to subject matter, students may work on a Bible story, a teaching, or an image or theme that runs through more than one such story or teaching. They may limit themselves to biblical passages, or they may make connections between those passages and some other field or medium, such as art, music, mythology, literature, historical backgrounds, or current affairs.

Here are some suggestions that teachers may wish to present to the class or keep in reserve for those who "can't think of anything." Such imagination stimulators may be offered either in the form of lists—written or oral, to a student with a problem or to a class—or, if copies or photographs are on file, as examples.

1. *IMAGINATIVE WRITING.* Biblical narrative is characteristically meager in detail, particularly as to the psychology of its characters: their inner conflicts, weighing of alternatives, confusions and complexities of emotion, reactions to events, doubts and fears, enthusiasms and satisfactions. Even in the most fascinating and crucial stories the Bible leaves us wondering. What thoughts and feelings did Adam and Eve have in the Garden? John Milton and Mark Twain supply wildly different answers. Kierkegaard suggests Abraham's possible musings on the way to sacrifice his son. Dialogue is equally sparse; dramatists have filled in from their knowledge of human nature and from their own humanity. Students may certainly be encouraged to use their imaginations as well.

In addition to those that supply the missing psychology and dialogue, other imaginative exercises are equally engaging, though perhaps less specially invited by the characteristics of biblical narrative style. Bible times were ancient times; let the student retell the stories or rephrase the teachings to fit our modern situation or our vernacular. Conversely, a student can put a modern story or preachment, out of his own experience or from current affairs, into a biblical setting or a biblical style. Still other techniques may be borrowed from creative exercises used with any other literature: What would have happened if—an event, a decision, a person had been different? How would the story have changed if told from the point of view of a minor character or of the loser or villain? What might have happened after the end of the narrative that appears in the Bible?

These are only reminders or thought-starters. So are the suggestions listed below (students should acknowledge ideas found in religious tradition or in secular authors):

- Jacob discovers he has the wrong bride. What is his reaction?
- Noah is loading the ark: What are his problems?
- A short biography of Rebekah before she met Isaac.
- A boyhood scene of Esau and Jacob.
- A newspaper account of the hardships and complaints of the

Israelites in the wilderness before Mt. Sinai, e.g., at the Red Sea, at Meribah.

- The story of the plagues and exodus from the point of view of an Egyptian.
- An editorial admonishing the Israelites about their idolatry at some point in their history, from the point of view of a priest, prophet, ruler, average person.
- What happened to Joseph's brothers after they settled in Goshen?
- What happened to the Roman soldiers who crucified Jesus?
- What happened to those of Samson's tormentors who survived?
- You are an Egyptian and saw Moses killing a fellow Egyptian.
- The spies argue what to tell Moses about what they saw in Canaan.
- Mrs. Noah's reaction to her husband's building the ark.
- The defenders of Jericho watch the Israelites marching around the walls.
- Adapt the story of Ruth or Esther for the theater, perhaps a musical: sketch key scenes, songs to crystallize key episodes, play backdrops, props, costumes.
- A series of biblical epitaphs in the manner of *Spoon River*.
- Satirical lyrics of religious and social ills during the times of the prophets.
- A ballad of several stanzas, each dealing thematically with stories of Jonah, Ruth, Jeremiah, Moses, Amos, Joseph.
- An original poem featuring a biblical character or incident.
- A letter such as a character in one of the biblical stories might have written.
- A "This Is Your Life" television script for Abraham, Moses, David, Jesus.
- An interview with Saul, Jacob, Solomon, Peter, Paul.
- A series of questions in preparation for "An Evening with _____."
- Rewrite a biblical story using modern symbols: planes, atomic bomb, moon landing, space satellites, automobiles.
- Character sketch of Mary Magdalene, Mary and Martha, Judas.
- A folk song based on a theme or story in the Bible.
- Treat a current figure—the President, a popular hero, a school character—in biblical style.
- Isaac's thoughts on the way to the sacrifice; Sarah's account of the event; Hagar tells Ishmael about it.

- An epic cycle, a la Abraham and descendants, of the local community.
- Adam and Eve converse after the expulsion.
- Moses' interior monologue on Mt. Nebo.
- Audience's reaction to the Sermon on the Mount.
- A viewer's reaction to a miracle of Moses, Elijah, Elisha, Joshua, Jesus.
- A poem in imitation of the psalms that applies to our experience.
- Create a series of twentieth-century proverbs.
- Write a philosophy of life after reading Ecclesiastes.
- Rewrite parts of Amos in terms of contemporary society.
- Write a modern parable.
- A letter (in Epistle form): Timothy to his mother after a journey with Paul.
- Judas' suicide note.
- Letter from Samuel to his mother, in training for temple service.
- An obituary notice for Job, Mordecai, Saul, Joseph (NT).
- A prophet denouncing racial discrimination, American foreign policy, immorality in government, educational practices, student apathy.
- An account of the boyhood of Jesus.
- Story of Job's friends after their punishment.
- Dialogue between a fourth comforter and Job.
- Newspaper account of the murder of Abel, destruction of Sodom and Gomorrah, fall of Jericho.
- Account of a trial of Cain—with both eyewitnesses and character witnesses.
- Television newscast of death of Moses, crucifixion and resurrection, Jonah's preaching.
- A Roman tourist who happens upon the crucifixion.

2. *EXPOSITORY COMPOSITIONS.* The subject matter of an assignment in exposition may grow out of reading the Bible as with any other worthwhile piece of literature—from paragraph to research paper, presented in writing or orally, to the teacher or to the class.

In a widely heterogeneous class, one day a very slow student read aloud to the group, from the security of his seat, a retelling of what he had laboriously read in a chapter or two of *The Greatest Story Ever Told* about the "hidden years" of Jesus, an imaginative biography. The class was as fascinated and approving as they were a few days later when an advance placement student lectured them on two versions of a Bible story, the biblical account of the rape of Tamar and an excerpt from Dan Jacobson's novel by that title, pointing out the differences in literary emphasis and the probable reasons for the differences as dictated by the intent of each story.

The Bible's many stories and teachings, its images, and its themes permit a wide variety of student compositions: reacting to the text, analyzing it, comparing it with other writing both within the Bible and outside it. In addition the vast field of Bible-related scholarship gives hints of the many directions in which the student may pursue and report on research, from a page to a "research paper": ancient backgrounds; biblical influences on history, on the arts, and on letters; the Bible in our contemporary culture and everyday life; interpretations and religious applications of biblical passages. Here are a few topics and treatments that have been successful:

- Write a summary of a biblical writer's attitude toward social reform, based on the text.
- Report on some aspect or aspects of the life of the Israelites: costumes, food, medicine, travel, trade, music.
- Explain the symbolic meanings of the various parts of the tabernacle and its major furnishings.
- Analyze closely David's elegy in II Samuel 1:19-27; focus on the character of Saul and of Jonathan.
- Report on Solomon's wisdom and wealth; give textual references.
- Write a character sketch of Jezebel in II Kings 20; compare with women of Bashan in Amos 4.
- Report on the Babylonian Empire during the time of the Exile.
- Report on the geography of Palestine.
- Report on archaeological finds in Palestine and their significance.
- Report on the Dead Sea Scrolls.
- Write on: "*My* Lost Eden," "*My* Ten Commandments."
- Give a sequential life of Jesus, with Bible references.
- Compare a biblical epic and one from another culture.
- Compare biblical characters: prophets, judges, women.
- Compare the Ten Commandments with Code of Hammurabi.
- Report on folk songs or spirituals that have grown out of the Bible.
- Compare Saul with a Greek tragic hero.
- Compare Job and Captain Ahab as quests for answers to the justice of human suffering.
- Analyze the psalms for poetic devices.

- Analyze one of the prophecies of Hosea.
- Compare Hebrews 11 with parallel passages in Genesis. What of Greek thought has been added, if anything?
- Report on Bible translations.
- Trace the vineyard image in the Bible.
- Trace the theme of sibling rivalry in the Bible.

3. *ARTS AND CRAFTS*. Students who are artistically talented will, of course, take pleasure in expressing themselves in their favorite medium. They may even get help and course credits from their art instructors. Particularly when such a student is only a fair academic performer, this is an excellent opportunity to involve him or her in the Bible course or unit and to reward interest, effort, and achievement. Furthermore, many boys have received credit in both shop and English courses through creative contributions that are often the envy of their more academically apt but mechanically inept or unimaginative fellow students.

Beyond the talented artist or craftsman, the less talented may also experience fulfillment from such a project. In any course it is unfair to reward, by a system of competitive grades, mere facile talent without some show of effort. It is especially unfair for an English course to set a higher value on purely artistic talent (which can, of course be acknowledged) than on effort and thoughtfulness.

Let a student give birth to his or her own idea, perhaps midwifed by the teacher, and then put time and energy into a project. If it enhances his or her own and fellow students' experience of the literature, it need not be a polished performance to be effective, satisfying, and worthy of recognition by the class and the teacher. And it is the teacher who sets the tone for that recognition.

In a writing exercise for an English class, however much a teacher may make allowances for individual differences, one of the purposes will be a language effort. The nonverbal student needs a chance now and then. True, with arts and crafts, students are, as with writing, trying to express themselves and to communicate to others through a medium, and clarity helps. When an arts or crafts project is created in the context of an English class, however, a student should feel less pressure to achieve artistic or technical excellence or to display great competence. Thus not only has the nonverbal but artistically or mechanically talented student a chance to shine through an arts or crafts project; the student who is both nonverbal and lacking in artistic or mechanical talent may also produce something of value for the class and be rewarded with the joy of creation.

A couple of general assignment possibilities: (1) Make something that will help you teach a Bible story to little children. (2) When you present your project to the class, explain how you went about it and what your main purpose was. Most of the items listed below have been preserved on slides made by students or teachers.

- Needlepoint: design copied from greeting card onto cloth: Jonah and whale
- Low relief string and tack design: Noah's ark and dove
- Mosaic of colored eggshell on wood: woman at well
- Mosaic: colored glass in plaster of Paris: Elijah fed by ravens
- Ceramics: Adam, Eve, serpent, and tree
- Felt on board: flight into Egypt
- Batik: burning bush
- Stained-glass mobile: Joseph in many-colored coat
- Shadow box: parable scenes on front and each end
- Silk screen: crucifixion
- Crayon drawings on related newspaper pages: Jesus lives today
- Ceramics: a tenth-century B.C.E. jug
- Illuminated manuscripts: series of four passages on theme of "all is vanity"
- Replicas of biblical musical instruments in working condition
- Noah's ark: popsicle stick sides; cork, toothpick, and felt animals
- "Quiet" book, cloth: Noah's ark of felt with plastic animals in zippered pocket; braidable hair for Ruth; weavable felt strips for tower of Babel, colored felt strips to snap on drawn figure of Joseph—all for little children to play with and learn from
- Jacob's ladder model in cardboard box: GI Joe doll figure fully dressed; angels on ladder; unseen light shining down ladder; landscaping included
- Stitchery on burlap: Balaam and ass
- Fluorescent paints: Moses
- Cake of tower of Babel; lower layers of styrofoam and frosted
- Pillows: embroidered original designs and Bible quotations
- Eden of living plants, watered every day in class
- Dice and ticket game: climb the mountain with Moses
- Balsa wood ark and animal cracker crew and passengers
- Model of the temple, done in sugar cubes
- Cartoon comic strip: story of Jonah

- Pop-up book illustrating Proverbs 31:10-31, selected verses in praise of a good woman
- Woodcut: Job and comforters
- Scale model of tabernacle
- Scale model of ark of the covenant
- Ceramics: whale with movable Jonah, positioned halfway in mouth or inside fish hollowed out on reverse side
- Maps: various journeys; Palestine or ancient Near East at various eras; the tribes and their symbols on the map
- "Ancient" manuscript: heavy paper, stained with lemon juice, scorched, and edges burned—hand-printed story of Adam and Eve
- Split, hinged log, with Decalogue numbers burned on inner surfaces
- Snipped out metal Hebrew letters attached to wood tablets for Decalogue
- Full-sized Joseph's coat, modeled by artist's boyfriend
- Plaster of Paris low relief: head of Jesus
- Political poster: the President as Moses speaking ironic commandments
- "Stained-glass" schoolroom window: colored cellophane—on theme of sin
- Beanbag game: throw beanbag Daniel into open jaws of papier-mâché lion
- "Mosaic" made of aquarium stones: Eve at the tree
- Classroom demonstration of a Passover seder
- Embroidery: composite of Moses, Jonah, and Eden
- Acrylics: Jonah episodes
- Wood engraving: Elijah and chariot, edges of wood burned for "antiquing"
- Collage: theme of "thou shalt not kill" with newspaper and magazine pictures and headlines chosen for irony
- Ticket game: turn the scroll, and figure out the cryptograms
- Block print: original design from Byzantine icon: head of Christ Pantocrator
- Poster: various Christian symbols with printed explanations
- Enameled copper tiles: Genesis scenes, mounted on wallboard
- Lettered computer-paper scroll: Genesis stories
- Aluminum tappings: Moses; a decorative cross
- Petit point: original design of Eden
- Flannelgraph: Joseph and his brothers

- Mobile: handpainted glass, Christian symbols
- Cartoon strips: illustrated Bible stories for little children
- Symbols and zodiac for twelve tribes: paint on cardboard, with titles
- Model of Ziggurat/Babel
- Model of scene: Lot's escape from Gomorrah

4. *AUDIO-VISUAL MEDIA PRESENTATIONS.* Recordings on reel or cassette tape, slides, overhead projectuals, filmstrips, mounted and framed materials, synchronized slide-tapes, videotapes, and movies, alone or in combination, are a bit more complicated than the usual arts and crafts projects. They require at least a minimum amount of specialized equipment, materials, technique (though less than the novice would think), and—unless the student has unusual talent and experience—help from the teacher with planning. In many instances, however, the degree of complexity of the media problems is the measure both of the student's involvement and of his or her satisfaction. (Note: There certainly are places in the curriculum for students to experience and react to audio visual materials produced commercially or by the teacher; generally, however, students learn more by working on their own less excellent productions, if the curriculum permits such activities.)

Experience has shown that students who have never used a camera but know more or less what they are looking for and those who have never used a tape recorder but have at least a partly developed idea in mind can produce excellent results for the course while sensitizing themselves to a new field of observation and perception. An average student can learn almost complete competence in synchronizing slides and taped materials—either created or selected by the student—in fifteen minutes. A student can usually find someone on the audio-visual squad to help record and show an original videotape or film of a prearranged performance or sequence of scenes if the school has the equipment.

Naturally, the hobbyist or member of a creative audio-visual production class will probably add an expertise to his or her media presentation, against which the beginner should not have to measure up. Again, the student's thoughtfulness and effort, what he or she did with whatever talent possessed, should be the basis for rewards: in terms of the student's own fulfillment, classmates' appreciation, teacher's approval, and mark, if any. If the equipment and materials are available, students should be encouraged to jump into audio-visual media waters and discover the pleasures of moving about in a new environment.

Here are a few examples of what some students have done:

- Videotape of student and friends pantomiming scenes from *Jesus Christ Superstar*
- Slide-tape: reading Bible passages on man in God's nature, with scenes of the ecology crisis
- Movie on Noah made in swimming pool, with hoses causing downpour
- Slide-tape: music played and sung by students, "How Great Thou Art"; pictures of scenic beauty
- Videotape of student and friends dancing original choreography of two Bible excerpts—Isaiah 52:7-8, Song of Songs 2:16-17; recorded Israeli music and Hebrew words; preceded by brief student talk
- Slide-tape: student speaking English, alternating with German excerpts from Haydn's *Creation;* one synchronized projector with illustrative pictures of nature, one independent projector automatically advancing from sun in total eclipse emerging to full sunlight
- Slide-tape: Bible readings, popular recordings, excerpts from assassination of Robert Kennedy; pictures of parts of original collage poster, booklet, and everyday objects—all on the theme of man's hypocrisy as he professes to value the Bible's injunction to love one's neighbor (joint project, two students)
- Slide-tape: Two Harry Belafonte recordings about nativity; interpretive slides from everyday life, with few art pictures; followed by student explanation on tape of how and why selections were made
- Slide-tape: excerpts of book of Revelation (KJV) from a recording, and introductory music; 110 full and detail pictures of Dürer's "Apocalypsis in Figuris" and introductory montage of parts of the eleventh-century Angers tapestry on the same subject
- Movies: choreographed and danced by student and friends from a modern dance class; series of three—Adam and Eve and serpent, parable of the sower, Lazarus and Dives; from representational to quite abstract in mode; to be accompanied by spoken narration
- Slide-tape: boys' glee club and woodcuts illustrating "Swing Low, Sweet Chariot"
- Videotape: collaboratively revised book of Job with fourth comforter

- Illustrated slide-tape lecture about stained glass with examples from many nearby churches
- Slide-tape illustrating and explaining the Catholic mass
- Live lecture with taped examples: the Bible in religious and secular music
- Lectures and exhibits of collections: the Bible in advertisements, in news headlines, in movie titles, titles of pieces of literature, common expressions, etymology of English words, music titles, modern dance titles, in biology and in geographical names; biblical stamps, graphics, greeting cards, picture postcards of religious sculpture or painting or architecture, political cartoons, humorous cartoons, book covers, dolls in biblical dress
- Tape: student barbershop quartet singing "Don't Sit Under the Apple Tree" and "In the Shade of the Old Apple Tree" for use with the Eden story

5. *DRAMA, DEBATE, AND MISCELLANY.* Here are some activities that proved successful and that other students might try:

- Write and act out a mystery or miracle play: Jacob wrestles with the angel, Abraham argues with God about Sodom, the shepherds visit the manger
- Debate the issue in the book of Job
- Act out a Bible-related play ("It Should Happen to a Dog," by Wolf Mankowitz)
- Direct a dramatic reading of James Weldon Johnson's "The Creation" with sound effects
- Direct a reading of *Green Pastures* excerpts
- Create a biblical crossword puzzle for the class to do
- Write a composition full of Bible quotations, which other students are to annotate
- Write biblical lyrics for a popular song, use a guitarist, and have the class sing
- Arrange role-playing: Moses and Aaron before Pharaoh, Joseph and his brothers, Saul and David and Jonathan, Jesus and the money changers
- Give an illustrated report on Russian icons
- Give an illustrated report on Greek church architecture

(The Indiana University Institute on Teaching the Bible in Literature Courses) has on file several hundred more project suggestions reported by over five hundred summer participants, based on their experiences as teachers of English. We urge teachers to send in their own ideas and sample slides or tapes of what their students produce so that others may be stimulated by them.)

Handouts and Exercises

Some Events in the Life of Jesus

	Matt.	Mark	Luke	John
Birth of John the Baptist foretold			1:5-23	
Annunciation to Mary			1:24-38	
Birth of John the Baptist			1:57-80	
Birth of Jesus	1:18-25		2:1-27	
Visit of the Magi/wise men	2:1-12			
Flight into Egypt	2:13-23			
Jesus teaches the doctors			2:41-52	
Ministry of John the Baptist	3:1-12	1:1-8	3:1-18	1:19-28
Baptism of Jesus	3:13-17	1:9-11	3:21-23	1:29-34
Temptation of Jesus	4:1-11	1:12-13	4:1-13	
First disciples/Draft of fishes	4:18-22		5:12-16	1:35-51
First miracle: wedding at Cana				2:1-12
Appointing of twelve apostles	10:2-4	3:13-19	6:12-19	
Healing of centurion's servant	8:5-15		7:1-10	
Death of John the Baptist	14:1-12	6:14-29	9:7-9	
Feeding of the five thousand	14:13-21	6:30-46	9:10-17	6:1-15
Jesus walks on the water	14:22-33	6:47-52		6:16-21
Peter's confession of faith	16:13-20	8:27-30	9:18-21	
Transfiguration of Jesus	17:1-13	9:2-13	9:28-36	
Healing of the man born blind				9:1-39
Raising of Lazarus				11:1-46
Visit to Zaccheus the publican			19:1-10	
Anointing by Mary	26:6-13	14:3-9		12:2-11
Entry into Jerusalem	21:1-11	11:1-11	19:29-44	12:12-19
Cleansing of temple, return to Bethany	21:12-17	11:15-19	19:45-48, 21:37-38	
Jesus' authority challenged	21:23-27	11:27-33	20:1-8	
Conspiracy of Judas	26:1-5, 14-16	14:1-2, 10-11	22:1-6	
Preparation for the Passover	26:17-20	14:12-17	22:7-14	
Last Supper, announcement of betrayal	26:21-25	14:18-21	22:15-23	13:21-35
Agony in the garden of Gethsemane	26:36-46	14:32-42	22:40-46	
Betrayal by Judas	26:47-50	14:43-45	22:47-48	18:4-9
Arrest of Jesus	26:50-56	14:46-52	22:49-53	18:10-12
Trial before Caiaphas	26:57-58	14:53-54	22:54-55	18:19-24
Denials by Peter	26:69-72	14:66-72	22:56-62	18:15-18, 25-27
Jesus mocked by enemies	26:67-68	14:65	22:63-65	
Jesus before Pilate	27:11-14	15:2-5	23:2-5	18:28-38

	Matt.	Mark	Luke	John
Jesus condemned, scourged, and mocked	27:26-30	15:15-19	23:24-25	19:1-3
Crucifixion and death	27:46-49		23:33-38, 46-49	
Jesus pierced in the side				19:31-37
Burial of Jesus	27:57-61	15:42-47	23:50-56	19:38-42
Morning of the resurrection	28:1-10	16:1-11	24:1-11	20:1-18
Walk to Emmaus		16:12-13	24:13-25	
Jesus appears to the apostles		16:14	24:36-48	20:19-29
Jesus ascends to heaven		16:19	24:50-53	

Parables in the Synoptic (First Three) Gospels

There are parables elsewhere in the Bible, in the Old Testament and in Acts and Epistles; and there are at least two discourses in the Gospel of John that might qualify as parables: the shepherd (10:1-5) and the true vine (15:1-5). Most often, however, the term is applied to those in Matthew, Mark, and Luke. Listed below are the opening verses only. (Titles are from the KJV.)

	Matt.	Mark	Luke
Parables that appear in only one Gospel			
The tares	13:24		
The hidden treasure	13:44		
The goodly pearl/pearl of great price	13:45		
The drawnet	13:47		
The unmerciful servant	18:23		
The laborers in the vineyard	20:1		
The two sons	21:28		
The marriage of the king's son	22:2		
The ten virgins	25:1		
The talents	25:14		
The sheep and goats	25:31		
The seed growing secretly		4:26	
The householder		13:34	
The two debtors			7:41
The good Samaritan			10:30
The importunate friend			11:5
The rich fool			12:16
Servants watching			12:35
The wise steward			12:42
The barren fig tree			13:6
The great supper			14:16
Building a tower or going to war			14:28
The piece of money			15:8
The prodigal son			15:11
The unjust steward			16:1
The rich man and Lazarus the beggar			16:19
Unprofitable servants			17:7
The unjust judge/importunate widow			18:2
The Pharisee and the publican			18:10
The pounds			19:12

Parables that appear in two Gospels			
The house built on rock and on sand	7:24		6:47
The leaven	13:33		13:20
The lost sheep	18:12		15:4
Parables that appear in three Gospels			
The candle under a bushel	5:15	4:21	8:16, 11:33
New cloth on an old garment	9:16	2:21	5:36
New wine in old bottles	9:17	2:22	5:37
The sower	13:3	4:3	8:5
The mustard seed	13:31	4:30	13:18
The wicked husbandman/the vineyard	21:33	12:1	20:9
The fig tree and all the trees	24:32	13:28	21:29

Background on the Bible as a Book

(Student research guide or lecture note sheet)

1. Old Testament/Jewish Bible

2. Pentateuch/Law

3. Prophets

4. Other writings

5. New Testament

6. Gospels and Acts

7. Epistles and Revelation/Apocalypse

8. Masoretic text

9. Septuagint

10. Vulgate

11. Apocrypha

12. Douay Version

13. King James Version

14. Later Catholic versions

15. Later Protestant versions

16. Jewish versions

17. Joint efforts and unusual versions

Four Roughly Contemporary Writings for Comparison

In the beginning God created the heaven and the earth. And the earth was without form, and void; and darkness was upon the face of the deep. And the Spirit of God moved upon the face of the water. And God said, Let there be light: and there was light. And God saw the light, that it was good: and God divided the light from the darkness. And God called the light Day, and the darkness he called Night. And the evening and the morning were the first day.

And God said, Let there be a firmament in the midst of the waters, and let it divide the waters from the waters. And God made the firmament, and divided the waters which were under the firmament from the waters which were above the firmament: and it was so. And God called the firmament Heaven. And the evening and the morning were the second day. (Gen. 1:1-8 KJV, 1611)

Great and manifold were the blessings, most dread Sovereign, which Almighty God, the Father of all mercies, bestowed upon us the people of England, when first he sent your Majesty's Royal Person to rule and reign over us. For whereas it was the expectation of many, who wished not well to our Sion, that, upon the setting of that bright Occidental Star, Queen Elizabeth of most happy memory, some thick and palpable clouds of darkness would so have overshadowed this Land, that men should have been in doubt which way they were to walk; and that it should hardly be known, who was to direct the unsettled State; the appearance of Your Majesty, as of the Sun in his strength, instantly dispelled those supposed and surmised mists, and gave unto all that were well affected exceeding cause of comfort; especially when we beheld the Government established in Your Highness, and Your hopeful Seed, by an undoubted Title, and this also accompanied with peace and tranquility at home and abroad. (from KJV translators' dedication, 1611)

Horatio, when thou shalt have overlooked this [letter], give these fellows some means to the King. They have letters for him.

Ere we were two days old at sea, a pirate of very warlike appointment gave us chase. Finding ourselves too slow of sail, we put on a compelled valor, and in the grapple I boarded them. On the instant they got clear of our ship; so I alone became their prisoner. They have dealt with me like thieves of mercy; but they knew what they did; I am to do a good turn for them.

Let the King have the letters I have sent, and repair to me with as much speed as thou wouldst fly death. I have words to speak in thine ear will make thee dumb; yet are they too light for the bore of the matter. These good fellows will bring thee where I am. (Shakespeare's *Hamlet,* ca. 1600)

(NOTE: Use either the preceding passage or the following one.)

They met me in the day of success; and I have learned by the perfectest report, they have more in them than mortal knowledge. When I burned in desire to question them further, they made themselves air, into which they vanished. Whiles I stood rapt in the wonder of it, came missives from the King, who all-hailed me "Thane of Cawdor"; by which title, before, these weird sisters saluted me, and referred me to the coming of the time with "Hail, King that shalt be!" This have I thought good to deliver thee, my dearest partner of greatness, that thou mightst not lose the dues of rejoicing by being ignorant of what greatness is promised thee. Lay it to thy heart, and farewell. (Shakespeare's *Macbeth,* ca. 1606)

Being thus arrived in a good harbor, and brought safe to land, they fell upon their knees and blessed the God of heaven who had brought them over the vast and furious ocean, and delivered them from all the perils and miseries thereof, again to set their feet on the firm and stable earth, their proper element. And no marvel if they were thus joyful, seeing wise Seneca was so affected with sailing a few miles on the coast of his own Italy, as he affirmed, that he had rather remain twenty years on his way by land than pass by sea to any place in a short time, so tedious and dreadful was the same unto him.

But here I cannot but stay and make pause, and stand half amazed at this poor people's present condition; and so I think will the reader, too, when he considers the same. Being thus passed the vast ocean, and a sea of troubles before in their preparation (as may be remembered by that which went before), they had now no friends to welcome them nor inns to entertain or refresh their weatherbeaten bodies; no houses or much less towns to repair to, to seek for succor. It is recorded in scripture, as a mercy to the apostle and his shipwrecked company, that the barbarians showed them no small kindness in refreshing them, but these savage barbarians, when they met with them (as after will appear), were readier to fill their sides full of arrows than otherwise. (William Bradford, 1620)

Notes on Language in the KJV

Words Ending in —en

Archaic Past Participles: brazen (serpent), shapen (in iniquity), etc.
Verbs (current or a bit old fashioned): past participles in —*n* or —*en:*
been, born, borne, bidden, bitten, blown, chidden, chosen, drawn, driven, eaten, fallen, flown, forsaken, frozen, given, gone, gotten,

grown, hewn, hidden, known, lain, mown, proven, ridden, risen,
riven, seen, sewn, shaken, shorn, shown, shrunken, slain, slidden,
sown, spoken, stolen, strewn, stricken, swollen, sworn, taken, torn,
thriven, thrown, trodden, woken, worn, woven, written

Adjectives (surviving —*en* past participles but archaic or obsolete as
verbs): beholden (to), bounden (duty), brazen (hussy), cloven (hoof),
drunken, graven (image), laden, misbegotten, misshapen, molten,
sodden, sunken

Nouns (plurals in —*n* and —*en*): Archaic—cow, kine; hose (legging),
hosen; shoe, shoon; eye, eyen. Modern remnants: men, children,
brethren, oxen

Archaic Inflections:
Pronouns and Verbs (Tense: Present Only)

	Number	1st Person	2nd Person	3rd Person
Subject	Sing.	I go	*thou *goest	he *goeth
	Plur.	we go	*ye go	they go
Object	Sing.	me	*thee	him
	Plur.	us	you	them

*Only five forms have changed

Different Becomes Bad

Gentile	nation ◗	foreign ◗	outlandish ◗	bad
Goy	nation	foreign	outlandish	bad
Barbarian	bearded	foreign	outlandish	bad
Insolent	unusual	different	subversive	bad
Pagan	villager	crude	uncivilized*	bad
Heathen	heath dweller	crude	uncivilized	bad
Boor	farmer, peasant	crude	uncivilized	bad
Vulgar	common	crude	uncivilized	bad
Churl	countryman, peasant	crude	uncivilized	bad
Savage	grove dweller	wild	uncivilized	bad
Rude	rustic	crude	uncivilized	bad
Lewd	laical	weaker, stupid	inferior	bad
Knave	boy	weaker, stupid	inferior	bad
Wench	woman	weaker, stupid	inferior	bad
Silly	innocent, sheeplike	foolish	inferior	bad

*Civilized: from both *civitas* ("one's city or nation") and *civicus* ("citizen"); an example of
the opposite development: one of *us* is good

Fish (Eng.) = Ichthus (Grk.) = Christ

I	Iesous	Jesus
Ch	Christos	Christ,
Th	Theou	God's
U	Uios	Son,
S	Soter	Savior

Paradise

Persian	pairi-daëza	means "enclosed, wooded pleasure garden"
Hebrew	pardes	word and idea borrowed from Persian
Greek	paradeisos	LXX—garden of Eden; NT—afterworld, good part
English	paradise	transliteration of the Greek term

James and John

Yaakov (Heb.)	Johanan (Heb.)	B'nai Regesh (Heb.) sons of tumult
Yakub (Arab.)	Johannus (Grk.)	B'nai Raam (Heb.) sons of thunder
Hagop (Armen.)	Johannes (Lat.)	? (Aram.) sons of thunder
Jakobus (Grk.)	Giovanni (It.)	Boanerges (Grk.) (from Heb. via
Jacobus, Jacomus (Lat.)	Juan (Sp.)	Aram.)—Mark uses this word
Giacopo, Giacomo (It.)	João (Port.)	and translates it as "Sons
Giacobo, Iacovo (It.)	Jean (Fr.)	of Thunder," a nickname for
Jiacobo, Jaime (Sp.)	Johann (Ger.)	James and John, sons
Iago, Diego (Sp.)	Johannes (Ger.)	of Zebedee
Tiago, Jaime (Port.)	Johan (Swed.)	
Jacques (Fr.)	Jan (Pol.)	
Jakob (Ger.)	Ivan (Rus.)	
Jakub (Pol.)	Eoin, Sean	
Yakov (Rus.)	(Irish)	
Seamus (Irish)	Shane (Irish)	
Jacob, James (Eng.)	Iaian (Scot.)	
	John (Eng.)	

Judah/Jew

Yehudah (Heb.); Judas (Grk., Lat.); Judah, Judea, Judith, Jude (Eng.).
Note: The Russian word, *Yuda,* also means "traitor."

Yehudi (Heb.), Judaeus (Grk., Lat.), judio (Sp.), judeu (Port.), giu
(OF.), juif (Fr.), Jude (Ger.), Jood (Du.), jøde (Dan.), jude (Swed.),
ebreo (It.), Yid/Yiddish (Yid.), zyd (Pol.), yevrei or (insulting) zhid
(Rus.), Jew/Jewish (Eng.)

Entymological Etymology

English	Ladybug; ladybird ("Our Lady's* bug"); Lady cow
Hebrew	Parat Mosheh Rabbēnu ("Moses our teacher's cow")
Yiddish	Moshe rabbenus kielach ("Moses our teacher's little cow")
Latin	Coccinella ("little scarlet one")
French	Coccinelle; poulette á Dieu ("God's hen")
Spanish	Vaquita de San Antón ("little cow of St. Anthony")
Portuguese	Joaninha ("little John")
Italian	Palomilla ("little dove/hen")
German	Marienkäfer ("Mary's beetle")
Dutch	Lievenheersbeestje ("dear Lord's little animal")
Danish	Mariehøne ("Mary hen")
Russian	Bozhjz Koróvka ("God's little cow")
Polish	Zazula**
India	habitat of dead souls (as also in some American Negro folklore)

*Ladybird and Lady Day are possessives but have no *'s*, following the rule with Anglo-Saxon feminine possessives.

**In Polish there is the rhyme: Ladybird, ladybird, go up to heaven
Bring me a piece of bread

Esther and Mordecai

Esther: Hebrew equivalent of Ishtar; Persian or Babylonian name for the Jewish queen, whose original name was Hadassah (myrtle)

Mordecai: Hebrew form of Marduk, chief Babylonian god, who is the creator and is also called Bel (ruler), Mesopotamian counterpart of Canaanite Baal—who represented order and who subdued the chaos of the waters (or sea dragon)

Stara, reh: Persian word for *star*

Ishtar: Babylonian, Assyrian goddess

Ashtart/Athtareth (Canaanite); Ashtaroth (Heb.); Astarte (Grk.) —forms of Ishtar

Asherah (Phoenician); Athirat (Ugaritic); Aphrodite (Grk.) — goddesses, vaguely related

Saturday/Sunday/Sabbath

	Sunday	*Saturday*
Hebrew	Yom rishon ("first day")	Shabbat ("rest, cease")
Greek	Kyriaki ("Lord's")	Sávaton
Latin	Solis dies ("sun's day")	Saturni dies ("Saturn's day")
	Dominica ("Lord's")	Sabbatum ("sabbath")
Italian	Domenico	Sábato
Spanish	Domingo	Sábado

Portuguese	Domingo	Sabado
French	Dimanche (from *dies domini-cus*—"Lord's day")	Samedi
German	Sonntag	Sonnabend ("sun's evening")
		Samstag (in southern Germany)
Dutch	Zondag	Zaterdag
Swedish	Söndag	Lördag
Danish/Norwegian	Søndag	Lørdag
Russian	Voskresénje	Subótta
Polish	Niedziela (in Old Polish: a week)	Sobota
Turkish	Pazar (market day)	
Mandarin Chinese	Li Bai (prayer day)	

Passover/Paschal/Easter

Hebrew	Pesach—"leap (over)"
Greek	Pascha, Paska—"leap"
Latin	Pascha
Italian	Pasqua
Spanish	Pascua (de Resurrección/Florida)
French	Pâques (singular = "Passover")
Danish	Paske
Dutch	Pasen
Swedish	Pask
Russian	Pascha
Polish	Wielkanoc—"great night"
So. German	Pasch
German	Ostern
English	Easter

Anglo-Saxon spring festival:

Easter monath, named for Easter, goddess of dawn, light, and spring

Symbolism in Apocalpytic Literature:
Two Comparable Modern Situations

"Posibilismo"—the art of writers adapting themselves to censorship—has, in effect, become second nature to Spanish writers, with all the usual consequences: self-censorship, elliptical prose, allegory, vague allusions, and so forth. This bizarre literary climate has produced a subtle reader—one marvelously adept in decoding allusions and reading between the lines. The self-banished Spanish intellectual, Joseph Blanco-White, quite rightly summed it up: "Citizens accustomed to governments that don't permit the freedom of expression have the agility of deaf mutes to understand each other by quick signals."

—Juan Goytisolo, "Writing in an Occupied
Language," *New York Times Book Review*,
March 31, 1974

A great many spirituals were disguised songs of earthly freedom or, failing that remote possibility of literal freedom for their creators, of heavenly release from worldly bondage. Quite simply, the spirituals were often songs of protest, the only kind of protest that in slavery days could be made without great physical danger. And sometimes to be caught singing a spiritual was to court drastic punishment.

Not all spirituals were by any means as forthright in their statements of Negro thought as "I been 'buked and I been scorned," or "Oh, freedom! Freedom over me," or "Go down, Moses, way down in Egypt land, and tell old Pharaoh to let my people go," which few slave masters were stupid enough to imagine concerned *only* the Hebrew children.

—Langston Hughes, from the jacket of Harry
Belafonte's *My Lord What a Mornin'*

CHAPTER 10

Fun and Games

Biblical Riddles

Experience has shown that most people find all but a dozen of these riddles pretty silly or inane. Unfortunately, no two people agree on which twelve the list should include. Use in small doses; students will express their approval by groaning.

When was baseball first played in the Bible?
   In the big inning.

On what did the earliest people do arithmetic lessons?
   God told them to multiply on the face of the earth.

Who was the champion runner of all time?
   Adam, first in the human race.

What was the longest day in the Bible?
   The one with no Eve.

At what time of day was Adam created?
   A little before Eve.

What was the first theatrical performance?
   When Eve appeared for Adam's benefit.

Why couldn't Eve have the measles?
   Because she'd Adam.

To what church did Eve probably belong?
   Adam thought Eve angelical.

Did Eve ever have a date with Adam?
   No, it was an apple.

Why did Adam bite the apple?

Because he didn't have a knife.

Why were the gates of the garden of Eden closed after Adam and Eve were expelled?
To keep the damned pair out.

How were Adam and Eve prevented from gambling?
They lost their paradise.

What did Adam and Eve never have but left to each of their children?
Parents.

What was the first gift mentioned in the Bible?
When Eve presented Adam with Cain.

What evidence is there that Adam and Eve were pretty noisy?
They raised Cain.

How long did Cain hate his brother?
As long as he was Abel.

What family, when named, make an order that a boy be punished?
"Adam," Seth Eve, "Cain Abel."

How do we know that three people went into the ark before Noah?
The Bible says that Noah came forth.

When was meat first mentioned in the Bible?
When Noah took Ham into the ark.

What animal took the most baggage into the ark; what one took the least?
The elephant took his trunk, but the fox and rooster took only a brush and comb between them.

Who was the best financier in the Bible?
Noah: He floated his stock while the whole world was in liquidation.

Where did Noah keep bees?
In the ark hives.

Why didn't the worms enter the ark in pairs?
They went in apples instead of pears.

What living creatures were not in the ark?
Fish.

Where did all the people in the world hear one rooster crow?
In the ark.

Why couldn't the people play cards on the ark?
Noah sat on the deck.

Where was Noah when the lights went out?
In d'ark.

Why couldn't Noah catch many fish while on the ark?
He had only two worms.

When is paper money first mentioned in the Bible?
When the dove brought the green back to the ark.

What did the cat say when the ark landed?
Is that Ararat?

Who was the first electrician?
Noah, who made the ark light on the mountain.

Why was Lot's wife turned into a pillar of salt?
Because she was dissatisfied with her Lot.

Where is cash-and-carry buying mentioned in the Bible?
When Joseph said, "All the days of my appointed time will I wait
until my change comes."

When was tennis first played?
When Joseph served in Pharaoh's court.

Who was the straightest man in the Bible?
Joseph: Pharaoh made a ruler out of him.

What was the first financial transaction in the Bible?
When Pharaoh's daughter took a little prophet from the bulrushes.

What did the Egyptians do when it got dark?
They turned on the Israelites.

What evidence is there that Moses wore a wig?
Sometimes he was seen with Aaron and sometimes not.

How were the Egyptians paid for what the Israelites took when they
fled?
They received a check on the bank of the Red Sea.

Where are automobiles mentioned in the Bible?
When Moses went up on high.

When Moses didn't feel well, what did God give him?
Two tablets.

What biblical king was often in his people's mouths?
  Agag.

What biblical man had no parents?
  Joshua, the son of Nun.

What simple affliction caused the death of Samson?
  He died of fallen arches.

How do we know that Samson was an excellent actor?
  He brought down the house.

How was Ruth rude to Boaz?
  She pulled his ears and stepped on his corn.

Why was Goliath astonished when David hit him with a stone?
  Such a thing had never entered his head before.

Who was older, David or Goliath?
  David: he rocked Goliath to sleep.

From the name of what biblical king can you take away six and leave his father?
  David: Take VI from his name and leave Dad.

What evidence is there of sewing in the time of David?
  He was hemmed in on all sides.

Why was the prophet Elijah like a horse?
  He was fed from aloft.

What did Job have with which to cover his sackcloth and ashes?
  Only three miserable comforters.

Who is the shortest man in the Bible?
  Bildad, the Shuhite.

Who was the most successful doctor in the Bible?
  Job: he had the most patience.

Who was the strongest man in the Bible?
  Jonah: the whale couldn't keep him down.

Who was Jonah's guardian?
  The whale brought him up.

How is the story of Jonah an inspiration?
  Jonah was down in the mouth but came out all right.

How was John the Baptist like a penny?
He was one sent.

Who were the three tiniest apostles?
Peter, James, and John: they all slept on a watch.

What is the sharpest tool in the New Testament?
The Acts of the Apostles.

How was St. Paul like a horse?
He liked Timothy, hey?

What is the worst insect in the Bible?
The wicked flee.

How were sandwiches made in the Bible?
Ham left the ark with his followers, who were bred and mustered; and when Lot's wife became salt, all the rest went into the desert.

How was a baseball game played in the Bible?
Eve stole first, Adam stole second, Rebecca walked with the pitcher; then Gideon rattled the pitchers, Saul was put out by David, and the prodigal son stole home.

Who were the shortest men in the Bible?
It is commonly believed that they were Knee-high Meyer and Bildad the Shuhite; but Paul said, "Silver and gold have I none," and no one could be shorter than that.

What three noblemen are mentioned in the Bible?
Barren fig tree, Lord how long, and Count thy blessings.

Who set the record for the high jump in the Bible?
Probably Jesus, when he cleared the temple.

Puzzles, Word Games, and Miscellany

Biblical Name Search

Hidden below are well over forty biblical names (people, places, ideas), forward or backward in a straight line—horizontally, vertically, or diagonally. Some overlap others; a few appear more than once. Circle those you find and write them on a separate paper.

```
A  J  O  E  L  E  I  R  B  A  G  A  C  N  T  N  N  I  S  A  N
R  D  F  N  H  S  E  L  T  S  O  P  A  A  O  L  O  R  D  U  E
Z  I  A  O  A  U  R  E  H  T  D  R  A  D  B  D  I  D  N  I  V
E  N  T  M  N  R  D  P  T  E  A  E  S  R  G  O  T  A  I  O  A
O  A  H  O  I  E  A  S  A  P  V  H  I  O  A  H  C  N  T  S  E
M  H  E  L  D  V  G  O  B  H  I  P  G  J  T  C  E  C  E  E  H
A  O  R  O  G  O  Y  G  B  E  D  E  O  N  H  I  R  O  R  T  T
L  R  E  S  O  S  V  A  A  N  I  S  H  T  U  R  R  M  Y  S  E
E  E  Y  E  L  S  H  E  S  H  A  O  N  M  L  E  U  M  T  A  R
I  B  A  L  G  A  M  A  R  Y  J  J  E  D  U  J  S  A  I  I  A
N  E  R  P  O  P  R  T  E  W  E  H  T  T  A  M  E  N  E  S  Z
A  K  P  I  T  A  S  H  T  V  S  L  S  M  P  H  R  D  N  E  A
D  A  L  C  H  Y  A  O  E  K  U  L  U  A  S  T  R  M  A  L  N
O  H  A  S  A  B  D  M  P  R  S  I  R  B  N  E  E  E  M  C  A
N  A  A  I  L  O  U  A  E  A  E  K  A  R  A  B  L  N  E  C  R
I  I  B  D  R  J  J  S  P  M  S  B  Z  A  I  A  B  T  S  E  A
J  M  A  E  U  M  O  E  I  A  O  R  A  H  S  Z  A  S  H  B  H
A  E  B  M  L  J  O  M  L  C  M  E  L  A  E  I  R  S  T  T  M
H  R  E  B  E  C  C  A  A  R  L  O  I  M  H  L  A  U  E  O  O
J  E  L  H  A  N  O  J  T  I  H  L  S  L  P  E  P  S  G  L  A
E  J  U  D  G  E  S  M  E  H  E  L  H  T  E  B  F  Z  A  O  B
```

Biblical Names

(Key to Search Puzzle)

Abba
Abel (2)
Abraham
Adam
Adonijah
Ahab
Amen (2)
Amos
Apostles
Ark (2)
Asa (4)
Asher

Baal
Babel
Bar [Jonah, etc.]
    (2)
Barak
Bel (3)
Beth [Shean,
    etc.] (2)
Bethlehem
Boaz

Commandments

Dan (3)
Daniel
David
Dinah (2)
Disciples
Dove

Ecclesiastes
Ehud
Eli (4)
Elias
Elizabeth

Ephesians
Ezra

Father

Gabriel
Gad
Gath
Gethsemane
God
Gog
Golgotha
Gospel

Ham
Haran
Heaven
Horeb

Isaac
Ish [Bosheth,
    etc.] (3)

Jacob
Jah
James
Jehu
Jeremiah
Jericho
Jesus
Job
Joel
John
Jonah
Jordan
Jose (2)
Joseph
Judah

Judas
Jude
Judges

Lazarus
Lord
Lot
Luke

Mark
Mary
Matthew
Mene
Moab
Moses

Nahor
Nazareth
Nisan
Noah
Nod(4)
Noe
Nun

Oded
Omri
Onan

Parable
Paran
Passover
Paul
Peter
Pilate
Pray
Prayer

Rebecca
Rebekah

Resurrect	Saul	Stephen
Resurrection	Seth	
Ruth	Shem	Thomas
	Sidon	Tyre
Sabbath	Sin(2)	
Sarah	Solomon	Any others?

Answers to Biblical Name Search

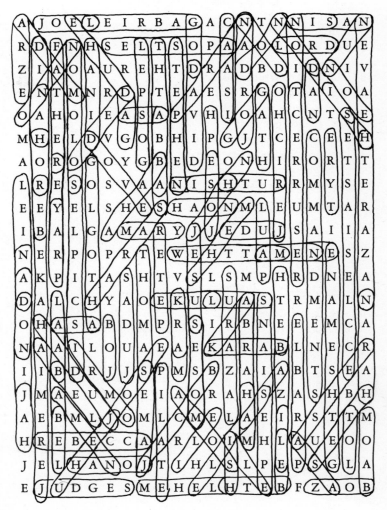

Games to Play with Titles of
Books of the Bible

Underline the names of the books of the Bible concealed in the following words and sentences. There's one in each sentence.

15 correct—excellent; 13—good; 11—fair

1. One of our new tracts will be printed soon.
2. The Johnstown flood was catastrophic.
3. She brews delicious coffee.
4. The markets are laden with fruit.
5. Can you put the garden hose along the walk?
6. Pete really has grown up.
7. The steps almost are too steep.
8. That is a most precious book.
9. Test her knowledge with this one.
10. Gene's is the fastest.
11. Joe laughed out loud.
12. They put Jon ahead of Leslie.
13. The jam especially was good.
14. A Negro man sat on the chair.
15. Jud entered a contest.

Can you compose another set of similar sentences containing other books of the Bible?

Biblical Anagrams That Make Sense

Adam and Eve.
    A man evaded.

The Ark of the Covenant.
    Noah voteth craft keen.

As the twig is bent, the tree is inclined.
    See treatise's intent: "Begin with child."

The bottomless pit.
    Hottest step—limbo.

Christian.
    Rich saint!

Christianity.
    I cry that I sin.
    Charity's in it.

Christmastime.
    It charms mites.

Destruction of Jerusalem.
    Judea mourns for its elect.

Devil in man.
    An evil mind.

Episcopalianism.
    Claim a pope is sin.

Epistler.
    Repliest.

The evangelist.
  List! Get heaven.

An everlasting life.
  Safe, eternal living.

Evil.
  Vile.

"The First Apostle"
  St. Peter's fit halo.

The forbidden fruit.
  Both fed; rift; ruined.

Garden of Gethsemane.
  E'en God-man fags there.

A good name is better than great riches.
  Be not a hoarder; right acts gain esteem.

Jesus Christ, the savior of the world.
  'Tis the just child who saves of error.

The judgment day of the blessed saviour.
  Jesus, thy advent so famed be our delight.

The Lord's Prayer.
  Thy errors plead.
  Pester "Old Harry."

Mephistopheles.
  The hopeless imp.
  He, Sheol's pet imp.

Our Father who art in heaven.
  In woe, haven for a hurt heart.

Pharisaicalness.
  A precisian's lash.

Presbyterian.
  Best in prayer.

The Prince of Darkness.
  Archfiend sent pokers.

Revised edition.
  Edited revision.

Star of Bethlehem.
  Halts before them.
  Blest the far home.

Ten Commandments.
  Can't mend most men.

Testament.
  Statement.

Three score years and ten.
  So thy career nearest end.

To cast pearls before swine.
  One's labor is perfect waste.

Tree of knowledge of Good and Evil.
  God grew food in Eden! Eve took fall.

The valley of the shadow of death.
  What have fools had to defy Lethe?

The wages of sin is death.
  Gee! Fate's shadow in this.
  High fees owed satanist.

Biblical Palindromes

Are we not drawn onwards, we Jews, drawn onward to new era?
Do Good's deeds live on? No, Evil's deeds do, O God.
Eve damned Eden, mad Eve.
Madam, in Eden I'm—Adam.
Naomi, did I moan?
So may Obadiah, even in Nineveh, aid a boy, Amos.
St. Simon sees no mists.

In Eden, I

Adam: Madam—
  Eve: Oh, who—
Adam: Named under a ban
      A bared, nude man—
  Eve: Heh?
Adam: Madam, I'm Adam.
  Eve: Name of a foeman?
Adam: O stone me! Not so.
  Eve: Mad! A maid I am, Adam.
Adam: Mad as it is, it is Adam.
  Eve: Eve mine. Denied, under a ban,
      a bared nude in Eden, I'm Eve.
Adam: Even in Eden I win Eden in Eve.
  Eve: I'm a Madam Adam, am I?
Adam: Aha!

  Abel: Name's Abel, a male base man.
  Eve: No, son.

  Cain: Miss, I'm Cain, a monomaniac.
      Miss, I'm—
  Eve: Name not so, O stone man!

Adam: Tut-tut.

"MY GOD, MY GOD . . . "

Now it came to pass early in the morning, toward the last day of the term,
that there arose a multitude smiting their books and wailing. There was
much weeping and gnashing of teeth, for the day of judgment was at hand;

and they were sore afraid. For they had left undone those things which they ought to have done, and had done those things which they ought not to have done; and there was no help for it.

And there were many abiding in the town which kept watch over their books all night, but it availeth naught. And some of them repented of their evil ways and of their riotous living, but they have not any hope. Yet others there are who arise peacefully, for they had prepared themselves and had made straight the paths of knowledge: and these were known as the faithful burners of the midnight oil.

And the multitude arose and ate the morning meal: some with a light heart, some with a heavy heart, but for the most part with no heart at all. And at the house of study they came to pass. Some few were to pass out.

At the Final hour there came among them one called Teacher and Master; and with a smile of Satan he strewed papers among them and went his way.

Many and varied were the answers they wrote: for some of his teachings had been sown in fertile minds, others had fallen among weeds, still others had fallen on hard rock, and some by the wayside. And of the multitude there were those who wrote for one hour, others for two. But some turned their faces away sorrowfully and wept, for these were the ones who had not any hope.

And when all had finished, they gathered up their belongings and quietly went their separate ways, each one on his own path and each one vowing to himself: "I shall not pass this way again!"

—Lamentations 0:0

A Biblical Cake

1 cup Judges 5:25
3½ cups I Kings 4:22
2 cups I Samuel 30:12
2 cups I Samuel 30:12
1 cup Genesis 24:17
1 cup Genesis 43:11 (last word)
    a little Leviticus 2:13
6 Isaiah 10:14
    I Kings 10:2 to taste
1 tbs. Exodus 16:31

Sift two teaspoonsfuls of baking powder with flour; blanch almonds; chop figs. Follow Solomon's advice for making good boys—Proverbs 23:14: "Thou shalt beat him with the rod."

Judges 5:25. She brought forth *butter* in a lordly dish.
I Kings 4:22. Solomon's provision for one day was thirty measures of fine *flour*.

I Samuel 30:12. They gave him a piece of cake of *figs,* and two clusters of *raisins.*

Genesis 24:17. Let me, I pray thee, drink a little *water.*

Genesis 43:11. Carry down the man a present, a little balm, and a little honey, spices, and myrrh, nuts, and *almonds.*

Leviticus 2:13. With all thine offerings thou shalt offer *salt.*

Isaiah 10:14. As one gathereth *eggs* that are left, have I gathered all the earth; and there was none that moved the wing, or opened the mouth, or peeped.

I Kings 10:2. She came to Jerusalem with a very great train, with camels that bare *spices.*

Exodus 16:31. The taste of it was like wafers made with *honey.*

Nickname Bibles

(Based on publishing boners or odd translations)

Affinity Bible: Included a table of affinity as appendix, which read, "A man may not marry his grandmother's wife."

Breeches Bible 1560: "They sewed fig leaves together, and made themselves *breeches*" (KJV: "aprons," Gen. 3:7).

Bug Bible 1551: "Afraid of *bugs* (bugges) by night" (KJV: "terror," Ps. 91:5).

Camels Bible 1823: "And Rebekah arose, and her *camels,* and they rode upon the camels" (KJV: "damsels," Gen. 24:61).

Discharge Bible 1806: "I *discharge* thee before God" (KJV: "charge," I Tim. 5:21).

Ears to Ear Bible 1810: "Who hath ears to *ear* let him hear" (KJV: "hear," Matt. 13:9).

Fool Bible ca. 1630: "The fool hath said in his heart there *is a* God" (KJV: "is no God," Ps. 14).

He Bible 1611, first edition of KJV: "*He* took it up and went into the city, and her mother-in-law" (KJV: "she," Ruth 2:18).

Judas Bible: Contains various misprints, one substituting Judas for Jesus.

Lions Bible: Contains many typographical errors, among which is "Kings shall come out of thy *lions*" (KJV: "loins," Gen. 35:11).

Murderer's Bible ca. 1801: "These are the murderers, complainers" (KJV: "murmurers," Jude 16).

Murderer's Bible: "The murderer shall surely be put *together* (KJV: "to death," Num. 35:18).

Murderer's Bible: "Let the children first be *killed* " (KJV: "filled," Mark 7:27).

Place-Makers Bible ca. 1562: "Blessed are the *place-makers*" (KJV: "peacemakers," Matt. 5:9).

Printer's Bible ca. 1702: "*Printers* have persecuted me without cause" (KJV: "princes," Ps. 119:61).

Rosin Bible 1609, Douay: "Is there no *rosin* in Gilead?" (KJV: "balm," Jer. 8:22).

Sin on Bible: "Go, and sin *on* more" (KJV: "no," John 8:11).

Standing Fishes Bible 1806: "The *fishes* shall stand upon it" (KJV: "fishers," Ezek. 47:10).

To Remain Bible 1805: In Galatians 4:29 the words *to remain* were inserted in place of a comma.

Treacle Bible 1568: "Is there no *treacle* in Gilead?" (KJV: "balm," Jer. 8:22).

Unrighteous Bible 1653: "The unrighteous *shall* inherit the kingdom of God" (KJV: "shall not," I Cor. 6:9).

Vinegar Bible 1717: "Parable of the *Vinegar*" (KJV: vineyard, title for Luke 20:9).

Wicked/Adulterous Bible 1631: "Thou shalt commit adultery" (Exod. 20:14).

Wife-beater Bible 1549: "Beat the fear of God into her head" (note to I Peter 3:7).

Wife-hater Bible 1810: "If a man come to me and hate not his . . . own *wife* " (KJV: "life," Luke 14:26).

Biblically Inspired Boners

These are some student answers to earlier versions of the KJV quizzes (see Part IV of this handbook, below) and to the pretest (Part III, chapter 9, above). Students enjoy them—even their own, if anonymous, but only when they are familiar with the correct answers.

Gen.	2:8	"And the Lord God planted a garden of *herbs* in Eden."
	2:22	Eve was created from *an apple tree.*
	3:6	Eating the forbidden fruit is often called the *Immortal* Sin.
	3:16	Eve's punishment: "In sorrow thou shalt bring forth *bread.*"

3:16	Eve was told, "In *conception* thou shalt bring forth children."
3:16	Eve was told, "In *labor* thou shalt bring forth children."
3:19	"In the sweat of thy face shalt thou eat *dirt.*"
3:19	"In the sweat of thy face shalt thou eat *dust.*"
4:9	Cain said, "Am I my brother's *son*?"
4:13	Cain said, "My punishment is greater than I can *bare.*"
4:13	Cain said, "My *cross* is greater than I can bear."
4:15	The mark of Cain was *a coat of many colors.*
8:7	Before sending a dove, Noah first sent out a *hawk.*
12:7	God *planted* the land of Canaan to Abraham's seed.
14:12	Lot was Abraham's *task.*
16:12	Every man's hand was against Hagar's son, named *Isthmus.*
16:12	The angel said *Eve's* "hand will be against every man."
16:12	Ishmael's "hand will be against every *Semite.*"
19:24	Sodom and Gomorrah were *twins.*
19:24	Sodom and Gomorrah were *lovers.*
19:26	Lot's wife turned into a pillar of *fire.*
19:26	Lot's wife turned *Christian.*
22:2	God asked Abraham to sacrifice Isaac on Mount *Montezuma.*
22:2	Abraham took his son Isaac up the mountain to be *baptized.*
22:2	Abraham took his son Isaac up the mountain to be *circumcized.*
22:2	Abraham took his son Isaac up the mountain to be *washed.*
24:67	Isaac's wife was named *Rebuka.*
25:24	Esau sold to his brother Jacob his *ladder.*
25:24	Esau sold to his brother Jacob his *wife.*
25:24	Esau was Jacob's *wife.*
29:10	Rachel was both Jacob's wife and his *daughter.*
29:28	Rachel was Jacob's cousin, wife, and *friend.*

	32:24	Jacob wrestled all night with *his conscience.*
	32:24	Jacob wrestled all night with *a serpent.*
	32:24	Jacob wrestled all night with *Isaac.*
	37:3	Jacob made Joseph a *"rainbow* of many colors."
	41:5	Joseph said the thin corn meant seven years of *bad luck.*
	42:38	"Shall ye bring down my gray hairs with sorrow to the *roots.*"
	49:33	"He gathered up his feet into the bed, and *drew* up the ghost."
Exod.	2:5	Moses was set adrift in an ark made of *driftwood.*
	3:5	"Put off thy *feet*. . . , for the place whereon thou standest is holy ground."
	3:8	The promised land was "flowing with milk and *blood.*"
	3:8	God first spoke to Moses from a burning *cross.*
	3:8	God first spoke to Moses from a burning *chariot.*
	3:8	Moses first heard God's voice coming from a *bulrush* bush.
	5:1	"Thus saith the Lord God of Israel, 'Let my people *sleep.*'"
	5:7	Pharaoh forced the Hebrew slaves to make *bread* without straw.
	5:7	Pharaoh forced the Hebrew slaves to make *beds* without straw.
	12:7	The Israelites put the *leg* of a lamb on their doorposts.
	12:17	At Passover Jews were to eat the paschal lamb and *unLevin* bread.
	14:22	After the Israelites crossed, the Egyptians were drowned in the *Red River.*
	14:22	The Israelites crossed the Red Sea by *diving the waters.*
	14:24	The Egyptians were drowned in the *dessert.*
	16:15	The food sent from heaven for the Israelites was *locusts & honey.*
	16:15	The food sent from heaven for the Israelites was *bread and fish.*

	16:15	For food in the wilderness God sent to the Israelites *matzoh*.
	20:1	The ten commandments are known (in Greek) as the *Decadent*.
	20:1	Moses was given the ten commandments on Mount *Synide*.
	20:1	Moses was given the ten commandments on Mount *Ida*.
	20:1	Moses received the ten commandments on Mount *Olympus*.
	20:7	"Thou shalt not take the name of the Lord thy God in *vein*."
	20:14	"Thou shalt not commit *adlutery*."
	20:17	"Thou shalt not *stone* thy neighbor's house."
	28:29	The holy of holies is the inner sanctum or sanctum *Saint Toram*.
	32:4	While Moses was gone, Aaron made for the people a *cross*.
Lev.	13:45	When he came among people a *lepod* had to cry, "Unclean!"
	25:4	The sabbatical year was originally to give *God* a rest.
	25:4	The sabbatical year was originally to give *liberty* a rest.
Num.	1:50	Members of the tribe of Levi served in the *tabaccle*.
	13:23	Two men had to carry on a staff one cluster of *serpents*.
	22:23	Balaam's ass saw the *angle*, but Balaam did not.
Deut.	8:3	"Man doth not live by bread *and water*."
	8:3	"Man doth not live by *sweat alone*."
	24:3	A man could divorce a wife he hated by giving her *an endowment*.
Josh.	6:4	The priests blew trumpets of *bull* horns before Jericho.
	6:20	Joshua opened Jericho's walls with *keys*.
	9:27	"Hewers of wood and *drinkers* of water."
	9:27	"Hewers of wood and drawers of *pictures*."

	10:12	In a battle God helped Joshua by making the sun and moon *collide*.
	10:12	God helped Joshua by making the sun and moon *flood*.
Judges	7:16	Gideon's men carried *spies* inside pitchers.
	7:16	Gideon's men carried lamps hidden inside *pumpkins*.
	13:5	A Nazarite was consecrated to God and did not cut his *throat*.
	16:17	The secret of Samson's strength was in his *head*.
	16:17	The secret of Samson's strength was in his *mind*.
	16:17	The secret of Samson's strength was in his *coat of many colors*.
	16:17	The secret of Samson's strength was in his *heel*.
	20:1	"From Dan to *dusk*."
	20:1	"From Dan to *Mizhap*."
Ruth	1:16	"Entreat me not to *kill thee*."
	1:16	"Entreat me not to *eat thee*."
	1:16	"Entreat me not to *sin*."
	2:3	Ruth gleaned in the fields of Boaz after the *foxes* were through.
	2:3	Ruth *bathed* in the field of Boaz after the reapers were done.
	2:3	Ruth *grazed* in the field of Boaz after the reapers were done.
	4:7	Boaz fulfilled Ruth's claim of *adultery* by marrying her.
	4:17	Ruth and Boaz were David's *daughters*.
	4:17	David was the great grandson of Ruth and *Baez*.
I Sam.	3:20	"From Dan to *Danube*" they knew Samuel to be a prophet.
	10:1	As first king of Israel, Samuel anointed the head of *Jesus Christ*.
	13:9	Saul offered a *holocaust* [hecatomb] unto God.
	16:23	David soothed the troubled Saul with *ointment*.
	16:23	To soothe King Saul, David played the *liar*.
	16:23	To soothe King Saul, David played the *mute*.
	16:23	To soothe King Saul, David played the *lure*.

	18:7	"Saul hath slain his *brother,* and David his ten thousands."
	18:7	"Saul hath slain his thousands, and David his *harp.*"
	28:12	To raise the dead Samuel, Saul called on the *winch* of Endor.
II Sam.	1:19	David's lament: "How are the mighty *smote!*"
	1:20	"Tell it not in Gath, publish it not in the *papers* of Askelon."
	1:20	"Tell it not in Gath, publish it not in the *journals* of Askelon."
	18:9	Absalom was killed when he was held fast by his *chair.*
	18:9	Absalom was killed when he was held fast by his *thumbs.*
	23:1	"Sweet *palmist* of Israel."
I Kings	3:9	"Give therefore thy servant an understanding *woman.*"
	6:1	In Jerusalem Solomon built the first *House of Lords.*
	10:1	Hearing of his wealth and wisdom, the Queen of Sheba visited *the Sheik.*
	11:11	God was angry with Solomon because his wives *outnumbered* him.
	16:31	Jezebel was Ahab's *donkey.*
	17:6	Elijah hid near a brook and was fed by *elves.*
	18:19	Elijah challenged the *profits* of Baal.
	18:21	"How long halt ye between two *pillars?*"
	18:21	"How long halt ye between two *thieves?*"
	18:44	"A little *wave* out of the sea, like a man's hand."
	18:46	Elijah "*picked* up his loins," and ran.
	18:46	Elijah "*looked* up his loins," and ran.
II Kings	2:11	The prophet who was carried to heaven in a chariot was *Eliza.*
	2:11	Elijah was carried to heaven in a flaming *cup of wine.*
	2:11	Elijah was carried to heaven in a flaming *boat.*
	2:11	Elijah was carried to heaven in a flaming *coffin.*

	2:14	Elisha "took up also the *conch*" of Elijah and became his successor.
	5:27	Because of his disobedience, Elisha's servant became a *leaper.*
	5:27	Because of his disobedience, Elisha's servant became a *leopard.*
	24:1	Nebuchadnezzar the Chaldean looted the *stores* in Jerusalem.
Esther		Two Old Testament books are named for women: Ruth and Queen *Elizabeth.*
	2:9	Esther was made *prophet* by King Ahasuerus.
	5:14	Haman built a *gibblet* for Mordecai but used it himself.
Job	1:7	Satan came from "*swinging* to and fro in the earth."
	1:12	God and Satan agreed to test the patience of *Jesus.*
	1:12	God and Satan agreed to test the patience of *each other.*
	5:7	Eliphaz said, "Man is born unto *woman,* as the sparks fly upward."
	19:20	"I am escaped with the skin of my *brother.*"
	19:20	"I am escaped with the skin of my *ancestors.*"
	19:20	"I am escaped with the skin of my *bones.*"
	19:25	Job insisted, "I know that my *savoir* liveth."
	40:15	"Behold now *Bohemian,* which I made with thee."
	41:1	"Canst thou draw out *water* with an hook?"
Psalms	8:2	"Out of the *womb* of babes and sucklings."
	8:4	"What is man, that thou art *afraid* of him?"
	8:5	"Thou hast made him a little lower than the *ants.*"
	8:5	"Thou hast made him a little lower than the *serpent.*"
	19:1	"The heavens declare the glory of God; and the *filament* showeth his handiwork."
	19:2	"Day unto day uttereth speech, and night unto night showeth *silence.*"
	22:16	"They pierced my hands and my *ears.*"

22:18	"They part my *lips* among them, and cast lots upon my vesture."
23:1	Psalm 23 begins, "The Lord is my *sheeper*."
23:2	"He maketh me to lie down in green *waters*."
37:35	"The wicked . . . spreading himself like a green bay *packer*."
42:5	"Why art thou cast down, O my *prophetic soul?*"
51:5	"I was shapen in iniquity, and in *the womb* did my mother conceive me."
51:17	"A broken and a *misshapen* heart, O God, thou wilt not despise."
103:15	"As for man, his days are as *nights*."
107:23	"They that go down to the sea in *shifts*."
107:23	"They that go down to the sea in *Hades*."
127:1	"Except the Lord build the house, they *sweat* in vain that build it."
137:1	"By the rivers of *Bethlehem*."
137:2	"We hanged our *heads* upon the willows."
137:2	"We hanged our *flowers* upon the willows."
137:2	"We hanged our *necks* upon the willows."
137:2	"We hanged our harps upon the *wall*."
137:2	"We hanged our harps upon the *books*."
137:2	"We hanged our harps upon the *waters*."
137:2	"We hanged our *hearts* upon the willows."
137:2	"We hanged our *troubles* upon the willows."
137:5	"If I forget thee, O Jerusalem, let my right hand forget her *left*."

Prov.		Two books, Proverbs and Song of Songs, are said to have been written by *Shakespeare*.
	3:18	"She is a *beauty* of life to them that lay hold upon her."
	3:18	"She is a tree of *wrath* to them that lay hold upon her."
	6:6	"Go to the ant, thou *bug*."
	15:1	"A soft answer turneth away *no one*."
	22:13	"The slothful man saith, 'A lion is in the *bed*.'"
Eccles.	11:1	"Cast thy bread upon the *street:* for thou shalt find it after many days."
	12:12	"Of making many books there is no *bindings*."

Isaiah	2:4	"They shall beat their swords into *the ground*."
	2:4	"They shall beat their *bread* into plowshares."
	2:4	"They shall beat their swords into plowshares, and their *forks* into pruninghooks."
	2:4	"They shall beat their swords into plowshares, and their *souls* into pruninghooks."
	2:4	"Nation shall not lift up sword against nation, neither shall they learn *nothing* any more."
	6:11	Isaiah asked, "Lord, how *come?*" would Israel not see and hear.
	9:6	"His name shall be called . . . The *Justice* of Peace."
	11:6	"And a little child shall *feed them*."
	11:6	"The wolf shall dwell with the lamb, . . . and a little child shall *eat* them."
	11:6	"The wolf shall dwell with the lamb, . . . and a little child shall *cry*."
	14:12	"How art thou fallen from heaven, O *Jenifer!*"
	14:12	"How art thou fallen from heaven, O *Christ!*"
	22:13	"Let us eat and drink; for tomorrow we shall *fast*."
	22:13	"Let us eat and drink; for tomorrow we shall *fight*."
	22:13	"Let us eat and drink; for tomorrow we shall *diet*."
	49:4	"I have labored in *pain*."
Jere.	13:23	"Can the Ethiopian change his skin, or the *leper* his spots?"
Lam.	3:19	"The *woodworm* and the gall."
Ezek.	1:16	Ezekiel saw a wheel inside a *bottle*.
	37:1	In a valley Ezekiel saw a heap of dry *water*.
Dan.	3:12	The three Jews in the furnace were *Shamrock*, Meshach, and Abednego.
	3:22	The men who threw the three Jews into the furnace were *Mene, Mene, and Tekel*.
	5:5	At Belshazzar's feast there appeared handwriting on the *lamb*.
	5:27	Belshazzar was weighed in the balances and found *too heavy*.

	6:16	The prophet who was thrown into the lions' den was named *Richard*.
	6:16	The prophet who was thrown into the lions' den was named *Hecate*.
	6:16	The prophet who was thrown into the lions' den was named *Androcles*.
	6:16	Daniel was saved by an angel from a den of *iniquity*.
Jonah	1:17	Jonah spent some time inside a *church*.
Sirach	13:1	"He that toucheth *me* shall be defiled therewith."
	38:34	"He that *kills* his son causeth him oft to feel the rod."
Gospels		The four Gospels were written by *Matthew, Mark, Luther, & John*.
		Matthew, Mark, Luke, and John wrote the *Gossiples*.
Matt.	2:9	"And, lo, the star, which they saw in the east, went *down*."
	2:11	Two of the gifts of the magi were *gold & myrrth*.
	2:13	The king of Judea at the time of Jesus was named *Herald*.
	3:2	Because "the kingdom of heaven is at hand," John warned people to *flee*.
	3:3	"The voice of one crying in the *manger*."
	3:4	John wore rough clothes; he ate "locusts and *mild* honey."
	3:15	Jesus was baptized by *Moses*.
	4:1	In the wilderness Jesus was tempted by *Mary Magdalene*.
	4:18	One of Jesus' miracles for Peter was the Great *graft* of Fishes.
	5:8	"Blessed are the *young* in heart: for they shall see God."
	5:9	"Blessed are the *Jews:* for they shall be called the children of God."
	5:13	"Ye are the salt of the *water*."
	5:13	"Ye are the *scum* of the earth."
	5:17	"I am not come to *empty*, but to fulfill."
	5:18	Not "one *jobble* or one tittle" of the law would change.

5:38	"It hath been said, 'An eye for an eye, and a *toot* for a tooth.'"
5:41	"Whosoever shall compel thee to go a mile, go with him *train*."
5:41	"Whosoever shall compel thee to go a mile, go with him *twine*."
6:3	"Let not thy left hand *undo* what thy right hand doeth."
6:9	"Hallowed be thy name. Thy kingdom *done*."
6:13	This version of the Lord's Prayer ends in a *dioxide*.
6:13	This version of the Lord's Prayer ends in a *trilogy*.
6:13	"Thine is the kingdom, and the power, and the *light*."
6:20	"Lay up for yourselves *a bed* in heaven."
6:24	"Ye cannot serve God and *Merman*."
6:28	"Consider the *laborers* of the field, how they grow."
6:30	"O ye of little *people?*"
6:34	"Sufficient unto the day is the evil *eye*."
7:12	"All things whatsoever ye would that men should do to you, do ye even *worse* to them."
7:15	"False prophets" are like wolves "in sheep's *skin*."
7:16	"Ye shall *eat* them by their fruits."
7:26	In the parable, the *sand* man built his home upon the sand.
8:22	"Let the dead bury their *grudges*."
9:17	"Neither do men put new wine into old *skins*."
10:6	"Go rather to the lost *horizon*."
10:15	Jesus warned the unheeding against the "*lack* of judgment."
10:39	"He that loseth his *mind* for my sake shall find it."
12:25	"Every . . . house divided against itself shall not *beget*."
13:18	The stories by which Jesus taught were called *probables*.
13:18	The stories by which Jesus taught were called *parodies*.

13:46   Jesus likened the kingdom of heaven to a *mustard seed* of great price.

13:57   "A prophet is not without honor, save in his own *mind.*"

14:4   John the Baptist criticized Herod for *marring* Herodias.

14:8   After Salome danced, she asked Herod for John the Baptist's *coat.*

14:19   Jesus fed the multitude of five thousand with five loaves and two *jugs.*

16:23   "Get thee behind me, *James.*"

16:23   "Get thee behind me, *quick.*"

16:24   "Let him deny himself, and take up his cross, and *strike* me."

17:1   James, John, and Peter saw Jesus talking with Elias and Moses during the *transgression* of Jesus.

18:20   "Where two or three are gathered *sin* in my name, there am I."

18:20   "There am I in the *mist* of them."

18:22   Jesus told Peter to *beat* a sinner "until seventy times seven times."

18:22   Jesus told Peter to *be* a sinner "until seventy times seven times."

21:13   Jesus said they had made the temple a "den of *inequity.*"

23:24   "Ye blind guides, which strain at a *leash,* and swallow a camel."

24:2   "There shall not be left one stone upon *thee.*"

26:31   Jesus foretold that Peter would three times *arise.*

26:36   Jesus was in agony in the garden of *Eden.*

26:41   "The spirit indeed is willing, but the flesh is *cold.*"

26:41   "The spirit indeed is willing, but the flesh is *drowsy.*"

27:24   Feeling no responsibility, Pilate publicly washed his *body.*

27:46   One of the "seven last words of Christ" was *"Verily, verily, I say unto you."*

27:49   The soldiers mocked Jesus and put on him a crown of *thrones.*

	28:5-6	"He is not here: for he is *dead.*"
Mark	5:41	Mark quotes Jesus' words in the *Aromatic* language and translates.
	9:17	Jesus cured a boy with a "dumb *head,*" probably an epileptic.
	10:14	"Suffer the little *pain* to come unto me."
	14:22	At the Last Supper Jesus said the bread they ate was *burnt.*
	14:22	At the Last Supper Jesus said the bread they ate was *poisoned.*
	14:22	At the Last Supper Jesus said the bread they ate was *stale.*
Luke		The Last of the three Synoptic Gospels is the Gospel of *Luck.*
	1:26	Although Jesus was born in Bethlehem, he and his family lived in *a manger.*
	1:28	"Hail, . . . the Lord is with thee; blessed art thou among *sinners.*"
	1:28	Mary learned of the coming of Jesus in the episode known as the *conception.*
	1:28	Mary learned of the coming of Jesus in the episode known as the *assumption.*
	1:28	Mary learned of the coming of Jesus in the episode known as the *enunciation.*
	1:28	Mary learned of the coming of Jesus in the episode known as the *visitation.*
	1:42	"Blessed is the fruit of thy *moon.*"
	1:42	"Blessed is the fruit of thy *labor.*"
	2:1	"There went out a decree from *Saint* Augustus."
	2:4	Joseph and Mary left Nazareth to be *born* in Bethlehem.
	2:29	The Nunc Dimittis begins, "Lord, *Jesus* lettest thou thy servant depart."
	2:32	"A light to lighten the *lamp.*"
	2:32	"A light to lighten the *genitil.*
	2:46	When Jesus was twelve, he sat in the temple *conducting his father's business.*
	10:33	The man beaten by thieves was helped by the good *shepherd.*

15:29	"Lo, these many *ears*."
16:2	The rich man said, "Give an *inkling* of thy stewardship."
16:22	In the parable, the dead beggar Lazarus went to "Abraham's *bossem*."
16:22	Lazarus died and was carried by angels to Abraham's *womb*.
19:5	Jesus ate at the house of Zaccheus, the *chef publican*.
21:2	"He saw also a certain poor widow casting in thither two *smites*."
22:3	"Then entered *Jesus* into Judas surnamed Iscariot."
22:3	"Then entered *Caesar* into Judas surnamed Iscariot."
22:12	Jesus and the disciples ate the passover in a "large *banquet* room."
22:15	The occasion of the Last Supper was probably the Jewish holiday of *Yom Kippur*.
22:20	"This cup is the new *juice* in my blood."
22:20	"This cup is the new *wine* in my blood."
22:42	"Father, if thou be willing, remove this *thorn* from me."
22:42	"If thou be willing, *drink* this cup from me."
22:48	"*God*, betrayest thou the Son of man with a kiss?"
23:34	"They parted his raiment and cast *stones*."
23:34	"They *shed* his raiment, and cast lots."
24:30	Jesus opened his disciples' eyes at Emmaus when he broke *Passover*.
John 1:1	Both Genesis and the last Gospel start with "*Brethern*."
1:1	"In the beginning was the *flesh*."
1:14	"And the word was made *good*."
1:14	"And the word was made *by God*."
1:14	"And the word was made *fresh*."
1:14	"And the *bread* was made flesh."
2:11	Jesus' first miracle was at Cana, where he created *the three Kings*.

8:32	"The truth shall make you *shudder*."
8:32	"The truth shall make you *poor*."
10:14	"I am the *lost* shepherd."
10:14	"I am the good *earth*."
12:13	They "took branches of palm trees . . . and cried, '*help*.'"
12:13	They "took branches of palm trees . . . and cried, '*O'Hannah*.'"
12:15	"Behold, thy King cometh, sitting on an *woman*'s colt."
13:26	Jesus indicated who would betray him by giving him a *sod*.
13:26	Jesus indicated who would betray him by giving him a *sob*.
13:26	To show that it was Judas who would betray him, he *sopped him*.
14:2	"In my Father's house are many *enemies*."
14:2	"In my Father's house are many *windows*."
14:2	"In my Father's house are many *women*."
14:2	"I go to prepare a *supper* for you."
14:6	"No man cometh unto the Father, but by *woman*."
19:5	The priests delivered Jesus up to *Ponchas Piolet*.
19:25	"There stood by the cross of Jesus his *garments*."
20:17	Jesus told Mary Magdalene at the tomb, "Touch me *again*."

Acts	1:9	The Ascension was when Jesus finally went to heaven for good.
	2:4	On the Pentecost "they were all *stricken* with the Holy Ghost."
	2:4	On the Pentecost the apostles spoke to the pilgrims "with *split* tongues."
	2:4	The apostles spoke to the pilgrims "with *spiked* tongues."
	5:3	"Ananias, why hath Satan filled thine heart to *listen* to the Holy Ghost?"
	6:6	Believers received the Holy Ghost through *sitting* on of hands.
	7:51	Stephen said non-Christian Jews were "uncircumcised in *common*."

	7:59	When he was young, Saul of Tarsus *revoked God.*
	8:1	At the stoning of Stephen "Saul was *lifted* unto his death."
	9:3	Saul saw the light, and was converted, on the road to *recovery.*
	9:3	Saul saw the light, and was converted, on the road to *Catholicism.*
	9:4	"Saul, Saul, why persecutest thou *self* ?"
	9:4	"Saul, Saul, why *persuadest* thou me?"
	17:28	"In him we live, and move, and have our *children.*"
	19:19	"Many . . . brought their *clothes* together, and burned them."
	21:24	After his missionary trip, Paul, with four who got haircuts on completion of their Nazarite vows, *circumcized* himself.
	21:39	Paul was "a Jew of Tarsus, . . . a citizen of no mean *Roman.*"
	25:11	Rather than be tried in Jerusalem as a Jew, Paul *repealed* to Caesar.
Romans		The Epistle to the Romans was written by *Pauline.*
I Cor.	11:3	"The *envy* of the woman is the man."
	13:1	"Though I speak with the tongues of men and of angels, and have not *sinned,* I am become as sounding brass, or a tinkling cymbal."
	13:1	"I am become as *strumpeting* brass or a tinkling cymbal."
	13:1	"Charity" in the King James Version of the New Testament is now taken to mean *"give."*
	13:12	"For now we see through a glass *bottle.*"
	13:12	"For now we see through a glass *eye.*"
	13:12	"For now we see through a glass *vase.*"
	13:13	"And now abideth faith, hope, and *prosperity.*"
	15:50	"*Bread* and blood cannot inherit the kingdom."
Gal.	6:7	"Whatsoever a man soweth, that shall he also *wear.*"
II Tim.	4:7	"I have fought a *losing* fight . . . I have kept the faith."

Titus	1:15	"Unto the pure all things are *bad.*"
Heb.		The Epistle to the Hebrews went to unidentified Christians who were *dead.*
James		The Epistle of James is called a *Scarlet* (general) letter.
I Peter	4:8	"Charity shall cover the multitude of *angles.*"
Rev.	6:8	"The four horsemen appear in the *Acropolis.*"
	7:14	"Washed . . . in the blood of the *babes.*"
	7:14	"Washed . . . in the blood of the *Red Sea.*"
	17:5	The *Scarlot* woman was "Babylon the Great, the Mother of Harlots."

And from essays:

The Old Testament is used by Jews, Christians and Catholics; and the New Testament is used by Catholics and Christians.

The Bible shows us a style . . . filled with inversions, cliches, metaphors, and allusions.

I feel the course has enlightened my knowledge of the scared life of Christ.

The Bible teaches the wrong way of doing things and the right way. Jewish students learn about Jesus and Christian students learn about Mosses.

The Pentateuch is the first five books of the Bible. It is generally found in the Old Testament.

The first five books of the Old Testament are Genius, Exodus . . .

And some deliberate wise answers:

Gen.	32:24	Jacob wrestled all night with *insomnia.*
	41:27	The seven thin cows in Pharaoh's dream meant *no milk.*
Prov.	1:1	The wise sayings in proverbs are generally attributed to *parents.*
	16:18	"Pride goeth before *Prejudice.*"
Matt.	14:8	Salome danced for Herod in order to get *ahead.*

PART IV
The Bible *for* Literature

CHAPTER	Study Questions
11	**and Quizzes**

The following pages are designed to help students become familiar with what is in the Bible, so that they will recognize biblical allusions in literature and elsewhere. If that is the main objective of a course or unit, then the principal emphasis should be on learning and remembering biblical quotations, stories, and names.

Toward this end, these study questions and quizzes may be useful. They cover Bible passages that students will meet most often in our culture. The selections aim at broad coverage but are broken down into manageable reading assignments. Thus, the teacher may select assignments that will best suit the course.

For each of the forty-seven assignments there are two sets of questions:

Study questions focus students' attention on those passages that are most commonly quoted or referred to in the humanities and in everyday life. Occasionally, we have formulated these questions so that they furnish extratextual information that may be useful for literary allusions (e.g., the "forbidden fruit") or simply for understanding the language of the text.

Students can find the answers to these study questions in the biblical text, except for a few questions (marked *) that they may look up in a dictionary or a simple reference book—a Bible encyclopedia or even a Bible storybook. If a student cannot find the answer in such a case, little is lost: nearly always, the corresponding quiz question does not depend on that information.

To save teachers time, we have filled in the blanks in the questions with suggested answers. In some instances, more than one answer is acceptable. In others, only one is appropriate. Where it is a matter of direct quotation, it seems proper for the teacher to insist on the exact words of the text.

Quizzes constitute a police action, to make sure that students actually read the words of the Bible. They also can provide learning reinforcement if used thoughtfully. Quiz questions vary from their related study questions in three respects: (a) they appear in a different order and sometimes in slightly different language; (b) they call for different spaces to be filled in; and (c) a few of them are new questions that were not among the study questions.

For the teacher's convenience we have furnished, in addition to the answers, two other bits of information: the biblical citation and the number of the corresponding study question. New quiz questions carry a symbol (**#**) instead of a study question number.

Quizzes are fairly simple. For example, students will have to remember only the most important of the names. And those that are asked for usually appear, spelled correctly, elsewhere on the page. Academically able students should get nearly all of them correct. For the less able, see a suggestions about grading, below. A student instruction sheet (reproduced below) explains to students the relation of the quizzes to the study questions and the best way to handle both the reading and the tests.

How a teacher uses these questions—or others like them—depends on his or her individual purposes, methods, materials, and students. The teacher may prefer to cover considerably less ground. In such a case, the teacher may either select from among the following assignments or change them and adapt the sets of questions. Conversely, the teacher may wish to insert a favorite quotable verse that we have omitted because it is fairly isolated. A rather complete list of familiar quotations appears in Part III, chapter 8, of this handbook.

We hope eventually to provide an abridged KJV text adapted to these assignments (with occasional transitional links between the selections) and printed question sheets. Without such material, however, students can easily find the assigned passages in a complete Bible.

Teachers have many procedural options: one assignment a week, or more; more passages to memorize than the seven listed here, or fewer; the addition of games and/or audio-visual materials (provided by teacher or students); the presentation of student projects at the end of the course or unit; time for discussion, cumulative review tests, and other activities—all affecting the number and kind of assignments one can make. Unless accompanied by other teaching methods and materials, this routine of study questions and quizzes can become monotonous and self-defeating.

Question sheets are least effective as learning aids in the case of biblical poetry, where there is no story line to provide a context that will help fix the passage in the student's memory. Aside from rote memorizing, one of the best ways of setting poems in students' minds is through a combination of aural and visual experiences. Students may follow the text while hearing it read in class; they may look at interpretive pictures presented to or by the students. They can listen to recordings on their own, and they must read them aloud.

A general audio-visual suggestion: As a rule, Bible-related music and pictures are particularly helpful before the quiz takes place—provided that they do not become a substitute for homework. They are also valuable as reinforcement afterward. The quizzes themselves, while serving a serious purpose, may be treated lightheartedly. In going over the answers in class, the teacher may want to read some anonymous but particularly good student boners, both for reinforcement and as a relief from the tension of testing. Part III, chapter 10, above, records some boners in their pristine state, accumulated by one teacher over many years. The class will enjoy those that refer to passages they have studied.

In the matter of grading, there are the usual offsetting problems. If a teacher does grade the quizzes, students may come to overemphasize the grade or to dislike the entire operation and begin to look for ways to pass without really studying—and without remembering much after the quiz. Further, if the teacher grades, he or she must decide how much leeway to allow for answers that are close but not exact and whether to use the same standard for the entire class. Will the nonacademic student be guaranteed defeat yet again? On the other hand, if the teacher does not grade, students are likely to get into the habit of not doing the homework, a practice that would seem excusable only for the very poorest readers.

One compromise is not to give a grade but merely to check each answer on the students' quizzes before handing them back and going over them in class. Then the teacher and student may measure the student's performance against his or her own ability. If a good student suddenly gets half of the answers wrong, or if an average student suddenly gets only three or four right, then both the teacher and the student know that the student probably did not do he homework. This may be forgivable on occasion; two or three consecutive incidents, however, might warrant a conference.

To protect the future usefulness of the quizzes, the teacher will most likely want to take them back from the students. As for study questions, one might want to collect them as well, at the end of the course or before the end, so that future students will have less temptation to bypass the text and study only completed worksheets.

In keeping with the purpose of studying the Bible *for* literature, the text is the KJV because nearly all quotations in literature and elsewhere use that language. In dealing with the Gospels, our principle has been to take most of Matthew and fill in from what is unique to Luke and John, with only two stories from Mark's version. In addition, the spelling and punctuation come from the American Bible Society's edition, which may vary a bit from other Bibles in the school or in students' homes because some archaisms in the 1611 edition have been updated.

Student Instruction Sheet

How to study for Bible quizzes—and for real learning:

1. You will not learn what you need to know, nor remember it for very long, if you do not follow these three steps:
   a) First, read the assigned Bible text.
   b) Then, try to answer the *study questions* from memory.
   c) And finally, check back with the book for answers.
   Copying someone else's answers or reading the book only to find answers to the *study questions* simply will not do the job. The *study questions* are different from the ones on the *quiz sheets.*
   Even if you do squeeze by a quiz now and then without following the three steps, you will never remember the information later, when you may want it or need it. Below are some details about the *study questions* and the *quizzes.*

2. You should read short assignments more than once. Read poetry aloud (more than once). Do not skip section titles, if your Bible has them. A few *study questions* (marked *) cannot be answered from the Bible text; you may have to use a dictionary or a simple Bible encyclopedia. And there are seven passages to memorize: the Ten Commandments (in abbreviated form), Psalm 23, the opening poem in Isaiah, the Beatitudes, the Lord's Prayer, the list of apostles, and the hymn to charity in I Corinthians (the *study sheets* will remind you).

3. Most of the questions in the *quizzes* will be similar to those on the study question sheets, but with three differences:

   a) The questions are in a different order and sometimes are worded a bit differently.

   b) The quiz question omits a word different from the one left out of the study question.

   c) Some new questions are thrown in—story facts, not quotations.

4. When you fill in a quotation on a *quiz sheet,* the answer should be the precise word used in the Bible. In most other cases, only one word can be correct; but a few questions permit more than one answer. As for spelling and grading, your teacher makes the rules. You will usually be able to find important names printed elsewhere on the *quiz sheet* so that you can check the spelling.

5. Do not leave the assignment until the last moment. Do it early; then read the passage again before the quiz. Finally, to make it really stick after the quiz, look for biblical references, allusions, and quotations in the newspaper and elsewhere—wherever you are. Then you will be doing more than just passing the course: You will be truly learning—and learning something worthwhile.

Assignments

1. Genesis 1:1-3:24 (Creation, Eden)

2. Genesis 4:1-16; 5:21-27; 6:1-9:19; 10:8-10; 11:1-9 (Cain and
   Abel, Enoch, Methuselah, Noah, Nimrod, Babel)

3. Genesis 11:31-12:9; 15:1-19:28; 21:1-21; 22:1-19; 24:1-4,10,
   11,15-27,50,51 (Abraham, Isaac)

4. Genesis 25:19-34; 27:1-29:30; 30:25-31:20; 32:1-33:11; 35:9-
   29 (Jacob)

5. Genesis 37:1-36; 39:1-23; 41:1-45:28; 49:29-33 (Joseph)

6. Exodus 1:8-4:20; 5:1-6:9; 7:14-24; 11:1-12:36; 13:1-10; 13:
   19-14:31 (Moses, Deliverance)

7. Exodus 15:27-17:16; 19:1-20:22; 31:18-34:29 (Wilderness)
   MEMORIZE the Ten Commandments, 20:2-17

8. Leviticus 13:9-17,45,46; 19:13-18; 25:1-12
   Numbers 13:1,2; 13:17-14:10; 14:26-45; 18:1,6-10,21-24; 20:1-
   13; 21:4-9; 22:15-23:12

9. Deuteronomy 6:1-9; 14:3-21; 19:1-7; 23:19,20; 24:1-6; 25:1-10;
   31:14-18; 34:1-12
   Joshua 2:1-24; 3:14-4:24; 5:13-6:27; 9:3-27; 10:6-14; 24:29-33

10. Judges 2:6-23; 4:1-5:8; 5:19-7:25; 10:6-12:7 (Deborah, Gideon,
    Jephthah)

11. Judges 13:1-5; 13:24-16:31 (Samson)
    Ruth 1:1-4:22

12. 1 Samuel 1:1-3,9-11; 2:12-26; 3:1-21; 8:1-11:15; 15:1-35
    (Samuel, Saul)

13. 1 Samuel 16:1-18:16; 28:3-25; 31:1-13 (Saul and young David)

14. 2 Samuel 1:1-2:4a; 5:1-10; 6:1-23; 11:1-12:25; 14:25,26; 15:
    1-37; 16:15-17:23; 18:1-19:8; 23:1-7 (David, Bathsheba,
    Absalom)

15. 1 Kings 1:5-8,11-14,28b-31,47-53; 3:3-9,16-28; 4:20-25; 6:1,
    17-22; 10:1-12,21-25; 11:1-13,29-31,37-43; 12:1-5,12-24;
    16:29-33; 17:1-19:18; 21:1-22:4; 22:29-40 (Solomon,
    Elijah, Ahab, Jezebel)

16. 2 Kings 2:1-3,8-14,19-25; 4:1-37; 4:42-6:7; 6:24-7:20; 9:1-
    13,21b-37; 10:18-27; 13:14-21; 17:7-9,15-20; 25:1-15,21b-
    24 (Elisha, Jehu, the end of both kingdoms)

17. Esther 1:1-3:11; 4:1-8:17; 9:23-28

18. Job 1:1-6:3; 6:24-27; 7:9-8:3; 8:20-9:6; 9:19-10:8; 11:1-8;
    12:1-5; 13:1-15; 14:1-4; 14:14-15:13; 16:1-3; 19:20-29

19. Job 21:1-16; 23:1-7; 27:1-6; 28:12-29:16; 31:5-32:10; 33:1-17;
    35:1-16; 38:1-41; 39:19-41:7; 41:31-42:17

20. Psalms 1; 8; 19; 22-24; 42

    MEMORIZE Psalm 23

21. Psalms 46; 51; 55; 63; 84; 90; 91; 96; 103; 107

22. Psalms 115; 118; 119:97-112; 121; 122; 127; 130; 133; 137;
    139; 146; 150

23. Proverbs 1:1-10; 3:1-20; 6:6-11; 9:13-10:2; 13:12-24; 15:1-5;
    16:18,19; 20:11,12; 22:1-6; 25:20-22; 26:1-14,27,28; 29:18-
    20; 30:15-28; 31:10-31

24. Ecclesiastes 1:1-4:16; 7:1-18; 8:2-15; 9:11,12; 11:1-12:13
    Song of Solomon 1:1-2:17

25. Isaiah 1:18-20; 2:1-4; 5:1-7; 6:1-13; 7:10-17; 9:1-7; 11:1-9
    MEMORIZE poem, 2:2-4

26. Isaiah 14:3,4,12-15; 21:11,12; 28:5,6,9,10; 32:1-8; 35:1-8;
    37:21-38:8; 40:1-16; 42:1-9; 48:20-22; 52:1-53:12; 61:1-9

27. Jeremiah 1:4-10; 4:23-28; 6:9-15; 13:20-27; 31:15-17

    Lamentations 1:1-4; 2:1-4; 3:18,19

    Ezekiel 1:1-28; 18:1-4; 37:1-14

    Hosea 8:1-12

    Joel 2:1-3,21-29

    Amos 1:1-2:12; 5:10-24; 7:10-15

28. Daniel 1:1-7; 2:1-6,10-15; 2:24-3:1; 3:3-6,8,12; 3:14-4:9; 4:
    19-6:24

    Jonah 1:1-4:11

29. Judith 4:1-3; 5:1-4; 7:1,2,19-27; 8:32-9:4; 10:1-23; 12:1-4;
    12:10-13:20; 14:11-15:11; 16:18-25

    Ecclesiasticus 13:1-8; 30:1-13; 44:1-15

    Susanna 1-64

30. Matthew 1:18-5:11

    <u>MEMORIZE</u> the <u>Beatitudes</u>, 5:3-10

31. Matthew 5:12-7:6

    <u>MEMORIZE</u> the <u>Lord's Prayer</u>, 6:9<u>b</u>-13

32. Matthew 7:7-8:27; 9:1-17; 10:1-42

    <u>MEMORIZE</u> the <u>apostles' names</u>, 10:2-4

33. Matthew 11:1-15,25-30; 12:22-14:36; 15:10-28

    Mark 5:1-24,35-43

34. Matthew 16:13-17:13; 18:1-22; 19:1-20:28

35. Matthew 21:1-22; 22:1-22,34-40; 23:23-36; 24:1-8; 25:1-46

36. Matthew 26:1-28:20

37. Luke 1:1-2:52

38. Luke 3:15-17; 4:16-32; 5:1-11; 10:1,17-42; 15:8-32; 16:10-31;
       18:9-14; 23:1-17,32-34,39-46; 24:13-53

39. John 1:1-29; 2:1-11; 3:1-21; 4:1-46; 5:1-9a; 6:25-40; 8:1-20,
       31-59; 10:1-18

40. John 11:1-45; 13:1-19; 13:31-14:7; 14:15-24; 15:1-17; 18:33-
       38; 19:1-5,25-27; 20:1-21:25

41. Acts 1:1-2:15; 2:29-42; 3:1-11; 4:32-5:11; 5:17-32; 6:1-7:2a;
       7:51-8:24; 9:1-31; 10:1-11:3

42. Acts 11:19-27; 12:1-25; 14:8-15:29; 15:36-41; 17:1-9; 17:16-
       18:6; 19:1-20

43. Acts 21:17-22:1; 22:22-23:24; 24:22-26:1; 26:24-28:30

44. Romans 1:1-7; 2:12-16,27-29; 3:19-31; 5:1-11; 6:20-23; 13:1-14
    1 Corinthians 5:1-5; 6:19-7:9; 9:19-23; 11:1-34

45. 1 Corinthians 13:1-13; 15:47-58
    Galatians 5:1-6:10
    1 Timothy 1:1,2; 3:1-7; 6:1-10
       MEMORIZE hymn to charity, 1 Cor. 13:1-13

46. Hebrews 11:1-40
    James 1:1,12-25; 2:14-26; 5:7-11
    1 Peter 2:18-3:8; 4:7-11
    1 John 2:18-25; 4:7-21

47. Revelation 1:1-20; 4:1-6:8; 7:1-4,9-17; 12:1-17; 17:1-18; 20:
       1-22:21

STUDY QUESTIONS 1 — Genesis 1:1-3:24 (Creation, Eden)

1. "In the _beginning_ God created the heaven and the earth."

2. On the first day God said, "Let there be _light_."

3. God made "the _lesser_ light to rule the night."

4. God "created man in his own _image_."

5. The sabbath is the day on which God _rested_ from all his work.

6. God "_blessed_ the seventh day, and sanctified it."

7. Adam [Hebrew: earth/man] was formed of the "_dust_ of the ground."

8. "And the Lord God planted a _garden_ eastward in Eden."

9.*The _Garden_ of Eden is known as Paradise [Persian: pleasure garden].

10. In its midst were a tree of _life_ and a tree of knowledge.

11. Forbidden fruit was on "the tree of the knowledge of _good and evil_."

12. "It is not good that the man should be _alone_."

13. God decided to make "a _help_ meet [helper suitable]" for Adam.

14. _Adam_ gave names to every living creature.

15. Eve was created out of Adam's _rib_.

16. Adam said, "This is now bone of my bones, and flesh of my _flesh_."

17. The story says that man and wife are "_one_ flesh."

18. The first clothing was made of _fig_ leaves.

19.*Eating the forbidden fruit is often called the _Original_ Sin.

20.*According to some traditions, the _serpent/snake_ was Satan.

21.*A man's Adam's apple is located in his _throat/neck_.

22. Eve's punishment was, "In sorrow shalt thou bring forth _children_."

23. Adam had to earn his bread by the "_sweat_ of his face" (or brow).

24. "Dust thou art, and unto dust shalt thou _return_."

25. Eve was so named because she was the "_mother_ of all living."

26.*The expulsion from Eden is often called the _Fall_ of Man.

*The answer is not in the Bible text

QUIZ 1 — Creation, Eden

1. God "blessed the _seventh_ day, and sanctified it."(2:3) (6)

2. God "created man in his _own_ image." (1:27) (4)

3. "The Lord God planted a garden _eastward_ in Eden." (2:8) (8)

4. _Eve_ ate the forbidden fruit first. (3:6) (#)

5. The expulsion from Eden is often called the Fall of _Man_ . (26)

6. The story says that man and wife are "one _flesh_ ."(2:24)(17)

7. "In the beginning God _created_ the heaven and the earth." (1:1) (1)

8. "It is not good that the _man_ should be alone."(2:18)(12)

9. In its midst were a _tree_ of life and a tree of knowledge. (2:9) (10)

10. Adam said he hid himself because he was _naked/afraid_. (3:10) (#)

11. The first _clothing/etc._ was made of fig leaves. (3:7) (18)

12. God made "the lesser _light_ to rule the night." (1:16) (3)

13. The Garden of _Eden_ is known as Paradise. (9)

14. Eve was told, "In _sorrow_ shalt thou bring forth children." (3:16) (22)

15. Eve was so named because she was the "mother of all _living_ ." (3:20) (25)

16. Adam gave _names/a name_ to every living creature. (2:19) (14)

17. Eating the forbidden fruit is often called the Original _Sin_ . (19)

18. On the first day God said, "_Let_ there be light." (1:3) (2)

19. "Dust thou art, and unto _dust_ shalt thou return." (3:19) (24)

20. "The tree of the _knowledge_ of good and evil" had forbidden fruit. (2:9) (11)

21. As punishment, the _serpent/snake_ had to crawl on its belly. (3:14) (#)

22. "In the sweat of thy face shalt thou eat _bread_ ."(3:19)(23)

23. The serpent tempted _Eve_ to eat of the forbidden fruit. (3:6) (#)

24. God decided to make "a help _meet_ " for Adam. (2:18) (13)

25. Eve was created out of _Adam_ 's rib. (2:22) (15)

26. According to tradition the forbidden fruit was an _apple_ . (21)

#Not a Study Question

STUDY QUESTIONS 2 — Genesis 4:1-16; 5:21-27; 6:1-9:19; 10:8-10;
11:1-9 (Cain & Abel, Enoch, Methuselah, Noah, Nimrod, Babel)

1. Abel was Cain's __brother__ .

2. "Am I my __brother's__ keeper?"

3. "My __punishment__ is greater than I can bear."

4. To protect the outcast Cain, "the Lord set a __mark__ " upon him.

5.*According to most traditions, the "mark of Cain" is on the __forehead__ .

6. Enoch was unusual because he "__walked__ with God."

7.*According to tradition, Enoch, like Elijah, was taken alive up to __heaven/God__ .

8. Methuselah lived __969__ years, longer than anyone else in the Bible.

9. "There were __giants__ in the earth in those days."

10. Noah had three __sons__ : Shem, Ham, and Japheth.

11.*According to tradition, the Semites are descended from __Shem__ .

12.*According to tradition, the Hamites are the __black/Negro__ race.

13. Noah took __two__ of every living thing into the ark.

14. During the flood it __rained__ for forty days and nights.

15. The ark rested upon the mountains of __Ararat__ .

16. The first __bird__ Noah sent out was a raven.

17. Noah felt at peace when the dove brought back an __olive__ leaf/branch.

18. "Whoso sheddeth man's blood, by __man__ shall his blood be shed."

19. As a sign of no such future floods, God put a __(rain)bow__ in the sky.

20. Tradition says that Nimrod, the "mighty __hunter__ ," built great cities.

21. The confusion of tongues resulted from the tower of __Babel__ .

QUIZ 2 — Cain & Abel, Enoch, Methuselah, Nimrod, Babel

1. Noah had three sons: Shem, ___Ham___, and Japheth.(6:10) (10)

2. According to tradition, Enoch was _alive/etc._ when he
   went to heaven with God. (5:24)   (7)

3. "Am I my brother's ___keeper___?" (4:9)   (2)

4. Noah was at peace when the ___dove___ brought back an
   olive leaf/branch. (8:11)   (17)

5. The confusion of tongues took place at the ___tower___ of
   Babel. (11:9)   (21)

6. Cain and ___Abel___ were brothers. (4:2)   (1)

7. Methuselah was unusual because he ___lived___ for a very
   long time. (5:27)   (8)

8. According to tradition, ___Shem___ is the ancestor of the
   Semites.   (11)

9. Tradition says that Nimrod the hunter built great
   cities. (10:9)   (20)

10. Enoch was unusual because he "walked with ___God___."(5:22)(6)

11. The ark rested upon the _mountain(s)_ of Ararat. (8:4)   (15)

12. "Whoso sheddeth man's blood, by man shall his ___blood___
    be shed." (9:6)   (18)

13. Most traditions say that the "mark of ___Cain___" is on
    the forehead.   (5)

14. Before sending a dove, Noah first sent a ___raven___. (8:7)(16)

15. To protect the outcast ___Cain___, God set a mark upon
    him. (4:15)   (4)

16. God's rainbow was a sign of no more such _floods_.(9:15)(19)

17. During the flood it rained for ___forty___ days and
    nights. (7:12)   (14)

18. Tradition says that ___Ham___ is the ancestor of the
    black race.   (12)

19. "My punishment is greater than I can ___bear___." (4:13)   (3)

20. Noah took two of every living thing into the
    ___ark___ (6:19)   (13)

21. "There were giants in the ___earth___ in those days." (6:4) (9)

STUDY QUESTIONS 3 — Genesis 11:31-12:9; 15:1-19:28; 21:1-21; 22:1-19; 24:1-4,10,11,15-27,50,51 (Abraham, Isaac)

1. God promised to make of Abram a "great __nation__" and a blessing.

2. Lot was Abram's (Abraham's) __nephew__.

3. God promised the __land__ of Canaan to Abraham's seed.

4. Because he had no __son/heir__, Abraham made his head servant his heir.

5. To the sleeping Abraham, God foretold the slavery and return to the land of __Canaan__.

6. Abraham took his wife's maid, __Hagar__, to have children.

7. Out of pity, Hagar's son was called __Ishmael__ [God hears].

8. The angel said his "hand will be against every __man__."

9. God made a __covenant__ with Abraham to be a "father of many nations."

10. God named Abraham's son __Isaac__ [he laughs] because Abraham had laughed.

11.*According to tradition, Abraham washed the __feet__ of the three angels at his tent.

12. Sodom and Gomorrah were destroyed by brimstone (sulfur) and __fire__.

13. Lot's wife looked back and became a "pillar of __salt__."

14. Isaac was Abraham's "son in his __old__ age."

15. Abraham banished __Hagar__ and Ishmael into the wilderness.

16.*Traditionally, the __Arabs__ are Ishmaelites (descended from Ishmael).

17. As a test God asked Abraham to sacrifice _Isaac/his son_ on Mount Moriah.

18. Instead of his son, Abraham sacrificed a __ram__.

19. Abraham wanted a __wife__ for his son from among his own relatives.

20. Rebekah drew __water__ for Abraham's servant at the well.

21. Rebekah was the granddaughter of Abraham's __brother__.

22. Laban and Bethuel, Rebekah's brother and __father__, gave their consent.

QUIZ 3 — Abraham, Isaac

1. Isaac was ___Abraham___'s "son in his old age." (21:2)   (14)

2. At _his wife/Sarai/h_'s request, Abraham took her maid, Hagar, to have children. (16:3)   (6)

3. Instead of his ___son___, Abraham sacrificed a ram. (22:13) (18)

4. God promised to make of Abraham a "great nation" and a ___blessing___. (12:2)   (1)

5. As a test God asked Abraham to _sacrifice/kill_ Isaac on Mount Moriah. (22:2)   (17)

6. Sarai/Sarah was Abraham's ___wife___. (12:5)   (#)

7. God destroyed the wicked cities of ___Sodom___ and Gomorrah. (19:25)   (12)

8. God _promised/etc._ the land of Canaan to Abraham's seed. (12:7) (3)

9. ___Lot___'s wife looked back and became a pillar of salt. (19:26)   (13)

10. Abraham wanted a wife for his ___son___ from among his own relatives. (24:4)   (19)

11. Of ___Ishmael___ it was said, "Every man's hand [will be] against him." (16:12)   (#)

12. ___Abraham___ banished Hagar and Ishmael into the wilderness. (21:14)   (15)

13. Rebekah was the _granddaughter_ of Abraham's brother. (24:15) (21)

14. With God's covenant, he changed the _names/lives_ of Abram and Sarai. (17:5,15)   (#)

15. Tradition says the Arabs are descended from _Ishmael/Hagar_. (16)

16. Because he had no son, Abraham made his head servant his ___heir___. (15:3)   (4)

17. God named Abraham's son Isaac because Abraham had ___laughed___. (17:17)   (10)

18. _Lot/Bethuel_ was Abraham's nephew. (12:5; 24:15)   (2)

19. Hagar's son was called Ishmael because God ___heard___ her complaint. (16:11)   (7)

20. God foretold the slavery to Abraham while he was _asleep/sleeping_. (15:13)   (5)

21. According to tradition, Abraham ___washed___ the feet of the three angels at his tent. (18:4)   (11)

22. Rebekah drew water for Abraham's servant at the ___well___. (24:15)   (20)

23. God made a covenant with Abraham to be a "___father___ of many nations." (17:4)   (9)

24. Laban and Bethuel, Rebekah's ___brother___ and father, gave their consent. (24:50)   (22)

STUDY QUESTIONS 4 — Genesis 25:19-34; 27:1-29:30; 30:25-31:20; 32:1-33:11; 35:9-29 (Jacob)

1. Esau was Jacob's _twin/older_ brother.

2. Isaac loved ___Esau___ , but Rebekah loved Jacob.

3. For a "mess of pottage [meal of (lentil) soup]" Esau sold his _birthright_ .

4. "The voice is Jacob's voice, but the hands are the hands of ___Esau___ .

5. ___Rebekah___ and Jacob tricked Isaac into giving Jacob Esau's birthright blessing.

6. Jacob fled from Esau after getting his father's _blessing_ .

7. With a stone for a pillow, Jacob dreamed of angels [messengers (of God), Greek] climbing on a ___ladder___ .

8. Jacob called the place where he dreamed ___Beth-el___ [house of God].

9. Like others before her, Jacob's future wife first appears at a ___well___ .

10. Jacob's wait of seven years "seemed unto him but a few ___days___ ."

11. ___Laban___ tricked Jacob by giving him Leah as a bride.

12. Leah was Jacob's wife, his sister-in-law, and his ___cousin___ .

13. ___Laban___ tricked Jacob by giving the spotted sheep and goats to his sons.

14. ___Jacob___ tricked Laban by making the strongest white sheep and goats produce spotted ones.

15. For revenge, Rachel stole ___Laban___'s images (household figures that were proof of inheritance).

16. Jacob _wrestled_ all night with a man/angel, who finally blessed him.

17. At Peniel [face of God] Jacob got a new name: ___Israel___ .

18. After the wrestling episode, ___Esau___ forgave Jacob.

19. At Beth-el God promised the land of ___Canaan___ to Jacob/Israel.

20. Tradition says that Jacob buried ___Rachel___ just outside Bethlehem.

21. Rachel had two sons: Joseph and ___Benjamin___ .

QUIZ 4 — Jacob

1. At Beth-el God *promised/etc.* Canaan to Jacob. (35:12) (19)

2. Jacob made Laban's strongest white sheep and goats produce ___*spotted*___ ones. (30:41) (14)

3. ___*Jacob*___ was Esau's twin brother. (25:26) (1)

4. Jacob fled from Esau to Laban, who was his mother's ___*brother*___. (27:43) (#)

5. Jacob called the place where he ___*dreamed*___ of the ladder Beth-el. (28:19) (8)

6. Tradition says ___*Rachel*___ was buried close to Bethlehem. (35:19) (20)

7. Laban gave the spotted *sheep/goats* to his sons. (30:35) (13)

8. "The voice is ___*Jacob*___'s voice, but the hands are the hands of Esau." (27:22) (4)

9. For a pottage of lentils, ___*Esau*___ sold Jacob his birthright. (25:33) (3)

10. Rebekah and ___*Jacob*___ tricked Isaac into giving Jacob Esau's blessing. (27:25) (5)

11. After the wrestling episode, Esau *forgave/etc.* Jacob. (33:4) (18)

12. The man/angel changed Jacob's name to ___*Israel*___. (32:24) (17)

13. Laban tricked Jacob by giving him Leah as a *bride/wife* instead of Rachel. (29:24) (11)

14. Isaac loved Esau, but Rebekah loved ___*Jacob*___. (25:28) (2)

15. For revenge, Rachel *stole/etc.* Laban's images. (31:19) (15)

16. Jacob's wait of seven ___*years*___ "seemed unto him but a few days." (29:20) (10)

17. Like Rebekah, ___*Rachel*___ first appears at a well. (29:9) (9)

18. Rachel was Jacob's wife, cousin, and *sister-in-law*. (29:28) (12)

19. With a *stone/rock* for a pillow, Jacob dreamed of angels on a ladder. (28:11) (7)

20. Rachel's two sons were ___*Joseph*___ and Benjamin. (35:24) (21)

STUDY QUESTIONS 5 — Genesis 37:1-36; 39:1-23; 41:1-45:28;
49:29-33 (Joseph)

1. Jacob made for Joseph a "coat of many ___colors___."

2. In Joseph's first dream his brothers' _sheaves/corn_ bowed down to his.

3. In Joseph's second dream the sun, moon, and ___stars___ bowed down to him.

4. "Behold, this ___dreamer___ cometh."

5. Joseph's ___brothers___ sold Joseph into slavery.

6. When ___Jacob___ saw Joseph's coat, he thought Joseph was dead.

7. Joseph's first owner in Egypt was named _Potiphar_.

8. ___Joseph___ was falsely accused by his master's wife.

9. In Pharaoh's dream the thin kine (cows) _ate/etc._ the fat kine.

10. In his second dream the _thin/etc._ ears of corn (wheat) ate the full ears.

11. Joseph said the fat kine meant ___seven___ years of plenty.

12. Pharaoh appointed Joseph _ruler/governor_ of Egypt at the age of thirty.

13. Joseph demanded that his brothers bring _Benjamin_ back with them.

14. After the first trip, the brothers found their _silver/money_ in their sacks.

15. Ye shall "bring down my ___gray___ hairs with sorrow to the grave."

16. Joseph's own silver ___cup___ was put into Benjamin's corn.

17. ___Judah___'s offer to replace Benjamin showed that Judah had reformed.

18. "I am Joseph; doth my ___father___ yet live?"

19. Jacob lived in the "land of Goshen" and ate "the fat of the ___land___."

20. ___Jacob___ was buried in the cave of Machpelah (in Hebron).

QUIZ 5 — Joseph

1. "Behold, this dreamer _cometh_ ." (37:19)   (4)

2. His master's _wife_ falsely accused Joseph. (39:14)   (8)

3. Pharaoh appointed _Joseph_ to be ruler of Egypt. (41:40)   (12)

4. Joseph's silver cup was found in _Benjamin_ 's sack of
   corn. (44:2)   (16)

5. Jacob was buried in the _cave_ of Machpelah. (49:29ff)   (20)

6. Jacob made Joseph a "_coat_ of many colors." (37:3)   (1)

7. Joseph's brothers sold _Joseph/him_ into slavery. (37:28)   (5)

8. In Pharaoh's dream, the thin cows ate the _fat_
   ones. (41:4)   (9)

9. Joseph demanded that his _brothers_ bring Benjamin to
   Egypt. (42:15)   (13)

10. _Judah_ pleaded for his brother Benjamin's life in
    Egypt. (44:18)   (17)

11. In Joseph's dream his _brothers'_ corn bowed to his. (37:7) (2)

12. In Pharaoh's dream, the thin ears of corn ate the full
    ones/etc. . (41:7)   (10)

13. After the first trip, the brothers found their money in
    their _sacks/corn_ . (42:27)   (14)

14. "I am _Joseph_ ; doth my father yet live?" (45:3)   (18)

15. In Joseph's dream, the sun, moon, and stars _bowed/knelt_
    to him. (37:9)   (3)

16. When Jacob saw Joseph's _coat_ , he thought Joseph
    was dead. (37:33)   (6)

17. Joseph said the thin corn meant seven years of
    famine/starving . (41:27,29)   (#)

18. Ye shall "bring down my gray hairs with sorrow to the
    grave ." (42:38)   (15)

19. Jacob, in the "land of _Goshen_ ," ate "the fat of the
    land." (45:10,18)   (19)

20. Joseph's first owner in _Egypt_ was Potiphar. (37:36)   (7)

STUDY QUESTIONS 6 — Exodus 1:8-4:20; 5:1-6:9; 7:14-24; 11:1-
12:36; 13:1-10; 13:19-14:31 (Moses, Deliverance)

1. "There arose up a new king over Egypt, which knew not
    Joseph ."

2. Pharaoh ordered the midwives to kill the Hebrews' _sons_ .

3. The parents of Moses belonged to the tribe of _Levi_ .

4. The infant Moses was set adrift in an "ark of _bulrushes_ ."

5. Moses fled from Egypt because he had _slain/killed_ an Egyptian.

6. Moses said he was "a _stranger_ in a strange land."

7. Moses kept the _flock/sheep_ of Jethro/Reuel, his father-in-law.

8. "The bush _burned_ with fire, and the bush was not consumed."

9. "Put off thy shoes from off thy feet, for the place whereon
    thou standest is _holy_ ground."

. God promised them a land "flowing with _milk_ and honey."

11. God said his name was "_I AM_ ."

12. God gave Moses confidence by turning his rod into a _serpent_ .

13. Because Moses was slow of speech, _Aaron_ went with him.

14. "Thus saith the Lord God of Israel, 'Let my _people_ go.'"

15. Pharaoh forced the Hebrew slaves to make bricks without
    straw .

16. Pharaoh's cruelty brought upon Egypt a series of _plagues_ .

17. After each plague, Pharaoh's "heart was _hardened_ ."

18. Finally, "all the _firstborn_ in the land of Egypt shall die."

19. The Israelites put the blood of a _lamb_ on their door-
    posts.

20. They ate the unleavened bread, the paschal lamb, and
    bitter herbs.

21. They ate the meal in haste because "it is the Lord's
    Passover ."

22. On the Passover/Pesach, God passed over the houses of the
    Jews/etc. .

23. Moses took _Joseph_ 's bones with him to bury in Canaan.

24. At the _Red_ Sea the Israelites complained to Moses.

25. The pillar that protected Israel by day gave it _light_
    at night.

26. Pharaoh's army was finally _drowned/etc._.

284

QUIZ 6 — Moses, Deliverance

1. Moses kept the flock of Jethro, his wife's _father_. (3:1) (7)

2. "Thus saith the Lord God of Israel, 'Let my people
   _go_.'" (5:1) (14)

3. The infant Moses was set adrift in "an _ark_ of
   bulrushes." (2:3) (4)

4. The last plague was the _slaying/etc._ of every Egyptian
   firstborn. (11:5) (18)

5. God promised them a land "flowing with milk and
   honey." (3:8) (10)

6. "Pharaoh's _army_ got drowned." (14:28) (26)

7. "There arose up a new king over _Egypt_, which knew
   not Joseph." (1:8) (1)

8. They ate unleavened _bread_, the paschal lamb, and
   bitter herbs. (12:8) (20)

9. "Put off thy _shoes_ . . . for the place whereon thou
   standest is holy ground." (3:5) (9)

10. Moses was Aaron's _brother_. (4:14) (#)

11. Moses stretched out his hand over the Red Sea and
    divided/etc. it. (14:21) (#)

12. Moses first heard God's voice coming from a _burning/flaming_
    bush. (3:4) (#)

13. They put the _blood_ of a lamb on their doorposts.(12:7) (19)

14. Pharaoh's _daughter_ had the baby Moses drawn out of the
    water. (2:5) (#)

15. After each plague, _Pharaoh_'s "heart was hardened."
    (7:22) (17)

16. Pharaoh ordered the midwives to _kill/slay_ the Hebrews'
    sons. (1:16) (2)

17. The Hebrew slaves had to make _bricks_ without
    straw. (5:7) (15)

18. The _pillar/column_ that shaded the way by day gave light at
    night. (14:20) (25)

19. _God/The Lord_ said his name was I AM. (3:14) (11)

20. Moses was a "stranger in a _strange_ land." (2:22) (6)

21. God reassured Moses by turning his _rod_ into a
    serpent. (4:3) (12)

22. At the Red Sea, the Jews _complained/etc._ to Moses. (14:11) (24)

23. Moses fled because he had killed an _Egyptian_. (2:15) (5)

24. Pharaoh brought upon his _people/land_ ten plagues. (7:17) (16)

25. They ate hastily because "it is the _Lord's_ Pass-
    over." (12:11) (21)

26. Moses took Joseph's _bones/body_ to bury in Canaan.(13:19) (23)

285

STUDY QUESTIONS 7 — Exodus 15:27-17:16; 19:1-20:22; 31:18-34:29
(Wilderness. MEMORIZE Ten Commandments: 20:2-17)

1. The Israelites longed for the " _fleshpots_ " (for meat) of Egypt.

2. In the wilderness God sent food called ___manna___ from heaven.

3. The Israelites were commanded to ___rest___ on the seventh day.

4. Moses struck a rock with his rod to bring forth ___water___ .

5. To encourage the army, Moses had two men hold up his _hands/arms_ .

6. Moses received the commandments on Mount ___Sinai___ (also called Horeb).

7. *The Decalogue is another name for the ___Ten Commandments___ .

8. "I am the Lord thy ___God___ , which have brought thee out . "

9. "Thou shalt have ___no___ other gods before me."

10. "Thou shalt not make unto thee any ___graven___ [carved] image."

11. Children suffer for the sins of the fathers who ___hate___ God.

12. "Thou shalt not take the name of the Lord thy God in ___vain___ ."

13. "Remember the ___sabbath___ day, to keep it holy."

14. " ___Honor___ thy father and thy mother."

15. "Thou shalt not _kill/steal_ ." (one word)

16. "Thou shalt not ___commit___ adultery [sexual immorality]."

17. "Thou shalt not bear false ___witness___ against thy neighbor."

18. "Thou shalt not covet [desire] thy neighbor's _wife/house_ ." (one word)

19. Aaron made a "molten ___calf___ " by melting golden earrings.

20. In anger, God called the Israelites " ___stiff___ -necked."

21. In anger, Moses _broke/smashed_ the tables/tablets of the testimony/covenant.

22. After Moses talked with God, the skin of his face _shone/etc._ .

QUIZ 7 — Wilderness

1. Moses struck a rock with his ___rod___ to bring forth
   water. (17:6) (4)

2. "Thou shalt not covet thy ___neighbor___'s wife." (20:17) (18)

3. Moses received the ten commandments on ___Mount___
   Sinai. (19:20) (6)

4. "Thou shalt not take the ___name___ of the Lord thy God
   in vain." (20:7) (12)

5. After Moses talked with God, the skin of his ___face___
   shone. (34:29) (22)

6. "Thou shalt not ___kill/steal___." (one word) (20:13,15) (15)

7. "Thou shalt not ___steal/kill___." (different word) (20:13,15) (15)

8. In the wilderness God sent food called manna from
   ___heaven/etc.___ (16:15) (2)

9. "Thou shalt have no other gods ___before___ me." (20:3) (9)

10. "Thou shalt not bear ___false___ witness against thy
    neighbor."(20:16) (17)

11. To encourage the army, two men held up the hands of
    ___Moses___. (17:2) (5)

12. "I am the Lord thy God, which have ___brought___ thee out of
    the land of Egypt." (20:2) (8)

13. "Honor thy father and thy ___mother___." (20:12) (14)

14. In anger, God called the ___Israelites/etc.___ a "stiffnecked
    people." (32:9) (20)

15. "Thou shalt not make unto thee any graven
    ___image___." (20:4) (10)

16. "___Remember___ the sabbath day, to keep it holy." (20:8) (13)

17. Aaron made a molten calf out of melted ___gold(en)___
    earrings. (32:4) (19)

18. "Thou shalt not commit ___adultery___." (20:14) (16)

19. The Israelites were ordered to rest on the ___seventh/sabbath___
    day. (16:29) (3)

20. In anger, ___Moses___ broke the two tablets. (32:19) (21)

21. Children suffer for the sins of the ___fathers___ who hate
    God. (20:5) (11)

22. The Israelites longed for the "___flesh___-pots" of
    Egypt. (16:3) (1)

STUDY QUESTIONS 8 — Leviticus 13:9-17,45,46; 19:13-18; 25:1-12.
Numbers 13:1,2; 13:17-14:10; 14:26-45; 18:1,6-10,21-24; 20:1-13;
21:4-9; 22:15-23:12

1. *The book of _Leviticus_ deals with priestly laws (of Levites).

2. A leper had to cry " _Unclean!_ " when he came among people.

3. "Thou shalt not . . . put a _stumbling_ block before the blind."

4. "Thou shalt not hate thy brother in thine _heart_ ."

5. "Thou shalt love thy neighbor as _thyself_ ."

6. On every seventh/sabbatical _year_ the land was allowed to rest.

7. Every _fiftieth_ year was a jubilee.

8. "Proclaim liberty throughout all the _land_ to all the inhabitants thereof."

9. Moses' spies brought back from Canaan a huge cluster of _grapes_ .

10. In fear, the spies spread (false) reports of _giants_ in Canaan.

11. "We were in our own sight as _grasshoppers_, and so we were in their sight."

12. Only _Joshua_ and Caleb did not complain against Moses and God.

13. Only the _children/etc._ of the complainers could enter the promised land.

14. The _ark_ of the covenant/testimony represented God's protection of the Israelites.

15. Aaron and his sons became the _priests_ of Israel, responsible for the sanctuary/holy place.

16. Members of the tribe of _Levi_ served in the tabernacle/tent of meeting (later, the Temple).

17. The "most _holy_ place" is the holy of holies [Lat.: sanctum sanctorum], or inner sanctum.

18. The _Levites_ were supported by tithes (a tenth of the people's income).

19. Instead of speaking to the rock for water, as ordered this time, Moses _smote/etc._ it.

20. As punishment, Moses was not allowed to enter the _promised land_.

21. To punish the complaining people, God sent _fiery_ serpents.

22. To cure snake bites, Moses made a brass/brazen _serpent_ .

23. Balak summoned the heathen prophet Balaam to _curse_ Israel.

24. Balaam's _ass_ saw the angel, but Balaam did not.

QUIZ 8 — Leviticus, Numbers

1. "Thou shalt ___love___ thy neighbor as thyself." (L19:18) (5)

2. The ark of the covenant represented ___God___'s protection of the Israelites. (N14:44) (14)

3. Only Balaam's ass saw the ___angel___. (N22:23) (24)

4. ___Aaron___ and his sons became priests of Israel. (N18:1) (15)

5. To punish the complaining prople, God sent fiery ___serpents___. (N21:6) (21)

6. "Thou shalt not . . . put a stumbling block before the ___blind___. (L19:14) (3)

7. God changed ___Balaam___'s words from a curse to a blessing. (N23:11) (#)

8. Only their children could enter the ___promised land___. (N14:30) (13)

9. "We were in our own sight as grasshoppers, and so we were in their ___sight___." (N13:33) (11)

10. As punishment, Moses was not allowed to ___enter___ the promised land. (N20:12) (20)

11. A ___leper___ had to cry "Unclean!" when he came among people. (L13:45) (2)

12. Every ___seventh___ year the land rested. (L25:4) (6)

13. Balak summoned the heathen prophet Balaam to curse the ___Jews/etc.___ (N22:17) (23)

14. Members of the tribe of Levi served in the ___tabernacle___. (N18:6) (16)

15. Every fiftieth year was a ___jubilee___. (L25:11) (7)

16. Instead of speaking to the ___rock___, Moses struck it twice. (N20:11) (19)

17. A cluster of ___grapes___ had to be carried on a staff by two men. ((N13:23) (9)

18. To cure snake bites, God helped ___Moses___ make a brazen serpent. (N21:9) (22)

19. Only Joshua and ___Caleb___ did not complain. (N14:6-9) (12)

20. "Thou shalt not ___hate___ thy brother in thine heart." (L19:17) (4)

21. The Levites were supported by ___tithes___: a tenth of people's income. (N18:21) (18)

22. "Proclaim ___liberty___ throughout all the land to all the inhabitants thereof." (L25:10) (8)

23. The "most holy place" is the holy of ___holies___, or inner sanctum. (N18:10) (17)

24. In fear, the two ___spies/etc.___ spread (false) reports of giants in Canaan. (N13:33) (10)

STUDY QUESTIONS 9 — Deuteronomy 6:1-9; 14:3-21; 19:1-7; 23:19,20;
24:1-6; 25:1-10; 31:14-18; 34:1-12. Joshua 2:1-24; 3:14-4:24;
5:13-6:27; 9:3-27; 10:6-14; 24:29-33

1. "Hear, O Israel: The Lord our God is one ___Lord___."

2. "Thou shalt love the Lord thy God with all thine heart, all
   thy soul, and all thy ___might___."

3. Swine were unclean (not kosher); they did not chew a
   ___cud___.

4. An accidental ___killer/etc.___ went to one of the three sanctuary
   cities for protection.

5. "Thou shalt not lend upon ___usury___ [interest] to thy brother."

6. A man could ___divorce___ a wife who sinned (was found "unclean")
   by merely giving her a paper.

7. A newly ___married___ man could not be drafted into the army for
   a year.

8. A bachelor had to ___marry___ his brother's widow if she had no
   son.

9. On Nebo, atop ___Pisgah___, God showed Moses the promised land.

10. Moses named ___Joshua___ his successor in command of the Israel-
    ites.

11. Rahab, the harlot of Jericho, hid Joshua's spies on her
    ___roof___.

12. For hiding the spies, Rahab asked that all her ___family/etc.___ be
    spared.

13. They crossed over River ___Jordan___ into the promised land.

14.*Israel entered Canaan from the ___east___ (on the compass).

15. The Israelites crossed the river on their ___feet___.

16. Each tribe took a ___stone___ from the river bed as a memorial.

17. The priests blew trumpets of ___rams'___ horns before Jericho.

18. Seven priests circled Jericho ___seven___ times on the seventh
    day.

19. God warned Israel not to take booty from what was "___accursed___"
    (to be destroyed).

20. The Gibeonites pretended to be from a ___far___ country.

21. Slaves were called "hewers of wood and drawers of ___water___."

22. God gave Joshua more time to fight by making the sun
    ___stand still___.

23.*Deuteronomy [___second___ laws] repeats laws of earlier books.

24.*The Pentateuch [___five books___] is also called "the Law" [Hebrew:
    Torah].

25. The book of ___Joshua___ continues the story of the Five Books
    of Moses.

QUIZ 9 — Deuteronomy, Joshua

1. ___Joshua___ succeeded Moses as commander of the Israelites (D34:9)   (10)

2. Deuteronomy [second ___laws___] repeats earlier laws.   (23)

3. An accidental murderer went to one of three ___cities___
   for sanctuary/protection. (D19:4)   (4)

4. Altogether, the tribes took ___twelve___ stones from the
   river bed. (J4:5)   (16)

5. Rahab, the harlot of ___Jericho___, hid two spies on her
   roof. (J2:6)   (11)

6. The book of Joshua continues the ___Five___ Books of
   Moses.   (25)

7. "Hear, O ___Israel___ : The Lord our God is one Lord."(D6:4) (1)

8. The priests ___blew/sounded___ rams' horns before Jericho. (J6:8) (17)

9. The Pentateuch is also called ___the Law/Torah___.   (24)

10. "Thou shalt ___love___ the Lord thy God with all thine
    heart, all thy soul, and all thy might." (D6:5)   (2)

11. Israel crossed over Jordan into the ___promised___
    land. (J3:16)   (13)

12. God helped Joshua by making the ___sun___ stand
    still. (J10:13)   (22)

13. On Nebo, atop Pisgah, God showed ___Moses___ the promised
    land. (D34:1)   (9)

14. Gibeonites were made "hewers of wood and ___drawers___ of
    water." (J9:21)   (21)

15. "Thou shalt not ___lend___ upon usury to thy broth-
    er." (D23:19)   (5)

16. A man had to marry his dead brother's ___wife/widow___ if she
    had no son. (D25:5)   (8)

17. God warned Israel not to take "the ___accursed___ thing."(J6:18)(19)

18. Israel entered Canaan going toward the ___west___ .   (14)

19. A man could divorce a wife who sinned by giving her a
    ___paper/etc.___. (D24:1)   (6)

20. The Gibeonites lied about where they ___lived/etc.___ (J9:6) (20)

21. Miraculously, the Israelites crossed the ___(Jordan)river___ on
    foot. (J3:17)   (15)

22. A newly married man could not be drafted into the army
    for a ___year___ . (D24:5)   (7)

23. Swine were unclean: they did not ___chew___ a cud. (D14:8) (3)

24. Seven priests circled Jericho seven times on the
    ___seventh___ day. (J6:15)   (18)

25. As a reward, the ___harlot/betrayer___ of Jericho won her fam-
    ily's safety. (J2:13; 6:25)   (12)

STUDY QUESTIONS 10 — Judges 2:6-23; 4:1-5:8; 5:19-7:25; 10:6-12:7
(Deborah, Gideon, Jephthah)

1. "And the children of Israel did evil in the ___*sight*___ of the Lord."

2. "And they forsook the ___*Lord*___, and served Baal and Ashtaroth."

3. "And the children of Israel cried unto ___*the Lord*___."

4. ___*Deborah*___ was a judge, a prophetess, and a military leader of Israel.

5. Jael killed Sisera with a ___*(tent) nail*___ through his temples/head.

6. Deborah and Barak sang, saying that Deborah "arose a mother in ___*Israel*___."

7. Deborah's song contrasts Jael with ___*Sisera*___'s mother.

8. The angel caused a fire to consume ___*Gideon*___'s offering.

9. Gideon tested God by the miracles of the dew and the ___*fleece*___.

10. Gideon chose his 300 valiant men by their manner of ___*drinking*___.

11. Gideon's men carried lamps hidden inside ___*pitchers*___.

12. The Gileadite elders asked ___*Jephthah*___, the outlaw, to lead them.

13. ___*Jephthah*___ vowed to sacrifice whatever first met him on his return if he won.

14. Because of his rash oath, Jephthah had to sacrifice his ___*daughter*___.

15. Jephthah used "Shibboleth" as a password to discover his ___*enemies/etc.*___.

QUIZ 10 — Deborah, Gideon, Jephthah

1. Because of his rash _oath/etc._ , Jephthah had to sacrifice his daughter. (11:35)   (14)

2. "They forsook the Lord, and served _Baal(im)_ and Ashtaroth." (2:13)   (2)

3. The _angel_ caused a fire to consume Gideon's offering. (6:21)   (8)

4. Repenting, "the children of Israel _cried_ unto the Lord." (4:3)   (3)

5. Ephraimites could not _pronounce/say_ the password: "Shibboleth." (12:6)   (15)

6. God convinced Gideon by miracles with _dew_ and the fleece. (6:37)   (9)

7. Deborah was a _judge/mother_, prophetess, and military leader of Israel. (4:4)   (4)

8. Jephthah vowed to _sacrifice/etc._ whatever first met him if he won. (11:31)   (13)

9. Deborah and Barak sang that Deborah "arose a _mother_ in Israel." (5:7)   (6)

10. The Gileadites asked Jephthah, the outlaw, to _lead/etc._ them. (11:5)   (12)

11. Gideon chose only _300_ valiant men. (7:6)   (10)

12. "The children of Israel did _evil_ in the sight of the Lord" every time they were at peace. (2:11)   (1)

13. Jael nailed Sisera's _head/temple_ to the ground. (4:21)   (5)

14. Gideon's men carried _lamps/torches_ hidden inside pitchers. (7:16)   (11)

15. Deborah's song contrasts _Jael_ with Sisera's mother. (5:28)   (7)

STUDY QUESTIONS 11 — Judges 13:1-5; 13:24-16:31. Ruth 1:1-4:22.

(Samson, Ruth)

1. A Nazarite/Nazirite, consecrated to God, did not cut his
   hair .

2. On his way to woo the Philistine woman, Samson slew a
   lion .

3. Samson saw bees and _honey_ inside the carcass of a lion.

4. Samson's first wife got the answer to his _riddle_ from him.

5. "If ye had not _plowed_ with my heifer, ye had not found out
   my riddle."

6. Samson burned the corn/wheat with pairs of _foxes(tails)_ and
   torches.

7. Samson "smote them hip and _thigh_ " with a great slaughter.

8. Samson slew a thousand men with the jawbone of an _ass_ .

9. Samson took the doors of the gates of the city to the top of
   a _hill_ .

10. Delilah pestered Samson about the source of his great
    strength .

11. Delilah was the second woman to fool Samson into telling her
    a _secret_ .

12. Samson suffered eyeless in _Gaza_ , where he ground grain
    in prison.

13. Samson pulled the middle _pillars_ , killing himself and many
    others.

14. Ruth, the Moabitess, was the _daughter-in-law_ of Naomi, the
    Israelite.

15. "Entreat me not to _leave_ thee."

16. "Whither thou _goest_ , I will go."

17. "Thy _people_ shall be my people, and thy God my God."

18. "Where thou diest, will I die, and there will I be _buried_ ."

19. Ruth _gleaned_ (collected the leavings) in the field of Boaz
    after the reapers were done.

20. Boaz was kind to Ruth for her loyalty to her mother-in-law,
    Naomi .

21. Ruth asked Boaz to marry her ("spread his _skirt_ over"
    her), as was his duty.

22. Boaz fulfilled Ruth's _claim/etc._ of kinship by marrying her.

23. _David_ was the great grandson of Ruth and Boaz.

QUIZ 11 — Samson, Ruth

1. Samson got his strength from his ___*hair*___. (J16:17)   (#)

2. Ruth asked Boaz to "___*spread*___ his skirt" over her.(R3:9)   (21)

3. Samson "___*smote*___ them hip and thigh" with a great slaughter. (J15:8)   (7)

4. "Entreat me not to leave ___*thee*___." (R1:16)   (15)

5. Samson destroyed the corn with pairs of foxes and *torches/fire*. (J15:4)   (6)

6. "___*Where*___ thou diest, will I die, and there will I be buried." (R1:17)   (18)

7. Ruth gleaned in the field of Boaz after the *reapers/etc.* were done. (R2:3)   (19)

8. On his way to woo the ___*Philistine*___ woman, Samson slew a lion. (J14:6)   (2)

9. David was the ___*great grandson*___ of Ruth and Boaz. (R4:22)   (23)

10. At Gaza Samson ground grain while in ___*prison/etc.*___. (J16:21)   (12)

11. Samson saw bees and honey inside the carcass of a ___*lion*___. (J14:8)   (3)

12. A Nazarite was under a vow not to ___*cut*___ his hair. (J13:5)   (1)

13. "___*Whither*___ thou goest, I will go." (R1:16)   (16)

14. Samson slew a thousand men with the ___*jawbone*___ of an ass. (J15:15)   (8)

15. Boaz fulfilled Ruth's claim of ___*kinship*___ by marrying her. (R4:13)   (22)

16. "If ye had not plowed with my ___*heifer*___, ye had not found out my riddle." (J14:18)   (5)

17. ___*Delilah*___ was the second woman to get a secret from Samson. (J16:17)   (11)

18. Naomi was Ruth's *mother-in-law*. (R1:4)   (14)

19. Samson's first ___*wife*___ got the answer to his riddle from him. (J14:17)   (4)

20. "___*Thy*___ people shall be my people, and thy God my God." (R1:16)   (17)

21. Delilah pestered ___*Samson*___ about the source of his great strength. (J16:6)   (10)

22. Boaz admired ___*Ruth*___'s loyalty to Naomi. (R2:11)   (20)

23. Samson left the *doors/gates* of the city on the top of a hill. (J16:3)   (9)

STUDY QUESTIONS 12 — 1 Samuel 1:1-3,9-11; 2:12-26; 3:1-21;
8:1-11:15; 15:1-35 (Samuel, Saul)

1. __Hannah__ vowed that her son would be dedicated to God as a Nazirite.

2. Eli's __sons__ were called "sons of Belial [wicked]," unworthy to be priests.

3. The child Samuel heard the call from the __Lord__ at night.

4. "From Dan to __Beersheba__" people knew Samuel was a prophet.

5.*A prophet [Greek: one who __speaks__ for] was God's spokesman.

6. Samuel, last of the judges, was also a __priest__ and prophet.

7. Samuel's sons, like those of __Eli__, were unfit to succeed him.

8. The people demanded from Samuel a __king__ to judge them.

9. Samuel foretold that a king would __oppress/etc.__ them.

10. Saul came from the tribe of __Benjamin__.

11. Saul went to Samuel for advice about his father's lost __asses__.

12. Samuel anointed Saul with oil when God chose Saul to be __king__.

13. The people wondered, "Is Saul also among the __prophets__?"

14. __Saul__ was chosen the second time, in a public drawing.

15. All the people shouted, "God __save__ the king."

16. Saul was crowned after slaying the __Ammonites__ who besieged Jabesh.

17. The Lord told Saul to destroy every one of the __Amalekites__ and their animals.

18. Saul disobeyed God by __sparing/etc.__ the best Amalekite livestock.

19. For disobeying God, __Saul__ was abandoned by Samuel and by God.

20. Begging forgiveness, Saul grabbed __Samuel__'s robe, and it tore.

_296_

QUIZ 12 — Samuel, Saul

1. The child __Samuel__ heard the call from the Lord at night. (3:4) (3)

2. Samuel, last of the __judges__, was also a priest and a prophet. (3:20) (6)

3. Samuel advised the people not to replace judges by a __king__. (8:10) (9)

4. Samuel anointed Saul with __oil__ as a sign of divine kingship. (10:1) (12)

5. All the people shouted, "God save the __king__." (10:24) (15)

6. Saul disobeyed God by sparing the __best__ Amalekite livestock. (15:9) (18)

7. Hannah vowed that her __son__ would be dedicated to God as a Nazirite. (1:11) (1)

8. "From __Dan__ to Beersheba" people knew that Samuel would be a prophet. (3:20) (4)

9. Samuel's __sons__, like those of Eli, were unfit to succeed him. (8:3) (7)

10. Saul was from Benjamin, one of the smallest of the __tribes__. (9:2) (10)

11. Saul went to Samuel for advice about his __father__'s lost asses. (9:14) (11)

12. Saul was __crowned/etc.__ after slaying the Ammonites who besieged Jabesh. (11:15) (16)

13. For disobeying God, Saul was abandoned by __Samuel__ and by God. (15:14) (19)

14. Eli's sons were called "sons of Belial," unworthy to be __priests__. (2:12) (2)

15. A prophet was God's __spokesman__. (5)

16. The people demanded from __Samuel__ a king to judge them. (8:5) (8)

17. "Is __Saul__ also among the prophets?" (10:11) (13)

18. Saul was chosen the second time, in a public __drawing/lottery__. (10:21) (14)

19. Begging forgiveness, Saul grabbed Samuel's __robe/etc.__, and it tore. (15:27) (20)

20. The Lord told __Saul__ to destroy every one of the Amalekites and their animals. (15:3) (17)

1. God sent Samuel to the city of _Bethlehem_ in the tribe of Judah for a new king.

2. David was Jesse's ___son___.

3. At God's command, Samuel _anointed_ David with oil, to be Saul's successor.

4. To soothe ___Saul___, David played the harp and sang psalms.

5. Goliath, the Philistine champion, was about ten and a half feet tall ("six cubits and a ___span___").

6. _Goliath_ insultingly challenged the Israelites to single combat.

7. While David's brothers fought, he worked at home as a _shepherd_.

8. David's ___brother___ resented David's inquiry about the fearsome giant.

9. Saul said to David, "Go, and the Lord be ___with___ thee."

10. David took only his staff, five smooth ___stones___, and a sling.

11. "I come to thee in the ___name___ of the Lord of hosts."

12. David slew Goliath with a ___sling___ and a stone.

13. ___David___ and Jonathan, Saul's son, made a covenant of brotherhood.

14. "Saul hath slain his _thousands_, and David his ten thousands."

15. The jealous Saul cast a javelin to smite ___David___ to the wall with it.

16. Saul had banished all _witches_ with "familiar spirits" and all wizards.

17. Saul had the witch of Endor raise the spirit of ___Samuel___.

18. ___Saul___ met his death by suicide.

QUIZ 13 — Saul and young David

1. Saul had the ___witch___ of Endor raise the spirit of
   Samuel. (28:12)   (17)

2. At God's command, Samuel anointed David to be
   ___Saul___'s successor. (16:13)   (3)

3. David took only his staff, ___five___ smooth stones, and
   a sling. (17:40)   (10)

4. ___Saul___ took a sword and fell on it. (31:4)   (18)

5. Jesse was David's ___father___. (16:11)   (2)

6. Saul said to David, "Go, and ___the Lord___ be with
   thee." (17:37)   (9)

7. Saul had banished all witches with "familiar ___spirits___"
   and all wizards. (28:3)   (16)

8. Jesse and David originally lived in the city of
   ___Bethlehem___ in Judah. ((16:1)   (1)

9. David's brother resented ___David___'s inquiry about the
   fearsome giant. (17:28)   (8)

10. The jealous Saul cast a ___javelin/etc.___ to smite David to the
    wall with it. (18:11)   (15)

11. To soothe Saul, David played the ___harp___ and sang
    psalms. (16:23)   (4)

12. While David's brothers ___fought/etc.___, he worked at home as a
    shepherd. (17:15)   (7)

13. "Saul hath slain his thousands, and David his
    ___ten thousands___." (18:7)   (14)

14. "I come to thee in the name of the Lord of ___hosts___,"
    said David to Goliath. (17:45)   (11)

15. The champion of the Philistines was named ___Goliath___. (17:4) (5)

16. David and Jonathan made a covenant of ___brotherhood/etc___. (18:3) (13)

17. Goliath insultingly challenged the Israelites to
    ___single___ combat. (17:9)   (6)

18. David slew Goliath with a ___sling___ and a stone. (17:50) (12)

STUDY QUESTIONS 14 — 2 Samuel 1:1-2:4a; 5:1-10; 6:1-23;
11:1-12:25; 14:25,26; 15:1-37; 16:15-17:23; 18:1-19:8; 23:1-7
(David, Bathsheba, Absalom)

1. "Thy __blood__ be upon thy head."

2. "How are the __mighty__ fallen!"

3. "Tell it not in Gath, __publish__ it not in the streets of Askelon."

4. "I am distressed for thee, my __brother__ Jonathan."

5. At first David was king of his native tribe, __Judah__ , in Hebron.

6. __Jerusalem__ (in Benjamin) was called Zion and "the city of David."

7. David brought the __ark__ to the tabernacle in Jerusalem, his capital city.

8. __David__ publicly leaped and danced before the ark, dressed only in a scanty garment (an ephod).

9. David committed adultery with __Bathsheba__ .

10. David sent __Uriah__ to a treacherous death with a note to Joab.

11. __Nathan__ rebuked David with a parable of the ewe lamb.

12. Nathan said to David, "Thou art the __man__ ."

13. As punishment, the __child__ of David and Bathsheba died.

14. Bathsheba was Solomon's __mother__ .

15. Absalom polled/cut his handsome __hair__ once a year.

16. Absalom stole men's hearts by acting as a generous __judge__ .

17. Absalom's headquarters were in David's old capital city, __Hebron__ .

18. David did not let the ark leave __Jerusalem__ with him.

19. __David__ sent Hushai, his counselor, to lead Absalom astray.

20. Ahithophel gave Absalom good __counsel/etc.,__ but it was not accepted.

21. A woman hid Hushai's __messengers__ to David in a well.

22. The disappointed Ahithophel finally __hanged/killed__ himself.

23. Joab disobeyed David's orders to "deal gently" with __Absalom__ .

24. Absalom was killed when he was held fast in a __tree__ .

25. "Would God I had __died__ for thee, O Absalom, my son, my son!"

26. David is referred to as the "sweet __psalmist__ of Israel."

QUIZ 14 — David, Bathsheba, Absalom

1. David brought the ark to the tabernacle he had built in the city of __Jerusalem__. (6:12) (7)

2. David was Absalom's __father__. (14:25) (#)

3. Nathan said to David, "Thou __art__ the man." (12:7) (12)

4. Jerusalem was called Zion and "the city of __David__." (6:12) (6)

5. __Absalom__ stole men's hearts by acting as a generous judge. (15:6) (16)

6. "Would __God__ I had died for thee, O Absalom, my son, my son!" (18:33) (25)

7. "Tell it not in Gath, publish it not in the __streets__ of Askelon." (1:20) (3)

8. David sent Hushai, his counselor, to lead __Absalom__ astray. (15:34) (19)

9. __David__ committed adultery with Bathsheba. (11:4) (9)

10. "Thy blood be upon thy __head__." (1:16) (1)

11. David is called the "__sweet__ psalmist of Israel."(23:1) (26)

12. Absalom did not accept Ahithophel's good __advice/etc.__ (17:14) (20)

13. God punished David's betrayal of Uriah by killing David and Bathsheba's __child__. (12:18) (13)

14. Solomon was Bathsheba's __son/child__. (12:24) (14)

15. David sent Uriah to his death with a note to the general, __Joab__. (11:14) (10)

16. Joab disobeyed David's order to "deal __gently__" with Absalom. (18:5,14) (23)

17. At first David was king of Judah, in the city of __Hebron__. (2:4) (5)

18. "How are the mighty __fallen__!" (1:19) (2)

19. "I am distressed for thee, my brother __Jonathan__." (1:26) (4)

20. Absalom cut his golden hair once a __year__. (14:26) (15)

21. Nathan rebuked __David__ with the parable of the ewe lamb. (12:1) (11)

22. A woman hid Hushai's messengers to David in a __well__. (17:19) (21)

23. Absalom was killed when he was held fast by his __hair__. (18:14) (24)

24. David had to __flee/etc.__ Jerusalem for safety from Absalom. (15:14) (#)

25. Bathsheba was Uriah's __wife__. (11:3) (#)

26. As king of Israel, David made the city of __Jerusalem__ his capital. (5:5) (#)

STUDY QUESTIONS 15 — 1 Kings 1:5-8,11-14,28b-31,47-53; 3:3-9,16-
28; 4:20-25; 6:1,17-22; 10:1-12,21-25; 11:1-13,29-31,37-43; 12:1-
5,12-24; 16:29-33; 17:1-19:18; 21:1-22:4; 22:29-40
(Solomon, Elijah, Ahab, Jezebel)

1. Solomon was the third ___king___ of Israel.

2. Holding the horns/corners of the ___altar___ saved the
   usurper (illegal ruler) Adonijah.

3. "Give therefore thy servant an _understanding_ heart,"

4. After the judgment of Solomon, the right _woman/mother_ got the
   child.

5. They "dwelt ___safely___, every man under his vine and under his
   fig tree."

6. At ___Jerusalem___ Solomon built a temple of cedars of Lebanon and
   pure gold.

7. The Queen of ___Sheba___ saw Solomon in all his glory and with
   all his wisdom.

8. Every three years ships brought "ivory, and apes, and
   ___peacocks___."

9. Solomon's wives and concubines totaled ___1,000___.

10. Solomon angered God by turning after his ___wives'___ false gods.

11. Ahijah foretold the revolt by tearing up Jeroboam's _garment/etc._.

12. The country was divided into two kingdoms: Judah in the
    south and ___Israel___ in the north.

13. The kingdom of Judah had two tribes: Judah and _Benjamin_.

14. Jezebel was Ahab's ___wife___.

15. Elijah hid from Ahab near a brook and was fed by _ravens/birds_.

16. Elijah made the "widow's cruse [jar] of ___oil___" last for
    many days.

17. Elijah _revived/etc._ the widow's son.

18. Elijah challenged the prophets of ___Baal___ on Mount Carmel.

19. "How long halt ye between ___two___ opinions?"

20. "A little cloud out of the sea, like a man's ___hand___."

21. Elijah "girded up his ___loins___" and ran.

22. Elijah hid from Jezebel in a ___cave___ on Mount Horeb/Sinai.

23. Elijah heard God in a "still ___small___ voice."

24. Jezebel helped Ahab get the ___vineyard___ of Naboth by treachery.

25. The northern city of Samaria was Ahab's capital of the kingdom
    of ___Israel___.

26. As prophesied, Ahab was killed and ___dogs___ licked up his
    blood.

QUIZ 15 — Solomon, Elijah, Ahab, Jezebel

1. The country was divided into two kingdoms: __Judah__ and Israel. (12:16) (12)

2. For the ark Solomon built the first _temple/etc._ (6:1ff) (6)

3. Elijah made the "__widow__'s cruse of oil" last for many days. (17:16) (16)

4. "Every man under his ___vine___ and under his fig tree." (4:25) (5)

5. Elijah challenged the ___prophets___ of Baal on Mount Carmel. (18:19) (18)

6. Adonijah saved himself by holding the _horns/corners_ of the altar. (1:51) (2)

7. Elijah hid from Jezebel in a cave on Mt. _Horeb/Sinai_.(19:9) (22)

8. Solomon's ships brought "ivory, and ___apes___, and peacocks." (10:22) (8)

9. _Jezebel_ helped Ahab get the vineyards of Naboth by treachery. (21:7) (24)

10. After the judgment of Solomon, the right woman got the _baby/etc._ . (3:27) (4)

11. Ahijah prophesied that Jeroboam would win the ___ten___ northern tribes. (11:31) (#)

12. The ___Queen___ of Sheba saw Solomon in all his glory and wisdom. (10:1) (7)

13. Elijah hid from Ahab near a _brook/stream_ and was fed by ravens. (17:6) (15)

14. Solomon said, "Give therefore thy servant an understanding ___heart___." (3:9) (3)

15. "How long halt ye between two _opinions_?" (18:21) (19)

16. _Solomon_ angered God by turning after his wives' false gods. (11:9) (10)

17. Elijah heard God in a "___still___ small voice." (19:12) (23)

18. _Solomon_ was the third king of Israel. (1:30,51) (1)

19. "A little ___cloud___ out of the sea, like a man's hand." (18:44) (20)

20. Ahab was Jezebel's ___husband___. (16:31) (14)

21. Solomon had ___700___ wives and 300 concubines. (11:3) (9)

22. Elijah revived the widow's _son/child_. (17:22) (17)

23. The new kingdom of ___Judah___ had two tribes: Judah and Benjamin. (12:21) (13)

24. As prophesied, ___Ahab___ was killed and dogs licked up his blood. (22:38) (26)

25. Samaria was the capital city of the northern kingdom of ___Israel___. (21:17) (25)

STUDY QUESTIONS 16 — 2 Kings 2:1-3,8-14,19-25; 4:1-37; 4:42-6:7;
6:24-7:20; 9:1-13,21b-37; 10:18-27; 13:14-21; 17:7-9,15-20;
25:1-15,21b-24 (Elisha, Jehu, end of both kingdoms)

1. Elijah crossed over the River _Jordan_ before entering heaven.

2. Elijah was carried to heaven in a flaming _chariot_ .

3. Elisha "took up the _mantle_ " of Elijah as his successor in Israel.

4. Elisha showed that he had Elijah's spirit by performing similar _miracles/etc._.

5. Elisha put his mouth on the dead boy's _mouth/lips_ and revived him.

6. Elisha fed a hundred men with twenty _loaves_ made of barley.

7. Naaman, the Syrian captain, asked the prophet to cure his _leprosy/etc._.

8. Naaman was told to wash in the River _Jordan_ seven times.

9. For taking money from Naaman, Elisha's servant, Gehazi, got Naaman's _leprosy/etc._ and his skin became white.

10. In one miracle, Elisha made an iron _axe-head_ float.

11. Elisha, like Elijah, was blamed for a _famine_ in Samaria/Israel.

12. When the Syrians fled from Samaria/Israel, _grain/food_ became cheap again.

13. Elisha's messenger _anointed_ Jehu king of Israel and fled.

14. A taxi driver is called a Jehu, "for he _driveth_ furiously."

15. Jezebel "painted her _face_ " and sat looking out at the window.

16. Jehu wiped out the worship of _Baal_ .

17. A dead man's body, on touching Elisha's bones, _revived/etc._.

18. As Elijah had prophesied, Jezebel was eaten by _dogs_ .

19. The lost ten tribes of _Israel_ disappeared as captives of Assyria.

20. The pagan Samaritans of Samaria worshiped _idols/etc._

21. Nebuchadnezzar the Chaldean was king of _Babylon_ .

22. Nebuchadnezzar took the southern kingdom, _Judah_ , into captivity.

QUIZ 16 — Elisha, Jehu, end of both kingdoms

1. Elisha fed a hundred men with only __*twenty*__ barley loaves. (4:44)   (6)

2. Nebuchadnezzar of Babylon looted the __*temple*__ in Jerusalem. (25:13)   (#)

3. Elisha "__*took*__ up the mantle" of Elijah to succeed him. (2:14)   (3)

4. In one miracle, Elisha made an iron axe-head __*float*__. (6:6)   (10)

5. Naaman, a Syrian captain, asked Elisha to cure his __*leprosy/etc.*__ (5:9)   (7)

6. __*Jehu*__ wiped out the worship of Baal. (10:25)   (16)

7. The painted Jezebel was thrown to her death through a __*window*__. (9:33)   (#)

8. Elisha showed that he had __*Elijah*__'s spirit by performing similar miracles. (2:14)   (4)

9. The prophet __*Elijah*__ crossed over Jordan before going to heaven. (2:8)   (1)

10. Elisha's __*servant*__ took money from Naaman and ended up with white skin. (5:27)   (9)

11. The wicked tribes of __*Israel*__ were lost to the king of Assyria. (17:6)   (19)

12. Elisha put his __*mouth/lips*__ on the dead boy's mouth and revived him. (4:34)   (5)

13. The __*flaming/etc.*__ chariot swung low and carried Elijah home to God. (2:11)   (2)

14. A __*taxi driver*__ is called a Jehu, "for he driveth furiously." (9:20)   (14)

15. Elisha's messenger anointed __*Jehu*__ king of Israel and fled. (9:6,10)   (13)

16. As Elijah had prophesied, __*Jezebel*__'s body was eaten by dogs. (9:35)   (18)

17. Nebuchadnezzar took the people of Judah with him back to __*Babylon*__. (25:11)   (22)

18. A dead man's body revived when it touched Elisha's __*bones*__. (13:21)   (17)

19. After washing in the Jordan __*seven*__ times, Naaman was cleansed of his disease. (5:10)   (8)

20. Hearing the noise of chariots, the Syrians fled from __*Samaria/Israel*__. (7:6)   (#)

21. Blamed for the __*famine*__, Elisha said that grain would soon be cheap. (6:31)   (11)

22. The pagan Samaritans, who lived in __*Samaria/etc.*__, worshiped idols. (17:29)   (20)

STUDY QUESTIONS 17 — Esther 1:1-3:11; 4:1-8:17; 9:23-28

1. The Persian King Ahasuerus deposed his ___queen___ for refusing to appear at a banquet.

2. The laws of the Medes and the _Persians_ could not be altered.

3. The Jewess Hadassah was given the name of _Esther_, who was a Persian goddess.

4. Esther was Mordecai's _cousin_.

5. _Esther_ won the beauty contest to become the new queen.

6. Esther did not reveal to the court that she was a _Jew(ess)_.

7. Mordecai saved the king from the plot of two _chamberlains_.

8. Mordecai made _Haman_ angry by refusing to bow down.

9. Haman got permission to _destroy/kill_ all the Jews.

10. Mordecai asked _Esther_ to speak to the king for the Jews.

11. Esther bravely replied, "If I perish, I _perish_."

12. Haman was overjoyed that _Esther_ invited him to a banquet with the king.

13. On the advice of his _wife_, Haman built a high gallows.

14. The king finally learned of _Mordecai_'s loyalty when the chronicles were read to him.

15. "What shall be done unto the man whom the king _delighteth_ to honor?"

16. Haman had to lead _Mordecai_ on his horse throughout the city.

17. At the banquet, Esther said that _Haman_ was the enemy of her people.

18. Haman used his _gallows_ himself instead of for Mordecai.

19. _The Jews_ were allowed to avenge themselves on their enemies.

20. The Jewish _holiday/etc._ of Purim [lots] commemorates their deliverance from the threat of being wiped out.

306

QUIZ 17 — Esther

1. Esther bravely said, "If I __*perish*__, I perish." (4:16) (11)

2. Mordecai was given the dead Haman's __*ring*__ to
   wear. (8:2) (#)

3. The __*laws*__ of the Medes and the Persians could not
   be altered. (1:19) (2)

4. Haman was overjoyed that Esther invited him to a private
   __*banquet/etc.*__ (5:12) (12)

5. The gallows that had been built for Mordecai were used
   by __*Haman*__. (7:10) (18)

6. Esther won the beauty contest and became the new
   __*queen*__. (2:9) (5)

7. Mordecai asked Esther to speak to __*the king/etc.*__ for the
   Jews. (4:8) (10)

8. The Jewish holiday of Purim commemorates the Jews'
   __*deliverance/etc.*__ (9:26) (20)

9. "__*Esther*__" was the Persian name given to the Jewess
   Hadassah. (2:7) (3)

10. Haman got permission to destroy all the __*Jews*__. (3:11) (9)

11. The king thought Haman was assaulting the __*queen*__ on
    the bed. (7:8) (#)

12. Mordecai was Esther's __*cousin/guardian*__. (2:7) (4)

13. Mordecai made Haman angry because Mordecai refused to
    __*bow (down)*__. (3:5) (8)

14. Haman had to lead Mordecai on his __*horse*__ throughout
    the city. (6:11) (16)

15. Esther kept her relationship to Mordecai a __*secret*__
    from the king. (2:10) (6)

16. On his wife's advice, Haman built a high __*gallows*__. (5:14) (13)

17. King Ahasuerus got rid of his queen when she __*refused*__
    to appear at the banquet. (1:12,22) (1)

18. The king finally heard about Mordecai's loyalty from the
    __*chronicles/etc.*__ (6:2) (14)

19. Mordecai saved __*the king*__ from a plot by two of his
    chamberlains. (2:22) (7)

20. Haman thought that the king's question showed he intended
    to __*honor/etc.*__ Haman. (6:6) (15)

STUDY QUESTIONS 18 — Job 1:1-6:3; 6:24-27; 7:9-8:3; 8:20-9:6;
9:19-10:8; 11:1-8; 12:1-5; 13:1-15; 14:1-4; 14:14-15:13;
16:1-3; 19:20-29

1. Satan came from "going to and fro in the ___earth___ ."

2. "I only am ___escaped___ alone to tell thee."

3. "___Naked___ came I out of my mother's womb, and naked shall I return thither."

4. "The Lord gave, and the Lord hath taken away; ___blessed___ be the name of the Lord."

5. "All that a man ___hath___ will he give for his life."

6. Job's wife advised him, "Curse God, and ___die___ ."

7. ___Three___ of Job's old friends came to comfort him.

8. Job lamented, "Let the day ___perish___ wherein I was born."

9. Job complained, "Why did I not give up the ___ghost___ ?"

10. Eliphaz said, "Man is born unto trouble as the ___sparks___ fly upward."

11. Job answered Eliphaz, "How ___forcible___ are right words!"

12. "I would not live ___alway___ ."

13. Bildad said, "God will not cast away a ___perfect___ man."

14. Zophar asked, "Canst thou by ___searching___ find out God?"

15. "No doubt but ye are the people, and ___wisdom___ shall die with you."

16. "Though he slay me, yet will I ___trust___ in him."

17. "Man that is born of a woman is of few days and full of ___trouble___ ."

18. Disgusted, Job said, "___Miserable___ comforters are ye all."

19. "I am escaped with [RSV: by] the skin of my ___teeth___ ."

20. Job insisted, "I know that my redeemer ___liveth___ ."

21. "The ___root___ of the matter is found in me."

QUIZ 18 — Job, through 19:29

1. "The Lord ___gave___ , and the Lord hath taken away; blessed be the name of the Lord." (1:21) (4)

2. Job lamented, "Let the day perish wherein I was ___born___." (3:3) (8)

3. Job answered Eliphaz, "How forcible are right ___words___!" (6:25) (11)

4. "Man that is born of a woman is of few ___days___ and full of trouble." (14:1) (17)

5. "The root of the ___matter___ is found in me." (19:28) (21)

6. "Naked came I out of my mother's womb, and naked shall I ___return___ thither." (1:21) (3)

7. Three old friends came to comfort ___Job/him___. (2:11) (7)

8. "I would not ___live___ alway." (7:16) (12)

9. "No doubt but ye are the people, and wisdom shall ___die___ with you." (12:2) (15)

10. Job insisted, "I know that my ___redeemer___ liveth." (19:25) (20)

11. "I only am escaped to ___tell___ thee." (1:15) (2)

12. Job's wife advised him, "___Curse___ God, and die." (2:9) (6)

13. Eliphaz said, "Man is born unto ___trouble___ as the sparks fly upward." (5:7) (10)

14. Zophar asked, "Canst thou by searching find out ___God___?" (11:7) (14)

15. "I am escaped with the ___skin___ of my teeth." (19:20) (19)

16. Satan came from "going to ___and fro___ in the earth." (1:7) (1)

17. "All that a man hath will he give for his ___life___." (2:4) (5)

18. Job complained, "Why did I not ___give up___ the ghost?" (3:11) (9)

19. Bildad said, "God will not cast away a perfect ___man___." (8:20) (13)

20. Disgusted, Job said, "Miserable ___comforters___ are ye all." (16:1) (18)

21. "Though he ___slay___ me, yet will I trust in him." (13:15) (16)

STUDY QUESTIONS 19 — Job 21:1-16; 23:1-7; 27:1-6; 28:12-29:16; 31:5-32:10; 33:1-17; 35:1-16; 38:1-41; 39:19-41:7; 41:31-42:17

1. "Wherefore do the wicked live, become old, yea, are mighty in ___power___?"

2. "I would know the words which he would ___answer___ me."

3. "Neither is it found in the land of the ___living___."

4. "The price of wisdom is above ___rubies___."

5. "I was eyes to the ___blind___, and feet was I to the lame."

6. "My desire is, that the Almighty would ___answer___ me."

7. The men ceased answering Job because he was "___righteous___ in his own eyes."

8. Elihu, ___younger___ than Job and the comforters, had to wait his turn to speak.

9. Finally, "the Lord answered Job out of the ___whirlwind___."

10. "Where wast thou when I laid the ___foundations___ of the earth?"

11. "Hitherto shalt thou come, but no ___further___."

12. "Shall he that contendeth with the Almighty ___instruct___ him?"

13. "Behold, I am vile; what shall I ___answer___ thee?"

14. "Behold now ___behemoth___ [the largest beast], which I made with thee."

15. "Canst thou draw out ___leviathan___ [the largest fish] with an hook?"

16. "I uttered that [RSV: what] I ___understood___ not; things too wonderful for me, which I knew not."

17. "The Lord blessed the ___latter___ end of Job more than his beginning."

310

QUIZ 19 — Job, from 21:1

1. "I was eyes to the blind, and ___*feet*___ was I to the lame."(29:15) (5)

2. They ceased answering Job because he was "righteous in his own ___*eyes*___." (32:1) (7)

3. "Where wast thou when I laid the foundations of the ___*earth*___?" (38:4) (10)

4. "Behold, I am ___*vile*___; what shall I answer thee?"(40:4) (13)

5. "The Lord ___*blessed*___ the latter end of Job more than his beginning." (42:12) (17)

6. "Canst thou draw out leviathan with an ___*hook*___?"(41:1) (15)

7. Job and his friends were ___*older*___ than Elihu. (32:4) (8)

8. "Neither is it found in the ___*land*___ of the living." (28:13) (3)

9. "I uttered that I understood not; things too *wonderful* for me, which I knew not." (42:3) (16)

10. "___*Hitherto*___ shalt thou come, but no further." (38:11) (11)

11. "___*Behold*___ now behemoth, which I made with thee."(40:15) (14)

12. "Shall he that contendeth with the ___*Almighty*___ instruct him?" (40:2) (12)

13. Finally, "the ___*Lord*___ answered Job out of the whirlwind." (38:1) (9)

14. "My ___*desire*___ is, that the Almighty would answer me." (31:35) (6)

15. "The price of ___*wisdom*___ is above rubies." (28:18) (4)

16. "I would know the ___*words*___ which he would answer me."(23:5) (2)

17. "Wherefore do the ___*wicked*___ live, become old, yea, are mighty in power?" (21:7) (1)

STUDY QUESTIONS 20 — Psalms 1; 8; 19; 22-24; 42 (MEMORIZE 23)

1. "Blessed is the man that walketh not in the counsel of the _ungodly_ ."

2. "Out of the mouth of _babes_ and sucklings."

3. "What is man, that thou art _mindful_ of him?"

4. "Thou hast made him a little _lower_ than the angels."

5. "The heavens declare the glory of God; and the firmament showeth his _handiwork_ ."

6. "Day unto day uttereth speech, and night unto night showeth _knowledge_ ."

7. "Sweeter also than honey and the _honeycomb_ ."

8. "Let the words of my mouth, and the _meditation_ of my heart, be acceptable in thy sight, O Lord, my strength and my redeemer."

9. "My God, my God [Hebrew: Eli, Eli], why hast thou _forsaken_ me?"

10. "They _pierced_ [NEB: hacked off] my hands and my feet."

11. "They part my garments among them, and cast lots upon my _vesture_ ."

12. "He maketh me to lie down in _green_ pastures."

13. "Yea, though I walk through the valley of the shadow of _death_ ."

14. "My cup _runneth_ over."

15. "The earth is the Lord's, and the fulness _thereof_ ."

16. "Lift up your heads, O ye _gates_ ; and be ye lifted up, ye everlasting doors."

17. "As the hart [deer] panteth after the _water_ brooks, so panteth my soul after thee, O God."

18. "Why art thou cast _down_ , O my soul?"

19. "Deep _calleth_ unto deep."

312

QUIZ 20 — Psalms, through 42

1. "The heavens declare the __glory__ of God, and the firmament showeth his handiwork." (19:1)   (5)

2. "The __earth__ is the Lord's, and the fulness thereof." (24:1)   (15)

3. "What is __man__, that thou art mindful of him?" (8:4)   (3)

4. "The Lord is my __shepherd__; I shall not want." (23:1)   (#)

5. "Let the words of my __mouth__, and the meditation of my heart, be acceptable in thy sight, O Lord." (19:14)   (8)

6. "They part my __garments__ among them, and cast lots upon my vesture." (22:18)   (11)

7. "Sweeter also than __honey__ and the honeycomb." (19:10)   (7)

8. "I will fear no __evil__, for thou art with me." (23:4)   (#)

9. "Blessed is the man that __walketh__ not in the counsel of the ungodly." (1:1)   (1)

10. "As the hart panteth after the water brooks, so __panteth__ my soul after thee, O God." (42:1)   (17)

11. "Thou hast made him a little lower than the __angels__." (8:5)   (4)

12. "Deep calleth unto __deep__." (42:7)   (19)

13. "They pierced my hands and my __feet__." (22:16)   (10)

14. "Lift up your __heads__, O ye gates; and be lifted up, ye everlasting doors." (24:7)   (16)

15. "Day unto day uttereth __speech__, and night unto night showeth knowledge." (19:2)   (6)

16. "Why art thou cast down, O my __soul__?" (42:5)   (18)

17. "Thou anointest my head with __oil__." (23:5)   (#)

18. "My God, my God, why hast thou forsaken __me__?" (22:1)   (9)

19. "Out of the mouth of babes and __sucklings__." (8:2)   (2)

<u>STUDY QUESTIONS 21</u> — Psalms 46; 51; 55; 63; 84; 90; 91; 96;
<u>103; 107</u>

1. "God is our refuge and <u>*strength*</u>, a very present help in trouble."

2. "I was shapen in <u>*iniquity*</u>; and in sin did my mother conceive me."

3. "A broken and a <u>*contrite*</u> heart, 0 God, thou wilt not despise."

4. "Oh that I had wings like a <u>*dove*</u>!"

5. "We took sweet counsel <u>*together*</u>."

6. "The words of his mouth were smoother than <u>*butter*</u>."

7. "Early will I <u>*seek*</u> thee."

8. "They go from strength to <u>*strength*</u>."

9. "I had rather be a doorkeeper in the house of my <u>*God*</u>, than to dwell in the tents of wickedness."

10. "A thousand years in thy sight are but as <u>*yesterday*</u> when it is past."

11. "We spend our years as a tale that is <u>*told*</u>."

12. "The days of our years are <u>*threescore*</u> years and ten [i.e., seventy]."

13. "So teach us to <u>*number*</u> our days, that we may apply our hearts unto wisdom."

14. "Establish thou the work of our <u>*hands*</u> upon us; yea, the work of our hands establish thou it."

15. "He is my refuge and my <u>*fortress*</u>."

16. "Sing unto the Lord a new <u>*song*</u>."

17. "As for man, his <u>*days*</u> are as grass."

18. "They that go down to the sea in <u>*ships*</u>."

19. "They reel to and fro, and stagger like a drunken man, and are at their wit's <u>*end*</u>."

QUIZ 21 — Psalms, 46 through 107

1. "The words of his mouth were _smoother_ than butter."(55:21)(6)

2. "A _thousand_ years in thy sight are but as yesterday when it is past." (90:4) (10)

3. "Establish thou the _work_ of our hands upon us; yea, the work of our hands establish thou it." (90:17) (14)

4. "They that go down to the _sea_ in ships." (107:23) (18)

5. "I was shapen in iniquity; and in _sin_ did my mother conceive me." (51:5) (2)

6. "_Early_ will I seek thee." (63:1) (7)

7. "We spend our years as a _tale_ that is told." (90:9) (11)

8. "He is my _refuge_ and my fortress." (91:2) (15)

9. "They reel to and fro, and stagger like a drunken man, and are at their _wit_'s end." (107:27) (19)

10. "God is our refuge and strength, a very present help in _trouble_." (46:1) (1)

11. "They go from _strength_ to strength." (84:7) (8)

12. "The days of our _years_ are threescore years and ten." (90:10) (12)

13. "_Sing_ unto the Lord a new song." (96:1) (16)

14. "A _broken_ and a contrite heart, O God, thou wilt not despise." (51:17) (3)

15. "I had rather be a _doorkeeper_ in the house of my God, than to dwell in the tents of wickedness." (84:10) (9)

16. "So teach us to number our days, that we may apply our hearts unto _wisdom_." (90:12) (13)

17. "Oh that I had _wings_ like a dove!" (55:6) (4)

18. "As for man, his days are as _grass_." (103:15) (17)

19. "We took sweet _counsel_ together." (55:14) (5)

STUDY QUESTIONS 22 — Psalms 115; 118; 119:97-112; 121; 122; 127;

130; 133; 137; 139; 146; 150

1. "They have mouths, but they speak not; eyes have they, but
   they ___*see*___ not."

2. "O give thanks unto the Lord; for he is good: because his
   ___*mercy*___ endureth forever."

3. "The stone which the builders refused is become the head stone
   of the ___*corner*___."

4. "Blessed is he that cometh in the name of the ___*Lord*___."

5. "I have more understanding than all my ___*teachers*___."

6. "Thy word is a lamp unto my ___*feet*___."

7. "I will lift up mine ___*eyes*___ unto the hills, from whence
   cometh my help."

8. "Peace be within thy walls, and prosperity within thy
   ___*palaces*___."

9. "Except the Lord build the house, they ___*labor*___ in vain that
   build it."

10. "Out of the ___*depths*___ have I cried unto thee, O Lord."

11. "How good and how pleasant it is for brethren to dwell to-
    gether in ___*unity*___!"

12. "By the rivers [RSV: waters] of ___*Babylon*___, there we sat down,
    yea, we wept."

13. "We hanged our harps upon the ___*willows*___."

14. "If I forget thee, O Jerusalem, let my right hand forget her
    ___*cunning*___."

15. "I take the wings of the ___*morning*___."

16. "Put not your trust in ___*princes*___."

17. "Let every thing that hath ___*breath*___ praise the Lord."

18. "Praise ye the ___*Lord*___ [Hebrew: hallelujah]."

QUIZ 22 — Psalms, from 115

1. "I have more _understanding_ than all my teachers." (119:99)   (5)

2. "Except the Lord build the house, they labor in
   vain that build it." (127:1)   (9)

3. "O give _thanks_ unto the Lord; for he is good:
   because his mercy endureth forever." (118:1)   (2)

4. "We hanged our _harps_ upon the willows." (137:2)   (13)

5. "Let every thing that hath breath _praise_ the
   Lord." (150:6)   (17)

6. "The stone which the _builders_ refused is become the
   head stone of the corner." (118:22)   (3)

7. "Thy word is a _lamp_ unto my feet." (119:105)   (6)

8. "Out of the depths have I _cried_ unto thee, O
   Lord." (130:1)   (10)

9. "If I forget thee, O _Jerusalem_, let my right hand
   forget her cunning." (137:5)   (14)

10. "_Praise_ ye the Lord." (150:1)   (18)

11. "_Blessed_ be he that cometh in the name of the
    Lord." (118:26)   (4)

12. "I will lift up mine eyes unto the hills, from whence
    cometh my _help_." (121:1)   (7)

13. "Behold, how good and how pleasant it is for _brethren_
    to dwell together in unity!" (133:1)   (11)

14. "I take the _wings_ of the morning." (139:9)   (15)

15. "They have _mouths_, but they speak not; eyes have
    they, but they see not." (115:5)   (1)

16. "Peace be within thy _walls_, and prosperity within
    thy palaces." (122:7)   (8)

17. "By the _rivers_ of Babylon, there we sat down, yea,
    we wept." (137:1)   (12)

18. "Put not your _trust_ in princes." (146:3)   (16)

STUDY QUESTIONS 23 — Proverbs 1:1-10; 3:1-20; 6:6-11; 9:13-10:2;
13:12-24; 15:1-5; 16:18,19; 20:11,12; 22:1-6; 25:20-22
26:1-14,27,28; 29:18-20; 30:15-28; 31:10-31

1. "The proverbs of ___*Solomon*___ the son of David."

2. "Whom the Lord loveth he ___*correcteth*___ ."

3. "She is a ___*tree*___ of life to them that lay hold upon her."

4. "Go to the ant, thou sluggard; consider her ways, and be
___*wise*___ ."

5. "Stolen waters are ___*sweet*___ ."

6. "A wise son maketh a ___*glad*___ father."

7. "Hope deferred maketh the heart ___*sick*___ ."

8. "The way of *transgressors* is hard."

9. "He that spareth his ___*rod*___ hateth his son."

10. "A soft answer turneth away ___*wrath*___ ."

11. "Pride ___*goeth*___ before . . . a fall."

12. "The hearing ear, and the seeing ___*eye*___ ."

13. "A good name is rather to be chosen than great ___*riches*___ ."

14. "Train up a ___*child*___ in the way he should go: and when he
is old, he will not depart from it."

15. "Thou shalt heap coals of ___*fire*___ upon his head."

16. "Answer a fool according to his ___*folly*___ ."

17. "The slothful [lazy] man saith, . . . 'A ___*lion*___ is in the
streets.'"

18. "Whoso diggeth a pit shall ___*fall*___ therein."

19. "Where there is no vision, the people ___*perish*___ ."

20. "The way of a man with a ___*maid*___ ."

21. "Who can find a virtuous woman? For her price is far above
___*rubies*___ ."

QUIZ 23 — Proverbs

1. "Go to the ant, thou _sluggard_ ; consider her ways, and be wise." (6:6) (4)

2. "The way of transgressors is ___hard___ ." (13:15) (8)

3. "The hearing ear, and the ___seeing___ eye." (20:12) (12)

4. "Answer a ___fool___ according to his folly." (26:5) (16)

5. "The ___proverbs___ of Solomon the son of David." (1:1) (1)

6. "___Stolen___ waters are sweet." (9:17) (5)

7. "He that ___spareth___ his rod hateth his son." (13:24) (9)

8. "A good ___name___ is rather to be chosen than great riches." (22:1) (13)

9. "The slothful man saith, . . . 'A lion is in the ___streets___ .'" (26:13) (17)

10. "Whom the Lord ___loveth___ he correcteth." (3:12) (2)

11. "A ___wise___ son maketh a glad father." (10:1) (6)

12. "A ___soft___ answer turneth away wrath." (15:1) (10)

13. "___Train___ up a child in the way he should go: and when he is old, he will not depart from it." (22:6) (14)

14. "Whoso diggeth a ___pit___ shall fall therein." (26:27) (18)

15. "She is a tree of ___life___ to them that lay hold upon her." (3:18) (3)

16. "Hope ___deferred___ maketh the heart sick." (13:12) (7)

17. "Pride goeth before . . . a ___fall___ ." (16:18) (11)

18. "Where there is no ___vision___ , the people perish."(29:18) (19)

19. "Thou shalt heap ___coals___ of fire upon his head."(25:22) (15)

20. "Who can find a virtuous ___woman___ ? For her price is far above rubies." (31:10) (21)

21. "The way of a ___man___ with a maid." (30:19) (20)

STUDY QUESTIONS 24 — Ecclesiastes 1:1-4:16; 7:1-18; 8:2-15;
9:11,12; 11:1-12:13. Song of Solomon 1:1-2:17

1.*According to some traditions, King __Solomon__ was the
"preacher" [Heb.: koheleth] quoted in Ecclesiastes.

2. "'Vanity of vanities,' saith the __preacher__ . . . 'all is
vanity.'"

3. "The __sun__ also ariseth [RSV: rises], and the sun goeth
down."

4. "There is no __new__ thing [RSV: nothing new] under the
sun."

5. The writer says he pursued both pleasures and wisdom and
found them all __empty/etc.__

6. "To every thing there is a __season__ ."

7. "A time to love, and a time to hate; a time of __war__ ,
and a time of peace."

8. "Be not righteous __over__ [too] much."

9. "There is no __discharge__ in that war."

10. "To eat, and to drink, and to be __merry__ ."

11. "The race is not to the __swift__ , nor the battle to the
strong."

12. "Cast thy __bread__ upon the waters: for thou shalt find it
after many days."

13. "Or ever the silver cord be loosed or the __golden__ bowl be
broken."

14. "The dust return to the earth as it was, and the spirit shall
return unto __God__ who gave it."

15. "Of making many __books__ there is no end."

16. "Much __study__ is a weariness of the flesh."

17.*The Song of Solomon is also called Song of Songs and Canticle
of __Canticles__ .

18. "I am the __rose__ of Sharon, and the lily of the valleys."

19. "For, lo, the __winter__ is past, and the rain is over and
gone."

20. "The __voice__ of the turtle [dove] is heard in our land."

21. "The little __foxes__ , that spoil the vines: for our vines
have tender grapes."

22. "My beloved is mine and I am __his__ ."

320

QUIZ 24 — Ecclesiastes, Song of Solomon

1. "The little foxes, that spoil the vines: for our vines have tender _grapes_ ." (S2:15) (21)

2. The Song of Solomon is often called the Song of _Songs_ . (S1:1) (17)

3. "Or ever the silver cord be loosed or the golden bowl be _broken_ ." (E12:6) (13)

4. "There is no discharge in that _war_ ." (E8:8) (9)

5. The writer pursued both pleasures and _wisdom_ and found them all empty. (E2:17) (5)

6. Ecclesiastes/Koheleth may have been King _Solomon_ . (E1:1) (1)

7. "For, lo, the winter is past, the _rain_ is over and gone." (S2:11) (19)

8. "Much study is a _weariness_ of the flesh." (E12:12) (16)

9. "Cast thy bread upon the _waters_ : for thou shalt find it after many days." (E11:1) (12)

10. "Be not _righteous_ over much." (E7:16) (8)

11. "There is _no_ new thing under the sun." (E1:9) (4)

12. "My _beloved_ is mine and I am his." (S2:16) (22)

13. "The voice of the _turtle_ [dove] is heard in our land." (S2:12) (20)

14. "The _race_ is not to the swift, nor the battle to the strong." (E9:11) (11)

15. "A time to love, and a time to _hate_ ; a time of war, and a time of peace." (E3:8) (7)

16. "The sun _also_ ariseth, and the sun goeth down." (E1:5) (3)

17. "I am the rose of Sharon, and the _lily_ of the valleys." (S2:1) (18)

18. "Of making many books there is no _end_ ." (E12:12) (15)

19. "To eat, and to _drink_ , and to be merry." (E8:15) (10)

20. "To every _thing_ there is a season." (E3:1) (6)

21. "'Vanity of _vanities_ ,' saith the preacher . . . 'all is vanity.'" (E1:2) (2)

22. "The _dust_ return to the earth as it was, and the spirit shall return unto God who gave it." (E12:7) (14)

STUDY QUESTIONS 25 — Isaiah 1:18-20; 2:1-4; 5:1-7; 6:1-13;
7:10-17; 9:1-7; 11:1-9 (MEMORIZE 2:2-4)

1. "Come now, and let us reason _together_ ."

2. "Though your sins be as scarlet, they shall be as white as
snow ."

3. "The Lord's house shall be established in the top of the
mountains ."

4. "Out of _Zion_ shall go forth the law."

5. "They shall beat their swords into _plowshares_ ."

6. "Nation shall not lift up _sword_ against nation."

7. "The vineyard of the Lord of hosts is the house of _Israel_ ."

8. Isaiah saw over God's throne seraphim [angels] with six
wings .

9. "Holy, holy, holy, is the Lord of _hosts_ ." [The "tersanctus": three times holy]

10. Fearfully, Isaiah said, "Woe is me! for I am _undone_ ."

11. After his _lips_ were touched with fire, Isaiah said,
"Here am I; send me," and became a prophet of God.

12. Isaiah asked, "Lord, how _long_ ?" would Israel not see and
hear.

13. "Behold, a virgin [RSV: young woman] shall _conceive_ and bear
a son."

14. "The people that walked in _darkness_ have seen a great light."

15. "Unto us a child is born, unto us a _son_ is given."

16. "His name shall be called . . . The Prince of _Peace_ ."

17. "The wolf also shall dwell with the lamb, . . . the calf and
the young _lion_ ."

18. "And a little child shall _lead_ them."

19.* _Isaiah_ 's vision is of a "peaceable kingdom."

322

QUIZ 25 — Isaiah, through 11:9

1. "Come now, and let us ___reason___ together." (1:18) (1)

2. "They shall beat . . . their ___spears___ into pruning hooks." (2:4) (#)

3. "Holy, holy, holy, is the ___Lord___ of hosts." (6:3) (9)

4. "Behold a ___virgin___ shall conceive, and bear a son." (7:14) (13)

5. "The wolf also shall dwell with the ___lamb___, . . . the calf and the young lion." (11:6) (17)

6. "Though your sins be as ___scarlet___, they shall be as white as snow." (1:18) (2)

7. "Neither shall they learn ___war___ any more." (2:4) (#)

8. Fearfully, Isaiah said, "___Woe___ is me! for I am undone." (6:5) (10)

9. "The people that walked in darkness have seen a great ___light___." (9:2) (14)

10. "And a little ___child___ shall lead them." (11:6) (18)

11. "And all the ___nations___ shall flow unto it." (2:2) (#)

12. "The ___vineyard___ of the Lord of hosts is the house of Israel." (5:7) (7)

13. Isaiah said, "Here am I; ___send___ me," and became a prophet. (6:8) (11)

14. "Unto us a child is ___born___, unto us a son is given." (9:6) (15)

15. Isaiah's vision is of a "peaceable ___kingdom___." (11:6-9) (19)

16. "And the word of the ___Lord___ from Jerusalem." (2:3) (#)

17. Isaiah saw over God's throne seraphim, each with ___six___ wings. (6:2) (8)

18. Isaiah asked, "Lord, ___how___ long?" would Israel not see and hear. (6:11) (12)

19. "His name shall be called . . . The ___Prince___ of Peace." (9:6) (16)

STUDY QUESTIONS 26 — Isaiah 14:3,4,12-15; 21:11,12; 28:5,6,9,10;
32:1-8; 35:1-8; 37:21-38:8; 40:1-16; 42:1-9; 48:20-22;
52:1-53:12; 61:1-9

1. "How art thou fallen from heaven, O _Lucifer_, [RSV: day star] son of the morning!"

2. "Watchman, what of the _night_?"

3. "Line upon line; here a little, and _there_ a little."

4. "The shadow of a great rock in a _weary_ land."

5. "The desert shall rejoice, and blossom as the _rose_."

6. "Out of _Jerusalem_ shall go forth a remnant."

7. As prophesied, Judah, the southern kingdom, was saved by God from Sennacherib, king of _Assyria_.

8. "Set thine house in _order_."

9. "Comfort ye, comfort ye my _people_."

10. "The voice of him that crieth in the _wilderness_."

11. "The nations are as a drop of [RSV: from] a _bucket_."

12. "Behold my servant, whom I uphold; mine _elect_."

13. "I . . . will give thee . . . for a light of the _Gentiles_."

14. "There is no peace . . . unto the _wicked_."

15. "They shall see eye to _eye_."

16. "He [i.e., the Lord's suffering servant] is _despised_ and rejected of men; a man of sorrows."

17. "We like sheep have gone _astray_."

18. "He is brought as a _lamb_ to the slaughter."

19. "He bare [bore] the sin of many, and made intercession for the _transgressors_."

20. "The Lord hath anointed me to preach good _tidings_ unto the meek."

QUIZ 26 — Isaiah, from 14:3

1. "We like ___sheep___ have gone astray." (53:6)   (17)

2. "Line upon line; here a little, and there a
   ___little___." (28:10)   (3)

3. "Set thine ___house___ in order." (38:1)   (8)

4. "Behold my ___servant___, whom I uphold; mine elect."(42:1) (12)

5. "He is brought as a lamb to the ___slaughter___." (53:7) (18)

6. "The shadow of a great ___rock___ in a weary land."(32:2) (4)

7. "Comfort ye, comfort ye ___my___ people." (40:1)   (9)

8. "I . . . will give thee . . . for a ___light___ of the
   Gentiles." (42:6)   (13)

9. "How art thou ___fallen___ from heaven, O Lucifer, son of
   the morning!" (14:12)   (1)

10. "The ___desert___ shall rejoice, and blossom as the
    rose." (35:1)   (5)

11. "The ___voice___ of him that crieth in the wilder-
    ness." (40:3)   (10)

12. "There is no ___peace___ . . . unto the wicked." (48:22) (14)

13. "___Watchman___, what of the night?" (21:11)   (2)

14. As prophesied, the Assyrians were driven away from the
    kingdom of ___Judah___, in the south. (37:36)   (7)

15. "The nations are as a ___drop___ of a bucket." (40:15)   (11)

16. "They shall ___see___ eye to eye." (52:8)   (15)

17. "He bare the ___sin___ of many, and made intercession
    for the transgressors." (53:12)   (19)

18. "He is despised and rejected of men; a man of
    ___sorrows___." (53:3)   (16)

19. "The Lord hath anointed me to preach good tidings
    unto the ___meek___." (61:1)   (20)

20. "Out of Jerusalem shall go forth a ___remnant___." (37:32) (6)

STUDY QUESTIONS 27 — Jeremiah 1:4-10; 4:23-28; 6:9-15; 13:20-27;
31:15-17. Lamentations 1:1-4; 2:1-4; 3:18,19. Ezekiel 1:1-28;
18:1-4; 37:1-14. Hosea 8:1-12. Joel 2:1-3,21-29.
Amos 1:1-2:12; 5:10-24; 7:10-15

1. *A Jeremiad is a long __*sad/etc.*__ kind of speech or essay.

2. "The whole land shall be a __*desolation*__."

3. "Peace, peace; when there is no __*peace*__."

4. "Can the Ethiopian change his skin, or the leopard his __*spots*__?"

5. "Rachel weeping for her children refused to be __*comforted*__."

6. "How lonely sits the __*city*__ that was full of people!"

7. "The wormwood and the __*gall*__." (i.e., both taste bitter)

8. In his first vision, Ezekiel saw four creatures with wings and with faces of a man, a lion, an ox, and an __*eagle*__.

9. Ezekiel's flying object had a "wheel in the middle of a __*wheel*__."

10. "The fathers have eaten sour grapes, and the children's __*teeth*__ are set on edge."

11. Ezekiel had a vision of a valley full of dry __*bones*__.

12. The bones in Ezekiel's vision represented the "whole house of __*Israel*__."

13. "They have sown the wind, and they shall reap the __*whirlwind*__."

14. "Your old men shall dream dreams, your young men shall see __*visions*__."

15. "For three transgressions of Israel, and for four, I will not turn away the __*punishment*__ thereof."

16. "They afflict the just, they take a bribe, and they turn aside the __*poor*__."

17. "I __*despise*__ your feast days . . . and your meat offerings, I will not accept them."

18. "I was no prophet, neither was I a prophet's __*son*__."

QUIZ 27 — Jeremiah, Lamentations, Ezekiel, Hosea, Joel, Amos

1. "For three transgressions of Israel, and for ___*four*___,
   I will not turn away the punishment thereof." (A2:6)   (15)

2. A ___*Jeremiad*___ is a long complaining/sad kind of speech
   or essay. (Je1:1ff)   (1)

3. "The ___*wormwood*___ and the gall." (L3:19)   (7)

4. Ezekiel had a vision of a ___*valley*___ full of dry
   bones. (E37:1)   (11)

5. "Your old men shall dream ___*dreams*___; your young men
   shall see visions." (Jo2:28)   (14)

6. Ezekiel saw four winged creatures with faces of a man,
   a ___*lion*___, an ox, and an eagle. (E1:10)   (8)

7. "Rachel weeping for her ___*children*___ refused to be comforted." (Je31:15)   (5)

8. "The fathers have eaten sour ___*grapes*___, and the children's teeth are set on edge." (E18:2)   (10)

9. "They have sown the ___*wind*___, and they shall reap
   the whirlwind." (H8:7)   (13)

10. "I despise your feast days . . . and your meat offer-
    ings, I will not ___*accept*___ them." (A5:21,22)   (17)

11. "Peace, peace; when there is ___*no*___ peace." (Je6:14)   (3)

12. "I was no ___*prophet*___, neither was I a prophet's
    son." (A7:14)   (18)

13. The ___*bones*___ in Ezekiel's dream represented the
    "whole house of Israel." (E37:11)   (12)

14. "They afflict the just, they take a ___*bribe*___, and
    they turn aside the poor." (A5:12)   (16)

15. Can the Ethiopian change his skin, or the ___*leopard*___
    his spots?" (Je13:23)   (4)

16. The flying object had a "___*wheel*___ in the middle of
    a wheel." (E1:16)   (9)

17. "The whole ___*land*___ shall be a desolation." (Je4:27)   (2)

18. "How lonely sits the city that was so full of
    ___*people*___!" (L1:1)   (6)

STUDY QUESTIONS 28 — Daniel 1:1-7; 2:1-6,10-15; 2:24-3:1;
3:3-6,8,12; 3:14-4:9; 4:19-6:24. Jonah 1:1-4:11

1. _Nebuchadnezzar_, the king, took Judah into Babylonian captivity.

2. They named the three Jews Shadrach, _Meshach_ , and Abednego.

3. The king dreamed of a statue with feet of _clay_ and iron.

4. Everyone was ordered to bow down to the huge statue in the plain of _Dura_ .

5. The three Jews were thrown into a "burning fiery _furnace_ ."

6. Instead of three men, Nebuchadnezzar found _four_ alive in the furnace.

7. Nebuchadnezzar went mad, and he ate _grass_ .

8. At _Belshazzar_'s feast they drank to idols out of sacred cups taken from the temple.

9. Daniel was called in to interpret the handwriting on the _wall_ .

10. The words were _MENE_ , MENE, TEKEL, UPHARSIN.

11. "Thou art _weighed_ in the balances, and art found wanting."

12. "The law of the _Medes_ and Persians, which altereth not."

13. Daniel was saved in the _lions_' den by an angel.

14. Jonah brought _bad_ luck to the sailors on his ship.

15. Jonah spent three days in the belly of a _fish/whale_.

16. "Out of the belly of hell [Heb.: sheol] _cried_ I."

17. As God had instructed, Jonah prophesied that _Nineveh_ would surely be overthrown.

18. The king of Nineveh repented, sitting in _sackcloth_ and ashes.

19. _Jonah_ was angry because God changed his mind about Nineveh.

QUIZ 28 — Daniel, Jonah

1. Jonah prophesied, "Yet forty days, and ___Nineveh___
   shall be overthrown." (J3:4)   (17)

2. ___Shadrach___, Meshach, and Abednego were Babylonian
   names given to the three Jews. (D1:7)   (2)

3. In addition to the ___three___ Jews, Nebuchadnezzar
   found an angel alive in the furnace. (D3:25)   (6)

4. "This . . . was written, MENE, ___MENE___, TEKEL,
   UPHARSIN." (D5:25)   (10)

5. ___Jonah___ brought bad luck to the sailors of his
   ship. (J1:12)   (14)

6. The king of Nineveh repented, sitting in sackcloth
   and ___ashes___. (J3:6)   (18)

7. Nebuchadnezzar dreamed of a statue with ___feet___ of
   clay and iron. (D2:33)   (3)

8. Nebuchadnezzar went ___mad/etc.___ and ate grass, as Daniel had prophesied. (D4:33)   (7)

9. Belshazzar was warned that he had been tried and
   "found ___wanting___." (D5:27)   (11)

10. Jonah spent ___three___ days in the belly of a great
    fish. (J1:17)   (15)

11. ___God/The Lord___ was merciful to Nineveh, as he had been
    to Jonah. (J3:10)   (19)

12. Everyone was ordered to bow down to the huge ___statue/idol___
    in the plain of Dura. (D3:5)   (4)

13. At Belshazzar's ___feast/etc.___ they drank to idols from
    sacred Jewish cups. (D5:3)   (8)

14. "The law of the Medes and ___Persians___, which altereth
    not." (D6:8)   (12)

15. "Out of the ___belly___ of hell cried I." (J2:2)   (16)

16. Nebuchadnezzar took ___Judah/etc.___ into Babylonian cap-
    tivity. (D1:2)   (1)

17. The three Jews were thrown into a "burning ___fiery___
    furnace." (D3:23)   (5)

18. Daniel was called to interpret the ___(hand)writing___ on the
    wall. (D5:13)   (9)

19. Daniel was saved in the lions' den by an ___angel___. (D6:22)(13)

STUDY QUESTIONS 29 — Judith 4:1-3; 5:1-4; 7:1,2,19-27; 8:32-9:4;
   10:1-23; 12:1-4; 12:10-13:20; 14:11-15:11; 16:18-25.
   Ecclesiasticus 13:1-8; 30:1-13; 44:1-15. Susanna 1-64

1.*Some of the Catholic Old _Testament_ is called Apocrypha in
   other Bibles.

2.*In some places _Nebuchadnezzar_ is called Nebuchadrezzar, Nabucho-
   donosor, or Nabucco (really king of Babylon, not Assyria, as
   in this story).

3. _Bethulia_ was a hill town under siege by Holofernes.

4. Judith and the Assyrian commander ate and drank inside his
   tent .

5. Judith brought back to the Jews Holofernes' _head_ .

6. When the Assyrians found they were without a _head/etc._ ,
   they fled.

7.*Ecclesiasticus is also called The Wisdom of Jesus the Son of
   [Heb.: ben] _Sirach_ .

8. "He that toucheth pitch [tar] shall be _defiled_ therewith."

9. "He will speak thee _fair_ , and . . . will laugh thee to
   scorn."

10. "He that loveth his son causeth him oft to feel the
    rod ."

11. "Let us now _praise_ famous men."

12.*The story of Susanna is part of the book of _Daniel_ in
   Catholic Bibles.

13. The elders spied on Susanna as she washed in her _garden_ .

14. Falsely accused, Susanna was condemned to _die/death_ .

15. The youth who came to Susanna's judgment was named _Daniel_ .

16. Daniel caught the _elders/men_ in their lie by questioning them
    separately.

QUIZ 29 — Judith, Ecclesiasticus, Susanna

1. Judith cut off Holofernes' ___head___ . (J13:8)   (5)

2. "He that ___loveth___ his son causeth him often to
   feel the rod." (E30:1)   (10)

3. The youth who came to ___Susanna___'s judgment was
   named Daniel. (S45)   (15)

4. ___Judith___ and the Assyrian commander ate and drank
   inside his tent. (J12:19)   (4)

5. "He will ___speak___ thee fair, and . . . will laugh
   thee to scorn." (E13:6,7)   (9)

6. Falsely accused, ___Susanna___ was condemned to death. (S41) (14)

7. Bethulia was a hill town under ___siege/etc.___ by
   Holofernes. (J7:1)   (3)

8. Daniel caught the elders in their lie by questioning
   them ___apart/etc.___ . (S51)   (16)

9. The ___elders/men___ spied on Susanna as she washed in
   garden. (S16)   (13)

10. In the book of Judith, Nebuchadnezzar is king of the
    Assyrians, not the ___Babylonians___, as elsewhere. (J4:1)   (2)

11. "Let us now praise ___famous___ men." (E44:1)   (11)

12. The story of Susanna is part of the book of Daniel
    in ___Catholic___ Bibles.   (12)

13. "He that toucheth ___pitch___ shall be defiled there-
    with." (E13:1)   (8)

14. When the Assyrians found they were without a head,
    they ___fled/etc.___ . (J15:2)   (6)

15. Ecclesiasticus is also called The Wisdom of ___Jesus___
    the Son of Sirach.   (7)

16. Some parts of the Catholic ___Old___ Testament are
    called Apocrypha in other Bibles.   (1)

STUDY QUESTIONS 30 — Matthew 1:18–5:11
(MEMORIZE Beatitudes, 5:3-10)

1. "The ___Gospel___ [good news, AS = Grk.: evangel] According to Matthew."

2. *Jesus is the Greek form of ___Yeshua___ [he will save, Heb.].

3. When Jesus was born, King ___Herod___ ruled the Jews under the Romans.

4. "Where is he that is born ___King___ of the Jews?"

5. "The star, which they saw in the ___east___, went before them."

6. The gifts of the magi (wise men) were gold, frankincense, and ___myrrh___.

7. *The holiday of Epihany [showing forth, Grk.] celebrates the visit of the _magi/wise men_.

8. Because of Herod's threat, the family took flight into ___Egypt___.

9. ___Herod___ ordered the "Slaughter/Massacre of the Innocents."

10. "___Repent___ ye, for the kingdom of heaven is at hand."

11. John the Baptist wore rough clothes and ate "locusts and wild ___honey___."

12. "O generation [offspring] of ___vipers___."

13. "He that cometh after me is ___mightier___ than I."

14. "He shall baptize you with the ___Holy___ Ghost [RSV: Spirit]."

15. Jesus saw the "Spirit of God descending like a ___dove___."

16. "This is my beloved Son, in whom I am well ___pleased___."

17. Jesus went into the wilderness, where he was tempted by the ___devil___.

18. "Man shall not live by ___bread___ alone."

19. Jesus told Simon Peter [Simon the rock, Grk. = Aram.: Cephas] and Andrew that he would make them "___fishers___ of men."

20. The next disciples [Lat.: pupils] were also brothers: James and ___John___.

21. *The Beatitudes [blessedness, happiness] begin the ___Sermon___ on the Mount.

22. "Blessed are they that mourn: for they shall be ___comforted___."

23. "Blessed are the ___meek___: for they shall inherit the earth."

24. "Blessed are the merciful: for they shall obtain ___mercy___."

332

QUIZ 30 — Matthew, through 5:11

1. Jesus told Peter and Andrew to become "fishers of
   __men__." (4:19)   (19)

2. Herod ordered the "Slaughter/Massacre of the
   __Innocents__." (2:16)   (9)

3. The Sermon on the Mount begins with the __Beatitudes__. (5:3) (21)

4. "He that cometh after me is mightier than
   __I__." (3:11)   (13)

5. "Blessed are the __poor__ in spirit: for theirs
   is the kingdom of heaven." (5:3)   (#)

6. "The __star__, which they saw in the east, went
   before them." (2:9)   (5)

7. "0 __generation__ of vipers." (3:7)   (12)

8. "Blessed are the __peacemakers__: for they shall be
   called the children of God." (5:9)   (#)

9. "This is my beloved __Son__, in whom I am well
   pleased." (3:17)   (16)

10. John the Baptist wore rough clothes and ate "locusts
    and __wild__ honey." (3:4)   (11)

11. Jesus insisted that John the Baptist should __baptize__
    him. (3:15)   (#)

12. When Jesus was born, Herod was __king/ruler__ of the
    Jews under the Romans. (2:1)   (3)

13. The gifts of the magi were __gold__, frankincense,
    and myrrh. (2:11)   (6)

14. __Jesus__ is the Greek form of the Hebrew Yeshua.   (2)

15. The celebration of the wise men's visit is called
    __Epiphany__.   (7)

16. "Man shall not __live__ by bread alone." (4:4)   (18)

17. "Where is he that is __born__ King of the Jews?" (2:2)   (4)

18. Jesus saw the "__Spirit__ of God descending like a
    dove" at his baptism. (3:16)   (15)

19. Jesus went into the __wilderness__, where he was tempted
    by the devil. (4:1)   (17)

20. The second two disciples were __James__ and John. (4:21) (20)

21. "Repent ye, for the kingdom of heaven is at
    __hand__." (3:2)   (10)

22. "The Gospel [__good news__, AS] According to Matthew."   (1)

23. Because of __Herod__'s threat, the family took flight
    into Egypt. (2:13)   (8)

STUDY QUESTIONS 31 — Matthew 5:12-7:6
(MEMORIZE Lord's Prayer, 6:9b-13)

1. "Ye are the ___*salt*___ of the earth."

2. Salt that has lost its savor/taste is "good for ___*nothing*___."

3. "A city that is set on an ___*hill*___ cannot be hid."

4. "Neither do men light a ___*candle*___, and put it under a bushel [basket]."

5. "I am not come to destroy, but to ___*fulfill*___."

6. Jesus promised that not "one jot [Grk.: iota] or one ___*tittle*___ [dot]" of law would change.

7. "If thy right ___*eye*___ offend thee, pluck it out."

8. Jesus ___*forbade/etc.*___ swearing oaths: let your yea be yea; your nay, nay.

9. The Lex Talionis [law of revenge, Lat.] was, "An eye for an eye, and a tooth for a ___*tooth*___."

10. When struck on one cheek, one should ___*turn*___ the other.

11. When forced to go a ___*mile*___, one should "go a second mile."

12. "Love your ___*enemies*___, bless them that curse you."

13. "He . . . sendeth ___*rain*___ on the just and on the unjust."

14. "Let not thy left hand know what thy right ___*hand*___ doeth."

15. "When thou prayest, enter into thy ___*closet*___ [private room]."

16. The Lord's Prayer begins, "Our ___*Father*___" [Lat.: Pater Noster].

17. "Lay up for yourselves treasures in ___*heaven*___."

18. "Where your ___*treasure*___ is, there will be your heart also."

19. "The ___*light*___ of the body is the eye."

20. "No man can serve two masters . . . Ye cannot serve God and ___*mammon*___."

21. "Consider the ___*lilies*___ of the field."

22. "Even ___*Solomon*___ in all his glory was not arrayed like one of these."

23. "O ye of ___*little*___ faith."

24. "Sufficient unto the day is the ___*evil*___ thereof."

25. "Judge not, that ye be not ___*judged*___"; i.e., measure for measure.

26. "First cast out the ___*beam*___ [RSV: log] out of thine own eye."

27. "Neither cast ye your pearls before ___*swine*___."

334

QUIZ 31 — Matthew 5:12-7:6

1. "I am not come to _destroy_, but to fulfill." (5:17) (5)

2. "First cast out the beam out of thine own _eye_." (7:5) (26)

3. "Give us this day our daily _bread_." (6:11) (#)

4. Forced to go a mile, one should "go a _second_ mile." (5:41) (11)

5. "_Sufficient_ unto the day is the evil thereof." (6:34) (24)

6. The old law was, "An eye for an eye, and a _tooth_ for a tooth." (5:38) (9)

7. "Solomon in all his _glory_ was not arrayed like one of these." (6:29) (22)

8. "Let not thy left hand _know_ what thy right hand doeth." (6:3) (14)

9. "Love your enemies, bless them that _curse_ you."(5:44) (12)

10. "No man can serve two _masters_ . . . ye cannot serve God and mammon." (6:24) (20)

11. The Lord's Prayer begins, "_Our_ Father." (6:9) (16)

12. "Ye are the salt of the _earth_." (5:13) (1)

13. "Consider the lilies of the _field_." (6:28) (21)

14. "Hallowed be thy name. Thy kingdom _come_."(6:9,10) (#)

15. Jesus forbade swearing oaths: let your _yea_ be yea; your nay, nay. (5:34) (8)

16. "_Judge_ not, that ye be not judged," measure for measure. (7:1) (25)

17. Jesus promised that not "one _jot_ or one tittle" of the law would change. (5:18) (6)

18. "Where your treasure is, there will your _heart_ be also." (6:21) (18)

19. "O ye of little _faith_." (6:30) (23)

20. When struck, one should "turn the other _cheek_."(5:39) (10)

21. "Neither cast ye your _pearls_ before swine." (7:6) (27)

22. "He . . . sendeth rain on the _just_ and on the unjust." (5:45) (13)

23. Salt that has lost its savor is "_good_ for nothing." (5:13) (2)

24. "When thou _prayest_, enter into thy closet." (6:6) (15)

25. "A city that is set on an hill cannot be _hid_."(5:14) (3)

26. "Lead us not into _temptation_." (6:13) (#)

27. "Lay up for yourselves _treasures_ in heaven." (6:20) (17)

STUDY QUESTIONS 32 — Matthew 7:7-8:27; 9:1-17; 10:1-42
(MEMORIZE Apostles' names, 10:2-4)

1. "Seek, and ye shall ___*find*___ ; knock, and it shall be opened."

2. "All things whatsoever ye would that men should do to
   ___*you*___ , do ye even so to them."

3.*The Golden Rule is called the "law and the ___*prophets*___ " of the
   Hebrew scripture.

4. "Strait [tight] is the gate and ___*narrow*___ is the way."

5. "False ___*prophets*___ " are like wolves "in sheep's clothing."

6. "By their ___*fruits*___ ye shall know them."

7. In the parable the wise man built his house upon a ___*rock*___ .

8. "It fell: and ___*great*___ was the fall of it."

9. Jesus healed a ___*leper*___ and made his skin clean.

10. "I have not found so great faith, no, not in ___*Israel*___ ."

11. The third person Jesus healed was Peter's *mother-in-law*.

12. "Let the dead bury their ___*dead*___ ."

13. While on a ___*ship/etc.*___ with his disciples, Jesus calmed the
    storm/sea.

14. "Be of ___*good*___ cheer."

15. "I am not come to call the righteous, but ___*sinners*___ to
    repentance."

16. "Neither do men put new wine into old [leather] ___*bottles*___ ."

17. Two apostles [messengers, Grk.] were named Simon and two
    were named ___*James*___ .

18. Matthew was a ___*publican*___ : he bought the right to collect
    Roman taxes and charge a profit.

19. "Go rather to the lost ___*sheep*___ ."

20. Jesus told his ___*disciples*___ to travel without money or
    possessions.

21. "When ye depart . . . shake off the dust of your ___*feet*___ ."

22. A sparrow "shall not fall on the ___*ground*___ without your
    Father."

23. "I came not to send peace but a ___*sword*___ ."

24. "He that loseth his life for my sake shall ___*find*___ it."

QUIZ 32 — Matthew 7:7 to 10:42

1. "___Seek___, and ye shall find; knock, and it shall
   be opened." (7:7)   (1)

2. "When ye depart . . . shake off the ___dust___ of
   your feet."(10:14)   (21)

3. "By their fruits ye shall ___know___ them." (7:20)   (6)

4. "I have not found so great ___faith___, no, not in
   Israel." (8:10)   (10)

5. The apostles James and ___John___ were sons of
   . Zebedee. (10:2)   (#)

6. "All things whatsoever ye would that men should do to
   you, do ye even so to ___them___." (7:12)   (2)

7. A ___sparrow___ "shall not fall on the ground without
   your Father." (10:29)   (22)

8. "False prophets" are like wolves "in sheep's
   ___clothing___." (7:15)   (5)

9. Jesus healed a leper and made his ___skin___ clean. (8:3)   (9)

10. The third person Jesus healed was ___Peter___'s
    mother-in-law. (8:15)   (11)

11. "Neither do men put new ___wine___ into old bottles."(9:17) (16)

12. Disciples were told to travel without ___money/etc.___
    or possessions. (10:10)   (20)

13. "He that loseth his ___life___ for my sake shall
    find it." (10:39)   (24)

14. "___Strait___ is the gate and narrow is the way." (7:14)   (4)

15. "It fell: and great was the ___fall___ of it." (7:27)   (8)

16. "Let the dead ___bury___ their dead." (8:22)   (12)

17. "I am not come to call the ___righteous___, but sinners
    to repentance." (9:13)   (15)

18. "Go rather to the ___lost___ sheep." (10:6)   (19)

19. "I came not to send ___peace___ but a sword." (10:34)   (23)

20. "Do as you would be done by" is one form of the
    ___Golden___ Rule.   (#,3)

21. In the parable the ___foolish___ man built his house
    upon the sand. (7:26)   (#)

22. While on a ship, Jesus ___calmed/etc.___ the storm. (8:26) (13)

23. Matthew was a publican: he bought the right to
    collect ___taxes___. (10:3)   (18)

24. "Be of good ___cheer___." (9:2)   (14)

STUDY QUESTIONS 33 — Matthew 11:1-15,25-30; 12:22-14:36; 15:10-28

Mark 5:1-24,35-43

1. Jesus said John the Baptist was ___Elijah___ , the messenger of the deliverer/savior.

2. "He that hath ears to hear, let him ___hear___ ."

3. "Come unto me, all ye that labor and are heavy laden, and I will give you ___rest___ ."

4. "Every city or house divided against itself shall not ___stand___ ."

5. "He that is not with me is ___against___ me."

6. "Blasphemy against the Holy Ghost shall not be ___forgiven___ . . . neither in this world, neither in the world to come."

7. Jesus said he would be in the earth for three days, like ___Jonah___ in the whale.

8. In the parable of the sower "some seed fell by the ___wayside___ ."

9. The enemy sowed ___tares___ [weeds] among the wheat.

10. The kingdom of heaven is like a "grain of ___mustard___ seed."

11. Jesus also likened the kingdom of heaven to a "goodly [fine] ___pearl___ . . . of great price."

12. Jesus had four "brothers": James, Joses/Joseph, Simon, and ___Judas___ .

13. "A prophet is not without honor, save in his own ___country___ ."

14. Salome, daughter of Herodias, danced for ___Herod___ 's birthday.

15. As a reward, Salome was served John's ___head___ on a charger (platter).

16. Jesus fed a multitude with only a few loaves and ___fish(es)___ .

17. Jesus met his disciples on the ship by ___walking___ on the water.

18. "If the blind lead the ___blind___ , both shall fall into the ditch."

19. "Dogs eat of the crumbs which fall from their masters' ___table___ ."

20. "My name is Legion [i.e., thousands]: for we are ___many___ ."

21. Jesus drove the ___devils/etc.___ out of the Gadarene [RSV: Gerasene] demoniacs into a herd of swine.

22. "Sitting, and clothed, and in his right ___mind___ ."

23. Jairus' daughter "lieth at the point of ___death___ ."

338

QUIZ 33 — Matthew 11:1 to 15:28. Mark 5:1 to 5:43

1. "Dogs eat of the __crumbs__ which fall from their masters' table." (Mt15:27) (19)

2. "He that is __not__ with me is against me." (Mt12:30) (5)

3. "My name is __Legion__: for we are many." (Mk5:9) (20)

4. Jesus likened the kingdom of heaven to a "grain of mustard __seed__." (Mt13:31) (10)

5. As a reward, Salome was served __John__'s head on a platter. (Mt14:11) (15)

6. "If the blind __lead__ the blind, both shall fall into the ditch." (Mt15:14) (18)

7. Jesus drove the devils out of the possessed Gadarenes into a herd of __swine/pigs__. (Mk5:13) (21)

8. "Every city or house __divided__ against itself shall not stand." (Mt12:25) (4)

9. The __enemy/devil__ sowed tares among the wheat. (Mt13:25) (9)

10. Salome, daughter of Herodias, __danced__ for Herod's birthday. (Mt14:6) (14)

11. "Sitting, and clothed, and in his __right__ mind." (Mk5:15) (22)

12. "Come unto me, all ye that labor and are heavy __laden__, and I will give you rest." (Mt11:28) (3)

13. In the parable of the sower, "some seeds __fell__ by the wayside." (Mt13:4) (8)

14. "A prophet is not without __honor__, save in his own country." (Mt13:57) (13)

15. Jesus went to his disciples on the ship by walking on the __water/sea__. (Mt12:25) (17)

16. Jairus' daughter "lieth at the __point__ of death." (Mk5:23) (23)

17. "He that hath __ears__ to hear, let him hear." (Mt11:15) (2)

18. Jesus said he would be in the earth for __three__ days, like Jonah in the whale. (Mt12:40) (7)

19. Jesus had four "brothers": __James__, Joses, Simon, and Judas. (Mt13:55) (12)

20. Jesus fed the multitude with only a few __loaves__ and fish(es). (Mt14:20) (16)

21. Jesus said John the Baptist was Elijah, the __messenger__ of the deliverer/savior. (Mt11:14) (1)

22. "Blasphemy against the Holy __Ghost/Spirit__ shall not be forgiven . . . neither in this world, neither in the world to come." (Mt12:31,32) (6)

23. "The kingdom of heaven is likened to a "goodly pearl . . . of great __price__." (Mt13:45) (11)

STUDY QUESTIONS 34 — Matthew 16:13-17:13; 18:1-22; 19:1-20:28

1.*Peter confessed his faith that Jesus was the Christ [anointed one, Grk. = Heb.: __messiah__].

2. "Thou art Peter, and upon this __rock__ I will build my church."

3.*In some traditions, __Peter__ founded the Christian church and was the first pope, in Rome.

4. "I will give unto thee the __keys__ of the kingdom of heaven."

5.*Peter is often shown with keys, as gatekeeper of __heaven__ .

6. "Get thee __behind__ me, Satan."

7. "Let him deny himself, and take up his cross, and __follow__ me."

8. "What is a man __profited__ , if he shall gain the whole world, and lose his own soul?"

9. Jesus met Moses and __Elijah__ on a mountain and was trans-figured.

10. "Whoso shall receive one such little child in my name __receiveth__ me."

11. "He rejoiceth more of that sheep, than of the __ninety__ and nine."

12. "Where two or three are gathered together in my name, there am I in the __midst__ of them."

13. Jesus said to forgive a sinner "until __seventy__ times seven" times.

14. "What therefore God hath joined together, let no man put __asunder__ ."

15. "Suffer [permit] little children . . . to come unto me; for of such is the kingdom of __heaven__ ."

16. "It is easier for a camel to go through the eye of a __needle__ than for a rich man to enter into the kingdom of God."

17. "With God all things are __possible__ ."

18. "The first shall be last; and the __last__ shall be first."

19. In the parable the "laborers in the __vineyard__ " each got a penny.

20. The complaining laborers had "borne the burden and heat of the __day__ ."

21. "The Son of man came . . . to give his life a __ransom__ for many."

340

QUIZ 34 — Matthew 16:13 to 19:28

1. "It is easier for a ___camel___ to go through the eye of a needle than for a rich man to enter into the kingdom of God." (19:24) (16)

2. "The Son of man came . . . to give his ___life___ a ransom for many." (20:28) (21)

3. Peter is often shown with keys, as the ___gatekeeper___ of heaven. (16:19) (5)

4. On a mountain, Jesus met ___Moses___ and Elijah and was transfigured. (17:2) (9)

5. Jesus said to ___forgive___ a sinner "until seventy times seven" times. (18:22) (13)

6. "With ___God___ all things are possible." (19:26) (17)

7. "Thou art Peter, and upon this rock I will build my ___church___." (16:18) (2)

8. The laborers in the parable had "borne the burden and ___heat___ of the day." (20:12) (20)

9. "Whoso shall receive one such little ___child___ in my name receiveth me." (18:5) (10)

10. "What therefore ___God___ hath joined together, let not man put asunder." (19:6) (14)

11. "The ___first___ shall be last; and the last shall be first." (19:30) (18)

12. In some traditions, Peter founded the church and was the first ___pope___, in Rome. (3)

13. "Let him deny himself, and take up his ___cross___, and follow me." (16:24) (7)

14. "He rejoiceth more of that ___sheep___, than of the ninety and nine." (18:13) (11)

15. "Suffer little ___children___ . . . to come unto me; for of such is the kingdom of heaven." (19:14) (15)

16. In the parable, the "laborers in the vineyard" each got a ___penny___. (20:10) (19)

17. "I will give unto thee the keys of the ___kingdom___ of heaven." (16:19) (4)

18. "Get thee behind me, ___Satan___." (16:23) (6)

19. "Where two or three are gathered together in my ___name___, there am I in the midst of them." (18:20) (12)

20. "What is a man profited, if he shall gain the whole world, and lose his own ___soul___?" (16:26) (8)

21. Peter confessed his faith: "Thou art the ___Christ___." (16:16) (1)

STUDY QUESTIONS 35 — Matthew 21:1-22; 22:1-22,34-40; 23:23-36;
24:1-8; 25:1-46

1. At Jesus' entry into _Jerusalem_ they strewed palm branches before the ass on which he rode.

2. "_Hosanna_ [save, we pray thee—Heb.] in the highest."

3. Jesus cleansed the _temple_ of money changers and sellers of doves.

4. Jesus said they had made the temple a "den of _thieves_."

5. Jesus cursed the _fig_ tree because it did not welcome him.

6. The invited guests in the parable "made _light_ of it."

7. "There shall be weeping and _gnashing_ of teeth."

8. "Many are called, but few are _chosen_."

9. Concerning the tribute money, Jesus said, "Render therefore unto Caesar the things which are _Caesar's_."

10. "Thou shalt love the Lord thy God with all thy _heart_."

11. "This is the first and great commandment, and the _second_ is like unto it."

12. "Thou shalt love thy neighbor as _thyself_."

13. "Ye blind guides, which strain at a gnat and swallow a _camel_."

14. "Ye are like unto whited _sepulchres_ [RSV: whitewashed tombs]."

15. "There shall not be left here one stone upon _another_."

16. "Ye shall hear of wars and rumors of _wars_."

17. In the parable there were five wise and five foolish _virgins_.

18. "Well done, thou good and faithful _servant_."

19. In the parable the master punished the man who did not use his _talent/money_ for the benefit of the master.

20. "Unto every one that _hath_ shall be given."

21. At the last judgment, the king will separate the _sheep_ from the goats.

22. "I was a _stranger_, and ye took me in."

23. "Inasmuch as ye have done it unto one of the least of my _brethren_, ye have done it unto me."

24. Those who did not accept Jesus will be "cursed into _everlasting_ fire."

QUIZ 35 — Matthew 21:1 to 25:46

1. "Unto every one that hath shall be ___given___ ." (25:29) (20)

2. At his entry into Jerusalem, they strewed palm ___branches___ before the ass on which Jesus rode. (21:8) (1)

3. The invited guests in the parable "___made___ light of it." (22:5) (6)

4. "Ye blind guides, which ___strain___ at a gnat and swallow a camel." (23:24) (13)

5. In the parable the master punished the man who did not ___use/etc.___ his talent for the master's benefit. (25:28) (19)

6. Those who did not accept Jesus will be "cursed into everlasting ___fire___ ." (25:41) (24)

7. Jesus ___cursed___ the fig tree for not welcoming him. (21:19) (5)

8. "This is the first and great ___commandment___ , and the second is like unto it." (22:38,39) (11)

9. In the parable there were five wise and ___five___ foolish virgins. (25:2) (17)

10. "Inasmuch as ye have done it unto one of the ___least___ of these my brethren, ye have done it unto me." (25:40) (23)

11. "Thou shalt love thy ___neighbor___ as thyself." (22:39) (12)

12. Jesus said they had made the temple a "___den___ of thieves." (21:13) (4)

13. Of the tribute money, Jesus said, "___Render___ therefore unto Caesar the things which are Caesar's." (22:21) (9)

14. "Ye shall hear of wars and ___rumors___ of wars." (24:6) (16)

15. "I was a stranger, and ye ___took___ me in." (25:35) (22)

16. Jesus ___cleansed/rid___ the temple of money changers and sellers of doves. (21:12) (3)

17. "Many are ___called___ , but few are chosen." (22:14) (8)

18. "There shall not be left here one ___stone___ upon another." (24:2) (15)

19. At the last judgment the king will separate the sheep from the ___goats___ . (25:32) (21)

20. "Hosanna in the ___highest___ ." (21:9) (2)

21. "There shall be weeping and gnashing of ___teeth___ ." (22:13) (7)

22. "Ye are like unto ___whited___ sepulchres." (23:27) (14)

23. "Well done, thou good and ___faithful___ servant." (25:23) (18)

24. "Thou shalt ___love___ the Lord thy God with all thy heart." (22:37) (10)

STUDY QUESTIONS 36 — Matthew 26:1-28:20

1. Jesus came to Jerusalem with other pilgrims at the _Passover_ holiday.

2. A woman in Bethany anointed Jesus with a precious _ointment_ .

3. Judas agreed to betray Jesus for thirty pieces of _silver_ .

4.*The Last Supper was probably a Passover festive meal called a _seder_ .

5. "Verily [truly] I say unto you that one of you shall _betray_ me."

6. "Take, eat; this is my _body_ ."

7. "This is my _blood_ of the new testament [covenant]."

8. Jesus said that before cockcrow Peter would _deny_ that he knew Jesus.

9. In the Garden of Gethsemane on the Mount of Olives/Olivet, Jesus _prayed_ in agony.

10. "Let this cup _pass_ from me."

11. "The spirit indeed is willing, but the _flesh_ is weak."

12. Judas pointed out Jesus to the soldiers by _kissing_ his cheek.

13. Jesus was first tried before Caiaphas, the high _priest_ .

14. Jesus was then tried before Pontius _Pilate_ , the Roman governor.

15. Judas repented, hanged himself, and was buried in the potter's _field_ .

16. Pilate publicly washed his _hands_ of the blood of Jesus.

17. Pilate released _Barabbas_ instead of Jesus, as a holiday gift.

18. The soldiers scourged/whipped Jesus and mocked him as king, with a royal robe and a crown of _thorns_ .

19. On the way to Golgotha/Calvary Simon of Cyrene carried the _cross_ .

20. _Two_ thieves were crucified with Jesus.

21. Jesus cried out, "My God, my God, why hast thou _forsaken_ me?"

22. The Roman centurion said, "Truly this was the _Son_ of God."

23. Joseph of Arimathea buried _Jesus_ in Joseph's new tomb.

24. At dawn on Sunday, the angel told the two Marys, "He is not here: for he is _risen_ ."

25. After the resurrection, Jesus appeared to the _disciples_ as he had promised.

26. "Go ye therefore, and teach all nations, _baptizing_ them in the name of the Father, and of the Son, and of the Holy Ghost."

QUIZ 36 — Matthew 26:1-28:20

1. Roman soldiers scourged Jesus, then mocked him with
   a royal ___*robe*___ and crown of thorns. (27:26,29)   (18)

2. The Roman centurion said, "Truly this was the Son
   of ___*God*___." (27:54)   (22)

3. "Go ye therefore, and ___*teach*___ all nations, baptizing
   them in the name of the Father, and of the Son, and of
   the Holy Ghost." (28:19)   (26)

4. In the ___*Garden*___ of Gethsemane on the Mount of Olives,
   Jesus prayed in agony. (26:39)   (9)

5. Jesus said that before ___*cockcrow*___ Peter would deny that
   he knew Jesus. (26:34)   (8)

6. At the Last Supper, Jesus said, "Take, ___*eat*___; this
   is my body." (26:26)   (6)

7. Pilate released Barabbas instead of ___*Jesus*___ on the
   holiday. (27:26)   (17)

8. "My God, my God, why hast thou forsaken ___*me*___?" (27:46) (21)

9. After the resurrection, Jesus *appeared/etc.* to the
   disciples. (28:17)   (25)

10. Judas betrayed Jesus for ___*thirty*___ pieces of
    silver. (26:15)   (3)

11. "This is my blood of the new *testament* [covenant]." (26:28) (7)

12. Jesus was first tried before Caiaphas, the ___*high*___
    priest. (26:57)   (13)

13. Pilate publicly ___*washed*___ his hands of Jesus' blood. (27:24)(16)

14. Two thieves were ___*crucified*___ with Jesus. (27:38)   (20)

15. "He is not ___*here*___: for he is risen." (28:6)   (24)

16. "Let this ___*cup*___ pass from me." (26:39)   (10)

17. A ___*woman*___ in Bethany gave Jesus costly ointment. (26:7) (2)

18. Jesus was sentenced by Pontius Pilate, the Roman
    ___*governor*___. (27:2)   (14)

19. "Verily I say unto you, that one of you shall betray
    ___*me*___." (26:21)   (5)

20. Judas pointed out Jesus by kissing his ___*cheek*___. (26:49) (12)

21. ___*Simon*___ of Cyrene helped Jesus carry his cross. (27:32) (19)

22. Judas hanged himself and was buried in the ___*potter's*___
    field. (27:5,7)   (15)

23. ___*Joseph*___ of Arimathea buried Jesus in his own new
    tomb. (27:60)   (23)

24. Jesus came to ___*Jerusalem*___ with other Passover pilgrims. (26:2)(1)

25. "The spirit indeed is ___*willing*___, but the flesh is
    weak." (26:41)   (11)

STUDY QUESTIONS 37 — Luke 1:1-2:52

1. Luke addressed both his gospel and book of Acts to _Theophilus_.

2. Zechariah/Zacharias and his wife, _Elisabeth_, were of priestly descent.

3. The angel, _Gabriel_, told Zechariah he would have a son.

4.*In the Annunciation, Mary learned of _Jesus_' coming.

5. Through Joseph, Mary's husband, Jesus was descended from King _David_.

6.*"Hail, thou that art highly favored [Douay: Hail, full of _grace_], the Lord is with thee."

7. Elisabeth was Mary's _cousin_.

8. "Blessed art thou among women, and blessed is the _fruit_ of thy womb."

9.*The Ave Maria [Hail, Mary—Lat.] combines two greetings addressed to _Mary_.

10. The Magnificat begins, "My _soul_ doth magnify the Lord."

11. Zechariah was cured when his baby was named _John_.

12. The Benedictus begins, "_Blessed_ be the Lord God of Israel."

13. Joseph and Mary left Nazareth to be taxed in the city of _Bethlehem_.

14.*Jesus was a Nazarene: from _Nazareth_ (John was a Nazirite: under a vow).

15.*Both David's birthplace, _Bethlehem_, and his capital, Jerusalem, were called "the City of David."

16. "She . . . wrapped him in _swaddling_ clothes, and laid him in a manger, because there was no room for them in the inn."

17. "I bring you good _tidings_ [AS: gospel] of great joy."

18. "Glory to God in the _highest_ [Lat.: Gloria in excelsis deo] and on earth peace, good will toward men."

19. The Nunc Dimittis [now dismiss, Lat.] begins, "Lord, now _lettest_ thou thy servant depart in peace."

20. "A light to _lighten_ the Gentiles [foreign nations, Lat.]."

21. At Jesus' presentation in the temple, _Simeon_ and Anna recognized the messiah.

22. They found Jesus in the _temple_ with the "doctors" [learned men].

23. "I must be about my Father's _business_."

QUIZ 37 — Luke 1:1-2:52

1. "Blessed art thou among women, and blessed is the
   fruit of thy ___womb___." (1:42)   (8)

2. John the Baptist and Jesus were related: their
   mothers were ___cousins___. (1:36)   (#)

3. "She . . . laid him in a ___manger___, because there
   was no room for them in the inn." (2:7)   (16)

4. Joseph and Mary left the city of ___Nazareth___ to
   register for taxes. (2:4)   (13)

5. Through ___Joseph/etc.___, Jesus was related to King David. (1:27) (5)

6. "A light to lighten the ___Gentiles___." (2:32)   (20)

7. Luke wrote both a gospel and the book of ___Acts___
   to Theophilus. (1:3)   (1)

8. ___Mary___ learned of Jesus in the Annunciation. (1:26,31)   (4)

9. The angel told the ___shepherds___, "I bring you good
   tidings [news] of great joy." (2:10)   (17)

10. The Magnificat begins, "My soul doth magnify the
    ___Lord___." (1:46)   (10)

11. They found Jesus in the temple with the "___doctors___." (2:46) (22)

12. ___Zechariah___ was cured when his baby was named John. (1:64)   (11)

13. At Jesus' presentation in the temple, Simon and
    ___Anna___ knew he was the messiah. (2:34,38)   (21)

14. The Ave Maria combines greetings to Mary by Gabriel
    and ___Elisabeth___. (1:28,42)   (#)

15. The Benedictus begins, "Blessed be the Lord God of
    ___Israel___." (1:68)   (12)

16. "Glory to God in the highest, and on earth ___peace___,
    good will toward men." (2:14)   (18)

17. "Hail . . . the Lord is ___with___ thee." (1:28)   (6)

18. Jesus was a Nazarene; ___John___ was a Nazirite.   (14)

19. The Nunc Dimittis begins, "Lord, ___now___ lettest
    thou thy servant depart in peace." (2:29)   (19)

20. Zechariah was Elisabeth's ___husband___ (1:5)   (2)

21. "I ___must___ be about my Father's business." (2:49)   (23)

22. The ___angel___ Gabriel told Zechariah he would have
    a son. (1:13)   (3)

23. Both Jerusalem and Bethlehem were called "the City
    of ___David___." (2:11)   (15)

STUDY QUESTIONS 38 — Luke 3:15-17; 4:16-32; 5:1-11; 10:1,17-42;
15:8-32; 16:19-31; 18:9-14; 23:1-17,32-34,39-46; 24:13-53

1. John said Jesus would separate the ___wheat___ from the chaff (husks).

2. "Physician, heal ___thyself___."

3. One of Jesus' miracles for Peter was the great draft (catch) of ___fish(es)___.

4. "I beheld ___Satan___ as lightning fall from heaven."

5. When Jesus was asked, "Who is my ___neighbor___?" he told the parable of the good Samaritan.

6. "Go, and do thou ___likewise___."

7. The prodigal (wasteful) son ruined himself with "riotous ___living___."

8. The father welcomed back his son and killed the "fatted ___calf___."

9. The other son protested that he had served obediently for "Lo, these many ___years___."

10. The rich man [Lat.: dives] "fared ___sumptuously___ [feasted] every day."

11. In the parable poor man Lazarus went to "Abraham's ___bosom___."

12. One parable tells of two who prayed: a Pharisee and a ___publican___ (a profit-making tax collector).

13. "God, I thank thee, that I am not as other ___men___ are."

14. The other prayed, "God be ___merciful___ to me a sinner" and was "justified" (i.e., freed of guilt).

15. "Art thou the King of the Jews?" . . . "Thou ___sayest___ it."

16. Jesus was tried three times: before Caiaphas, Pilate, and ___Herod___.

17. "Father, ___forgive___ them; for they know not what they do."

18. Jesus said to the penitent thief, "Today shalt thou be with me in ___paradise___."

19. "Father, into thy hands I ___commend___ [entrust] my spirit."

20. Jesus revealed himself to two disciples at the village of ___Emmaus___ when he broke bread with them.

21. Jesus told his disciples to preach because they were "___witnesses___ of these things."

22. After his resurrection and appearances to his disciples, Jesus ascended into ___heaven___.

QUIZ 38 — Luke 3:15 to 24:53

1. "I beheld Satan as lightning __*fall*__ from heaven."(10:18)(4)

2. The elder son in the parable served obediently for
   "Lo, these __*many*__ years." (15:29)   (9)

3. One prayed, "God be merciful to me a __*sinner*__ ."(18:13) (14)

4. "Father, into thy hands I commend my __*spirit*__ ."(23:46) (19)

5. "Physician, __*heal*__ thyself." (4:23)   (2)

6. The prodigal son ruined himself in "__*riotous*__
   living." (15:13)   (7)

7. One parable tells of two who prayed: a __*Pharisee*__
   and a publican. (18:10)   (12)

8. "Father, forgive them; for they know not what they
   __*do*__ ." (23:34)   (17)

9. After his resurrection, Jesus appeared to his
   __*disciples/etc.*__ and then ascended into heaven. (24:51) (22)

10. One of Jesus' miracles for __*Peter*__ was the great
    draft of fishes. (5:6)   (3)

11. The father welcomed back his son and killed the
    "__*fatted*__ calf." (15:23)   (8)

12. "God, I thank thee, that I am not as __*other*__ men
    are." (18:11)   (13)

13. Jesus said to the penitent __*thief*__ , "Today shalt
    thou be with me in paradise." (23:43)   (18)

14. John said that __*Jesus*__ would separate the wheat
    from the chaff. (3:17)   (1)

15. "__*Go*__ , and do thou likewise." (10:37)   (6)

16. Poor man Lazarus went to "__*Abraham*__ 's bosom." (16:22) (11)

17. Jesus was tried three times: before Caiaphas,
    __*Pilate*__ , and Herod. (23:7)   (16)

18. Jesus told his disciples to preach among all __*nations*__
    because they were "witnesses of these things." (24:48) (21)

19. When asked "Who is my neighbor?" Jesus told the
    parable of the good __*Samaritan*__ . (10:29)   (5)

20. The __*rich*__ man "fared sumptuously every day."(16:19) (10)

21. "Art thou the __*King*__ of the Jews?" . . . "Thou
    sayest it." (23:3)   (15)

22. Jesus revealed himself to two disciples in Emmaus when
    he broke __*bread*__ with them. (24:31)   (20)

STUDY QUESTIONS 39 — John 1:1-29; 2:1-11; 3:1-21; 4:1-46; 5:1-9a;
6:25-40; 8:1-20,31-59; 10:1-18

1.*___John___'s gospel differs from the three synoptics [viewed
or viewing together, Grk.]

2. "In the _beginning_ [Lat.: in principio] was the Word [Grk.:
logos]."

3. "And the Word was made ___flesh___."

4. "He . . . whose shoe latchet [lace] I am not worthy to
___unloose___."

5. "Behold the ___Lamb___ of God [Lat. agnus dei], which taketh
away the sin of the world!"

6. Jesus turned water into ___wine___ at the marriage/wedding at
Cana.

7. "Except a man be born ___again___, he cannot see the kingdom of
God."

8. "The wind ___bloweth___ where it listeth [wishes]."

9. "God so loved the world, that he gave his ___only___ begotten
Son."

10. "That whosoever believeth in him should not perish but have
everlasting life."

11. "God sent . . . his Son . . . that the world through him might
be ___saved___."

12. At the well Jesus told the woman of ___Samaria___ that he was the
messiah.

13. "Rise, take up thy bed, and ___walk___."

14. "I am the bread of ___life___."

15. The self-righteous ones brought him a "woman taken in
___adultery___."

16. "He that is without sin among you, let him first cast a
___stone___."

17. "Go, and ___sin___ no more."

18. "I am the ___light___ of the world."

19. The Jews could not understand Jesus' hint that God was his
___Father___.

20. "Ye shall know the truth, and the truth shall make you
___free___."

21. "I am the ___good___ shepherd . . . [who] giveth his life for
the sheep."

QUIZ 39 — John 1:1 to 10:18

1. "He . . . whose ___*shoe*___ latchet I am not worthy
   to unloose." (1:27)   (4)

2. "Except a man be ___*born*___ again, he cannot see the
   kingdom of God." (3:3)   (7)

3. "That whosoever believeth in him should not perish,
   but have everlasting ___*life*___." (3:16)   (10)

4. "And the ___*Word*___ was made flesh." (1:14)   (3)

5. Jesus turned water into wine at the marriage at
   ___*Cana*___. (2:9)   (6)

6. "God so ___*loved*___ the world, that he gave his only
   begotten Son." (3:16)   (9)

7. "In the beginning was the ___*Word*___." (1:1)   (2)

8. "Rise, take up thy ___*bed*___, and walk." (5:8)   (13)

9. "He that is without ___*sin*___ among you, let him
   first cast a stone." (8:7)   (16)

10. Jesus mystified the Jews by implying that ___*God*___
    was his Father. (8:19)   (19)

11. At the well Jesus told the ___*woman*___ of Samaria
    that he was the messiah. (4:26)   (12)

12. The self-righteous ones brought him a "___*woman*___
    taken in adultery." (8:3)   (15)

13. "I am the light of the ___*world*___." (8:12)   (18)

14. John's gospel differs from the three so-called
    ___*synoptic*___ gospels.   (1)

15. "Behold the Lamb of ___*God*___, which taketh away the
    sin of the world!" (1:29)   (5)

16. "The ___*wind*___ bloweth where it listeth." (3:8)   (8)

17. "Ye shall ___*know*___ the truth, and the truth shall
    make you free." (8:32)   (20)

18. "God sent . . . his Son . . . that the ___*world*___
    through him might be saved." (3:17)   (11)

19. "I am the ___*bread*___ of life." (6:35)   (14)

20. "Go, and sin ___*no*___ more." (8:11)   (17)

21. "I am the good ___*shepherd*___ . . . [who] giveth his life
    for the sheep." (10:11)   (21)

STUDY QUESTIONS 40 — John 11:1-45; 13:1-19; 13:31-14:7; 14:15-24;
15:1-17; 18:33-38; 19:1-5,25-27; 20:1-21:25

1. "I am the resurrection, and the ___*life*___ ."

2. "By this time he stinketh: for he hath been ___*dead*___ four days."

3. In ___*Bethany*___ Jesus raised/revived the dead Lazarus, brother of Mary and Martha.

4. "I then, your Lord and ___*Master*___ , have washed your feet."

5. "A new commandment I give unto you, that ye ___*love*___ one another."

6. "Lord, whither ___*goest*___ thou?" [Lat.: quo vadis]

7. "In my Father's ___*house*___ are many mansions."

8. "I am the way . . . no man cometh unto the Father, but by ___*me*___ ."

9. "If ye ___*love*___ me, keep my commandments."

10. "He shall give you another Comforter [Grk.: paraclete; i.e., the Holy Ghost/Spirit], that he may ___*abide*___ [stay] with you forever."

11. "I am the true vine, and my Father is the ___*husbandman*___ [vine-grower]."

12. "Greater ___*love*___ hath no man than this."

13. Jesus said his followers were not servants but "___*friends*___ ."

14. "My kingdom is not of this ___*world*___ ."

15. Pilate asked, "What is ___*truth*___ ?" and would not stay for an answer.

16. Pilate presented Jesus and jeered, "___*Behold*___ the man!" [Lat.: ecce homo]

17. "There stood by the cross of Jesus his ___*mother*___ ." (Lat.: stabat mater)

18. "Woman, behold thy son! . . . Behold thy ___*mother*___ !"

19. Jesus' cry, "I ___*thirst*___ ," brought only vinegar; then he said, "It is finished."

20. "One of the soldiers with a ___*spear*___ pierced his side."

21. Mary Magdalene "stood without at the sepulchre ___*weeping*___ ."

22. Jesus told her, "___*Touch*___ me not." [Lat.: noli me tangere]

23. ___*Thomas*___ doubted until he felt the wounds in the body.

24. On his third visit Jesus repeated to Peter, "___*Feed*___ my sheep."

352

QUIZ 40 — John 11:1 to 21:25

1. Jesus told Mary Magdalene, "Touch me ___not___."(20:17) (22)

2. Jesus raised the dead Lazarus, ___brother___ of
   Mary and Martha. (11:44)   (3)

3. "I am the ___way___ . . . no man cometh to the
   Father, but by me." (14:6)   (8)

4. Jesus called his followers ___friends___, not servants.(15:15)(13)

5. Jesus said on the cross, "Woman, behold thy ___son___!"
   and then, "Behold thy mother!" (19:26,27)   (18)

6. Thomas doubted until he felt Jesus' _wounds/etc._ (20:27) (23)

7. "I then, your ___Lord___ and Master, have washed your
   feet." (13:14)   (4)

8. "If ye love me, keep my _commandments_." (14:15)   (9)

9. "My kingdom is not of ___this___ world." (18:36)   (14)

10. "He shall give you another _Comforter_, that he may
    abide with you forever." (14:16)   (10)

11. Jesus repeated to Peter, "Feed my ___sheep___." (21:16) (24)

12. "A new _commandment_ I give unto you, that ye love one
    another." (13:34)   (5)

13. Finally, Jesus on the cross said, "I thirst," and
    "It is _finished_." (19:28,30)   (19)

14. ___Pilate___ jestingly asked, "What is truth?" (18:38) (15)

15. "One of the soldiers with a spear pierced his
    ___side___." (19:34)   (20)

16. "I am the _resurrection_, and the life." (11:25)   (1)

17. "Lord, whither goest ___thou___?" (13:36)   (6)

18. "I am the true ___vine___, and my Father is the
    husbandman." (15:1)   (11)

19. Pilate presented Jesus to the crowd and jeered,
    "Behold the ___man___!" (19:5)   (16)

20. ___Mary___ Magdalene "stood without at the sepulchre
    weeping." (20:11)   (21)

21. "He stinketh: for he hath been dead ___four___
    days." (11:39)   (2)

22. "In my Father's house are many _mansions_." (14:2)   (7)

23. "Greater love hath no man than ___this___." (15:13)   (12)

24. "There ___stood___ by the cross of Jesus his mother."(19:25)(17)

STUDY QUESTIONS 41 — Acts 1:1-2:15; 2:29-42; 3:1-11; 4:32-5:11;
5:17-32; 6:1-7:2a; 7:51-8:24; 9:1-31; 10:1-11:3

1. The apostles saw Jesus for __forty__ days after his death.

2. They saw the bodily ascension of __Jesus__ into heaven.

3. The apostles lived and prayed in "an __upper__ room."

4. With his blood money, __Judas__ bought the field called Aceldema.

5. __Matthias__ replaced Judas as apostle and bishop [Grk.: episcopos = overseer].

6. On the __Pentecost__ holiday, "they were all filled with the Holy Ghost, and began to speak with other tongues [languages]."

7. Peter spoke of the line of King David, who was "dead and __buried__."

8. "Silver and gold have I none; but such as I have __give__ I thee."

9. "They had all things in __common__. And . . . distribution was made unto every man according as he had need."

10. __Ananias__ and Sapphira, accused by Peter of lying, both died.

11. An __angel__ [messenger (of God), Grk.] released them from prison.

12. "We ought to obey God rather than __men__."

13. Stephen, the first Christian martyr [witness, Grk.], died by __stoning__.

14. "And __Saul__ was consenting unto his death."

15. Believers received the Holy Ghost/Spirit by the laying on of __hands__.

16. Simon, the ex-sorcerer, offered __money/etc.__ for holy power.

17. "Saul, Saul, why __persecutest__ thou me?"

18. __Saul/Paul__ of Tarsus heard the voice, saw the light, and was stricken blind on the road to Damascus.

19. "He is a chosen __vessel__ [RSV: instrument] unto me."

20. Saul escaped over the wall of __Damascus__ in a basket.

21. "What God hath __cleansed__, that call thou not common [non-kosher/impure]."

22. "God is no __respecter__ of persons."

23. Peter showed that uncircumcized Gentiles (non-Jews) might become __Christians__.

354

QUIZ 41 — Acts 1:1 to 11:3

1. "God is no respecter of __persons__ ." (10:34) (22)

2. The apostles lived and prayed in "an upper
   __room__ ." (1:13) (3)

3. "We ought to __obey__ God rather than men." (5:29) (12)

4. __Peter__ showed that uncircumcized Gentiles might
   become Christians. (10:45) (23)

5. Saul of Tarsus heard the voice, saw the light, and was
   stricken __blind__ on the road to Damascus. (9:8) (18)

6. Peter spoke of the line of King David, who was
   " __dead__ and buried." (2:29) (7)

7. The apostles saw the bodily __ascen/t(sion)__ of Jesus into
   heaven. (1:9) (2)

8. An angel released them from __prison/jail__. (5:19) (11)

9. On the Pentecost, "they were all filled with the Holy
   Ghost, and began to __speak__ with other tongues."(2:4) (6)

10. "__Saul__ , Saul, why persecutest thou me?" (9:4) (17)

11. "What God hath cleansed, that call thou not
    __common__ ." (10:15) (21)

12. The apostles saw Jesus for forty days after his
    __death/etc.__ (1:3) (1)

13. " __Silver__ and gold have I none; but such as I have
    give I thee." (3:6) (8)

14. Stephen, the first Christian __martyr__ , died by
    stoning. (7:58) (13)

15. Saul escaped over the wall of Damascus in a
    __basket__ . (9:25) (20)

16. With his blood __money__ , Judas bought the field
    called Aceldema. (1:19) (4)

17. "They had all things in common. . . distribution was
    made unto every man according as he had __need__ ."(4:32) (9)

18. "And Saul was consenting to his __death__ ." (8:1) (14)

19. "He is a __chosen__ vessel unto me." (9:15) (19)

20. Simony, selling or buying holy things or power, is
    named after the ex-sorcerer, __Simon__ . (8:18) (16)

21. Matthias replaced __Judas__ as apostle and bishop.(1:20,26)(5)

22. Ananias and Sapphira, accused by Peter of __lying__ ,
    both died. (5:5,10) (10)

23. Believers received the Holy Ghost/Spirit by the
    __laying__ on of hands. (8:17) (15)

STUDY QUESTIONS 42 — Acts 11:19-27; 12:1-25; 14:8-15:29;
15:36-41; 17:1-9; 17:16-18:6; 19:1-20

1. "The disciples were called Christians first in __Antioch__."

2. The Passover [Heb.: pesach; Grk.: pascha] is first called __Easter__ at this point.

3. In a daze, __Peter__ was freed from chains and prison.

4.*John Mark is believed to have accompanied Peter to Rome and to have written the __Gospel__ of Mark.

5. Saul is called __Paul__ [short, Lat.] when he becomes a missionary.

6. The Lycaonians thought that Barnabas and Paul were Greek __gods__.

7. They ordained/appointed "__elders__" [Grk.: presbyter] to rule the churches they founded.

8. Some Christians wanted all __Gentile/etc.__ converts to become pious Jews first.

9. "Through the grace of the Lord Jesus Christ we shall be __saved__."

10. James, the leader, quoted Amos, after Barnabas and Paul "held their __peace__."

11. Citing the example of Simeon/Simon Peter, the council at __Jerusalem__ accepted uncircumcised Gentiles who abstained from idolatry, adultery, and nonkosher meat.

12. "Certain lewd [vulgar] fellows of the __baser__ sort."

13. The missionaries were accused of having "turned the world upside __down__."

14. Paul told the Athenians their "Unknown __God__" was the Lord God.

15. "In him we live, and move, and have our __being__."

16. "He hath appointed a __day__ in which he will judge the world." [doomsday, AS]

17. "Your blood be upon your own __heads__."

18. Having received the Holy Ghost/Spirit, "they spake with tongues [ecstatic utterances, "glossolalia"] and __prophesied__."

19. Many converts "brought their books [of magic] together and __burned__ them."

QUIZ 42 — Acts 11:19 to 19:20

1. _Saul_ is called Paul as a missionary. (14:9) (5)

2. "Through the _grace_ of the Lord Jesus Christ we shall be saved." (15:11) (9)

3. The missionaries were accused of having " _turned_ the world upside down." (17:6) (13)

4. "Your _blood_ be upon your own heads." (18:6) (17)

5. The holiday of _Passover_ is first called Easter in this passage. (12:4) (2)

6. The Lycaonians thought that Barnabas and _Paul_ were Greek gods. (14:11) (6)

7. After Barnabas and Paul " _held_ their peace," James quoted Amos. (15:13) (10)

8. Paul told the Athenians that their " _Unknown_ God" was the Lord God. (17:24) (14)

9. Having received the Holy Ghost/Spirit, "they spake with _tongues_ , and prophesied." (19:6) (18)

10. In a daze, Peter was freed from _chains_ and from prison. (12:7) (3)

11. They ordained "elders" to rule the _churches/etc._ they founded. (14:23) (7)

12. The council at Jerusalem accepted uncircumcised _Gentiles_ who abstained from idolatry, adultery, and nonkosher meat. (15:29) (11)

13. "In him we live, and _move_ , and have our being."(17:28)(15)

14. Many converts "brought their _books_ together and burned them." (19:19) (19)

15. John Mark is believed to have accompanied Peter to _Rome_ and to have written the Gospel of Mark.(12:25) (4)

16. Some Christians wanted all Gentile converts to become pious _Jews_ first. (15:1) (8)

17. "Certain lewd _fellows_ of the baser sort." (17:5) (12)

18. "He hath appointed a day in which he will _judge_ the world." (17:31) (16)

19. "The disciples were called _Christians_ first in Antioch." (11:26) (1)

STUDY QUESTIONS 43 — Acts 21:17-22:1; 22:22-23:24; 24:22-26:1; 26:24-28:30

1. After his missionary trip, Paul reported to the elders in Jerusalem and then _purified_ himself.

2. _Four_ of the men with him got haircuts on completion of their Nazirite vows.

3. Paul was a "Jew of Tarsus . . . a citizen of no _mean_ [small] city."

4. The chief captain freed Paul, who was a _Roman_ citizen.

5. Paul, who was a _Pharisee_ , caused dissension between them and the Sadducees.

6. Festus, the governor, kept Paul in protective custody in the city of _Caesarea_ .

7. As a Roman citizen, Paul demanded a _Roman_ , not a Jewish, trial, saying, "I appeal unto Caesar."

8. "Paul, thou art _beside_ thyself; much learning doth make thee mad."

9. Herod Agrippa said, "Almost thou _persuadest_ me to be a Christian."

10. "We sailed . . . unto a place called the Fair _Havens_ ."

11. Paul predicted trouble for the voyage, but the _centurion_ did not believe him.

12. The tempest drove the _ship/etc._ away from Crete and scared the sailors.

13. When his prediction came true, _Paul_ took charge.

14. The barbarians on Melita/Malta _helped/etc._ the stranded men.

15. Paul performed many miracles on the island of _Malta/Melita_.

16. Christians from Rome met Paul at the Three _Taverns_ .

17. Paul taught "with all confidence, no man _forbidding_ him."

18. *According to tradition, _Paul_ wrote some epistles (letters) while under house arrest, made other journeys, and was arrested again.

QUIZ 43 — Acts 21:17 to 28:30

1. Christians from Rome met Paul at the __Three__ Taverns. (28:15)   (16)

2. Four of the men with Paul got __haircuts__ on completion of their Nazirite vows. (21:24)   (2)

3. Herod Agrippa said to Paul, "Almost thou persuadest me to be a __Christian__." (26:28)   (9)

4. The tempest drove the ship away from Crete and scared the __sailors/etc.__. (27:30)   (12)

5. Paul taught in Rome "with all __confidence__, no man forbidding him." (28:31)   (17)

6. Paul was a "Jew of Tarsus . . . a citizen of no mean __city__." (21:39)   (3)

7. Tradition says Paul wrote some __epistles/etc.__ while under Roman house arrest.   (18)

8. "We sailed . . . unto a place called the __Fair__ Havens." (27:7,8)   (10)

9. The barbarians on __Malta/Melita__ gave much help to the stranded men. (28:2)   (14)

10. After his trip as a __missionary__, Paul reported to the elders in Jerusalem and then purified himself. (21:24)   (1)

11. Paul, a Pharisee, caused dissension between them and the __Sadducees__. (23:7)   (5)

12. "Paul, thou art beside thyself; much __learning__ doth make thee mad." (26:24)   (8)

13. When his prediction about the storm came true, __Paul__ took charge of the ship. (27:31,32)   (13)

14. Paul performed many __miracles/etc.__ while on the island of Malta. (28:9)   (15)

15. The chief captain freed Paul, who was a Roman __citizen__. (22:29)   (4)

16. As a Roman citizen, Paul said, "I __appeal__ unto Caesar." (25:11)   (7)

17. Paul predicted __trouble/etc.__ for the voyage, but the centurion did not believe him. (27:10,11) (11)

18. Festus, the __governor__, kept Paul in protective custody in Caesarea. (24:23)   (6)

STUDY QUESTIONS 44 — Romans 1:1-7; 2:12-16,27-29; 3:19-31; 5:1-11; 6:20-23; 13:1-14. 1 Corinthians 5:1-5; 6:19-7:9; 9:19-23; 11:1-34

1. *The New _Testament_ contains history (Gospels, Acts), letters, (Epistles), and an apocalypse (Revelation).

2. The _Epistle_ to the Romans, a church he had not yet visited, comes first and is the longest Pauline letter (i.e., by Paul).

3. "Gentiles, which have not the law . . . are a law unto _themselves_ ."

4. Paul demanded circumcision "in the spirit, and not in the _letter_ " of the law.

5. "All have sinned . . . being _justified_ [acquitted] freely by his grace."

6. "Do we then make void the law through faith? God _forbid_ ."

7. "We glory in _tribulations_" which "worketh patience [endurance]."

8. "The wages of _sin_ is death."

9. "The _powers_ that be are ordained of God."

10. "Now it is _high_ time to awake out of sleep."

11. "Absent in body, but present in _spirit_ ."

12. "Your _body_ is the temple of the Holy Ghost which is in you."

13. "It is good for a man not to touch a _woman_ ."

14. "It is better to marry than to _burn_ ."

15. "I am made all things to all _men_ ."

16. "The head of the woman is the _man_ ."

17. "If a man have long hair, it is a _shame_ unto him."

18. "If a woman have long hair, it is a _glory_ to her."

19. At the Lord's _Supper_ they ate bread and drank wine to "show the Lord's death till he come."

360

QUIZ 44 — Romans, 1 Corinthians to 11:34

1. "Gentiles, which have not the law . . . are a ___law___ unto themselves." (R2:14) (3)

2. "Do we then make void the law through faith? ___God___ forbid." (R3:31) (6)

3. "Absent in body, but ___present___ in spirit." (C5:3) (11)

4. "I am made ___all___ things to all men." (C9:22) (15)

5. At the ___Lord's___ Supper they ate bread and drank wine "to show the Lord's death till he come." (C11:26) (19)

6. Paul demanded circumcision "in the ___spirit___, and not in the letter" of the law. (R2:29) (4)

7. "We glory in tribulation" which "worketh ___patience___." (R5:3) (7)

8. "Your body is the ___temple___ of the Holy Ghost which is in you." (C6:19) (12)

9. "The ___head___ of the woman is the man." (C11:3) (16)

10. "The ___wages___ of sin is death." (R6:23) (8)

11. "The powers that ___be___ are ordained of God." (R13:1) (9)

12. "It is good for a man not to ___touch___ a woman." (C7:1) (13)

13. "If a man have ___long___ hair, it is a shame unto him." (C11:14) (17)

14. The New Testament contains history, ___letters/epistles___, and an apocalypse. (1)

15. "All have sinned . . . being justified freely by his ___grace___." (R3:23,24) (5)

16. "Now it is high ___time___ to awake out of sleep." (R13:11) (10)

17. "It is better to ___marry___ than to burn." (C7:9) (14)

18. "If a woman have long ___hair___, it is a glory to her." (C11:15) (18)

19. The Epistle to the Romans was written by ___Paul___. (R1:17) (2)

STUDY QUESTIONS 45 — 1 Corinthians 13:1-13; 15:47-58.
Galatians 5:1-6:10. 1 Timothy 1:1,2; 3:1-7; 6:1-10
(MEMORIZE hymn to love, 1 Corinthians 13:1-13)

1.*"Charity" [Lat.: __caritas__] in this passages is the translation of "agape" [divine or selfless love, Grk.].

2. "Though I speak with the __tongues__ of men and of angels, and
have not charity [RSV: love], I am become as sounding brass
or a tinkling cymbal."

3. "Though I have all faith, so that I could __remove__ mountains . . . and have not charity, I am nothing."

4. "Charity . . . believeth all things, __hopeth__ all things."

5. "When I was a child, I __spake__ as a child, I understood as
a child, I thought as a child."

6. "Now we see through a __glass__ [RSV: in a mirror], darkly,
but then face to face."

7. "And now abideth faith, __hope__, and charity, these three;
but the greatest of these is charity."

8. "The first man is of the earth, __earthy__." [the "old Adam"
in people]

9. "Flesh and __blood__ cannot inherit the kingdom of God."

10. "In the __twinkling__ of an eye, at the last trump [trumpet]."

11. "0 death, where is thy sting? 0 grave, where is thy
__victory__?"

12. "Ye are fallen from __grace__."

13. In Galatians, Paul contrasts the flesh and the __Spirit__.

14. "Be not deceived; God is not __mocked__."

15. "Whatsoever a man soweth, that shall he also __reap__."

16.*The __epistles__ to Timothy are Pauline and "pastoral" [on a
pastor's duties].

17. A bishop should not be "greedy of filthy __lucre__ [money]."

18. "We brought nothing into this world, and it is certain we can
carry __nothing__ out."

19. "The love of money is the root of all __evil__."

QUIZ 45 — 1 Corinthians from 13:1, Galatians, 1 Timothy

1. "Though I have all faith, so that I could remove
   mountains . . . and have not charity, I am
   nothing." (C13:2)   (3)

2. "And now abideth _faith_, hope, and charity,
   these three; but the greatest of these is
   charity." (C13:13)   (7)

3. "O death, where is thy _sting_? O grave, where
   is thy victory?" (C15:55)   (11)

4. "Whatsoever a man _soweth_, that shall he also
   reap." (G6:7)   (15)

5. "The _love_ of money is the root of all evil."(T6:10) (19)

6. "When I became a man, I put away _childish_
   things." (C13:11)   (#)

7. "The _first_ man is of the earth, earthy." (C15:47) (8)

8. "Ye are _fallen_ from grace." (G5:4)   (12)

9. Paul's epistles to _Timothy_ deal with pastoral
   duties.   (16)

10. "Now we know in _part_, and we prophesy in
    part." (C13:9)   (#)

11. "_Flesh_ and blood cannot inherit the kingdom
    of God." (C15:50)   (9)

12. In Galatians, Paul contrasts the _flesh_ and
    the Spirit. (G5:16)   (13)

13. Paul tells Timothy that a bishop should not be
    "greedy of _filthy_ lucre." (T3:3)   (17)

14. "Charity" in this passage means selfless _love_.   (1)

15. "Now we see through a glass, _darkly_, but then
    face to face." (C13:12)   (6)

16. "In the twinkling of an _eye_, at the last
    trump." (C15:52)   (10)

17. "Be not _deceived_; God is not mocked." (G6:7)   (14)

18. "We brought nothing into this _world_, and it
    is certain we can carry nothing out." (T6:7)   (18)

19. "Though I speak with the tongues of men and _angels_,
    and have not charity, I am become as sounding brass or
    a tinkling cymbal." (C13:1)   (2)

STUDY QUESTIONS 46 — Hebrews 11:1-40. James 1:1,12-25; 2:14-26;
5:7-11. 1 Peter 2:18-3:8; 4:7-11. 1 John 2:18-25; 4:7-21

1.*Neither the author nor the recipient of the (Pauline?) Epistle
to the ___Hebrews___ (Jewish Christians) is recorded in the
epistle.

2. A child was born to the aged Abraham, "and him as ___good___
as dead."

3. "They were strangers and ___pilgrims___ on the earth."

4. "He hath prepared for them a ___city___."

5. By faith Abraham "offered up his only ___begotten___ son," whom
God raised up "from the dead . . . in a figure [RSV: figuratively speaking]."

6. "By ___faith___" the Old Testament people acted, but they only
saw what was promised and did not receive it.

7.*The ___epistle___ of/by James is "catholic" (of general interest)
and "encyclical" (circulated among churches).

8. "Let every man be swift to hear, slow to speak, and slow to
___wrath___."

9. "Be ye doers of the word and not ___hearers___ only."

10. "By works a man is justified, and not by ___faith___ only."

11. "Faith without works is ___dead___."

12. "Ye have heard of the patience [suffering/endurance] of
___Job___."

13. "Husbands . . . giving honor unto the wife, as unto the
weaker ___vessel___ [RSV: weaker sex]."

14. "Be ye all of one ___mind___."

15. "Charity shall cover a multitude of ___sins___."

16. "Ye have heard that antichrist shall ___come___."

17. "He that loveth not, knoweth not God; for God is ___love___."

18. "There is no fear in love; but perfect love casteth out
___fear___."

19. "He that loveth not his brother whom he hath seen, how can he
love ___God___ whom he hath not seen?"

QUIZ 46 — Hebrews, James, 1 Peter, 1 John

1. "_Faith_ without works is dead." (Ja2:26)   (11)

2. "Husbands . . . giving honor unto the wife, as unto the _weaker_ vessel." (P3:7)   (13)

3. "Ye have heard that _antichrist_ shall come." (Jo2:18)   (16)

4. "He that loveth not his _brother_ whom he hath seen, how can he love God whom he hath not seen?" (Jo4:20)   (19)

5. "They were strangers and pilgrims on the _earth_." (H11:13)   (3)

6. The Epistle of James is "_catholic_" and "encyclical."   (7)

7. "Be ye _doers_ of the word, and not hearers only." (Ja1:22)   (9)

8. "Ye have heard of the _patience_ of Job." (Ja5:11)   (12)

9. "_Charity_ shall cover a multitude of sins." (P4:8)   (15)

10. "There is no fear in love; but perfect _love_ casteth out fear." (Jo4:18)   (18)

11. A child was born to the aged Abraham, "and him as good as _dead_." (H11:12)   (2)

12. The Old Testament people acted "by faith," but only _saw_ what was promised and did not receive it. (H11:39)   (6)

13. "Let every man be swift to hear, _slow_ to speak, and slow to wrath." (Ja1:19)   (8)

14. "By _works_ a man is justified, and not by faith only." (Ja2:24)   (10)

15. "Be ye all of _one_ mind." (P3:8)   (14)

16. "He that loveth not, knoweth not God; for _God_ is love." (Jo4:8)   (17)

17. The Epistle to the _Hebrews_ went to unidentified Christians who were Jewish.   (1)

18. "He hath _prepared_ for them a city." (H11:16)   (4)

19. By faith Abraham "offered up his only begotten _son_," whom God raised up "from the dead . . . in a figure." (H11:17,19)   (5)

365

STUDY QUESTIONS 47 -- Revelation 1:1-20; 4:1-6:8; 7:1-4,9-17;
12:1-17; 17:1-18; 20:1-22:21

1.*The _Revelation_ (Douay: Apocalypse) of John the Divine uses
   fantastic images to show the triumph of God at the end of
   time.

2. "I am the Alpha and the ___Omega___ [first and last Greek let-
   ters], the beginning and the ending."

3.*The four beasts—like a lion, a calf, a man, and an ___eagle___
   —are now the symbols of the four evangelists.

4. "Holy, holy, holy, Lord, God _Almighty_ , which was, and is,
   and is to come." [also a tersanctus]

5. Only the Lamb of God could ___open___ the book.

6. "Ten thousand times ten _thousand_ " were allowed around the
   throne of God.

7. The fourth horseman of the apocalypse was Death, on a pale
   ___horse___ .

8. The marked servants of God numbered _144,000_ .

9. "A great multitude" in "white robes" stood at the _throne/etc._
   of the Lamb.

10. They "washed their robes . . . white in the ___blood___ of the
    Lamb."

11. The archangel Michael and his angels cast out the dragon,
    "that old serpent called the Devil, and ___Satan___ " from
    heaven to the earth.

12. The scarlet woman was "_Babylon_ the Great, the Mother of
    Harlots."

13. The beast will ascend from the "_bottomless_ pit."

14. Satan was to be bound for a _thousand_ years (a millenium).

15. The final war on earth will be against Gog and ___Magog___ .

16. "I John saw the holy city, new _Jerusalem_ ."

17. At the last judgment the evil ones will be sent to the
    "___lake___ which burneth with fire and brimstone [sulfur]."

18. The great new city will be "the ___bride___ , the Lamb's wife."

19. "The twelve gates were twelve ___pearls___ . . . and the street
    of the city was pure gold."

20. The river, "clear as ___crystal___ ," had a "tree of life" on
    either side.

366

1. The fourth horseman of the apocalypse was Death,
   on a ___pale___ horse. (6:8)   (7)

2. Michael and his angels cast out the dragon, "that
   old ___serpent___ called the Devil, and Satan." (12:9)   (11)

3. The final ___war/etc.___ on earth will be against Gog
   and Magog. (20:8)   (15)

4. "The twelve gates were twelve pearls . . . and the
   street of the city was pure ___gold___." (21:21)   (19)

5. "Holy, holy, holy, ___Lord___ God Almighty, which
   was, and is, and is to come." (4:8)   (4)

6. The marked servants of ___God___ numbered 144,000. (7:4)   (8)

7. The scarlet woman was "Babylon the Great, Mother
   of ___Harlots___." (17:5)   (12)

8. "I John saw the holy city, ___new___ Jerusalem."(21:2)   (16)

9. The river, "clear as crystal," had a "tree of
   ___life___" beside it. (22:1,2)   (20)

10. Only the ___Lamb___ of God could open the book. (5:7)   (5)

11. "A great multitude" in "___white___ robes" stood
    at the throne. (7:9)   (9)

12. The four beasts were like a lion, a calf, a
    ___man___, and an eagle. (4:7)   (3)

13. At the last judgment the evil ones will go to "the
    lake which burneth with ___fire___ and brimstone."(21:8)   (17)

14. Revelation, by John the Divine, is also called
    ___Apocalypse___.   (1)

15. "Ten thousand ___times___ ten thousand" were around
    the throne of God. (5:11)   (6)

16. They "washed their robes . . . white in the blood
    of the ___Lamb___." (7:14)   (10)

17. ___Satan___ is to be bound for a thousand years. (20:2)   (14)

18. The great new city is called "the bride, the Lamb's
    ___wife___." (21:9)   (18)

19. "I am the ___Alpha___ and the Omega, the beginning
    and the ending." (1:8)   (2)

20. The beast will ascend from "the bottomless
    ___pit___." (17:8)   (13)

PART V
GLOSSARY

The purpose of this list is to provide a relatively simple reference of biblical, scholarly, and religious terms that a teacher may meet in teaching the Bible in a literature course.

The biblical items (e.g., *angel, messiah, temple*) explain what the terms meant in biblical times and/or what they mean today. Definitions of scholarly terms (e.g., *canon, hermeneutics, redaction criticism*) help the teacher who might be consulting reference books or introductions to biblical studies. Religious terms (e.g., *creed, infallibility, transubstantiation*) give some insight into the wide variety of assumptions about the Bible that students (and teachers themselves) bring to class.

We have selected terms from the humanities—mainly allusions and images found in literature but also some from art and music. We have drawn terms from religious beliefs, practices, and liturgies—mainly of Western Christianity (especially Catholicism and Protestantism) and Judaism but also from Eastern Orthodoxy and a few from Islam. Further, the emphasis is American: We speak of Episcopalians, not Anglicans; we take little note of religious movements that are oriental or are exclusively European. Finally, the terms and definitions represent the approaches to the Bible and religion of both critical scholarship and conservative tradition.

The process of selection often frustrates the most earnest efforts to avoid oversimplification and to be objective and evenhanded. The Bibliography at the end of the Glossary will help those for whom the list of terms or the definitions and explanations are inadequate.

In the interest of simplicity and of avoiding much (though not all) controversy, we have made some arbitrary decisions. People who have been canonized are not identified as saints: it is Matthew, not Saint Matthew. Jesus is referred to as Christ only when the title is identified as a synonym. Some readers will want to make mental changes in this language as they read.

In most cases, Hebrew words are transliterated as Sephardic, the Ashkenazic being added as an alternative for words that are most often apt to be heard in that pronunciation or seen in that spelling. Similarly, when a Latin term is often pronounced in its Italian (or Catholic or church) version, we have added that pronunciation.

In order to avoid diacritical marks, pronunciation guides follow neither the international phonetic alphabet nor Webster's system. The result is only partially successful. An exception is the symbol ḥ, which represents a guttural sound, as in Scottish *"loch"* or German *"ach."*

As elsewhere in this handbook, the words *sect, church, religion, denomination,* and *faith* are synonymous and neutral, applying equally to mainstream and divergent religious groups.

Definitions are more often descriptive than prescriptive, especially where a term is used in many different ways. Some definitions overlap or even contradict others. Some of them are given in a strict scholarly sense and some loosely. Generally, we have omitted definitions that are not relevant to the field of religion or, more specifically, to the Bible.

Many words used in the definitions and explanations are themselves listed in the Glossary. We have cross-referred such words (using SMALL CAPITALS), where the additional information seems necessary to understand the explanation.

References to handbook material that is not in the Glossary direct the reader to Part II of this handbook, entitled "Religious Sensibilities." If a biblical citation is accompanied by an asterisk (*), the text is quoted in Part II, chapter 7. A double asterisk (**) indicates that a related article appears in Part II, chapter 6.

Abbreviations

Aram	Aramaic
AS	Anglo-Saxon
B.C.E.	before the Christian/common era
C.E.	Christian/common era
c.	century
cf.	compare
EO	Eastern Orthodox (adjective; also plural noun); Eastern Orthodoxy
Ger	German
Grk	Greek
Heb	Hebrew
It	Italian
Lat	Latin
ME	Middle English
MSS	manuscripts
OE	Old English
ON	Old Norse
p.	page
RC	Roman Catholic (adjective; also singular noun)
RCs	Roman Catholics
/	separates synonyms and/or alternatives

ABSOLUTION [Lat: setting free] Remission of the guilt and penalty for a sin, by a priest following confession, in the RC or EO sacrament of PENANCE/reconciliation/confession (Matt. 16:19*).

ACCURACY INERRANCY.

ADONAI [Heb: my lords] (ahd-o-NIGH) A Hebrew word that is read orally by Jews as a substitute for the written TETRAGRAMMATON (YHWH/JHVH), which their tradition considers sacrilegious to pronounce. It is translated "the Lord" in most Bibles, "Jehovah" in a few.

ADORATION OF THE MAGI *In art,* a representation of the three wise men from the East, worshiping or offering their gifts to Mary and the infant Jesus. The scene may include other people and animals. Tradition has made the MAGI represent all ages: one young, one middle-aged, one old. They have also become kings, representing the parts of the whole world: Asia (Caspar/Gaspar), Europe (Melchoir), and Africa (Balthazar, depicted as black). Thus Jesus is presented to all people and the whole world, and the occasion is an EPIPHANY. Journey of the Magi: a representation of the kings, usually on camels, in a rich caravan, following a star.

ADORATION OF THE SHEPHERDS *In art,* a representation of Mary and the baby in the barn; worshiping shepherds in rough clothes, with staffs and/or a lamb; and, usually, an ox and ass (Luke 2:16). These last represent the humblest animals (Isa. 1:3); also, the ox was a sacrificial animal, and the ass foreshadows the entry into Jerusalem.

ADVENT [Lat: coming] (1) The season before Christmas: for Western churches, beginning with either the fourth Sunday before Christmas or the Sunday nearest November 30; for EO, a forty-day period of fasting/austerity, from November 15 to December 24. (2) SECOND COMING. (3) INCARNATION.

ADVENTISM A strong belief in the imminent SECOND COMING of the physical Jesus.

AFFUSION [Lat: pouring] INFUSION.

AGAPE [Grk: love] (AH-ga-pay, a-GAH-pay) (1) Selfless, spiritual love (vs. *eros,* physical love). (2) Love feast, or fellowship meal, of the early Christians, held in conjunction with the EUCHARIST; since revived by some sects without the Eucharist (John 13:4*).

AGONY IN THE GARDEN *In art,* a representation of Jesus praying in the garden of Gethsemane on the Mount of Olives, usually with Peter, John, and James sleeping nearby and soldiers, led by Judas, approaching in the distance (Matt. 26:39). Sometimes a supportive angel is added (Luke 22:43).

AGNUS DEI [Lat: lamb of God] (Lat: AHG-noos DAY-ee; It: AHN-yoos DAY-ee) A prayer in some Christian liturgies; the last part of the ordinary of the RC MASS.

   In art, a representation of a lamb, usually carrying a cross or a banner with a cross on it (symbolizing victory over death), sometimes with a halo (John 1:29*).

ALLELUIA HALLELUJAH.

AMORAIM [Heb: speakers, interpreters] (ahm-o-RAH-yim) Commentators on the MISHNAH (third to sixth c. C.E.), whose work became the GEMARA.

ANABAPTISM [Grk: rebaptism] (AN-a-BAP-tizm) Belief in adult baptism: originally (fifteenth c. Germany), rebaptism of those already baptized as infants. Anabaptists were forerunners of, among others, Mennonites, who carry on their pacifism, and Baptists, who share their emphasis on church-state separation, in addition to doctrines about baptism.

ANATHEMA [Grk: set aside (for God to deal with); similar to Heb. *herem,* devoted, accursed] (a-NATH-e-ma; HAY-rem) It usually involves condemning to hell; rarely employed today. It is stronger than EXCOMMUNICATION.

ANCIENT NEAR EAST Southwest Asia plus Egypt; i.e., most of what is now called the Middle East, which is usually extended beyond the Ancient Near East to include Pakistan in the east and Libya in the west. Until recently, the modern term *Near East* meant the Balkan peninsula; today it is vague and usually means countries bordering on the eastern Mediterranean, sometimes including the Arabian peninsula and northeastern Africa. Thus, today's Near East overlaps what most people call the Middle East.

ANGELS [Grk: messengers] Superhuman beings: (1) God's messengers. (2) Guardian spirits. (3) Fallen angels/demons. (4) The lowest order in the CELESTIAL HIERARCHY. (5) The entire hierarchy.

In art, they usually have young and beautiful human faces and bodies, with wings and often with harps or trumpets for praising God or announcing his messages (Eph. 1:21*).

ANGELIC HYMN/SONG GLORIA IN EXCELSIS.

ANGELUS (AN-jel-us) (1) A thrice daily RC prayer said/sung in memory of the angelic annunciation to Mary of the incarnation (Luke 1:21*). (2) The bell announcing the time for this prayer.

ANNUNCIATION (1) The announcement by Gabriel to Mary of the coming birth of Jesus. (2) The church festival commemorating this event, also called Lady Day (Luke 1:31*).

In art, a representation of Mary, usually interrupted while kneeling in prayer, in a white gown (for purity) and a royal blue robe (queen of heaven); Gabriel, holding a messenger's wand and sometimes a lily of purity; and a dove (the Holy Spirit/Ghost) descending on golden rays from heaven.

ANNUNCIATION TO THE SHEPHERDS *In art,* a representation of shepherds, with staffs and sheep, and angels in the sky (Luke 2:13*).

ANTEDILUVIAN (AN-ti-di-LOO-vi-an) Before the flood.

ANOINTING [Lat: smearing with oil or unguent] (1) An RC sacrament for the sick; EO, unction. (2) A ceremony of consecration, accompanying baptism, confirmation, ordination, coronation, and/or preparing for death (Matt. 6:13*). Some sects believe in spiritual anointing: by the Holy Spirit or by prayer for healing the spirit.

ANTHEM [Grk: antiphon, uttered responsively] (1) Choral music with words usually from the Bible. (2) A religious song or HYMN sung responsively; also called an antiphon. Cf. CANTICLE, CAROL.

ANTICHRIST [Grk: opponent of Christ] Usually identified biblically as Satan and the Beast of Revelation and historically as any powerful and vicious opponent of Christianity (I John 2:18*).

ANTINOMIANISM [Grk: opposition to law] (AN-ti-NO-mi-an-izm) Complete reliance on faith and grace for salvation, freeing one from observing moral law, whether Mosaic, "natural," or human.

APOCALYPSE [Grk: uncovering, revelation] (a-POK-a-lips) (1) A piece of APOCALYPTIC LITERATURE. (2) The Douay Bible's title for the last book of the NT.

APOCALYPTIC LITERATURE Writings that reveal the secrets of the END TIME and the new age beyond it. The visions of Daniel, in the OT, and of John, in the NT book of Revelation/Apocalypse, are examples. The apocalyptic movement was very strong in both Judaism and Christianity into the second c. C.E. and has its representatives today. See ESCHATOLOGY.

APOCRYPHA [Grk: hidden, spurious] (a-POK-ri-fa) Extracanonical writings.**

APOLOGETICS [Grk: speak in defense] A branch of theology that is occupied with the rational refutation of attacks on its faith. Apologist: a student or writer of apologetics.

APOSTASY [Grk: standing away, deserting] (A-POSS-ta-sy) (1) Leaving one's faith/religion. (2) Embracing a HERESY while claiming to retain one's religion. (3) Departure from monastic or clerical vows.

APOSTLE [Grk: messenger, envoy] (1) One of the twelve disciples (Matt. 5:1*). (2) These plus Paul and some other early missionaries. (3) Church leaders claiming apostolic succession (e.g., Mormons; Matt. 10:2*). Apostle to the Gentiles: Paul.

APOSTLES' CREED [Lat: belief] The revised version of the oldest (fourth c.) Christian CREED, attributed by tradition to the apostles.

APOSTOLIC SUCCESSION The RC and EO belief that bishops derive their powers (to ordain, administer sacraments, etc.) by direct descent from the apostles, transmitted through ordination (Matt. 16:19*). Some Protestant sects consider themselves apostolic because they preach the Word of God as the apostles transmitted it from Jesus and the Holy Spirit (Matt. 10:2*).

ARCHANGELS [Grk: chief angels] An order in the CELESTIAL HIERARCHY. Gabriel and Michael appear in the book of Daniel and in the NT; Raphael, in Tobit (apocrypha); and Uriel and several others, in Enoch (pseudepigrapha). EO recognizes only Michael and Gabriel. Islam considers Gabriel, Michael, Azrael, and Israfel/Uriel to be archangels. Jewish rabbinic tradition has its own lists.

ARIANISM (AIR-i-an-ism) The belief, proposed by Arius (ca. 256–336 C.E.), that the divine Jesus is not coeternal with, but created by, God the Father. Still held by some sects today, it was opposed by ATHANASIUS and condemned at the Council of Nicea (325 C.E.).

ARMAGEDDON [Heb: *har megiddo:* Mt. Megiddo] (ar-ma-GEDD-on; hahr-meh-GIDD-o) The scene and name of the coming battle between the powers of good and evil at the END TIME, prior to the establishment of the kingdom of God (Rev. 16:14*).

ARMINIANISM (ar-MINN-i-an-izm) Theology named for Jacob Arminius (1560–1609), which tempered strict Calvinist predestination and ELECTION with a belief in the ability of the believer, by virtue of free will, to accept grace through faith.

ARTICLES OF FAITH Official statements of beliefs, in addition to or in place of a sect's CREED or confession of faith: e.g., Episcopalians have their THIRTY-NINE ARTICLES; Methodists usually have such articles; many Jews accept the thirteen articles of faith stated by Maimonides. The term is also used generically, to include creeds, catechisms, and confessions of faith.

ASCENSION (1) The bodily ascension of Jesus into heaven. (2) The feast commemorating this event (Acts 1:9*). Ascension differs from ASSUMPTION in that Jesus was first buried, then resurrected.

In art, Jesus is typically depicted in midair, with his disciples looking on in awe. The scene usually includes God the Father in the heavens and a dove (the Holy Spirit) to complete the trinity.

ASH WEDNESDAY The first day of LENT, when in some churches members receive a mark on their foreheads from the ashes of last year's palm leaves, as a symbol of repentence and a reminder of death.

ASPERSION [Lat: sprinkling] BAPTISM by sprinkling water, usually on the head (Heb. 10:22*).

ASSIMILATION [Lat: making similar] See EDITOR.

ASSUMPTION [Lat: taking up] (1) The reception of Mary bodily into heaven, according to RC and EO tradition, during her deep sleep (EO term: *dormition*). (2) The RC and EO feast, August 15. (3) The reception of Enoch and Elijah into heaven in place of death. (4) Traditionally, the temporary assumptions of Moses and Isaiah during their lifetime. Assumption fast (EO): August 1-14.

ATHANASIAN CREED (ath-a-NAYZ-i-an) A lengthy statement of beliefs, attributed to Athanasius (ca. 297–373 C.E.). Written in Latin, it is also known by its first words: *Quicumque vult* (kwee-COOM-kweh voolt), "whosoever will (be saved)." The EO version is in Greek.

ATHANASIANISM The belief that God the Son/*Logos* is divine and of the same substance as God the Father—as opposed to ARIANISM.

ATONEMENT [ME: at one] Reconciliation of God and human beings. For Christians: (1) The expiation for human sins by Jesus in his sacrifice, of which the sacrificial lamb is a symbol. (2) A person's individual redemption achieved through the sufferings of Jesus and through one's own acceptance of Jesus as the Christ and one's change of heart.

ATONEMENT, DAY OF [Heb: *yom kippur*] (yohm kee-POOR) The most solemn Jewish holiday, of fasting, prayer, and repentance. It occurs in the fall, concluding ten days of penitence that begin with ROSH HASHANAH. The liturgy begins on the holiday eve (Gen. 1:5*) with a prayer for forgiveness of sins: *kol nidrei* (kohl need-RAY), "all vows" (Lev. 23:7*).

AUGSBURG CONFESSION Written by Melanchthon (1497–1560), approved by Luther, and presented at the Diet (council/assembly) of Augsburg (1530), it sealed Protestant opposition to the RC Church and to much of its doctrine. The first part has twenty-one articles of doctrine; the second, seven accusations against the RC Church.

AUREOLE [Lat: golden] (AW-ri-ole) *In art,* (1) EO, like nimbus or HALO, surrounding the head; (2) in Western art, it usually means a light surrounding the entire body.

AUTHORITY God's unquestioned right to rule the universe he created and to exact unquestioning obedience, through: (1) his Word made flesh in Jesus/Christ; (2) his revealed/inspired Word in the Bible (II Tim. 3:15*); (3) TRADITION; (4) the Holy Spirit; and/or (5) his (RC or EO) church. Generally, many Protestant sects emphasize scriptural authority; RC practice—ecclesiastical; Quakers—spiritual (the inner light); Conservative Protestant, EO, and Orthodox Jews—tradition as well as scripture (see HALAKAH). See INFALLIBILITY.

AVE MARIA [Lat: hail, Mary] (ah-vay ma-REE-ya) (1) Latin title and first words of a prayer based on Gabriel's salutation at the ANNUNCIATION and Elisabeth's at the VISITATION. It is repeated at the *angelus* and with the rosary (Luke 1:28, 42*). (2) A small bead in the ROSARY. (3) A song based on the prayer.

BAPTISM [Grk: dipping, immersing] The Christian ritual of induction into the faith (Matt. 28:19*). Sects differ about the *method:* immersion (Matt. 3:16*; Col. 2:12*); pouring/infusion (Acts 2:17*); sprinkling/aspersion (Heb. 10:22*); trine/triune/triple immersion (Matt. 28:19*b*). anointing with oil rather than with water or combined with it; by the Spirit or by fire; with blood (i.e., martyrdom, recognized by EO as effective for those otherwise unbaptized).

Sects also differ about the *age,* for those born into the community: infancy; childhood; or adulthood, initially or rebaptism. Finally, sects differ about the *meaning* of the ceremony and its *relationship* to the ceremony of *confirmation* or chrismation, as well as its relation to repentance, regeneration, justification, sanctification, and salvation.

BAR/BATH MITZVAH [Heb: son/daughter of the commandment] (bahr/baht MITS-va) The synagogue ceremony of initiation, traditionally for boys at age thirteen; they then become members of the congregation with full religious duties and privileges. *Bath mitzvah,* for girls, is of recent origin and not practiced by Orthodox Jews; the age of the girl, the actual ritual, and its significance vary with different Jewish congregations.

BASILICA [Grk: royal (building)] (ba-SILL-i-ca) (1) A RC church building with special privileges. (2) A rectangular church building without a protruding transept (see CRUCIFORM CHURCHES) but with an apse (rounded end, facing east); characteristic of fourth c. Roman architecture and contemporary EO churches. Many other modern churches take this form (without the apse), with a raised chancel/dais, on which are the pulpit, lectern, altar or communion table, and/or choir stalls.

BEATITUDE [Lat: blessedness] (bee-ATT-i-tood) (1) One of the opening sentences of the Sermon on the Mount that begin with the word *blessed* in most translations (Matt. 5:3-11). (2) A title for the patriarch/head of some EO churches.

BENEDICITE [Lat: praise, speak well of] (ben-e-DEES-i-tay) (1) Latin title and first word of a canticle based on Psalm 148, sung in some churches during Lent (cf. LAUDS). (2) Latin title and first word of the Song of the Three Holy Children, which appears in the APOCRYPHAL/deuterocanonical verses inserted between Daniel 3:23 and 3:24 in some Greek MSS and in the Vulgate.

BENEDICTION (1) Invocation of God's blessing: during or concluding a religious service, before or after a meal or meeting, or in dedicating persons or things to God. (2) A blessing offered at various points during the EO and RC service. (3) Part of the RC service centering on the monstrance (vessel) containing the host.

BENEDICTUS [Lat: blessed (be)] (BEN-e-DIC-toos) (1) Latin title and first word of Zacharias' hymn (Luke 1:68*). (2) A canticle based on that hymn. (3)

The part of the mass that opens with the words from Psalm 118:26 (or Matt. 21:9).

BISHOP [OE, overseer; translation of the Grk *episcopus*] (1) A high ranking clergyman in many Christian sects, presiding over a diocese/bishopric/episcopate, in which he has his seat/see. In some sects, the bishop is believed to be ordained in APOSTOLIC SUCCESSION (Acts 1:20*). (2) The Mormon high priest, head of the Aaronic priesthood (Ex. 28:1*).

BREVIARY [Lat: short form] (BREH-vi-a-ry) A book of daily services and prayers (both ORDINARY and PROPER) for the CANONICAL HOURS, for use in RC and EO churches. Cf. MISSAL, which contains the liturgy for the mass; other sacraments are found in the "ritual" or the "pontifical."

BURNING BUSH *In art,* a representation of Moses, awestruck, looking at the flaming bush, with his shoes off or being removed (Ex. 3:2).

BYZANTINE RITE (BIZ-an-teen, by-ZAN-teen) (1) The form of worship, liturgy, and other religious practices of EO churches, distinguishing this group of sects from RC and other Christians; originating in Constantinople /Byzantium. (2) Churches practicing these rites. (See GREEK ORTHODOX.)

CABALA/KABBALAH [Heb: tradition] (kah-ba-LAH, ka-BAH-la) Jewish theosophical mysticism, stressing the occult meaning and the esoteric interpretation of the Bible, which reveal to the informed: that the creation occurred through emanation from God (hence a pantheism); that people must establish the supremacy of the human spirit over its desires; that there will surely be a messianic restoration of the world to a perfect state; and other predictions. It has influenced Christian mysticism since the Middle Ages and today is most widely credited by HASIDIC Jews.

CANON [Grk: measuring rod] (1) A collection or list of sacred things: authoritative beliefs and practices, scriptural books, RC hours/devotions, ecclesiastical laws, saints, a special group of EO prayers. (2) A clerical title. (3) The central portion of the mass.

CANONICAL HOURS (ca-NONN-i-cal) Eight stated (times of) prayers that form the "divine office": MATINS/nocturne (midnight), LAUDS (3 A.M.), prime (6 A.M., the first/*primus* daytime hour), terce (9 A.M., the third daytime hour), sext (midday, the sixth daytime hour), NONES (3 P.M.), VESPERS/evensong (6 P.M.), and compline (9 P.M. or at bedtime, the completion). The first two are often combined as the night office and said late at night or very early in the morning.

CANTICLE [Lat: little song] (1) A biblical hymn or song of praise chanted as part of the liturgy, in a church service; e.g., a psalm, the Benedicite, Magnificat, Nunc Dimittis, Jubilate, Benediction, Angelic Hymn. (2) Canticle of Canticles: the Douay Bible's name for the book called Song of Songs/Solomon in other Bibles.

CANTOR [Lat: singer] (1) A solo singer in a RC service. (2) The official who sings the liturgy and leads the congregation in Jewish services. (3) Choir leader/master. (4) The director of church music in German churches.

CARDINAL VIRTUES [Lat: hinge/basic strengths] (1) Seven fundamental Christian virtues. Four were stated by Plato and are called moral (RC: natural): prudence/wisdom, justice, fortitude/courage, and temperance/self-control. The other three are from scripture and are called Christian (RC:

theological): faith, hope, and charity/love. (2) EO: the first four of these.

CAROL [Lat: choral song] A hymn, song of praise, especially those sung at Christmas (sometimes at Easter or May Day) in imitation of the Angelic Hymn. Usually popular and joyous, it is often a ballad or folk song. (Luke 2:13*)

CASUISTRY [Lat: incident, case] (CAZ-yoo-ist-ry) (1) The application of general moral principles to particular cases; case law (if . . . , then . . .). Some sects have manuals to guide such decisions. (2) The study/doctrine of cases of conscience. (3) In common secular usage, the word is usually pejorative, implying legalistic sophistry.

CATECHISM [Grk: oral teaching (of religion)] (CAT-e-kizm) A textbook or manual for systematic instruction in religious beliefs and practices, usually by question and answer. It defines, supplements, or replaces a *creed* and constitutes an outline of the faith. It is often required to be recited before baptism, confirmation, or church membership. Catechumen (cat-e-KYOO-men): a person, usually adult, undergoing instruction. Catechesis (cat-e-KEE-sis): oral instruction of catechumens. Catechetics (cat-e-KET-ics): science or theology of teaching children or converts the Christian faith; considered a practical accompaniment of KERYGMA. Catechetical school: EO equivalent of the Protestant Sunday school.

CATHEDRAL [Grk: (bishop's) chair] The principal church of a diocese, because it contains the bishop's chair/seat/SEE.

CATHOLIC EPISTLES [Grk: universal letters] (1) Also called general and encyclical, they are non-Pauline Letters and are supposedly not addressed to an individual or a church but to the whole/universal church and probably were circulated among the churches. Traditionally non-Pauline: James; I and II Peter; I, II, and III John; Jude. (Those by John are often called JOHANNINE.) (2) These seven plus Hebrews and Revelation, which are not by Paul, though the latter is not usually grouped with the Epistles. (3) Some lists add some Pauline Letters that are nonpastoral and have universal interest. First Peter and II and III John identify the recipients and are therefore omitted from some lists.

CENACLE [Lat: dining room] (SENN-a-cle) The upper room: traditional site of the last supper, of the first meeting place/church of the early Christians, of Jesus' appearance to the disciples after his resurrection, and of the descent of the Holy Spirit.

CELESTIAL HIERARCHY The nine orders/classes of "angels," divided into three choirs; listed from highest to lowest; SERAPHIM, CHERUBIM, thrones; dominations, VIRTUES, powers; principalities, ARCHANGELS, ANGELS (Eph. 1:21*). The nine orders themselves are also called choirs or hierarchies. Some lists differ.

CEREMONY See RITE.

CHALICE [Lat: cup] (CHAL-iss) The cup used at the EUCHARIST, representing Jesus' cup at the Last Supper; stemmed or bowl shaped, it contains wine or wine and water. Some sects have only one, which only certain people may handle; others have one for each communicant.

CHANCEL [Lat: lattice] (CHAN-sel) The part of the church in front of the nave, facing the congregation, sometimes raised; it is usually set apart for the clergy, altar, etc.

CHANT [Lat: song] A melody used in canticles and anthems; usually unaccompanied, repetitive, and hymnic. Successive nonmetrical verses are fitted to the music by assigning as many syllables to each note as required, giving an impression of monotone. Plainsong: a chant with free rhythms, especially applied to Gregorian chants. The tones for Gregorian chants were standardized by Pope Gregory the Great (sixth c.). EO chants also follow an approved set of tones. Jewish chanting is often antiphonal, between cantor and congregation.

CHARISMA/TA [Grk: (spiritual) gift/s] (ca-RIZ-ma/ca-riz-MAH-ta) (1) A token of God's grace, an unmerited gift/ability for the benefit of others rather than the recipient. (2) The gift of tongues, in CHARISMATIC/pentecostal sects (I Cor. 12:4*). The EO list of gifts of the Holy Spirit differs from that in Western churches.

CHARISMATIC (1) A distinguishing characteristic of the PENTECOSTAL movement within Christianity and the focus of certain sects that emphasize a strong spiritual response to the gospel, baptism of the spirit, and speaking in tongues. (2) Certain OT leaders; e.g., heroes of the book of Judges.

CHARITY [Lat: love] AGAPE: (1) God's unmerited love for people. (2) A person's similarly unselfish love for other human beings. (3) One's pure love for God. A CARDINAL VIRTUE.

CHERUBIM [Heb: plural of cherub] (CHEH-roo-beem) The second highest order of angels in the CELESTIAL HIERARCHY. English usage accepts *cherubs* and *cherubims* as plurals.

    In art, (1) Ethereal human forms with large wings, like those in the throne or covering the ark in the tabernacle or in Solomon's temple; sometimes shown holding a book. (2) God's chariot throne, described in Ezekiel 1 and Isaiah 10 as having human limbs, wheels, wings, many eyes, and four heads apiece (of a man, ox, eagle, and lion; see EVANGELISTS); usually in golden yellow or blue. (3) Winged babies.

CHILIASM [Grk: 1,000 (years)] (KILL-i-asm) MILLENNIALISM.

CHRISM [Grk: ointment] A consecrated mixture of olive oil and balm (aromatic balsam resin) or a combination of forty ingredients (EO), used in ANOINTING and/or chrismation. The mixture represents the divine and human natures of Jesus/Christ.

CHRISMATION The EO equivalent of the Western sacrament of confirmation; it is given to the infant immediately after baptism.

CHRIST [Grk: anointed (one)] (1) A title applied to Jesus by Christians, who believe him to be the Lord's anointed/Messiah. (2) A synonym for *Jesus*. (3) Part of his name: Jesus Christ. (4) A symbol of the divine part of his nature.**

CHRIST STORIES A class of pericopes studied by FORM CRITICISM: e.g., infancy narratives, baptism, temptation, Peter's confession, entry into Jerusalem, institution of the eucharist, resurrection, etc.

CHRISTMAS, DATE OF [OE: Christ's mass] The earliest observances were on January 6, but the church (ca. 300 C.E.) set it at December 25, the ancient world's day for the winter solstice (and the legendary date of the birth of many pagan dieties). Most EO churches retain the old date either because of its history or because of the Julian (old) calendar. Besides the date, many Western customs at Christmas have pagan histories that have been reinterpreted and assimilated. (Matt. 1:24*)

CHRISTOLOGY (kris-TOL-o-jy) The study/interpretation/doctrinal exposition of the nature of the person and redemptive work of Jesus: e.g., as the messiah, Son of God, king, and savior; as the Logos, atonement, revelation of God's grace; his incarnation, sacrifice, resurrection. A christological reading of the OT emphasizes its foreshadowing of Jesus as the Christ; see TYPE.

CHURCH [Grk: lord's (house)] (1) A house of Christian worship, including CATHEDRALS and BASILICAS. (2) An organized religious group/congregation. (3) A denomination/sect or organized group of them. (4) Christianity as a whole body. (5) The RC Church. (6) The successor to Israel, according to the traditional Christian ecclesiological reading of the OT (see TYPE). (7) The mystical body of Jesus (RC).

CIRCUMCISION [Lat: cutting around] (1) The Jewish rite of cutting off the male foreskin eight days after birth, when the boy is named. The Hebrew term is *b'rith milah,* covenant of circumcision, often shortened to *b'rith,* covenant (Gen. 17:10*). (2) A similar ceremony for Moslem boys, at age five or six. (3) The Feast of the Circumcision commemorates that of Jesus (Luke 2:21*).

CITY OF DAVID (1) Jerusalem, where David had his capital. (2) Bethlehem, his birthplace.

CODEX [Lat: (tree) trunk] (1) A code of canonical laws. (2) An ancient copy of the Bible in book form (as opposed to scrolls), with leaves of papyrus or vellum; the most important codices are Sinaiticus, Vaticanus, Alexandrinus, Bezae, and Ephraemi.

COMFORTER Generally taken to refer to the Holy Spirit sent to help humanity as teacher and advocate/intercessor before God. For Christian Scientists, the science of Christ is the comforter. See PARACLETE (John 14:16*).

COMMUNION [Lat: mutual participation] The EUCHARIST/Lord's supper/mass. (1) The ceremony of the bread and wine at a Christian service. (2) The service at which this ceremony occurs. (3) The members of a sect taken as a group. (Luke 22:19*)

CONCORDANCE [Lat: agreeing] An alphabetical index of words used in the Bible (or other important literary work/canon), listing where they appear in the text and often giving additional information about them.

CONCORDAT (con-CORE-dat) (1) An agreement or treaty between a state and a religious group; e.g., between the Vatican and the ruler of a country. (2) An agreement between two religious groups.

CONFESSION (OF SINS) (1) At a worship service: part of the liturgy for Protestants; also for Jews, especially on the Day of Atonement. (2) Privately: to a priest, as part of the RC sacrament of PENANCE/reconciliation, which is called the sacrament of confession in EO churches.

CONFESSION (OF FAITH) (1) A formal statement of a sect's doctrinal beliefs and practices (e.g., Augsburg, Dort, Dordrech, Westminster). See CREED. (2) A personal declaration (e.g., Peter's confession, Matt. 16:16). (3) A synonym for sect/communion (e.g., one is a member of a confession).

CONFESSION OF DORT/DORDRECHT (A city in Holland) (1) Dort: The Calvinist statement of beliefs, 1618/19. (2) Dordrecht: the Mennonite statement of beliefs and practices, 1632.

CONFIRMATION [Lat: making firm] A public initiatory rite symbolizing the sealing or strengthening of one's commitment to a faith. (1) A Christian sacrament/ordinance/practice supplemental to baptism (and prerequisite for Communion in some sects) (John 17:19;* Acts 8:15*). See CHRISMATION. (2) A recent practice among Reform and some Conservative Jews.

Christian sects that practice this ceremony differ as to: (1) the age of confirmation—infancy, at age seven, adolescence, or adulthood; (2) the elements—anointing/chrismation on the head or body, laying on hands, signing with a cross; and (3) its theological significance (Acts 19:1-6).

For Jews, the ceremony usually culminates a period of study, at adolescence. It is not required by scripture nor by rabbinic literature, and the practice varies: Orthodox Jews have no confirmation; many Conservative and Reform congregations have it in addition to bar/bath mitzvah; a few use it in place of bath mitzvah for girls (which is also unscriptural) as a counterpart to the boy's bar mitzvah.

CONFLATION [Lat: blowing together] See EDITOR.

CONSUBSTANTIATION [Lat: joining substances] A term expressing Luther's theological doctrine that in the EUCHARIST ceremony the body and blood of Jesus are actually present as substances "in, with, and under" the bread and wine, which remain as substances themselves. Many Lutherans depart from both this doctrine and that of TRANSUBSTANTIATION.

CONTRITION [Lat: bruise (oneself)] See PENITENCE.

CORRUPT TEXT [Lat: broken text] A Bible (or other) passage altered from the original: parts lost, deleted, added, or changed. See EDITOR.

COVENANT [Lat: coming together] The English translation of the Hebrew *b'rith*, Greek *diatheke (digh-a-THEE-kee)*, and Latin *testamentum*. In the OT, God's covenant with his people may be made with the group as a whole or with the king as its representative; it may carry either individual or communal responsibility; it may be conditional or unconditional. See TESTAMENT, WITNESS. This last consideration is a matter of doctrinal difference among Christians (see ELECTION, GRACE).

CREATION OF EVE *In art*, a representation of God, often depicted as an old man with a beard, drawing Eve out of the side of the sleeping Adam.

CREDO [Lat: I believe] (CRAYD-o) (1) Latin title and first word of the Apostles' Creed and of the Nicene Creed. (2) The third item in the ordinary of the mass.

CREED A concise statement of religious doctrine, usually used in public Christian worship. The best known are the Apostles', Nicene, and Athanasian creeds. Credal statements appear elsewhere; in the Bible, in prayers, and within narratives outside the Bible.

CRUCIFIX [Lat: fastened to a cross] *In art*, a representation of Jesus on the cross. Early ones show him crowned and robed as a king; modern ones, suffering or dead. Rood: a cross or crucifix, usually large, at the chancel. The EO crucifix has three bars, the lowest one at an angle, with the corpus painted rather than sculpted. Protestants usually use only the empty cross.**

CRUCIFIXION An especially degrading and cruel mode of capital punishment by binding, nailing, or impaling on a stake or a cross. It was borrowed by the Romans from the Phoenicians and others.

In art, Jesus is usually shown in a loincloth, nailed to a cross that sometimes has the superscription *INRI* (Latin initials for "Jesus of Nazareth, King of the Jews"). He may be alone or between two other crosses; there may be people sorrowing at the foot of the cross, especially the three women.

CRUCIFORM CHURCHES The floor plan of EO churches is usually a BASILICA within the outlines of a Greek cross (four equal, broad arms), with the corners filled in to form a square building. It usually has a dome over the center, few pews (people generally stand), and an ICONOSTASIS separating the apse from the nave. Western cruciform churches follow the Latin cross (one longer vertical arm), with a long central aisle (called nave, from its naval shape and symbolism as the saving ark of Noah), and a cross aisle at front (transept). Like the basilica, its apsidal (rounded) end is opposite the front of the building (façade) and the vestibule (narthex). Salisbury Cathedral is a patriarchal cross (two crossarms).

D-SOURCE The tradition, oral and/or written, presumably used by the redactors of the Bible or by the hypothetical DEUTERONOMIC WRITER, thought to be the final redactor of Joshua through II Kings, ca. 570 B.C.E.

DAVID AND GOLIATH *In art,* a representation of: (1) David as a boy, wearing simple clothing and carrying a sling, confronting the giant; (2) David severing the dead Goliath's head. (3) In sculpture, David is usually alone, with the sling or the sword, sometimes with Goliath's head at his feet.

DEACON [Grk: servant] A subordinate clerical or lay official in a Christian church, whose duties and authority vary according to the sect (Acts 6:3*). The adjectival form is *diaconal* (digh-ACK-o-nal).

DEADLY SIN See SEVEN DEADLY SINS.

DECALOGUE [Grk: ten words] (DEC-a-log) The Ten Commandments (Ex. 20**).

DEISM [Lat: (belief in) God] The belief in God as only the creator of the universe and its laws (which are beneficial for humanity) but no longer involved in our world. It usually results in a religion of nature that rejects the supernatural, including the AUTHORITY of revelation and the afterlife. As a movement, deism flourished in the eighteenth c. Enlightenment, which sought to view experience rationalistically and scientifically.

DEPOSITION/DESCENT FROM THE CROSS *In art,* a representation of Jesus being lowered from the cross, sometimes by means of a winding sheet, usually with Joseph of Arimathea helping or directing, and sometimes with Nicodemus and others (John 19:38).

DE PROFUNDIS [Lat: out of the depths] (day pro-FOON-dees) Latin title and opening words of the penitential Psalm 130 (129 in the Vulgate), used in funeral liturgies and prayers for the dead.

DESCENT OF THE HOLY SPIRIT/GHOST PENTECOST (Acts 2:1*). *In art,* a representation of the apostles, in an attitude of awe as rays of light or little flames fill their upper room.

DESTRUCTION OF SODOM AND GOMORRAH *In art,* a representation of Lot and his two daughters, a flaming city, and in the background Lot's wife facing the city and turned into a pillar (Gen. 19:26).

DEUTEROCANONICAL [Grk: second canonical] (DOO-ter-o-can-ON-i-cal) (1) RC and EO term for parts of the OT included in the SEPTUAGINT but omitted from the MASORETIC text. See APOCRYPHA. (2) Some other biblical passages whose authenticity is questioned by some scholars; e.g., Mark 16:9-20 is omitted from some modern Bibles or added as a footnote, as a late addition to the original text.

DEUTERO-ISAIAH [Grk: II Isaiah] The hypothetical source of chapters 40–66 of the book of Isaiah, which differ from the earlier chapters in vocabulary, style, and content. Some scholars split these later chapters again, hypothecating a Trito-Isaiah for chapters 56–66.

DEUTERO-PAULINE EPISTLES Epistles traditionally attributed to Paul but whose authorship is challenged by some critical scholars, with varying degrees of consensus: Ephesians, II Thessalonians, Colossians, I and II Timothy, and Titus.

DEUTERONOMIC WRITER (doo-ter-o-NOM-ic) The author of a "D-document" posited by some critical scholars for certain material found primarily in the book of Deuteronomy; usually dated from the seventh c. B.C.E. and connected to the book found by Josiah in the temple in 621 B.C.E. (II Kings 22-23).

DEUTERONOMY [Grk: second laws] (doo-ter-ON-o-my) The fifth book of the Bible.

DIASPORA [Grk: scattering about, dispersion] (digh-ASS-po-ra) (1) The condition/location/movement of Jews outside of Palestine, from the time of the Babylonian exile until today. (2) Less frequently, EO churches in America and elsewhere, away from their land of origin.

DIDACHE [Grk: teaching] (DID-a-kee) (1) A NT apocryphal book, entitled "Teaching of the Twelve Apostles." Grouped with the writings of the Apostolic FATHERS, it is considered by scholars a valuable source of information about second c. Christianity, possibly influenced by the Gospel of Matthew. It consists mainly of moral precepts and rules for religious practice and church organization. (2) Ethical teaching as distinct from missionary preaching/KERYGMA.

DIES IRAE [Lat: day of wrath] (Lat: DEE-ace EE-righ; Eng: DIGH-ees IGH-ree) Opening words and title of a medieval Latin hymn about the last judgment; part of some REQUIEM masses.

DIOCESE [Grk: administration] (DIGH-o-sis) A bishop's jurisdiction/see/bishopric/episcopate. The adjective is *diocesan* (digh-OSS-e-zan)

DISCIPLES [Lat: pupils] Followers of Jesus: (1) in his lifetime—sometimes limited to the twelve apostles or to the seventy (Luke 10:1), but more often applied generally to his followers; (2) since then, the term is applied to individuals and sects (Matt. 5:1*).

DIVES [Lat: rich man] (DIGH-veez) A descriptive adjective (wealthy) for the man in the parable (Luke 16:19), it has been taken to be his name.

DIVINE OFFICE CANONICAL HOURS.

DOCETISM [Grk: seem] (DOH-set-ism) The belief, growing out of

GNOSTICISM, that Jesus was totally and purely divine; that his body only seemed real, since matter is evil; and that the incarnation, crucifixion, resurrection, and ascension were illusory manifestations of the Logos.

DOCTORS OF THE CHURCH [Lat: teachers] A title given to important Christian theologians. (1) Certain FATHERS OF THE CHURCH: Greek—Basil, Gregory Nazianus, and John Chrysostom; Latin—these three plus Ambrose, Augustine, Gregory the Great, and Jerome. (2) Later doctors (RC) include Thomas Aquinas, Anselm, Leo the Great, the Venerable Bede, John of the Cross, et al. Most of the doctors have been canonized.

DOCTRINE [Lat: teaching] Religious belief(s) or teachings of a sect. They may appeal exclusively to one's faith in the AUTHORITY of God or may also appeal to evidence and/or reason. Some beliefs that are DOGMA in some sects are considered doctrine in others or, in EO faith, "pious beliefs."

DOGMA [Grk: seeming (true, good)] Infallible and binding religious doctrine, to be received on faith as AUTHORITATIVE: as revealed by God in scripture and as interpreted by a church council or by a revered authority. Creeds, catechisms, confessions, and articles of faith are usually considered dogma.

DOOMSDAY [OE: judgment day] The day of the last judgment, at the end of time, when both the living and the resurrected dead will be sent to heaven or hell (Matt. 24:29*).

DORMITION [Lat: sleep] (dor-MISH-un) See ASSUMPTION.

DOUAY/DOUAI BIBLE (doo-ay) (1) An English translation of the Bible from the Vulgate, for Catholics (NT done at Rheims, France, 1582; OT at Douay, 1610). Sometimes called Rheims-Douay (rance doo-ay). (2) Any revision of that version; especially one by Challoner, 1752. (3) All Catholic translations into English; distinctive in their adherence to the SEPTUAGINT canon for the OT instead of the MASORETIC and, until recently, in the use of Greek version of Hebrew names in the NT.**

DOUBLET Two basically similar stories that differ only in details; e.g., OT—Abraham, Sarah, and Abimelech (Gen. 20) and Isaac, Rebecca, and Abimelech (Gen. 26); NT—feeding the five thousand (Mark 6:30) and feeding the four thousand (Mark 8:1). Critical scholars account for these parallels as coming from different traditions. Triplets also appear in the Bible.

DOVE *In art:* (1) With an olive branch, it represents peace, based on Noah's dove and its olive leaf—the sign of God's renewed peace with humankind (Gen. 8:11). (2) The symbol of the Holy Spirit, based on the description of the baptism of Jesus (Matt. 3:16); seven doves represent the *charismata.*

DOXOLOGY [Grk: opinion/belief (expressed) in words] (doks-OLL-o-jy) (1) A Christian liturgical formula or hymn in praise of God; e.g., the GLORIA, SANCTUS, HALLELUJAH, Matthew 6:13*b* (see PATER NOSTER), the Protestant hymn "Praise God from whom all blessings flow," and the doxology of the RC mass ("Through him, with him, in him") (2) Jewish equivalents; e.g., the KADDISH; not usually called doxologies, however.

E-SOURCE The tradition, oral and/or written, presumably used by the redactors of the Pentateuch or by the hypothetical ELOHIST WRITER.

EASTER [OE: AS/Teutonic goddess of spring; her festival] The most important Christian festival (also called the PASCHAL holiday), celebrating the resurrection of Jesus (Acts 12:3*). A movable feast, the date also differs for the Gregorian (Western) and Julian (Eastern) calendars.

ECCE HOMO [Lat: behold the man] (Lat: EKK-eh HO-mo; It: ETCH-eh HO-mo) *In art,* a representation of Jesus crowned with thorns, often shown at the moment when Pilate presents him to the crowd (John 19:5).

ECCLESIASTICAL [Grk: assembly] Pertaining to the church—its clergy, congregation, or building. The book of Ecclesiastes takes its name from the preacher who is introduced as the speaker in chapter 1.

ECUMENICAL COUNCILS [Grk: worldwide councils] (ek-yoo-MEN-i-cal; noun: ECK-yoo-men-ism) (1) Historical councils: Nearly all Christians recognize the authority of the first four, which took place after the emperor moved to Constantinople: Nicea I, 324 C.E.; Constantinople I, 381; Ephesus, 431; and Chalcedon, 451. EO recognize these and only the next three: Constantinople II, 553, Constantinople III, 680; and Nicea II, 787 (the eighth, Constantinople IV, 869, condemned the patriarch of Constantinople for his schism). RCs recognize 21, through Vatican II, 1962–65. (2) Modern (limited) attempts to unite major groups of Christian sects, both between RCs and Protestants (Vatican II) and among Protestants (e.g., World Council of Churches). (Acts 15:6*)

EDITOR A biblical writer who goes beyond "REDACTION" (in the limited sense of reducing oral tradition to writing) and scribal copying of the traditional material; he also comments on the text or shapes it interpretively in various ways. Assimilation: forcing conformity to another text. Conflation: bringing together variant material from different sources. Interpolation: adding new material. Gloss: marginal or interlinear explanation, synonym, translation, or commentary that becomes part of the text in reproduction. Corruption: error, omission, or addition in transcription made by redactors, editors, or scribes. These definitions are not uniform among scholars; e.g., *redaction criticism* examines what has here been called the work of an editor.

ELDER A church official (Acts 14:23*): e.g., Presbyterian—an elected officer, ordained to assist at Communion; Methodist—a fully ordained minister; Mormon—an ordained priest of Melchizedek (Ps. 110:4*).

ELECTION [Lat: choosing (by God)] (1) The Jewish belief in the chosenness of Israel for redemption and to bring peace and salvation to the entire world; not usually called election, however. (2) The belief of Christians in their inheritance of that role. (3) The belief of some Christians (especially Calvinists) that salvation will come (only) to those elected by the free and unmerited grace of God (Rom. 11:5*).

ELOHIM [Heb: God/gods] (el-o-HEEM) (1) The plural form of the name of God. Scholars differ about the reason for the plural form of a monotheistic deity: his majesty (the royal "we"), God acting in council, the totality of God's attributes, the absorption of earlier pagan gods, the remnant of an earlier polytheism (an ancient Canaanite custom), etc. ADONAI is also plural. (2) Pagan gods.

ELOHIST WRITER The author of an E-document posited by some critical scholars for portions (not generally agreed upon) of the Pentateuch; usually dated ca. 875–750 B.C.E. and thought to have arisen in northern Israel/Ephraim. See E-SOURCE and J-SOURCE.

ENCYCLICAL [Grk: circular (letter)] (en-SICK-li-cal) (1) A letter from the pope addressed to the entire RC hierarchy of a country or of the world. (2) a CATHOLIC EPISTLE.

END TIME Last days. It is usually taken to include the utter corruption of the world, the second coming, the final struggle between good and evil, the resurrection of the dead, and the last judgment (Matt. 24:29;* Rev. 20:2*).

ENTOMBMENT *In art,* a representation of the burial of Jesus by Joseph of Arimathea, in the ground/a sarcophagus/a cave/sepulcher hewn out of the rock; sometimes Nicodemus and others are present (John 19:41).

ENTRY INTO JERUSALEM *In art,* a representation of Jesus on an ass, surrounded by joyous people waving palm branches, and (often, children) strewing them before him (Mark 11:8). Sometimes Zacchaeus is shown in a tree in the background (Luke 19:2).

EPIPHANY [Grk: manifestation, showing forth] (e-PIFF-a-ny) A Christian festival on January 6 (Twelfth Day); the end of the Christmas season that began with Advent. It commemorates the manifestation to the world of Jesus' messiahship, or divinity (THEOPHANY). Western Christians generally relate the holiday to the visit of the MAGI (Matt. 2:11*). EO churches include the baptism of Jesus (Matt. 3:16*) and the miracle at Cana (John 2).

EPISCOPACY [Grk: bishopric] (e-PIS-co-pa-cy) (1) Government of a church by bishops and a HIERARCHY (Acts 14:23;* 1:20*). (2) Bishopric: its rank or jurisdiction.

EPISTLE [Grk: message; Lat: letter] One of twenty-one NT books, usually subdivided into CATHOLIC/general/encyclical and PAULINE, some of the latter being called PASTORAL. Some critical scholars consider some of the traditional Pauline Letters to be DEUTERO-PAULINE.

ESCHATOLOGICAL PROCLAMATION (ESS-cat-o-LOJ-i-cal) Preaching that the end of the world is at hand (and that people should repent) (e.g., Matt. 3:2).

ESCHATOLOGY [Grk: account of last/end things] (ESS-cat-OLL-o-jy) The doctrine/study of the ultimate destiny and purpose of the individual/humanity/history/this world/time—and what lies beyond. (1) Individual eschatology focuses on the afterlife and immortality of the soul. (2) Christian apocalyptic eschatology usually views the END TIME as being brought on by God's intervention, in which he destroys the ruling powers of evil and establishes his timeless/eternal Kingdom for the elect/righteous. (3) Jewish eschatology ranges in belief from the OT hope for deliverance and peace on earth (especially after the judgment represented by the exile) to an apocalyptically established universal new age or messianic era. See SALVATION.

ESSENES [Heb: righteous ones(?)] (ESS-eenz) An ascetic, monastic, communal sect (ca. 200 B.C.E.–ca. 100 C.E.) whose strict rules for the religious life prepared its members for the imminent end of this world. John the Baptist may have been an Essene. Distinguished from Pharisees, Sadducees, and other groups, they are described in the Dead Sea Scrolls, Josephus, and other ancient writings.

EUCHARIST [Grk: giving thanks] (YOO-ca-rist) (1) A biblically instituted Christian sacrament/ordinance/ceremony. (2) The service in which it occurs. (3) The bread (and wine) themselves. Instituted by Jesus at the last supper, the rite commemorates Jesus' sacrifice and symbolizes the new covenant. *Eucharist* is commonly synonymous with *Lord's Supper, Lord's Table, (Holy) Communion,* and *Mass.* Generally, *Communion/Holy Communion* is the term used by RC, EO, and Episcopalians, and *Lord's Supper,* by other Protestants. Quakers do not practice the ceremony.

Sects differ on these points: (1) Whether the wine—or unfermented grape juice in some cases—as well as the bread is an "element" of the Eucharist: Communion under one kind (Catholic) or under both kinds (generally, Protestants). (2) Whether other substances than bread/wafer—unleavened or, in some cases (e.g., EO), leavened—may be used. (3) Whether the bread is received in the mouth or in the hand. (4) Whether "This is my body" is to be taken literally, symbolically, or otherwise: transubstantiation, consubstantiation, impanation, representation, seal of faith, reminder/memorial, etc. (5) Whether members of other sects may participate: open, closed, or restricted Communion. (6) What the purpose, effect, and meaning are of the ceremony. (Luke 22:19*)

EVANGELICAL [Grk: good news; OE: gospel] (e-van-JELL-i-cal) (1) A conservative Christian position that emphasizes loyalty to the gospel, spiritual-mindedness, and Christian living; as distinguished from positions that emphasize ecclesiastical, social, ritualistic, or rationalistic aspects of Christianity. (2) A branch of Protestantism that followed Luther; as distinguished from the reformed churches, which followed Calvin, Zwingli, and Melanchthon (all in Switzerland) and Knox (Scotland). In the United States there are sects that descend from both branches: Evangelical Lutheran and Reformed.

EVANGELIST (1) An evangelical or conservative Christian who preaches the gospel of individual conversion, usually as a traveling revivalist (Matt. 28:19*). See PROSELYTE. (2) A writer of one of the four Gospels.

In art, each evangelist is often represented by a symbol from Revelation 4:7: Matthew, a winged man; Mark, a winged lion; Luke, a winged ox; and John, an eagle.

EXCOMMUNICATION [Lat: not sharing] Exclusion from the (religious) community or from certain central parts of the Christian worship service. Originally, it carried the penalty of death but not eternal damnation. In RC doctrine, it may be temporary, until forgiven, or permanent (anathematized/damned)—major and minor excommunication, both of which are practiced infrequently. Similarly, Orthodox Jews distinguish between a long-term *herem* (hay-rem) and a short-term ban, a *niddui* (nid-ooy).

EXEGESIS [Grk: explanation] (ex-e-JEE-sis) The critical examination of the historical/original meaning of a biblical (or other) passage. (Contrast with HERMENEUTICS: interpreting the meaning for humanity today.) Eisegesis (igh-se-JEE-sis): interpreting a text by reading one's own ideas into it. Exposition/expounding: practical religious interpretation—following exegesis, and considered by some religious authorities a necessary part of exegesis. Literary analysis/rhetorical criticism/structuralism: examining the text apart from its historical setting. In some sects, only the official exegesis is acceptable.

EXILE/EXILIC (ex-ILL-ic) Referring to the Babylonian exile of the kingdom of Judah (south Israel) (ca. 585–ca. 535 B.C.E.). *Pre-exilic* and *postexilic* refer to events and concepts of Jews before and after that episode, which was a watershed in Israel's history.

EXODUS [Grk: going out] (1) The second book of the Bible. (2) The departure from Egypt.

EXPULSION *In art,* a representation of Adam and Eve, inside or outside the Garden, being driven from Eden, usually with an angel holding a sword, sometimes with the voice of God symbolically portrayed.

EXTREME UNCTION See UNCTION.

FALL OF MAN (1) Traditional Christian view: Adam and Eve were perfect, innocent, and potentially immortal until the ORIGINAL SIN; their nature changed, introducing mortality and evil into the nature of all future human beings. (2) Most Jews, and some Christians, believe that the first man and woman were created with both good and bad inclinations (or seeds) (Gen. 3:6*); the Fall represented a change only in the human condition, not in human nature. (3) Some Christians posit a premundane fall of men/giants who were created (Gen. 1) before this world and Adam and Eve were created (Gen. 2). (4) Others reject the doctrine of a real Fall and see instead a valuable myth.

In art, the term is used synonymously with either ORIGINAL SIN or EXPULSION.

FATHERS OF THE CHURCH Revered Christian theologians and religious interpreters during the patristic era—from the end of the NT to ca. 700 C.E. (1) Narrowly, those designated as DOCTORS OF THE CHURCH. (2) Broadly, the doctors and many others, who are classified both chronologically and geographically (as well as by the language in which they wrote): Pre/Ante-Nicene Fathers (before 324 C.E.), including the earliest generation, the apostolic fathers (first and second c.), are subdivided into Greek, Roman, Alexandrian, and Carthaginian. Post-Nicene Fathers are subdivided into Western and Eastern. Some of the more commonly met names (in addition to the doctors): Athanasius, Boethius, Clement, Irenaeus, Justin Martyr, Origen, Papias, Tatian, Tertullian.

FIAT LUX [Lat: let there be light] (FEE-aht loox) (Gen. 1:3).

FLAGELLATION [Lat: whipping] (flaj-e-LAY-shun) (1) A late medieval form of penance, still practiced in some countries (e.g., Penitentes, in Mexico). (2) The scourging of Jesus by Roman soldiers after his sentencing by Pilate and before being mocked.

In art, Jesus is often shown clad in a loincloth and tied to a post, his hands tied behind him, with bloody stripes on his body and being whipped with metal-tipped thongs.

FLIGHT INTO EGYPT *In art,* a representation of: (1) Mary riding an ass, usually in a royal blue robe and holding the infant Jesus, while Joseph on foot leads the ass. (2) The rest on the flight: Mary, holding the infant, seated by the wayside; sometimes alone and sometimes with Joseph in the background, with the ass tethered nearby. (3) Less frequently the family is depicted leaving Jerusalem during the MASSACRE OF THE INNOCENTS.

FLOOD *In art,* a representation of the ark surrounded by water, usually including Noah protruding from it and either the raven or the DOVE and olive branch (Gen. 8:6-11).

FORM CRITICISM Critical study of the history and function of the typical kinds of structure, genre, setting, and/or purpose through which traditions or messages are expressed; attempting to determine the situations (SITZ IM LEBEN) in which biblical pericopes arose—speaker, audience, and function of the story or teaching. The psalms and Jesus' teachings especially have been successfully analyzed in this way.

FUNDAMENTALISM (1) An American, militantly conservative Christian movement whose ideas were published in "The Fundamentals" (1910–12), as a reaction against "modernist" tendencies in some sects. (2) Any quite conservative Protestant sect or position, characterized generally by a belief in biblical infallibility and literalism and by acceptance of text-related TRADITIONS. "EVANGELICAL conservatives" share some of these views but usually oppose "traditionalism" and allow for rationalistic inquiry into the Bible.

GEHENNA [Heb: valley of Hinnom] (ge-HEN-a) A symbolic name for hell, taken from a burning garbage dump near Jerusalem that was formerly used by pagans for burnt sacrifice of children to MOLOCH—even by some OT Jewish kings who worshiped "other gods."

GEMARA [Aram: completion] (ge-MAH-ra) RABBINIC writings by AMORAIM in Babylonia and Palestine (third to sixth c. C.E.); part of the oral Law, as distinguished from the written Law (the Hebrew Bible). It consists mostly of commentary on the MISHNAH, with which it forms the Babylonian and the Palestinian TALMUDS.

GENESIS [Grk: birth] (1) The first book of the Bible. (2) The word used by Matthew to begin his Gospel, relating it to the book of Genesis.

GENTILES [Lat: (foreign) nations] (1) A Christian term for pagans/heathens. (2) A Jewish term for non-Jews. (3) A Mormon term for non-Mormons (except Jews). Like the Hebrew word *goy,* of which it is a translation, the Latin word *gens* was originally neutral: nation/tribe. Both words have followed the common linguistic decline into condescension toward, or fear of, outsiders and now often mean people who are inferior, at least religiously.

GENTILE CHRISTIANS (Also called Hellenistic Christians; both terms contrast with JEWISH CHRISTIANS.) Early converts to Christianity who were not previously Jews—by birth or conversion. They were the subject of the dispute among the apostles and missionaries that led to the Jerusalem council (Acts 15; Gal. 2).

GIFT OF TONGUES (i.e., languages) One of the CHARISMATA from the Holy Spirit: (1) The sudden ability to speak in foreign languages (Acts 2:4*). (2) Intelligible ecstatic speech. (3) Unintelligible speech or sounds. (4) Sometimes the term is extended to include another charisma, the ability to interpret ecstatic speech. It is a key element in PENTECOSTALISM and among sects that believe in baptism of the Holy Spirit and/or fire (Matt. 3:11*).

GOOD FRIDAY The Friday before Easter. The most solemn day of the

Christian year, celebrated as the anniversary of the crucifixion of Jesus. It is called "good" because of the benefit to humanity from the sacrifice. (Mark 15:42*)

GLORIA IN EXCELSIS [Lat: glory (to God) in the highest] (Lat: ex-KEL-sees; It: ex-CHEL-sees) The greater DOXOLOGY, or angelic hymn, based on Luke 2:14*. Used in many liturgies, it is the second item of the ordinary of the RC MASS.

GLORIA PATRI [Lat: glory (be) to the father] The lesser DOXOLOGY; it is part of many Western liturgies, including the RC divine office. Other doxologies include the *gloria tibi* (glory to thee), used in EO and Anglican liturgies.

GLOSS [Grk: difficult word; language; tongue] See EDITOR.

GLOSSOLALIA [Grk: speaking in/with tongues] (gloss-o-LAYL-ya) GIFT OF TONGUES.

GNOSTICISM [Grk: knowledge] (NOSS-ti-sizm) (1) The belief that the material world is evil, unreal, and/or the creation of the demiurge; and that the best human goal is to escape from concrete existence and be rejoined with the godhead through esoteric, mystical knowledge. (2) A movement, based on the blending of the dualisms of Persian theology and Greek metaphysics, which was contemporary with and absorbed into early Christianity by some theologians, though it was condemned by the church. See DOCETISM.

GOSPEL [OE: good news/story] (1) Any of the first four books of the NT. (2) A title for some of the books of the NT APOCRYPHA. (3) The message taught by Jesus and the apostles (Matt. 4:23*). The Greek word is *evangelion:* good news.

GRACE [Lat: favor, pleasure] The English translation of the Vulgate *gratia* (Lat: GRAH-ti-a; It: GRAH-tsi-a), Greek *charis* (CAH-ris), and Hebrew *hen* (hayn). (1) A complex, controversial theological concept, usually meaning unmerited divine favor, a free gift to individuals, usually leading to salvation through justification or election, thus reuniting the person with God (Rom. 3:23*). (2) A prayer, usually at a meal, thanking God and asking for a blessing.

GREEK ORTHODOX A specific branch of EO Christianity, but also a term loosely used to include all EO branches because they use the Greek Bible, as distinct from Western Christianity. The term *Eastern Orthodox* is itself similarly used to represent all Orthodox sects, though some are now Western; e.g., those that broke away from a Communist-dominated establishment. Other acceptable terms are *Orthodox Catholic* and *Byzantine Rite.* See ORTHODOX and UNIAT.

HAGGADA(H)/AGGADA(H) [Heb: story] (h/ah-gah-DAH) (1) Instructive stories in RABBINIC LITERATURE, as distinct from HALAKAH. (2) The book used to conduct the Passover SEDER, containing such stories about the holiday.

HAGIOGRAPHA [Grk: holy/sacred writings] (hag-i-OGG-ra-fa) KETUBIM.

HALAKAH [Heb: way] (hah-lah-KAH) (1) RABBINIC LITERATURE, mainly found in the Talmud and Midrash, that consists of laws and customs, including comments upon them; distinguished from HAGGADA. It is also called oral Law (or part of the oral Law)—both those TRADITIONS that interpret the written Law/Torah and those that are not linked to Torah but are believed to have been communicated orally to Moses. (2) All binding Jewish law, including both oral and written Law. Halakah (in either definition) is considered by Orthodox Jews to be equally sacred and authoritative as the Bible. A halakic Jew practices halakic Judaism: orthodoxy.

HALLELUJAH [Heb: praise (ye) the Lord] A Jewish and Christian doxological expression of joy. Alleluia: the Latin title and first word of a prayer, part of the ordinary of the RC mass.

HALO [Grk: disk of, or aura around, the sun or moon] *In art,* a gold or white area or rays of light around a person's head: (a) circular with three spokes, or triangular for persons of the Trinity and their symbols (lamb, dove); (b) circular without spokes (i.e., heavenly) for saints; (c) square (mundane) for living people who are revered. Both the halo (also called nimbus) and the MANDORLA are AUREOLES, a term sometimes limited to light that emanates from the entire body.

HAMITES [Heb: of Ham (son of Noah)] (1) Traditionally, descendants of Ham, usually meaning the black tribes of North Africa, though popularly extended to all black people. (2) Speakers of Hamitic languages.

HANUKKA(H)/CHANUKAH [Heb: dedication] (hah-noo-KAH, HAH-noo-ka) The eight-day festival of dedication/lights, celebrating the victory of the Maccabees over their oppressive Syrian ruler, Antiochus Epiphanes (165 B.C.E.), and the cleansing and rededication of the temple, which he defiled. It usually occurs in December (II Macc. 10:5*). See MENORAH.

HARROWING OF HELL The belief that Jesus descended into hell or LIMBO between his burial and resurrection and freed captive souls, especially the OT saints; a popular subject for MYSTERY plays.

In art, Jesus, large and in gleaming garments and sometimes carrying the banner of the resurrection, stands at the entrance of (sometimes trampling the gates) of a cavelike place crowded with people who are rushing to meet him. Sometimes the devil is shown—small, black, and cowering. The scene is also called "Christ in Limbo."

HASIDEANS/ASSIDEANS [Heb: pious ones] (h/ah-sid-DEE-anz) A term used to distinguish early HASIDIM from later movements. They were conservative Jews (third and second c. B.C.E.) opposed to HELLENIZATION, both from without (e.g., Syrian rulers; see HANNUKAH) and from within (Jewish modernizers and assimilationists).

HASIDIM/CHASSIDIM (Hah-sid-DEEM, hah-SEED-im) (1) HASIDEANS. (2) A modern Jewish movement (from ca. 1750) opposing both rationalism and Torah literalism, in favor of mysticism (often CABALISTIC), closeness to God, and joy in worship. (3) Between the early and late movements, individual Jews and groups have been called Hasidim, especially a minor movement in the thirteenth and fourteenth c.

HEILSGESCHICHTE [Ger: salvation history] (HIGHLZ-ge-SHISH-teh) A view of biblical history—originated by biblical scholars and further developed by Christian theologians—as a series of God's saving acts, beginning with the creation and ending with the PAROUSIA, the central event being the resurrection of Jesus.

HELL [ON: hidden realm of the dead] The English translation for biblical *Sheol, Gehenna,* and *Hades;* it refers variously to a vague and neutral grave/depths/afterworld; a place or state of punishment; or the place of fire, brimstone, and eternal torment (as described by Dante). Christian sects interpret the term variously, as physical or spiritual, eternal or revocable, literal or metaphorical. The Koran describes hell in concrete terms for Moslems.

HELLENIZED JEWS Those Jews, especially the ones living away from Jerusalem or Judea, during the Hellenistic period (after Alexander, d. 323 B.C.E.), whose first language was Greek and who were influenced by Greek culture. Among other things, they translated Hebrew scripture into Greek and produced Philo (20 B.C.E.–ca. 50 C.E.), the first major figure in a long line of writers who sought to bring together biblical theology and Greek philosophy. They were opposed by the HASIDEANS and, later, by the PHARISEES.

HENOTHEISM [Grk: one god] (HENN-o-thee-ism) Belief in one god as supreme among many, as distinguished from monotheism, which is belief in only one god.

HERESY [Grk: choice] A doctrine, held by a member of a sect, that is contrary to the sect's established beliefs or dogma.

HERMENEUTICS [Grk: interpretation] (her-men-OO-tics) (1) The study of methodological principles of biblical interpretation—not only EXEGESIS (what it originally meant) but also exposition (what it means to people's lives). Thus hermeneutics is especially interested in principles, methods, and rules of interpretation from one historical context to another (e.g., the Hebrew scriptures were understood differently by the NT and the rabbinic writers). (2) The discipline of interpreting the Bible's meaning for the modern world.

HEXATEUCH The first six books of the Bible taken as a unit.

HIERARCHY [Grk: sacred government] (HIGH-er-ark-y) (1) An ecclesiastical establishment that is usually (but not always) authoritarian, with the flow of power from the top to the lower ranks. (2) CELESTIAL HIERARCHY.

HISTORICITY OF THE BIBLE The belief that the Bible reports actual events, including miracles and seeming anachronisms and inconsistencies; an aspect of biblical literalism, which is opposed to either reading the Bible metaphorically or attempting to explain it naturalistically or by human logic.

HOLY GRAIL [MF: holy bowl] The legendary cup/chalice owned by Joseph of Arimathea, used by Jesus at the Last Supper, used to catch the blood from his wounds on the cross, brought by Joseph of Arimathea (or a relative) to England, sought by King Arthur's knights and others, and now claimed to be in at least three places: Montserrat, Valencia, and Genoa. Wagner's *Parsifal* is one of the many variant stories.

HOLY OF HOLIES [Heb: most holy place; Lat: *sanctum sanctorum*] (1) The innermost chamber of the ancient tabernacle and temple, containing the ark of the covenant, and entered once a year by the high priest on the Day of Atonement. It is represented today in synagogues by the ark containing the Torah scrolls. (2) In EO churches, the raised area behind the ICONOSTASIS, containing the altar table, where the body and blood of Jesus are always kept.

HOLY ORDERS See ORDER.

HOLY WEEK See PASSION.

HOMILETICS [Grk: conversation] (ho-mi-LET-ics) The study of the principles of preparation and delivery of effective sermons—usually drawing modern theological applications and moral imperatives from a biblical passage and/or a topical theme. Homily: a shorter and less formal kind of preaching than a sermon, almost always on a biblical text.

HOSANNA [Heb: do save (us)] (ho-ZANN-a) An exclamation of joy/praise, said/sung in Jewish and Christian liturgies (Ps. 118:25; Matt. 21:9).

HOST [Lat: sacrificial victim] The Eucharist wafer or bread (before or) after consecration. The term sometimes includes the wine.

HYMN [Grk: song of praise] A religious poem giving praise and glory to God, sung in Jewish and Christian services. (1) Narrowly defined, those poems with biblical texts, such as anthems, canticles, and psalms. (2) Broadly, these plus nonscriptural poems, such as carols and others—some composed by famous religious figures; e.g., Ambrose, Gregory the Great, "the Venerable Bede," Bernard of Cluny, Bernard of Clairvaux, Luther, the brothers Wesley.

ICON/EIKON [Grk: image] (IGH-con) A venerated religious picture hung on the ICONOSTASIS of EO churches and in homes, usually of the deity, Mary, or a saint. Icons are done in a stereotyped Byzantine manner according to set rules, on wood (sometimes metal or mosaic), sometimes with an enshrining metal dust cover.

ICONOCLASM [Grk: image breaking] (igh-CON-o-clazm) A movement (seventh to eighth c. C.E.) that destroyed sacred statues and paintings because of possible idolatry (Exod. 20:4*). An issue in the East/West schism, it strongly influenced the EO churches, where such statues never reappeared, although icons (paintings) returned after the movement was condemned in 787 C.E. A similar but limited movement appeared temporarily in RC churches during the Reformation.

ICONOSTASIS [Grk: image stand] (igh-con-OSS-ta-sis) (1) The partition or screen between the nave/worship area of EO churches and the apse/sanctuary/altar/bema/platform/eastern end. It is hung with icons and generally has three doors, the middle one usually flanked by images of Jesus and Mary. (2) A smaller background plaque for icons in the home, usually with a candle or lamp protruding forward.

IMMACULATE CONCEPTION [Lat: spotless] The RC dogma that Mary, when conceived by Anna, was free of original sin. The feast is December 8 (Luke 1:28*). EO doctrine holds that Mary was cleansed of original sin just before she conceived Jesus. Not to be confused with the VIRGIN BIRTH of Jesus.

IMMANUEL/EMANUEL [Heb: God (is) with us] (im-MANN-yoo-el) A title applied by Christians to Jesus as the Messiah/Christ (especially at Christmas, as the Christ child), in the belief that he is the person predicted by Isaiah, who first uses the term in the Bible (Isa. 7:14*).

IMMERSION [Lat: dipping] BAPTISM by dipping or completely plunging a person into water. A variant is TRINE immersion. EO churches insist on complete submersion (Matt. 28:19*).

IMPANATION [Lat: becoming bread] (im-pan-AY-shun) The doctrine that in the EUCHARIST ceremony the body of Jesus exists as a substance "hypostatically" [Grk: standing under] with the bread—on the model of the human and divine natures of Jesus/Christ. Similar to CONSUBSTANTIATION, it is contrasted with TRANSUBSTANTIATION. The parallel term for "the wine" is *invination*. (Luke 22:19*)

IMPRIMATUR [Lat: let it be printed] (im-prim-AH-toor) The permission granted by a RC bishop or his delegate to publish a book, usually on a religious subject. The word is printed at the front of the book, together with the NIHIL OBSTAT, which is a prerequisite for the imprimatur.

INCARNATION [Lat: being made flesh] The uniting of divinity and humanity in Jesus; the embodiment of the Logos/Word. That Jesus had two natures is a traditional Christian doctrine that has nevertheless caused controversy, heresy, and schism. (John 1:14*)

INDULGENCE [Lat: kindness, favor granted] In RC belief, after PENANCE, contrition, and remission/forgiveness of the guilt and eternal punishment for a mortal sin, an indulgence remits the temporal/temporary punishment that is still due on earth and in purgatory. Indulgences may be for the living or dead, full/plenary or partial (i.e., so many days' punishment remitted).

INERRANCY [Lat: not wandering] Freedom from error; often applied to the Bible, in its present or its original/pristine form.

INFALLIBILITY (1) Of the Bible: a traditional Christian doctrine and an emphasis of conservative Protestantism; inerrancy. (2) Of the EO Church: applied to doctrinal decisions of an ecumenical council. (3) Of the RC Church: when an ecumenical council or the magisterium (bishop's council) makes a pronouncement that is ratified by the pope. (4) Of the pope, who, speaking *ex cathedra* [Lat: from the chair (of Peter)], is considered by RCs as inspired and infallible, as successor to Peter (Matt. 16:18*). See AUTHORITY.

INFUSION [Lat: pouring on] BAPTISM by pouring, usually water, on the communicant (usually on the head). The term is preferred to *pouring* and *affusion* by RCs, for whom it implies that supernatural grace is infused into the soul.

IN PRINCIPIO [Lat: in the beginning] (Lat, in prin-KIPP-ee-o; It: in prin-CHIP-ee-o) Opening words in the Vulgate for both Genesis 1:1 and John 1:1.

INSPIRATION [Lat: breathing into] The doctrine that the speaker or writer is consciously or unconsciously inspired or guided by divine influence or the Holy Spirit. Sects differ about how far to extend the concept of inspiration (and its resultant INFALLIBILITY and AUTHORITY) beyond the Bible: to tradition, the church, church councils, papal *ex cathedra* pronouncements, "the rabbis," the "comforter," postbiblical prophets, and/or other individuals—including recipients of the gift of tongues.

INSPIRED TEXT One that has divine AUTHORITY. The Bible, so considered, is the revealed truth, the Word of God. The concept is interpreted variously: from inerrant literalness to divinely directed metaphor; from direct dictation by God or the Holy Spirit to the holiness of fallible authors. These ranges apply to both Christians and Jews.

INTERPOLATION [Lat: polish, furbish between] (in-TER-po-LAY-shun) See EDITOR.

INTERTESTAMENTAL [Lat: between the (Old and New) Testaments] (IN-ter-TESS-ta-MENT-al) The period of about two hundred years (ca. 150

B.C.E.–ca. 50 C.E.) assigned by critical scholars between the composition of the last book of the Hebrew Bible (possibly Daniel) and the first ones of the NT (possibly some Pauline Letters).

INTROIT [Lat: entrance] (in-TRO-it, IN-tro-it) (1) The opening liturgy of some religious services. (2) The first part of the proper of a RC mass, usually consisting of an antiphon/chant, a verse from a psalm, and the Gloria Patri. (3) The antiphon itself.

J-SOURCE The tradition, oral and/or written, presumably used by the redactors of the Hebrew Bible or by the hypothetical YAHWIST WRITER. The discrepancy between *J* and *Yahwist* comes from the German transliteration of the Hebrew into Jahweh.

JACOB'S DREAM/LADDER *In art,* a representation of Jacob asleep on the ground, a ladder nearby reaching into the clouds, and winged angels on the ladder.

JANSENISM A French seventeenth and eighteenth c. reform movement by followers of Jansen (1585–1638). It opposed the Jesuits as having fallen away from Augustine's teaching on predestination. It held that redemption and rejection were determined solely by God and that people had no free will in the matter. The movement was responsible for the Port Royal circle, which included Pascal. Condemned as a RC heresy, it survives in Holland among self-styled RCs, who also reject the doctrines of the immaculate conception and papal infallibility. The term is also applied pejoratively to rigorous but negative, forbidding moral attitudes.

JEHOVAH A transliteration of the TETRAGRAMMATON formed by adding to the originally unpointed (vowel-less) Hebrew consonants vowels from the word ADONAI, with minor changes. Jehovah's Witnesses favor this term.**

JEW [Heb: of Judah] (1) Narrowly applied: people of the postexilic era and their descendants, as distinguished from the early Hebrews and later Israelites; sometimes, dated back to the southern kingdom, some four hundred years before the Exile. (2) Broadly, any member of the ethnic group, from Abraham, the first Jew, until today. Most Jews have acknowledged a common Semitic origin and history and have identified with the religion of Judaism, based on the Hebrew scriptures, but the term cannot be precisely defined to satisfy everyone.**

JEWISH CHRISTIANS The earliest Christians, Jewish followers of Jesus, who continued to be Jews, interpreting him within their Jewish tradition. They are differentiated from Hellenistic/GENTILE CHRISTIANS, who were not Jews, and from HELLENIZED JEWS, who might or might not follow Jesus.

JOHANNINE WRITINGS (jo-HANN-in, JO-ha-nine) Tradition attributes the Gospel of John, the three Epistles of John, and the Revelation of John the Divine (or Apocalypse of John the Apostle) to one writer, the apostle who was the brother of James and son of Zebedee, called the beloved disciple and given the care of Mary by Jesus on the cross. Critical scholars generally posit at least two, if not three, different writers for these books.

JOHN THE BAPTIST (PREACHING) *In art,* a representation of a gaunt figure dressed in an animal skin and holding a cross-shaped staff, alone or with an audience.

JONAH *In art,* a representation of Jonah: (1) being cast into the sea from the ship, into the waiting jaws of a sea serpent or whale; (2) being vomited onto the shore; (3) lying under the gourd tree. Often all three scenes appear in one piece of art.

JUBILATE DEO [Lat: make a joyful noise to the Lord] (joo-bi-LAH-tay DAY-oh) Latin title and first words of Psalm 100* (99 in the Vulgate), sung as an alternative to the Benedictus at the morning prayer. Jubilate Sunday: in the RC Church calendar, the third Sunday after Easter, so called because the introit begins with Psalm 66, whose first word in Latin is *jubilate*.

JUDGMENT OF SOLOMON *In art,* a representation of Solomon on his throne, the two women, the baby between them, and usually an executioner with a raised sword (I Kings 3:25).

JUDITH AND HOLOFERNES (holl-o-FER-neez) *In art,* a representation of Judith: (1) outside the tent of Holofernes, holding his severed head, sometimes accompanied by her maidservant; (2) inside the tent, cutting off the head of the sleeping Holofernes.

JUSTIFICATION [making right] Declaring, judging, or making a person just/righteous/worthy of salvation, through: (1) the person's faith in Jesus' saving sacrifice and his or her own life of loving acceptance of God's will; (2) being freed from the guilt of a serious sin; and/or (3) the actual saving of the person's soul by the infusion of God's grace (Rom. 3:23*, 28*).

KADDISH [Aram: holy] (1) A Jewish prayer praising God used at various points in the liturgy. (2) A Jewish prayer, essentially the same, recited by mourners.

KERYGMA [Grk: proclamation] (ke-RIG-ma) In Christianity, the act of preaching the gospel and/or the message itself—both the announcement and the exhortation. It is preaching, as contrasted with teaching, confrontation for commitment vs. instruction in beliefs and practices. Cf. DIDACHE, CATECHISM. Scholars see two emphases: (1) christological—the earthly ministry of Jesus and its importance for people's way of life. This is differentiated from a historical interest in the life of Jesus. (2) The "cross side"—the passion and resurrection and their saving/redemptive importance for people.

KERYGMATIC (keh-rig-MAT-ic) A kind of preaching or proclamation in which the hearer or reader is personally confronted with the implications of God's activity in history; evangelizing/missionary/hortatory teaching, as distinct from DIDACHE/ethical teaching.

KETUBIM [Heb: writings] (ke-too-BEEM, ke-TOO-beem) The third division of the Hebrew Bible, following Torah and Nebi-im, with which it forms the TANAK.**

KISS OF PEACE Also called pax [Lat: peace] and the kiss of love/charity. A ceremonial embrace or kiss at Communion/Mass or other worship service—especially the LOVE FEAST. People kiss one another or (RC) the pax tablet, an image of Jesus or some other designated object. (Rom. 16:16*)

KOINE [Grk: common] (koy-nay) The language spoken by common people in Hellenistic Greece and elsewhere in the Roman Empire and used in the NT. It is contrasted with the literary Greek of the poets, philosophers, and historians whose writings are extant.

KOINONIA [Grk: community] (koy-no-NEE-ya) The Christian fellowship of believers, with an emphasis on common religious commitment and spiritual community; similar to AGAPE.

KOSHER [Heb: proper, fit] (KOH-sher) Food permitted and/or prepared according to Mosaic laws. Orthodox Jews observe these dietary laws, as elaborated in rabbinic literature, as do many Conservative and some Reform Jews, with varying degrees of strictness. Some Christian Sabbatarians observe the Mosaic laws. (Lev. 11:2,* 17:14*)

KYRIE ELEISON [Grk: Lord, have mercy] (KEE-ree-ay ay-LAY-ee-son) (1) An invocation, said/sung in Greek before the Gloria as the first item of the ordinary of the Latin RC mass. (2) A response, used in Episcopal, Lutheran, and EO worship services.

L-SOURCE The hypothetical tradition, oral and/or written, to which the writer of the Gospel of Luke may have had access apart from the other evangelists. It is generally characterized by an interest in people who are discriminated against.

LAST DAYS END TIME.

LAST SUPPER The synoptics are clear that it was a Passover SEDER; John's Gospel is ambiguous.

In art, some representations focus on the Eucharist, but most depict the moment when Jesus announces his coming betrayal: He and the apostles are at table, John is next to him, and Judas is set apart. Many post-Renaissance artists follow da Vinci's arrangement.

LAUDS [Lat: praises] (Lat: louds; Eng: lawds) A CANONICAL HOUR, the dawn office/prayers. The name derives from the opening word in Latin (*laudate:* praise ye) of Psalms 148*, 149, and 150, which are traditionally central to the office.

LENT [ME: springtime] (Latin name: *quadrigesima*) In Western Christianity, the forty-day penitential period of self-denial before Easter, beginning with Ash Wednesday. The EO lent lasts fifty days, beginning seven weeks before Easter.

LEVITICUS [Lat: (law) of the Levites] (le-VITT-i-cus) The third book of the Bible.

LEX TALIONIS [Lat: law of retaliation] (tal-i-O-nis) Originally established to limit revenge (Exod. 21:23), it was later taken literally and became an embarrassment. The RABBIS repudiated it by reinterpreting the passage; Jesus did so on his own authority (Matt. 5:39).

LILITH [Heb: proper name; the context implies a predatory night bird or, from Assyrian myth, an evil demon] (LILL-ith) (1) In rabbinic legend, the evil first wife of Adam. (2) In Jewish mysticism, a succubus, consort of Satan, killer of infants, and symbol of lust. (Isa. 34:14*)

LIMBO [Lat: border] In RC doctrine, a neutral place or condition outside hell for those who have not sinned but whose Original Sin has not been washed away by baptism. It is often divided into the limbos of the Fathers (OT saints freed in the HARROWING OF HELL) and of children (for all ages, mostly infants). (Luke 16:22*)

LITANY [Lat: entreaty] (LIT-a-ny) A prayer of invocation and supplication read/sung by a clergyman with alternating responses by the congregation, usually with a repeated formula. Litanies are found in both Christian and Jewish liturgies.

LITERARY CRITICISM (1) Source analysis: the study of the process and of the purpose of creating and writing a document (particularly the Bible) or portion thereof. (2) The application to the Bible and/or its parts the same principles of analysis that are used by literary scholars with other works of literature.**

LITURGY [Grk: public duty, service] (LIT-er-jee) The prescribed ritual for public worship; sometimes only the Eucharist. It is neglected by some sects that prefer to emphasize preaching, evangelism, and less formalized worship.

LOGIA [Grk: little words] (LO-jee-a) (1) Plural of *logion* (LO-gee-on), a saying or teaching attributed to Jesus, which may be from one sentence to an entire discourse in length. (2) Collections of such sayings, such as one from the second or third c. on papyrus, found in Egypt. (3) A specific collection, such as one mentioned by Papias (ca. 60–ca. 130 C.E.) and considered the hypothetical basis of the Gospels, or of Matthew in particular, though thought by some to refer to the apocryphal Gospel of Thomas.

LOGOS [Grk: word, reason] (LO-goss, LOG-oss) (1) The Word that was made flesh as Jesus (John 1:18). (2) The second person of the Trinity, in traditional Christian theology. (3) The ideal truth, in Christian Science. (4) The personification of *wisdom* in the OT and Apocrypha. (5) Similar concepts of the "Word" as God's activity and expression, in rabbinic literature, Philo, and Jewish mysticism.

LORD'S DAY Sunday, the first day of the week, set aside because of the resurrection (Matt. 28:1*) and early Christian worship (Acts 20:7; I Cor. 16:27); also to distinguish Christianity from Judaism. The name comes from Revelation 1:10. See SABBATH.

LORD'S PRAYER PATER NOSTER.

LORD'S SUPPER The term preferred by many Protestant sects for the EUCHARIST ceremony or service.

LOVE FEAST AGAPE.

LUCIFER [Lat: light bearer, Roman god of the morning star] In traditional Christianity, Satan, chief of the fallen angels. The identification is derived from the Latin translation of the Hebrew for the fallen "day star" in Isaiah 14:12, as referred to by Luke (10:18*).

M-SOURCE The hypothetical tradition, oral and/or written, to which the writer of the Gospel of Matthew may have had access apart from the other evangelists. It is generally characterized by its many parables and sayings.

MADONNA [It: my lady] *In art,* a representation of Mary, often holding the infant Jesus, sometimes with minor figures as well. It is commonly found in a "madonna window" of RC churches and on the EO ICONOSTASIS.

MAGI [Grk: wise men, astrologers] (MAY-jigh) Plural of *magus* (MAY-gus), possibly a Persian priest. See ADORATION OF THE MAGI.

MAGNIFICAT [Lat: (my soul) magnifies] (mag-NIFF-i-caht) Latin title and first word of a canticle uttered by Mary (Luke 1:46*). It has a strong flavor of Hebrew poetry. It is sung especially at vespers/evensong.

MANDORLA [It: almond] (MAN-dor-la) *In art,* an almond-shaped aureole (circle of light), usually surrounding the entire body of the divinity or a saint.

It is differentiated from the HALO, an aureole that surrounds only the head.

MANICHAEISM (man-i-KEE-izm) A dualistic religion founded in Persia by Mani (ca. 242 C.E.) from elements of Zoroastrianism, Buddhism, and Christian GNOSTICISM. One of its central doctrines is that the universe (and man) consists of two irreducibly antagonistic principles: good, light, and God on one side; evil, darkness, Satan, matter, and the flesh on the other. It flourished in the Roman Empire and has influenced many Christian groups, though considered heretical by the RC Church.

MANUSCRIPT [Lat: hand written] An early hand-written copy of part or all of a biblical text, invaluable to scholarship. The term includes papyrus and parchment scrolls and CODICES; mostly in Hebrew, Greek, Old Latin, Syriac, and Vulgate Latin. Uncials: third to tenth c. manuscripts written in capital, unconnected letters, usually not separated into words nor punctuated. Cursives/miniscules: those with letters connected and words separated, as in modern handwriting; a later development (after ca. 800 C.E.).

MARK OF CAIN An unspecified mark placed on Cain by God to protect him from people who might kill him (Gen. 4:15). Tradition has placed the mark on his forehead and has changed its significance to a brand of shame. Mormons combined it with Noah's curse upon Ham's son, Canaan.**

MARKAN/MARCAN PRIORITY The theory, accepted by most NT critical scholars, that the Gospel of Mark was written down before the other Gospels and that Matthew and Luke had access to it.

MARTYR [Grk: witness] One who sacrifices one's life for being a "witness" for a religion. Stephen, considered the first Christian martyr (Acts 7:54-60), was canonized, like most of the early ones who suffered similar fates. Martyrology: a calendar of their holy days. Examples of early Jewish martyrdom are recorded in II Maccabees 6, 7.*

MASORETIC TEXT/MASORA(H) [Heb: tradition] (maz-o-RET-ic; ma-ZO-ra) The authoritative Hebrew text of the Jewish Bible, finally set (seventh to tenth c.) according to rules for transcription developed by the Masoretes (MAZ-o-reets), who also added vowels to the previously purely consonantal writing. It is accepted as canon by Jewish tradition, and by Protestant Bibles (with some changes), in preference to the SEPTUAGINT, which is accepted by the RC and EO churches.

MASS [Lat: dismissal] The name derives from the prayer near the end: *ite, missa est congregatio* ("go, the congregation is dismissed"). It is the preferred RC term for the EUCHARIST, Lord's Supper, (Holy) Communion. It is divided into the ORDINARY and the PROPER. Low Mass: celebrated by the priest alone, in simplified form. High/solemn Mass/MISSA SOLEMNIS: includes incense, music, acolytes, deacons. Pontifical mass: celebrated by a bishop, cardinal, or abbot.

MASSACRE/SLAUGHTER OF THE INNOCENTS *In art,* usually a violent, bloody scene of cruel soldiers, mutilated babies, and agonizing mothers (Matt. 2:16*). The infants are referred to as the "holy innocents."

MATINS [Lat: morning] (MAT-inz) The chief and longest CANONICAL HOUR: (1) The RC midnight office, usually combined with lauds. (2) The morning prayer for Episcopalians. Originally, it was a vigils service (the midnight before a holiday).

MENORA(H) [Heb: candlestick] (men-O-ra) A seven-branched candelabrum that stood in the ancient tabernacle and temple and stands in many synagogues today. *In Christian art,* it symbolizes Jesus, the light of the world. The menorah used for HANUKKAH is called a *hanukkiyyah* and has eight main candles or oil cups, one for each day of the holiday, plus a "servant" candle to light them.

MESSIAH [Heb: anointed (one)] (me-SIGH-ya; mess-ee-AN-ic; MESS-i-an-izm) (1) The expected personal king and deliverer of the Jews (still awaited today by Orthodox Jews). (2) The herald/symbol of a divinely established messianic age on earth (still awaited by most Jews). (3) The spiritual savior who establishes God's (messianic) kingdom. (4) Jesus, as that Christ [Grk: anointed] and savior. Theological interpretations and doctrines of both Jesus' messiahship and God's kingdom vary among Christians. (5) One of several "false" messiahs in Jewish history, including Bar Cocheba (second c. C.E. and Shabbetai Zevi (seventeenth c.). (6) One of several "new messiahs" within Christianity and Islam. See SALVATION and REDEMPTION.

MEZUZA(H) [Heb: doorpost] (me-ZOO-za) A small encased scroll (usually parchment) inscribed with Deuteronomy 6:4-9; 11:13-21.* It is affixed to the doorpost of buildings occupied by Jews: synagogues, home entrances, and (among Orthodox and some Conservative Jews) each room within. Sometimes it is worn around the neck, a modern practice.

MIDRASH [Heb: explanation] (MID-rahsh, mid-RAHSH) (1) Any Jewish exegesis, homily, or narrative on a biblical text; it may be either haggadah (edifying story) or halakah (precept). (Commonly used today to mean only the former.) (2) The collection of such RABBINIC WRITINGS (from fifth c. B.C.E. onward), much of it gleaned from the TALMUD. (3) Extending beyond the rabbinic literature, through the twelfth c.: commentaries on the earlier midrashim.

MILLENNIUM [Lat: 1,000 years] Also "millenium": 1,000. The period during which Jesus will reign over a righteous world (Rev. 20:2*).

MILLENNIALISM/MILLENARIANISM (mill-ENN-i-al-izm, mill-en-AYR-i-an-izm) A strong commitment to the doctrine that the MILLENNIUM is imminent. Also called adventism, chiliasm. Premillennialism: belief that the second coming/parousia, resurrection of the dead, and final judgment will precede the 1,000 years. Postmillenialism: belief that they will follow. Some believe that the millennium will come at some point among these events.

MINISTER [Lat: servant] A person ordained, or otherwise authorized, to conduct Christian worship, preach the gospel, and administer the sacraments: a priest, deacon, preacher, or other clergyman. The term is used most often in Protestant sects.

MIRACLE PLAY A medieval drama focusing on the wonder-working of a Christian saint or martyr. Sometimes the term includes mystery plays, which are usually considered a separate genre, mainly because of their subject matter. See also MORALITY PLAYS, which developed earlier than and flourished alongside miracle plays.

MIRACLE STORIES A genre of FORM-CRITICAL units in NT scholarship, generally having such common elements as setting, cure, and demonstration.

MISERERE [Lat: have mercy] (miz-e-RAY-reh) Latin title and first word of Psalm 51* (50, in the Vulgate), chief of the penitential psalms; it is usually chanted in the liturgy and often set to music.

MISHNA(H) [Heb: instruction] (MISH-na) A collection of rabbinic HALAKIC writings commenting on the Torah. It is considered part of the authoritative oral Law by Orthodox Jews and most Conservative Jews. Its redaction, completed according to tradition about 210 C.E., gave rise to the GEMARA, with which it comprises the TALMUD.

MISSAL (1) A book containing the texts of all the RC masses of the year, in Latin and/or the local language. (2) Any RC devotional book. See BREVIARY.

MISSA SOLEMNIS [Lat: solemn mass] High MASS. Choral masses are usually taken from the ORDINARY and include the following parts of the liturgy: Kyrie, Gloria, Sanctus and Benedictus, and Agnus Dei.

MOLOCH/MOLECH (MO-lek) The Hebrew name of an ancient pagan (Phoenician?) deity, whose worship called for child sacrifice in fire. A shrine was at the valley of Hinnom/GEHENNA outside Jerusalem. It is cited as the epitome of evil, although (or because?) some backsliding kings of Judah worshiped Moloch.

MORALITY PLAY A late medieval/early modern allegorical drama, especially popular in the fifteenth and sixteenth c., whose characters personify moral virtues, vices, and other abstractions (death, youth, etc.). Its purpose is moral teaching. Like the MIRACLE and MYSTERY play, it began as religious drama, sponsored by the clergy; it moved further into the secular repertoire, however, than the other two genres.

MORTAL SIN In RC doctrine, a serious or deadly sin committed willfully, thereby indicating loss of faith as well as virtue. It involves spiritual death, loss of divine grace, and eternal punishment (Matt. 12:32*). The only remedy is full confession and PENANCE. Sometimes the term is limited to the SEVEN DEADLY SINS; sometimes it goes beyond. It is contrasted with VENIAL SINS, which do not separate the sinner from God.

MYSTERY [Grk: religious initiation] (1) A religious truth, achieved only by revelation from God. (2) A term for Christian sacraments in EO churches, and formerly in RC. (3) A meditation on the ROSARY, of which there are fifteen mysteries of the faith, based on the lives of Jesus and Mary: five joyful, five sorrowful, and five glorious.

MYSTERY PLAY Earliest of the medieval religious drama genres, it centers on an episode from the Bible. Originally (ninth c.) a brief skit performed in the church, it expanded and moved to the church steps or yard, and finally to public squares and courtyards. Some English cycles of such plays survive and are periodically revived. Contemporary nativity and passion plays follow this tradition. See MIRACLE and MORALITY plays.

MYSTICISM (1) The theological or philosophical view that one can know God/ultimate reality/spiritual truth only by direct intuition or divine illumination rather than through rationalistic or empirical reasoning. (2) This doctrine plus a belief in the occult and in a required initiation into esoteric knowledge and rituals. Strong mystical strains have been found among Catholics, Protestants, Jews, and Moslems for many centuries.

NATIVITY *In art,* a representation of Mary and the infant in the manger, alone or with others. The child, in swaddling clothes, is the central focus, with Mary on a rude couch, a star above them, and sometimes Joseph lost in thought. Usually the scene includes an ox and an ass. When shepherds are added, it may alternatively be called the ADORATION OF THE SHEPHERDS. The adoration of the magi, though considered a nativity story and often depicted in the same setting, is not usually classified as a Nativity in art.

NATIVITY STORIES The collective name for those in Matthew 1 and 2 and Luke 1 and 2; a genre of FORM-CRITICAL units.

NAZARENE (1) A native or resident of Nazareth. (2) A title for Jesus. (3) The name of a sect. It is to be distinguished from NAZIRITE.

NAZIRITE/NAZARITE [Heb: consecrated (person)] In biblical times, a man under a lifetime (later, a temporary) vow to avoid drinking wine, cutting his hair, and touching a corpse; e.g., Samuel, Samson, John the Baptist, and some companions of Paul.

NEBI-IM [Heb: prophets] (ne-BEE-yim) The second division of the Hebrew Bible; together with TORAH and KETUBIM it makes up the TANAK.

NEOPLATONISM (NEE-o-PLAY-ton-izm) A semimystical religious philosophy, formulated by Plotinus (204–270 C.E.) and deriving from Platonic tradition and other elements. It emphasized the reality of the divine/spiritual world, of which our world is an emanation or a less real shadow, and the necessity for an ascetic life to reunite the soul to God. It shares many ideas with Christian and Jewish MYSTICISM; see GNOSTICISM, DOCETISM, CABALA.

NESTORIANS (ness-TORE-i-anz) An EO sect, followers of Nestorius (ca. 425 C.E.), who emphasized the independent reality and equal importance of both the human and divine Jesus—as when man and wife become "one flesh"—and held that Mary was not the mother of God but only of the human Jesus. The sect is called Chaldean Christians today. Other schismatics, the monophysites, said Jesus had only one completely fused nature; condemned by the 451 council, the view persists in the Jacobite church.

NICENE CREED (nigh-seen) The statement of fundamental religious beliefs that was formulated at the first ecumenical council, at Nicea/Nice, Asia Minor (325 C.E.) in response to a threat of ARIANISM, and was expanded at the next council. A further addition was not adopted by EO churches. It is the shortest and most widely accepted of the major CREEDS in Western Christianity; without the addition, it is also common among EO churches.

NIHIL OBSTAT [Lat: nothing hinders] A verbal formula indicating that an official RC censor finds the literature free of doctrinal or moral error. Necessary for an IMPRIMATUR, it may stand alone, however, as a more limited approval. It is usually printed at the front of a book or pamphlet.

NIMBUS HALO.

NOLI ME TANGERE [Lat: touch me not] (NO-lee may TAHN-ge-reh) *In art,* a representation of the risen Jesus, who is standing solemn and aloof, and of Mary Magdalene, standing or crouching in awe (John 20:16).

NONE/S [Lat: ninth (hour)] A RC CANONICAL HOUR, the midafternoon office/prayer. Its name is taken from the ancient reckoning of the hours of the day, beginning with dawn. Originally set for 3 P.M., it came to be said earlier, just after midday; hence our word *noon.*

NUNC DIMITTIS [Lat: now let (thy servant) depart] (noonk di-MITT-ees)

Latin title and first words of a canticle, Simeon's poem at Luke 2:29.* It is part of the RC compline office and the Episcopalian evening service; it is also used as a dismissal in other services.

OFFICE DIVINE OFFICE.

ORAL TRADITION Most critical scholars theorize that nearly all of the Bible existed, and was passed on, orally for varying periods of time before being written down. This is distinct from the Jewish oral Law (see HALAKAH) and from TRADITION.

ORANT/ORANS [Lat: praying (person)] (O-rant, O-ranz) *In art,* a figure standing upright, arms raised high, and looking toward heaven—the posture for prayer most often described in the Bible.

ORATORIO [Lat: prayer, speech] A dramatic musical composition for solo voices, chorus, and orchestra, sung in concert style; its words are usually based on scripture. Traditionally, it was first performed in the Oratory (place of prayer) of Philip Neri, in Rome (sixteenth c.).

ORDER (1) One of the nine grades of angels in the CELESTIAL HIERARCHY. (2) A religious body; e.g., brotherhood of monks, sisterhood of nuns. (3) A grade of Christian clergy/ministry. Qualifications, rites, powers, and duties of the clerical orders vary among sects: e.g., RC orders are major (priest/bishop, deacon, subdeacon) and minor (acolyte, exorcist, lector/reader, porter/door-keeper). EO are similar. Episcopalian are bishop, priest, deacon/deaconess, lay reader. Church government varies widely. (Acts 14:23*) (Holy) orders: the sacrament/ordinance of ordination.

ORDINANCE [Lat: arrangement] An established, authoritative religious ceremony/rite/practice that is not considered a SACRAMENT.

ORDINARY Prayers whose texts remain fairly constant for all occasions: (1) Part of the MASS; it includes the Kyrie, Gloria, Credo, Sanctus, and Agnus Dei. (2) Part of the BREVIARY.

ORIGINAL SIN (1) The sin of Adam (and Eve) in Eden (Gen. 3:6*). (2) The resulting congenital depravity/sin/tendency to sin inherited by their descendants (excepting Mary, for RCs, and Jesus, in most sects). For some Christian sects that hold this doctrine, baptism washes away this condition; for others, there must be a regeneration/rebirth; still others emphasize other requirements for SALVATION.

In art, a representation of Adam and Eve, with the tree, serpent, and apple. It is also called "Adam and Eve" and the "Fall of Man." Without Adam, it is the "Temptation of Eve." Without the serpent, it is usually the "Temptation of Adam."

ORTHODOX [Grk: right opinion] (1) Eastern Christian churches and their offspring in diaspora, as distinct from RC, Protestant, and other Western Christian churches. See GREEK ORTHODOX. (2) HALAKIC Jews, as distinct from Conservative, Reform, and Reconstructionist. (3) Sunnites in Islam, as distinct from Shi-ites. (4) Any religious position or group that proclaims itself (and may be considered by others) as AUTHORITATIVE according to its adherence to some original standard (usually of infallibility—of the Bible, the church, etc.), as opposed to error or heresy.

P-SOURCE The tradition, oral and/or written, presumably used by the redactors of the Pentateuch (or Hexateuch, including Joshua) or by the hypothetical PRIESTLY WRITER.

PAGAN [Lat: country person] (1) Ancient polytheist. (2) Modern polytheist/heathen. (3) A non-Christian. (4) Anyone who is not a Christian, Jew, or Moslem.

PALM SUNDAY The Sunday preceding Easter; the first day of holy week. It is also called Passion Sunday. The holiday is celebrated in commemoration of Jesus' ENTRY INTO JERUSALEM. Palmer: a medieval pilgrim to Jerusalem (the holy sepulcher) who brought back or wore a palm leaf as a token of his visit. (John 12:12*)

PANTHEISM [Grk: all god] The belief that all that is, is God: him, his being, his expression, his activity. The doctrine usually denies the existence of a divine personality or a transcendent being, thereby differing from *omnipresence.* It is especially associated with MYSTICISM.

PANTOCRATOR [Grk: ruler of all] (pan-TOCK-ra-tor) (1) *In Byzantine art,* especially icons, a picture of Jesus, half length, holding a book, and blessing with his right hand; often found in the dome of the church. (2) In Western art, the title is occasionally applied to a picture or sculpture otherwise entitled Maesta/Christ-in-Majesty/Christ-Enthroned.

PARABLE [Grk: juxtaposition, comparison] A figurative statement or story that teaches a religious truth. The best known of biblical parables are the "similitudes" of Jesus, most of which are either simple comparisons (it is like _____; as _____; when _____) or narratives (there was _____; a certain _____). The latter sometimes develop their metaphors into complete allegories. The images are generally homely, drawn from nature and everyday life, though sometimes, when the similitude is not clearly stated, as in an "example story," the audience misses the point.

PARACLETE [Grk: intercessor, comforter] (PAR-a-kleet) A title usually applied to the Holy Spirit as the COMFORTER (John 14:16, 26*), but also to Jesus as intercessor or advocate (I John 2:1).

PARADISE [Pers: enclosed park/garden] (1) The garden of Eden, the "earthly heaven." (2) Heaven, a place or state of bliss for the blessed. (3) A blissful place or stage prior to heaven (Dante's top of mount purgatory) or earthly paradise. For most Christians heaven is the promised "kingdom" of the NT. For Jews, it is a postbiblical concept: the abode of just souls. For Moslems, the Koran describes it materialistically.

PAROUSIA [Grk: presence] (par-oo-SEE-a) (1) The second coming/advent of Jesus to earth in power and glory. (2) This advent plus the establishment of the final kingdom of God, over which Jesus will reign both as king and as the Lord, after the judgment of the living and the risen dead. Sects differ over the time and order of these events (see MILLENNIALISM), as well as over the meaning of the kingdom of God (Matt. 24:29*); Rev. 20:2*). (3) The INCARNATION. (4) Jesus' embodiment in the (RC) church at the PENTECOST.

PASCHAL [Grk and Heb: pass over] (PASS-cal) Pertaining to the Passover or Easter.** The paschal lamb, slaughtered for the Passover, became the symbol for Jesus' sacrifice. The Greek word *pasch* and the Hebrew word *pesach* (PESS-ah) both apply either to the holiday or to the lamb (or symbolic bone at the Passover SEDER).

PASSION [Lat: suffering] (1) The sufferings and death of Jesus during the last week after the entry into Jerusalem. (2) The agony in Gethsemane and the crucifixion. (3) The suffering on the cross. (4) The narrative of these sufferings. (5) An oratorio or play about them. Passion play: a MYSTERY PLAY, performed at the Easter season, dramatizing these events. Passion week/holy week: (1) the week before Easter, beginning at Palm Sunday and including Maundy Thursday and Good Friday; (2) the week ending on Palm Sunday. Passion stories: a genre of FORM-CRITICAL units taken from the four Gospels.

PASSOVER A Jewish spring festival, of pilgrimage in ancient temple times, commemorating: (1) the angel of death's passing over the homes of Jews in the last plague, and (2) the subsequent liberation of the Jews from Egyptian slavery. Religious interpretations are given to elements of earlier spring festivals: (1) agricultural—the early/barley harvest (festival of unleavened bread/*matzot*); (2) pastoral—firstlings of the flocks (the PASCHAL holiday of *pesach*). The holiday starts with a SEDER and lasts eight days (or seven, in some cases). (Lev. 23:5*)

PASTORAL EPISTLES [Lat: letters of/to a shepherd] (PASS-to-ral) Pauline Epistles on pastoral matters, from Paul to individual pastors: I and II Timothy and Titus. Some critical scholars dispute the Pauline authorship of one or more of these.

PATER NOSTER [Lat: our father] (Lat/It: PAH-ter NO-ster; Eng: PAT-er NOSS-ter) Latin title and first words of a universal Christian prayer; usually called the "Lord's Prayer" by Protestants and the "Our Father" by RCs. RCs omit the closing doxology of Matthew 6:13*b* ("For thine is the kingdom . . . "), adding it as a response in the mass.

PATRIARCH [Grk: ruling father] (PAY-tree-ark) (1) In the OT, Abraham, Isaac, and Jacob; sometimes adding Joseph or all twelve brothers; sometimes expanded to include major earlier figures, from Adam to Noah. (2) The chief bishop of various EO and Uniat churches; originally five, there are now eight. (3) One of the Mormon priesthood of Melchizedek (Ps. 110:4*).

PATRISTIC [Grk: of fathers] (pa-TRISS-tic) Pertaining to the FATHERS OF THE CHURCH. Patrology/patristics: the study of the church fathers and of their writings.

PAULINE EPISTLES [Grk: Paul's letters] Traditionally: Romans, I and II Corinthians, Galatians, Ephesians, Philippians, Colossians, I and II Thessalonians, I and II Timothy, Titus, Philemon, Hebrews. Of these fourteen, three are called PASTORAL. Those whose authorship is questioned are sometimes called DEUTERO-PAULINE. Pauline Epistles are distinguished from CATHOLIC EPISTLES.

PELAGIANISM (pell-AY-ji-an-izm) A doctrine, originated by Pelagius (ca. 400 C.E.), denying inherited original sin and predestination, and emphasizing freedom of will to sin or not, to merit the "grace" needed for salvation. Baptism is also reinterpreted, as uniting a person with Jesus/Christ but unnecessary to enter heaven.

PENANCE [Lat: sorrow, penalty] (1) A RC sacrament (now also called "reconciliation"), the equivalent of the EO sacrament of confession. It consists of required steps: PENITENCE and REPENTANCE for a sin, confession to a priest, performance of the penalty imposed by the confessor, and absolution. It is the most common means for the REMISSION OF SINS. (2) The punishment itself, imposed by the church for the sin.

PENITENCE Contrition/sorrow for a sin. In RC belief, imperfect contrition, motivated by fear of punishment, cannot lead to salvation; perfect contrition grows out of love of God, recognition of one's failure to respond to his grace. Perfect penitence must lead to REPENTANCE, necessary for the sacrament of PENANCE/reconciliation (RC) or confession (EO).

PENITENTIAL PSALMS Septuagint/Vulgate: Numbers 6, 31, 37, 50, 101, 129, 142. Masoretic: Numbers 6, 32, 38, 51, 102, 130, 143. So designated in RC liturgy.

PENTATEUCH [Grk: five scrolls] (PEN-ta-took) (1) The first five books of the Bible, also called the "five books of Moses." (2) These books constitute the first of the three major parts of the TANAK, the Jewish Bible, and are called TORAH/Law/teaching or *humash* [Heb: five (books)].

PENTECOST [Grk: fiftieth (day)] (1) The Jewish festival of SHAVUOT.** (2) The Christian festival commemorating the descent of the Holy Spirit on the apostles on the occasion of the Jewish festival (Acts 2:1*). Also called Trinity Sunday by EO and Whitsunday by Episcopalians and others. It is considered by RCs to be the birthday of the church (see PAROUSIA). See DESCENT OF THE HOLY SPIRIT.

PENTECOSTALISM (pen-te-KOSS-tal-izm) An emphasis of some Christian sects and of movements within others, sharing most of these characteristics: belief in spiritual baptism and faith healing; charismatic speaking in tongues; conservative/fundamentalist attitude toward the Bible; strongly spiritual response to one's faith. Pentecostal: pertaining to a person, group, belief, or practice identified with pentecostalism; a member of such a group is sometimes called a pentecostal. (Acts 2:1*)

PERICOPE [Grk: cut around] (peh-RICK-o-pee) (1) A section of scripture used in church as a reading or as a text for a sermon. (2) A separate unit of the Bible, or other ancient writing, for examination by scholars.

PHARISEES [Aram: separated (ones)] (FAIR-i-seez) (1) A Jewish popular party (ca. 150 B.C.E.–ca. 100 C.E.). They were opponents of HELLENISTIC assimilationists but distinct from the anti-Roman, activist Zealots and the ascetic Essenes. They were mainly contrasted with the upper class, largely Hellenized SADDUCEES, with whom they differed in matters of religion. Distinctively, they were committed to both the written and oral Law/tradition; believed in the immortality of the soul, bodily resurrection of the dead, punishment and reward after death, the existence of angels, and an imminent messiah; made considerable ethical advances in reinterpreting the Mosaic law; and eventually became the dominant force in normative Judaism. (2) Prime Jewish enemies of Jesus and his followers. This pejorative picture of the Pharisees (and scribes, who were also guardians of tradition) in the NT emphasizes the bitter family feud between two factions, each claiming exclusive legitimacy as the heir of Jewish tradition.**

PIETA [It: pity] (pee-ay-TAH) *In art,* a representation of Mary mourning over the dead body of Jesus, which is generally lying across her knees. When other people are included, it may be classified as a "Lamentation at the Cross," which does not necessarily show Jesus on Mary's lap.

PIETISM [Lat: dutiful] (PIGH-et-izm) (1) Originally, a movement in modern Christianity emphasizing the personal, spiritual, and practical revitalization of a faith that had become deadened by orthodoxy, formalism, and institutionalism. (2) Now the term is itself used pejoratively to characterize excessive, or even affected, devotional practices and experiences.

POSTMILLENNIALISM See MILLENNIALISM.

POURING INFUSION.

PREDESTINATION [Lat: determine beforehand] The doctrine: (1) that all events throughout eternity have been foreordained by divine decree and purpose; (2) in particular, that each person's eternal destiny is fixed. Sects differ especially about when God made the decision and what role, if any, free will plays in salvation; e.g., extreme Calvinism sees salvation only through the unmerited grace shown to the elect; Arminianism, in particular, challenges that position.

PREMILLENNIALISM See MILLENNIALISM.

PRESBYTER [Grk: elder] (PRESS-be-tair) An official position in the governance of a sect: (1) elder; (2) priest; (3) the congregation (in some translations of the Bible). (Acts 14:23*) Presbytery: (1) the ruling board in Presbyterianism, consisting of ministers (teaching elders) and elders (ruling elders) standing between the local session and the synod; (2) the area of the church reserved for the clergy; (3) the residence of a RC priest.

PRESENTATION IN THE TEMPLE *In art,* a representation of Mary holding the infant Jesus, in the temple, with a priest and, sometimes, with Simeon and/or Anna standing nearby. The scene is often entitled the "Purification" (of Mary). (Luke 2:22*)

PRIESTLY WRITER The author of a "P-document" posited by some critical scholars for portions of the Pentateuch or Hexateuch, usually dated in the time of the exile. The name derives from an emphasis on ancient worship traditions, preserved by the Jerusalem priesthood, reflected in the material so labeled. See P-SOURCE.

PROOF TEXTS Scriptural passages adduced as proof for a belief, usually that the OT foretells the coming of Jesus as the Christ. (Mal. 4:5*)

PROPER Prayers whose text varies according to the occasion: (1) part of the RC mass, including the Introit, Gradual, Alleluia, Offertory, and Communion; (2) part of the BREVIARY.

PROPHETS [Grk: speakers for] (1) Inspired spokesmen for God. (2) Predictors of the future. (3) Writers of the prophetic books of the OT (Jewish and Christian lists differ.**) (4) NEBI-IM; the second main division of the TANAK, the Jewish Bible, (5) Founders of some sects; e.g., Muhammed is "the Prophet" to Moslems; Joseph Smith, to Mormons (James 1:5*).

PROSELYTE [Grk: come near] (PROSS-e-light) A convert from one religion to another (RC: catechumen; see CATECHISM). Proselytism is a controversial issue between evangelizers and the sects whose members they seek to influence.

PSALTER (SOLL-ter) (1) The book of Psalms. (2) A book containing a vernacular translation of the psalms, often in rhyme and set to music. (3) The psalms, printed as a separate book or as a part of a prayer book; e.g., in the Breviary or in the *Book of Common Prayer.*

PSEUDEPIGRAPHA [Grk: falsely titled] (SOO-de-PIG-ra-fa) See APOCRYPHA. **

PURGATORY [Lat: cleansing (place)] In RC doctrine, the place or state of punishment in which a soul that died in God's grace may expiate VENIAL sins or satisfy the remainder of punishment due for MORTAL sins, after which it goes on to heaven. (II Macc. 12:14*) It is defined in the modern imagination by Dante. See INDULGENCE.

PURIM [Heb: lots] (POO-rim, poo-REEM) A Jewish festival, in late spring, commemorating the deliverance of the Jews from Haman's planned genocide, as recorded in the book of Esther.

Q-SOURCE The hypothetical tradition, oral and/or written, to which the writers of the Gospels of Matthew and Luke may have had access apart from Mark (and John). The name derives from *quelle* [Ger: source]. It generally consists of ethical and eschatological sayings attributed to Jesus.

QUO VADIS [Lat: Where are you going?] (kwo VAH-dis) Peter's question (John 16:5).

QUMRAN (coom-RAHN) The location of the caves where the Dead Sea Scrolls were found. The term refers to both the scrolls and the sect that lived nearby and probably produced them.

RABBI [Heb: my master] Also rab/rabban. (1) An unordained Jewish scholar and/or teacher of religious laws and ceremonies. (2) An ordained Jewish clergyman, mainly distinguished from Christian counterparts by having no priestly/sacerdotal function. (3) "The rabbis"—writers of RABBINIC LITERATURE.

RABBINIC LITERATURE The recorded expositions and interpretations of Jewish written and oral Law. Set down between ca. 200 and ca. 500 C.E., its sources go back to ca. 200 B.C.E. (e.g., Hillel d. ca. 10 C.E.). The best known documents are the TALMUD and the MIDRASH.

RAISING OF LAZARUS *In art,* a representation of Jesus with Lazarus, who is emerging from a sarcophagus or a burial cave and from his funeral windings; often with a man nearby holding his nose, sometimes with Mary, Martha, and neighbors (John 11:44).

RECENSION [Lat: revision] See VERSION.

REDACTION CRITICISM The study of how biblical and other ancient literary materials and/or traditions were organized, interpreted, and/or modified by an author, redacter, or EDITOR and the attempt to arrive at the perspective from which the writer shaped the work.

REDACTOR [Lat: bring together] (1) A writer who reduces oral tradition to writing. (2) EDITOR, as in redaction criticism.

REDEMPTION [Lat: buying back, ransoming] Deliverance, through divine intervention, from evil: physical—bondage, slavery, a corrupt world; or spiritual—sin, error, alienation from God. For Jews, the redeemer is God (and a future *messiah*). For Christians, it is Jesus, as savior, through his sacrifice, who reconciles humanity with God and redeems from sin. In both faiths, beliefs vary as to: what is required for redemption and who is redeemed, what people are redeemed from, and what people are redeemed for. See SALVATION.

REGENERATION [Lat: rebirth] Spiritual rebirth/renewal, usually believed to be helped by the Holy Spirit, from preoccupation with oneself or the world into God-centeredness. Most Christian sects consider this necessary for salvation, but differ: (1) whether it is a prerequisite for baptism, an accompaniment of it, or an unrelated gift of the Holy Spirit, and (2) whether it carries with it justification and sanctification or these are separate steps in preparation for eternal glory. (John 3:3*)

RELIGIOUS (noun: singular and plural) Person(s) bound by vows and devoted to a life of piety: a member of a religious order, congregation, or institute; male or female; clerical or lay; attached to a monastery or convent.

REMISSION OF SIN [Lat: sending back] Pardon/forgiveness of sins, generally through the (RC) sacrament of PENANCE/reconciliation.

REPENTANCE [Lat: being sorry, turning back] Turning away from sin and toward God, out of true PENITENCE/contrition; a change of heart and of behavior that is necessary for PENANCE/reconciliation.

REQUIEM [Lat: rest] (REK-wee-em) Latin title and first word of the opening prayer of the introit in the Latin mass for the dead, the requiem mass. It is sung mainly on All Souls' Day (November 2), at funerals, and on the anniversary of death. (II Esd. 2:34*)

RESPONSA [Lat: answers] (res-PON-sa) Jewish literature consisting of authoritative answers to questions of faith, ethics, and religious practice—religious case law. Some instances are found in the Talmud and other rabbinic writings, but most are later, continuing down to the present day.

RESURRECTION [Lat: rising again/back] (1) Of Jesus, the climactic event of the NT; also called the "Easter event" (Matt. 28:5*). (2) Of the dead, at the end time. Resurrection of the body was a tenet of the Pharisees. Christian sects differ about it: whether it is spiritual, both bodily and spiritual, or only figurative. Some sects consider baptism to be a real spiritual resurrection.

In art, a representation of Jesus/Christ emerging from the tomb/sepulcher, often carrying a banner with a cross on it, in triumph over death. Sometimes the scene shows only the empty tomb, with soldiers and/or women in attitudes of amazement.

REVELATION [Lat: unveiling] The disclosure to human beings of superhuman knowledge or divine purpose, usually through "higher" means than reason and/or empirical investigation—which, unaided, lead at best to "natural" religion. (1) The name of the last book of the Bible, used in Protestant, and some recent RC, versions (the traditional RC name is Apocalypse). (2) God's AUTHORITATIVE word as it: (a) appears in scripture; (b) is INFALLIBLY announced by the RC Church or pope *ex cathedra*; (c) is pronounced by revered people or authorities in other sects; (d) is revealed through nature; and/or (e) is experienced in a personal illumination.

In art, it usually consists of a series of scenes from the book of Revelation and is called Apocalypse, especially in illustrated manuscripts, tapestries, and drawings.

REVISION [Lat: seen again] See VERSION.

RITE [OE: number] (1) A prescribed, formal religious ceremony/practice/ritual. See also LITURGY. (2) A branch of Christianity; e.g., Latin Rite, Byzantine (EO and Uniat) Rite.

ROSARY [Lat: rose garden] A prayer, or string of beads for counting prayers, used by RCs. Formally, the string consists of fifteen sets of ten small beads and a large one, corresponding to the fifteen MYSTERIES of the faith to be meditated upon while saying the AVE MARIA (Hail Mary) for each small bead and a PATER NOSTER (Our Father) and GLORIA PATRI for the large ones. Normally, however, only five sets/decades are strung with a crucifix, plus an additional two large and three small beads.

ROSH HASHANA(H) [Heb: head of the year] (rosh hah-shah-NAH, ha-SHOH-na) The Jewish New Year, which begins the ten penitential days culminating in Yom Kippur (Day of ATONEMENT), which is the second of the two "high holidays." The ritual is distinguished by the blowing of the ram's horn (Heb: *shofar*). Thus, based on various parts of the liturgy, the holiday is also called the Day of Sounding (the horn), of Judgment, and of Remembrance. It is celebrated for two days by Orthodox and Conservative Jews, for one day by Reform Jews and in Israel.

RUBRICS [Lat: red] (ROOB-riks) (1) Red letters used as headings, to contrast with the regular black print. (2) Directions for the conduct of a worship service; the rules of a ceremony.

SABBATARIAN [Heb: rest] (sabb-a-TAIR-i-an) (1) A Christian individual or sect that keeps Saturday, the seventh day of the week, as the sabbath rather than Sunday (the LORD'S DAY). (2) A strict observer of the day of rest, whether Saturday or Sunday. (Exod. 20:8*)

SABBATH [Heb: (day of) rest] (1) Saturday, the seventh day of the week, beginning at sunset on Friday, for Jews and Christian SABBATARIANS (Gen. 2:2; Exod. 20:8*). (2) Sunday, the first day of the week, the LORD'S DAY, for most Christians. (3) Friday, for Moslems.

SACRAMENT [Lat: sacred obligation] The physical sign of spiritual grace. (1) A religious ceremony specifically commanded/instituted by Jesus: narrowly, baptism and the eucharist. Many Protestant sects limit themselves to these, as sacraments or ordinances. (2) Such ceremonies, for RCs and EO, considered to have been practiced or recognized by Jesus and instituted by the church: the two mentioned and five others: penance/reconciliation (RC) or confession (EO), matrimony, anointing of the sick (RC) or unction (EO), confirmation (RC) or chrismation (EO), and order/ordination. (3) Some Protestants observe no sacraments at all, some three or more; as sacraments, as ordinances, or as "practices."

SACRIFICE OF ISAAC *In art,* a representation of Abraham, bearded and with a raised knife; Isaac, bound on a brushwood altar; and an animal (goat/sheep) in the background. It is also the "Sacrifice of Abraham."

SADDUCEES [Heb: probably Zadokites, after the high priest under David] (SAD-yoo-sees) The Jewish establishment party of the relatively Hellenized priests, merchants, and aristocracy (ca. 150 B.C.E.–70 C.E.). Religious conservatives, they accepted the authority of only the written Law of the Torah and rejected the PHARISEES' religious progressivism as well as their beliefs about resurrection, a messiah, and angels. Their opposition to Jesus, in contrast to that of the Pharisees, was as much political and social as religious.

SAINT [Lat: sacred, holy] (1) A person canonized (i.e., enrolled on the canon/official list of saints) by a church. (2) A blessed soul in heaven. (3) An angel or archangel. (4) Any baptized Christian. (5) A member of certain sects (e.g., Latter Day Saints). RC and EO recognize many more canonized saints than do Protestants; render them special veneration; pray to them as intercessors; and consider them patrons of countries, churches, occupations, individuals, etc.

SALVATION [Lat: saving] REDEMPTION. The rescue by divine power of humanity or individuals from evil or guilt, so that they may attain happiness/blessedness or complete sinlessness. According to Christianity, the atonement/sacrifice of Jesus has saved people or else allowed them to achieve salvation. This latter effort requires, according to various sects, some or all of the following: acknowledgment of sin, penitence, repentance, regeneration, baptism, confirmation, anointing, sanctification, justification, faith, good works, God's grace, intervention of the Holy Spirit, worship, observance of the sacraments/ordinances. See MESSIAH.

SALVATION HISTORY See HEILSGESCHICHTE.

SALVE REGINA [Lat: hail, queen] (Lat: SAHL-way re-GEE-na; Eng/It: SAL-vay re-JEE-na) A chant in praise of Mary, sung at vespers and after a low MASS.

SAMARITANS (1) People of Samaria (north Israel) after its conquest by the Assyrians in 722. Though they followed Mosaic law, they were considered heretics by Jews of Judea because they rejected scripture beyond the Pentateuch and rejected Jerusalem-centered Judaism. (2) Present-day remnants of this group, centered in Nablus, near their holy mountain, Gerizim. (3) Metaphorically, persons generous to those in need (Luke 10:30).

SANCTIFICATION [Lat: making holy] Moral purification through the Holy Spirit, in Christianity. Its importance and sequential position vary for different sects: It may be an accompaniment to baptism, a supplement to regeneration, and/or the final stage for salvation. Some sects do not acknowledge it as a necessary step toward salvation; others call the entire progress toward salvation sanctification. Jews differ from Christians, and among themselves, in interpreting holiness *(kedushah),* a quality that is required of people and is present in God.

SANCTUARY [Lat: holy place] (1) In RC churches, the apsidal area behind the altar; in EO, the altar/bema area behind the iconostasis. (2) In many Christian churches, the chancel. (3) For some Protestants and Jews, the area used for worship services. (4) The entire building housing all these.

SANCTUM SANCTORUM [Lat: HOLY OF HOLIES]

SANCTUS [Lat: holy] Latin title and thrice-repeated first word of some DOXOLOGIES: (1) "Holy, holy, holy, Lord of hosts . . ." (Isa. 6:3); in Jewish and, with additions, RC liturgy. (2) "Holy, holy, holy, Lord God almighty . . ." (Rev. 4:8). (3) Hymns that open similarly. Also called TERSANCTUS.

SATAN [Heb: adversary] (1) In early OT literature, the prosecuting attorney in God's council. (2) In later OT literature (e.g., Chronicles) and in rabbinic literature, at times also a demonic power that causes people to sin. (3) More fully developed in the NT and subsequent Christianity as the devil, Antichrist, fallen angel, etc. (4) In traditional Christianity: the evil force throughout the Bible, beginning with the serpent in Eden.

SCRIBES [Lat: scratchers, writers] (1) Originally, and again today, Jewish copyists of sacred writings. (2) After the exile, they became editors, interpreters, and teachers of Jewish scripture. (3) By Hellenistic times, they were religious jurists. (4) With the PHARISEES, they supported oral tradition as well as the written Law. (5) In the NT, they are depicted only in their role of opponents of Jesus.

SCRIPTURE/S The Bible.**

SECOND COMING See PAROUSIA.

SEDER [Heb: order (of service)] (SAY-der) The Jewish service and meal, generally eaten at home, that inaugurates the Passover holiday; occasionally, seders are communal.

SEE [Lat: seat] (1) A bishop's chair/seat/cathedra/throne. (2) A bishop's jurisdiction/diocese/bishopric/episcopate. (3) A cathedral, containing the bishop's chair. Holy see: the papacy or its jurisdiction.

SEMITES [Heb: of Shem] (1) Traditionally, descendants of Shem, eldest son of Noah. (2) Popularly, today, Jews, or Jews and Arabs, who speak Semitic languages and are (historically, were) Middle Eastern neighbors. (3) Ancient Semites, who included these plus Babylonians, Phoenicians, Arameans, Canaanites, and others in southwest Asia, related through their languages and some aspects of their religions.

SEPTUAGINT [Grk: seventy (translators)] (sep-TOO-a-gint/jint, SEP-too-a-gint/jint) (1) One or all of the Greek translations of the Hebrew Bible, beginning with the third c. B.C.E.. (2) An Alexandrine Greek version of the OT, including the APOCRYPHA, which is considered authoritative by the RC and EO churches. It is contrasted with the MASORETIC text. Both are quoted in the NT. Often abbreviated LXX.**

SERAPHIM [Heb: plural of seraph] (SEH-ra-feem) The highest order of angels in the CELESTIAL HIERARCHY; they guard God's throne.

In art, they are fiery and have six wings (as described in Isa. 6:2), usually colored red; sometimes they hold burning candles.

SEVEN DEADLY SINS As first listed by Gregory the Great: pride, covetousness, lust, anger, gluttony, envy, and sloth. Capital/MORTAL sins, they are regarded as the source of other sins as well.

SHAVUOT [Heb: weeks] (sha-VOO-ote) The Jewish holiday of PENTECOST/Feast of Weeks, seven weeks after the second day of Passover. It commemorates the giving of the Law on Mt. Sinai and celebrates the wheat harvest. In ancient temple times, it was one of the three pilgrimage festivals (Lev. 23:16*)**.

SHEOL (sheh-OLE) An OT name for the grave/netherworld/place of the dead. Originally a vague and neutral concept, it became more elaborate: although often translated as "hell" in Bibles, most critical scholars feel that the idea of an afterlife with rewards and punishments developed after OT times.

SH'MA/SHEMA [Heb: hear] (shmah) (1) Hebrew title and first word of the Jewish confession of faith (Deut. 6:4*). (2) This affirmation plus two other passages which often follow it in the liturgy and on MEZUZAHS: Deuteronomy 6:5-9; 11:13-21; Numbers 15:37-41.

SIMONY Buying or selling sacred things—spiritual or material; e.g., church office, indulgences, sacraments, sacred objects. The name comes from Simon

Magus (the sorcerer), a Samaritan who offered Peter money for the power to bestow gifts of the Holy Spirit (Acts 8:18).

SITZ IM LEBEN [Ger: setting in life] (zits im LAY-ben) A concept of FORM CRITICISM denoting the situation/occasion/aspect of life or religious practice that provided the context or function for certain kinds of texts; e.g., exhortation, apologetics, catechetical instruction, liturgy, etc.

SOTERIOLOGY [Grk: savior theory] (so-TEE-ri-OLL-o-jy) A branch of Christian theology dealing with SALVATION; e.g., regeneration, atonement, justification, sanctification; sin, grace, human destiny; and, especially, Jesus as the Redeemer.

SOURCE CRITICISM The attempt to analyze the various sources of a biblical passage where it is believed that the text has been conflated or EDITED. Until recently, this discipline was called by biblical scholars LITERARY CRITICISM. **

SPIRITUALISM (1) The belief that all that exists or is real is spirit. (2) The belief that departed spirits can cause psychic phenomena and can communicate with living people in supernatural ways, usually through a medium. A modern religious movement (from ca. 1850), some of its adherents combine it with Christianity. Also called spiritism. (I Sam. 28:14*)

SPEAKING IN TONGUES See GIFT OF TONGUES.

SPRINKLING ASPERSION.

STABAT MATER [Lat: (his) mother was standing] (STAH-baht MAH-ter) Latin title and first words of a RC hymn based on John 19:25.*

STATIONS OF THE CROSS (way of the cross) A series of scenes/stops for meditation on the way to, or within, a church (sometimes out in the open country). RCs and Episcopalians have 14: (1) Jesus is condemned to death by Pilate, (2) picks up and carries the cross, (3) falls the first time, (4) meets his mother, (5) is helped to carry the cross by Simon of Cyrene, (6) has his face wiped by Veronica, (7) falls the second time, (8) talks to women of Jerusalem, (9) falls the third time, (10) is stripped of his garments, (11) is nailed to the cross, (12) dies on the cross, (13) is taken down from the cross (deposition), (14) is laid in the tomb. Numbers 3, 4, 6, 7, and 9 are nonbiblical.

STIGMATA [Grk: marks; plural of *stigma*] (stig-MAH-ta) RC terminology: wounds or scars that appear supernaturally on a person's body, resembling those of the crucified body of Jesus.

SUKKOT [Heb: booths] (sook-ote) The Jewish feast of Tabernacles/Booths, commemorating the wandering in the wilderness and celebrating the autumn harvest; a pilgrimage festival in ancient temple times (Lev. 23:24*).

SUPPER AT EMMAUS (ee-MAY-us) *In art*, a representation of Jesus and his two traveling companions, usually at the point when Jesus breaks the bread, their eyes are opened, and they recognize him as their risen leader (Luke 24:28).

SUSANNA AND THE ELDERS *In art*, a representation of the (almost) nude Susanna in her garden or outdoor bath/pool, with two old men peering out of the foliage nearby (Apocrypha).

SYNAGOGUE [Grk: (place of) assembly] (1) A Jewish place of worship, learning, and communal activity, developed during the exile as a substitute for the temple in Jerusalem, many of whose architectural features it imitates. (2) An Orthodox Jewish place of worship, as distinct from a Reform Jewish "temple."

SYNCRETISM [Grk: gathering together] (SIN-cre-tizm) (1) A seventeenth c. movement in Lutheranism attempting to unite Protestant and RC denominations. (2) An attempt to fuse Hebraic and Hellenic elements in Christianity. (3) Other similar attempts to combine divergent philosophies or theologies.

SYNOPTIC GOSPELS [Grk: view together] The Gospels of Matthew, Mark, and Luke. They are so called because of their common contrast with John and the similarities among them of outline and content. Synoptic problem: tracing the common and divergent sources of these three Gospels and accounting for their similarities and differences. See MARKAN PRIORITY, Q-SOURCE, M-SOURCE, L-SOURCE.

TALLIT [Heb: cover] (tah-leet) The prayer shawl worn by most Jewish men for certain devotional occasions, having fringes at the four corners and black or blue stripes at the ends (Num. 15:38*).

TALMUD [Heb: instruction] (TAHL-mood) RABBINIC LITERATURE that is considered an authoritative body of Jewish Law and tradition, written in Aramaic. It consists of the MISNAH and GEMARA. The Jerusalem Talmud is 150 years earlier, far shorter, and less popular than the Babylonian Talmud, which closed in the late fifth c. C.E.

TANAK (tah-NAHK) An acrostic formed of the initial consonants of the Hebrew names of the three divisions of the Jewish Bible: Torah/Law/Pentateuch, Nebi-im/Prophets, and Ketubim/Writings/Hagiographa; thus the Tanak is the Jewish Bible.**

TANNAIM [Heb: teachers] (ta-NAH-eem) Palestinian rabbis of the first and second c. C.E. whose interpretations of biblical law and oral tradition are recorded mainly in the MISHNAH.

TARGUM [Heb: translation] (TAHR-goom) A free translation (i.e., not word for word) of the Hebrew Bible; especially into Aramaic, the common language of Jews for about one thousand years following the exile. One such translation emerged as authoritative: that attributed to Onkelos (ca. 100–130 C.E.), though there are several others.

TE DEUM [Lat: thee, O Lord (we praise)] (tay DAY-oom) (1) Latin title and first words of an ancient hymn of thanksgiving to the Trinity. (2) A religious service of thanksgiving.

TEMPLE (1) The first temple (the temple of Solomon), built ca. 970 B.C.E. on Mt. Moriah in Jerusalem; destroyed by Nebuchadnezzar, ca. 585 B.C.E. (2) The second temple, built by Zerubbabel, ca. 515 B.C.E.; its life extends either to 20 B.C.E. or 70 C.E., depending on the following. (3) The third temple (Herod's temple) or the renovated second temple, rebuilt ca. 20 B.C.E. by Herod; destroyed by the Romans, 70 C.E. (4) A synagogue, especially of Reform or Conservative Jews. (5) A Mormon religious building.

TEMPTATION (OF CHRIST) *In art,* a representation of Jesus and the devil/Satan, usually standing on the pinnacle of either the temple or a mountain. Satan is usually black, with horns, tail, wings, and a grotesque face.

TENEBRAE [Lat: shadows] (TEN-e-bree) (1) Special matins and lauds said/sung on Wednesday, Thursday, and Friday of holy week, commemorating the sufferings, death, and burial of Jesus; so called because candles are gradually extinguished during the ceremony. (2) Chants sung during this service.

TERSANCTUS [Lat: thrice holy] SANCTUS.

TESTAMENT COVENANT or agreement between unequals, in which the obligations are not evenly reciprocal: e.g., between testator and heir today, between an ancient Near Eastern suzerain and vassal states, between God and his people.

TESTIMONIA [Lat: evidence] PROOF TEXTS.

TESTIMONY Evidence of an eyewitness's knowledge or of a believer's conviction. (See WITNESS)

TETRAGRAMMATON [Grk: four letters] (tet-ra-GRAM-a-ton) Four Hebrew consonants used in the Hebrew Bible as a name for God: YHWH/JHVH. Without vowels, its original pronunciation is lost. It is read devotionally as ADONAI, as a euphemism, and is translated "Lord" in most Bibles. Others supply vowels, resulting in YaHWeH, JeHoVaH, etc. The alternative consonants result from transliteration from the Hebrew into German and into English: J = Y; W = V.

TEXTUAL CRITICISM The study of the differences in wording of various copies/recensions and early translations of scripture (and other literature). Its purpose is to determine the relationships among the variants and, if possible, to identify the original or earliest form.

THEISM [Grk: god] The belief in a transcendent and immanent God (usually monotheistic) who both created and is interested in the world. It is distinguished from DEISM and from atheism.

THEOPHANY [Grk: divine appearance] (thee-OFF-a-ny) The manifestation of a god (or of God) to a human being; e.g., to Moses on Mt. Sinai (Exod. 34:5), the transfiguration of Jesus (Matt. 17:1*). See EPIPHANY.

THEOSOPHY [Grk: divine wisdom] (thee-OSS-o-fy) (1) MYSTICAL knowledge of God; (2) an eclectic religion founded in 1875, in the tradition of Gnosticism and other mystical and spiritualistic religions, with some aspects of philosophy and science. Among its beliefs are pantheism, the need for universal brotherhood, and the existence of precurser theosophists (e.g., Jesus) still operating in the spirit world.

THIRTY-NINE ARTICLES The statement of fundamental beliefs of the Episcopal church. A CONFESSION OF FAITH, it does not stand alone; Episcopalians also express their faith through the Apostles', Nicene, and Athanasian creeds, the *Book of Common Prayer,* and a catechism.

TITHE [OE: tenth] (tighthe) One-tenth of one's income (or of one's surplus over expenses) given voluntarily or as a tax to the clergy or church. Also a verb: to pay a tithe, to exact a tithe (Lev. 27:30*).

TONGUES See GIFT OF TONGUES.

TORAH [Heb: teaching] (to-RAH, TOH-ra) (1) The Pentateuch/Law, the first division of the Jewish Bible/TANAK. (2) The parchment scroll on which the Pentateuch is inscribed. (3) The entire Tanak. (4) All Jewish Law, written and oral.

TRADITION [Lat: handing over] Religious beliefs and practices not specifically mentioned in the Bible but considered AUTHORITATIVE. RC: based on noninscribed oral teaching of Jesus and the apostles, plus the writings of the church fathers. EO: called "holy tradition" (John 16:13*). Orthodox Judaism: often called "oral Law," consisting of (1) laws given to Moses on Mt. Sinai apart from the written Torah, and recorded in the Mishnah; (2) commentaries on the Mishnah and on the Talmud (see HALAKAH).

REDACTION CRITICISM theorizes that much biblical material was traditionally used in various ways before being given its present form. Oral tradition: hypothetical sources that preceded biblical writings. Traditionists: Protestant fundamentalists who accept not only scripture as authoritative but also traditions connected to it.

TRANSLATION [Lat: carrying across] (1) See VERSION. (2) God's carrying off of Enoch (Gen. 5:24).

TRANSUBSTANTIATION [Lat: through substance] In RC and EO doctrine, the conversion/transformation of the bread and wine, in the EUCHARIST ceremony, into new substances (in the Cartesian sense: what lies beneath physical properties and is apprehended only by the mind). They become the real body and blood of Jesus; and only the "accidents"/appearances of the former substance remain: taste, color, shape, quantity, smell. See CONSUBSTANTIATION.

TRINE/TRIUNE IMMERSION See IMMERSION.

TWELFTH NIGHT The eve of EPIPHANY.

TYPE [Grk: image (for copying)] An event, person, thing, or condition that is a prophetic model/prefiguration/exemplar/hidden prediction/foreshadowing/symbol of something or somebody in the future. Most often, the term is used as a christological or ecclesiological reading of the OT, where OT events are "types" of events in the life of Jesus, and words addressed to Israel are seen as meant for the Christian Church or community. Antitype: the NT event to which the OT type refers.**

UNIAT/UNIATE [Lat: united] (YOO-ni-at) A person or church under an Eastern patriarch that is in communion with the RC Church (i.e., recognizes the pope's authority and generally accepts RC doctrine) but follows characteristically EO liturgy (the Byzantine rite) and canon law. Also called Greek Catholics. The situation arises from efforts of the counter-Reformation. The movement includes Armenian and Byzantine Catholic churches; parts of the patriarchates of Antioch and Lebanon; and others, some of whom are in the United States.

UNCTION [Lat: anointing] See ANOINTING. Extreme unction: former name of the RC sacrament of anointing the dying, now absorbed into "anointing the sick."

VANITAS VANITATUM [Lat: vanity of vanities] (VAN-i-tahs van-i-TAH-toom) Most worthless, emptiest (Eccles. 1:2).

VENIAL SIN [Lat: pardonable sin] In RC doctrine, a sin in a minor matter of divine law or an inadvertent offense in a MORTAL matter. It may be remitted by good works and need not be confessed to take Communion.

VERSION [Lat: turning] The result of a quite new translation, literal or free, from one language to another. A revision of an existing translation results in a revised version. A critical revision of a text in the original language results in a recension. A variant of the original text is also a recension.

VESPERS [Lat: evening] (1) A RC CANONICAL HOUR, the later afternoon office/prayer, said/sung between 3 and 6 P.M. (2) Episcopalian "evensong."

VIA DOLOROSA [Lat: sorrowful way] (VEE-a do-lo-RO-sa) Jesus' route from Pilate's judgment hall through Jerusalem to Golgotha/Calvary (John 19:17*). The STATIONS OF THE CROSS replicate events of that journey.

VIRGIN BIRTH The doctrine that Jesus was supernaturally begotten and born while Mary was still a virgin. A related doctrine: Mary remained a virgin throughout her life, meriting the title "Virgin Mary." (Matt. 1:18*)

VIRTUES (1) CARDINAL VIRTUES. (2) An order in the CELESTIAL HIERARCHY.

VULGATE [Lat: common/popular (language)] The Latin version of the Bible officially sanctioned by the RC Church. First translated by Jerome (fourth c.) and since revised, it generally follows the Septuagint where it varies from the Masoretic text—the major difference being the inclusion of the APOCRYPHA.

WESTMINSTER CONFESSION A statement of fundamental beliefs drawn up at Westminster during the Puritan period, as a reaction against the established church's THIRTY-NINE ARTICLES, and since revised. Identified with the Presbyterian church, it has strongly influenced Congregationalists, Baptists, and others.

WHITSUNDAY [OE: white Sunday] PENTECOST.

WISDOM LITERATURE (1) The books of Job, Proverbs, Ecclesiastes; Ecclesiasticus/Sirach, Wisdom of Solomon, and part of Baruch. (Some psalms are of this genre.) (2) These plus other ancient literature focusing on practical knowledge.

WITNESS One who sees, physically (or spiritually). Mosaic law requires that a witness must come forward and offer TESTIMONY of what he or she has seen or believes. See MARTYR.

WRITINGS KETUBIM.

YAHWEH/YAHVEH [Heb: name for God] (YAH-weh) See TETRAGRAMMATON and ADONAI. **

YAHWIST WRITER The author of a "J-document" posited by some critical scholars for portions of the Pentateuch (or Hexateuch, with Joshua), arising in Judah (southern Israel) and usually dated about 1,000–800 B.C.E. It is thought to have been fused with the E-SOURCE into "JE" before inclusion in the canon. See J-SOURCE.

YOM KIPPUR [Heb: day of atonement] See ATONEMENT, DAY OF.

ZEALOTS [Grk: jealous] First c. C.E. activist left-wing PHARISEES who wanted to use force to bring about deliverance from Rome. They were political as well as religious and cultural enemies of the SADDUCEES.

ZION Heb. name for a hill (also called Moriah) within Jerusalem, on which Solomon built his temple. Figuratively, the term is used for: (1) Jerusalem/city of David; (2) Palestine; (3) the city of God/new Jerusalem.

Bibliography

Single volumes

Appel, Willi, and Daniel, Ralph T. *Harvard Brief Dictionary of Music.* New York: Washington Square Press, 1961, paper. A standard reference book.

Broderick, Robert C. *The Catholic Encylopedia.* Nashville: Thomas Nelson, 1976. Most recent explanation of RC views.

Demetrakopoulos, George H. *Dictionary of Orthodox Theology.* New York: Philosphical Library, 1964. The only book of its kind, unfortunately out of print but available at specialized libraries. Otherwise, see the *Oxford Dictionary,* below.

Ferguson, George. *Signs and Symbols in Christian Art.* New York: Oxford University Press, 1961, paper. A most helpful survey of the field, illustrated.

Kauffman, Donald T. *The Dictionary of Religious Terms.* Old Tappan, N. J.: Fleming H. Revell, 1967. Over ten thousand terms very briefly defined; excellent quick reference.

Sonder, Richard N. *Handbook of Biblical Criticism.* Richmond: John Knox Press, 1976, paper. First book of its kind: basic tools for the academic study of the Bible; articles on terms, people, problems, and lists of other scholarly information.

Wigoder, Geoffrey. *Encyclopedic Dictionary of Judaica.* New York: Leon Amiel, 1974. Abridgment of the 16-volume work, below.

Webster's International Dictionary, 3rd ed. Springfield, Mass.: G. & C. Merriam.

For greater depth

Encyclopaedia Judaica. Jerusalem: Keter, 1972. 16 vols.

Encyclopedia Americana. New York: Americana, 1966. 30 vols.

The Interpreter's Dictionary of the Bible. Nashville: Abingdon, 1962, 1976. 5 vols.

New Catholic Encylopedia. New York: McGraw-Hill, 1967. 16 vols.

Other useful single volumes

Atwater, Donald. *A Catholic Dictionary.* New York: Macmillan, 1949. A bit outdated in some areas, but a scholarly supplement to the Broderick book.

Cross, F. L., and Livingstone, E. A. *The Oxford Dictionary of the Christian Church.* New York: Oxford University Press, 1974. A standard reference book.

Ferm, Vergilius. *An Encyclopedia of Religion.* New York: Philosophical Library, 1945.

Matthews, Shailer, and Smith, Gerald B. *A Dictionary of Religion and Ethics.* New York: Macmillan, 1923. Also somewhat outdated, but a classic: over one hundred contributors and over fifteen hundred items in the bibliography.

Pike, E. Royston. *Encyclopedia of Religion and Religions.* New York: World, 1958, paper. Slight Anglican flavor, but more depth in many articles than the Kauffman.

Shannon, Ellen C. *A Layman's Guide to Christian Terms.* Cranbury, N. J.: A. S. Barnes, 1969. Slight RC flavor, but the simple explanations are helpful.

Ware, Timothy. *The Orthodox Church.* Baltimore: Penguin Books, 1963, paper. Easy reading, narrative supplement to the Demetrakopoulos and the Oxford, but little about the American scene.

Note: See also references mentioned in the introduction to Part II, chapter 7, in this handbook.